D1271875

*The Wilder House Series in Politics, History, and Culture
is published in association with the Wilder House
Board of Editors and the University of Chicago.*

DAVID LAITIN, *Editor*
LEORA AUSLANDER, *Assistant Editor*
GEORGE STEINMETZ, *Assistant Editor*

*Reclaiming the Sacred: Lay Religion and Popular Politics in Revolutionary
France* by Suzanne Desan

ALSO IN THE SERIES

*State and Society in Medieval Europe: A Comparison of Gwynedd and
Languedoc under Outside Rule* by James Given

Language and Power: Exploring Political Cultures in Indonesia by
Benedict R. O'G. Anderson

Detail showing the people's resistance to an early attack on the church,
from *Persecution of the Roman Catholic Clergy in France, 1791*.
Courtesy of the Bibliothèque nationale.

Reclaiming the Sacred

Lay Religion and Popular Politics in Revolutionary France

SUZANNE DESAN

Cornell University Press

Ithaca and London

Copyright © 1990 by Cornell University

All rights reserved. Except for brief quotations in a review, this book, or parts thereof, must not be reproduced in any form without permission in writing from the publisher. For information, address Cornell University Press, 124 Roberts Place, Ithaca, New York 14850.

First published 1990 by Cornell University Press.

International Standard Book Number 0-8014-2404-6
Library of Congress Catalog Card Number 90–55120
Printed in the United States of America
*Librarians: Library of Congress cataloging information
appears on the last page of the book.*

⊗ The paper in this book meets the minimum requirements
of the American National Standard for Information Sciences—
Permanence of Paper for Printed Library Materials, ANSI Z39.48-1984.

LIBRARY
ALMA COLLEGE
ALMA, MICHIGAN

For my parents
and in memory of
Patricia Feeley

Contents

Illustrations

Maps

[ix]

Acknowledgments

Many people have helped me to complete this work. My first thanks go to Lynn Hunt, mentor and friend. She guided and encouraged me through the many stages of this project. Her friendship, inspiration, and advice have helped me more than I could express. Natalie Zemon Davis and Robert Darnton first taught me to love French history and have continued to inspire me ever since. During my years at the University of California at Berkeley, William Bouwsma provided reassuring support and a model of scholarship. Laird Boswell, Christine Hinshaw, Julie Liss, and Sarah Farmer have talked to me for years about this project, offering their ideas and solidarity. As the many celebrations of the bicentennial wore down even the most loyal fans of 1789, Bryant T. Ragan shared my enthusiasm and fascination with the French Revolution and energetically discussed with me his own discoveries about peasant politics. I thank Keith Luria for his insights into the nature of religious devotion in early modern France and Julia Adams for her perceptive comments and encouragement.

The French government, the Mabelle McLeod Lewis Foundation, the Thomas More–Jacques Maritain Institute, and the University of California at Berkeley aided me in the early stages of this project. Assistance from the American Council of Learned Societies and the Graduate School and Humanities Institute of the University of Wisconsin–Madison enabled me to complete it. The maps were drawn by Kathryn Chapin, with the support of the Cartography Laboratory of the University of Wisconsin.

    While I was in France, Jean-Paul Desaive, Marie-Laurence Netter, and Pierre Roudil shared their knowledge of the Yonne with me. I particularly thank Jean-Pierre Rocher for generously giving me access to his forthcoming article on the clergy of the Yonne during the French Revolution. Mary Ann Quinn offered me hospitality in Auxerre. She has since read the entire manuscript with the care and expertise of someone who truly knows the Yonne. Guillaume de Bertier de Sauvigny kindly allowed me to use the private archives of his family. In Auxerre the staffs of the Bibliothèque municipale and the Archives départementales de l'Yonne helped me pick my way through their rich collections. I also thank the staffs of the Archives nationales, the Bibliothèque nationale, the Bibliothèque de la Société de Port Royal, and the Archives départementales de la Côte-d'Or and of several departments in the west.

    I thank the following publishers for permission to use material from previously published articles here. Part of Chapter 4 was published as "Redefining Revolutionary Liberty: The Rhetoric of Religious Revival during the French Revolution," *Journal of Modern History* 60 (1988): 1–27, copyright © 1988 by the University of Chicago. Parts of Chapter 5 previously appeared as "The Role of Women in Religious Riots during the French Revolution," *Eighteenth-Century Studies* 22 (1989): 451–68; and, with part of Chapter 3, as "Religious Riots and Ritual during the French Revolution," *Proceedings of the Annual Meeting of the Western Society for French History* 14 (1987): 171–79.

    Caroline Ford and Bryan Skib both read my manuscript and shared with me their familiarity with western France and French religiosity. Timothy Tackett has given me useful advice and information from the earliest days of this project. Philip Hoffman's recommendations about research and writing were very much appreciated. I thank Dena Goodman for reading several versions of this work and for her uncanny ability to offer clear insights at the muddiest moments in the rewriting process. My sister, Christine Desan Husson, has listened tirelessly to my deepest doubts about this work and offered me countless suggestions and generous encouragement in return. My brother, Paul, cracked jokes at all the right moments. I am especially grateful to Barbara Forrest for her creative suggestions and warm support.

    I also thank John Ackerman and the staff of Cornell University Press, and Judith Bailey, my copyeditor, for their support, expertise, and care throughout the production of this book.

    In my years at the University of Wisconsin at Madison, I have benefited from the encouragement and inspiring example of many of my colleagues in the history department. I extend special thanks to Domenico Sella, Edward Gargan, and Charles Cohen for offering me such constructive and useful suggestions for revision. Discussions with members of the Women's History Program, especially Jeanne Boydston, Linda Gordon, and Gerda Lerner, have helped me re-direct some of my thinking about this project. Jane Schulenburg has shared with me her knowledge of female religiosity in the Middle Ages; her zest for history has sent me back to my manuscript with renewed vigor many times. I have also benefited from discussions with Michael MacDonald and Robert Kingdon. The graduate stu-dents in my seminars have often helped me to think along new lines. My research assistant, Robert Ingham, came through with some cru-cial work in the final days of revision.

My oldest debt is to my parents, Elizabeth and Wilfrid Desan. Both writers themselves, they have long been models of intellectual curi-osity and personal warmth. I thank them and dedicate this work to them. Finally, Patricia Feeley, whose rich life was cut short a year ago, was the only historian who knew me when I was five. I dedicate this book to her also.

SUZANNE DESAN

Madison, Wisconsin

Abbreviations

AB	*Annales de Bourgogne*
AC	Archives communales
AD	Archives départementales
AHRF	*Annales historiques de la Révolution française*
AN	Archives nationales
AP	Archives privées
BN	Bibliothèque nationale
BSPR	Bibliothèque de la Société de Port-Royal
BSSY	*Bulletin de la société des sciences historiques et naturelles de l'Yonne*
JMH	*Journal of Modern History*
PV	procès verbal

Reclaiming the Sacred

Religious or political, the two questions are deeply, inextricably intermingled at their roots. Confounded in the past, they will appear tomorrow as they really are, one and identical.

—Jules Michelet, *Histoire de la Révolution française*

CHAPTER ONE

Introduction: Religion and Politics in the French Revolution

In December 1794 when the town officers of Saint-Bris tried to enforce a departmental decree closing the village church, Catholic villagers gathered en masse before the church doors and demanded the right to assemble peacefully to pray to the "Supreme Being." The mayor locked the church, but when he returned the next day, the doors had been removed. When he replaced them, the villagers pried off the locks. Next they assembled on the front steps and drafted a petition demanding to benefit from "the decree in which the Convention assured them religious liberty." Finally the mayor threw up his hands in despair and conceded that perhaps his persistent Catholic villagers should be allowed to worship publicly. "It is impossible to close the temples," he wrote to a friend. "The people have decided."[1] The activism of the parishioners of Saint-Bris was hardly unusual, for in the spring of 1795 French Catholics launched an energetic and widespread revival of their religion. After the fall of Robespierre when the Thermidorean government partially relaxed the laws restricting religious worship, religious activists throughout France seized the keys to parish churches, sang hymns and offices, and petitioned for the right to practice their religion in public.

[1] AD Yonne L716, PV par le maire de la commune de Saint-Bris, 8 nivôse an III (28 December 1794), Pétition des habitants de Saint-Bris à l'administration du district d'Auxerre, 17 germinal an III (6 April 1795); Lettre du maire de la commune de Saint-Bris à "mon ami," 9 nivôse an III (29 December 1794); AC Saint-Bris, Dépôt 583, D2, PV de la commune de Saint-Bris, 11 nivôse au 24 pluviôse an III (31 December 1794–12 February 1795). All translations from the French are my own.

The French Revolution fundamentally altered the relationship between religion and politics. In 1789 Catholicism and the monarchy
offered each other mutual support. As the official religion of France,
Catholicism had a virtual monopoly of public religious expression. By
1795 church and state were separate by law in a tenuous experiment
that would last seven years. By 1795 the Revolution had not only
nationalized church lands, closed many churches throughout France,
and driven most of the clergy to abdicate, to go into hiding, or to leave
the country; it had also created a whole cultural system of revolutionary rituals, symbols, and language which aimed to replace Christianity
and reeducate people according to the political ideals of the Revolution. The revolutionaries appropriated to the realm of political
culture many of the former roles of religion, including the moral
formation of human nature, the festive commemoration of life's most
crucial moments, the education of the nation's youth, and the ceremonial support of the political regime and its ideology. Clearly the
rituals and symbols the Revolution generated to define and unify its
political and cultural goals forced Christianity onto the defensive.

But this modern transformation of politics into a secular, moraliz-
ing force that could create a culture independent of religion was not a
smooth process. Many French people vigorously resisted surrendering their traditional Catholic beliefs and practices. Particularly after
the fall of Robespierre, they fought hard for the political right to
practice their religion in public. Catholic villagers, often with women
in the lead, fused the symbolic power of religious ritual with the
political techniques and ideology of the Revolution in order to press
their claim for freedom of public worship. They also drew on traditional popular culture both to make their political demands felt and to
refashion their religious practice. Although Catholicism was profoundly challenged by the Revolution, the cultural fluidity of the
1790s and the breakdown of the clerical hierarchy also enabled lay
Catholics to transform their own rituals and to redefine the sacred
within the community.

In this book I explore the revival of Catholicism between 1794 and
1799 in the department of the Yonne, situated in Burgundy and the
Paris Basin, an area that was religious, yet not counterrevolutionary. I
focus on lay Catholic activism as a political and religious movement
and ask how the context of revolution influenced both the religious
practice and political activism of Catholic villagers. I want to untangle
Michelet's "inextricable intermingling" of politics and religion in

France during the revolutionary era. To that end, I use a two-pronged analysis of this fundamental interaction between religion and politics and between the traditional and the revolutionary. On the one hand, I attempt to understand the impact of the Revolution on popular politicization by asking how Catholic villagers and townspeople in a *prorevolutionary* region of France combined revolutionary politics with customary, Old Regime methods to demand the right to worship. Lay Catholic activists did not simply react against the Revolution; they learned from it and assimilated certain elements of revolutionary popular politics into their more traditional forms of activism. I also ask what effect the religious struggle had on power dynamics within the community.

On the other hand, I analyze lay religious change in the context of political and cultural turmoil and probe the long-term effects of revolutionary religious activism. Catholics did not simply seek to restore Old Regime religion unchanged; instead, the laity took advantage of the fluid revolutionary context to institute new religious practices as well as to revive old ones. Revolutionary ideology joined with traditional religiosity to shape certain new forms of devotion, such as lay-led masses. In some instances women forged new spiritual and communal power as leaders of local religious activism. Within the religious responses and actions of these crucial years lie clues to the more gradual evolution of French religiosity, including such nineteenth-century trends as the feminization of religion, the polarization of politics along religious lines, and even the development of secularism itself.

The Evolving Politics of Revolution and Christianity

The conflict between Christianity and the Revolution was not a given in 1789. Initially, the national legislature moved against the church to curtail its economic independence and political power. But by 1793, as the Revolution grew more radical and expanded its cultural and political aims, its opposition to Catholicism developed and intensified. It became increasingly clear that cultural transformation would require a more thorough rejection of Christianity.

Under the Old Regime, Christianity had acted as the cultural, ideological, and institutional basis for the monarchical claim to authority. As Jacques Bossuet had argued in his defense of the divine right of kings, "Princes act as ministers of God and as his lieutenants on earth"; the mystical alliance between crown and altar was forged in heaven but was acted out on earth as the monarchy and the Catholic Church offered each other mutual support.[2] The rituals of the church, ranging from the anointing of the king at the cathedral of Reims to the singing of the Te Deum on his birthday, provided a ceremonial framework that lent an aura of sacrality and divine legitimacy to the king's authority. Christian morality, inculcated through catechisms, sermons, and ritual, emphasized respect for hierarchy, social order, and the patriarchal authority of father, king, and God. Christianity supplied the political system of the Old Regime with a central metaphor for its power.[3] Beyond this symbolic and philosophical support, the church often acted as the crown's political or economic ally. Certain members of the upper clergy served as the king's ministers, offered him advice, and helped him to get his way in ecclesiastical affairs and to secure the subsidies he requested. Moreover, the king's right to name individuals to important benefices enabled him to use the church as a source of spoils in the elaborate system of monarchical clientage. Although the alliance of crown and altar was often riddled with tension or conflict, over the centuries French kings managed to exert increasing control over ecclesiastical affairs and to bind the clergy to the state in a web of mutual interdependence.[4]

In return for its institutional and cultural support of the monarchy, the Catholic Church was guaranteed a privileged position as the only

[2]Jacques Bossuet, *Politique tirée des propres paroles de l'écriture-sainte* (Paris, 1709), book III, article II, propositions 1–2, pp. 71–77.

[3]The model of vertical, paternal authority centered in the father or father figure was the fundamental underpinning of early modern social, political, and religious structure: the paternal power of the father within the family and household, the political authority of the king within the realm, and the cosmological authority of God the Father over all creation paralleled and reinforced one another. Various anthropologists and sociologists have discussed the importance of a "central metaphor" or "cultural frame" to support social structures. See, for example, Clifford Geertz, *Local Knowledge: Further Essays in Interpretive Anthropology* (New York, 1983), pp. 121–47; James Fernandez, "The Mission of Metaphor in Expressive Culture," in *Persuasions and Performances: The Play of Tropes in Culture* (Bloomington, Ind., 1986), pp. 28–70; Robert Nisbet, *Social Change and History: Aspects of the Western Theory of Development* (Oxford, 1969), p. 6. On the family-state compact, see Sarah Hanley, "Engendering the State: Family Formation and State Building in Early Modern France," *French Historical Studies* 16 (1989): 4–27.

[4]John McManners, *The French Revolution and the Church* (New York, 1969), pp. 5–6; André Latreille, *L'Eglise catholique et la Révolution française*, 2 vols. (Paris, 1946–50), 1: chap. 2.

legal and official religion of France. Catholicism had exclusive rights to public worship, and the state used its secular powers, including censorship, laws against blasphemy, enforced payment of the tithe, and even the billeting of troops, to protect the church's monopoly of religious ceremony and its exclusive role as guardian of morals and religious belief. Exemption from taxation enabled the clergy to preserve inordinate amounts of wealth. The church had extensive landholdings in some regions, ranging from only 3 to 4 percent of the land in parts of the south to as much as a third of local properties in regions such as Picardy and the Cambrésis. Historians estimate that the church held roughly 6 to 10 percent of French land overall.[5] On the national and regional level, bishops and abbots maintained great personal and political power, and in the villages the local clergymen benefited from their positions as representatives of royal authority. It was the parish priests who announced the decrees of the crown, kept registers of births, marriages, and deaths, and maintained contacts with the urban world. The "bons curés" of the eighteenth century were important parish notables and the main forces of education in the countryside.[6]

In the early stages of the Revolution, the deputies sought first to tap the church's wealth for the nation's benefit and, second, to assure the political subservience of the Catholic Church as an institution. In November 1789 the National Assembly nationalized church lands with the double purpose of weakening the Old Regime power of church and, through sale of the lands, of helping to repay the national debt. A few months later, on 13 February 1790, after a bitter debate, the deputies voted to withdraw any recognition of existing monastic vows and to offer all members of religious orders the option of returning to secular life with a pension. In July 1790 the National Assembly passed the Civil Constitution of the Clergy, which was designed to rationalize the structure of the church, free it from financial abuses and injustices based on privilege, and place it more fully under the control of the state. Essentially an attempt to create a state church,

---

[5]McManners, *French Revolution*, pp. 6–7. McManners adds that contemporaries estimated the total annual income of the church on the eve of the Revolution at a hundred million livres, "nearly enough to have paid a living wage twice over to all the priests of the Gallican Church."

[6]Timothy Tackett, *Priest and Parish in Eighteenth-Century France* (Princeton, N.J., 1977), chap. 6; Philip T. Hoffman, *Church and Community in the Diocese of Lyon, 1500–1789* (New Haven, Conn., 1984), chaps. 4, 5.

the Civil Constitution redrew the lines of dioceses and parishes to form more "rational and equitable" units. Bishops and parish priests alike became salaried state officials, to be elected by active citizens. All external sources of ecclesiastical income, such as fees for ceremonies and benefices without the cure of souls, were abolished. In short, the French church became a national institution; its priests civil servants. (See the Appendix for a list of the major national religious laws.)

Recognizing that the Civil Constitution provided necessary ecclesiastical reforms, many of the clergy and even a majority of the bishops were willing to find a way to make it acceptable. Louis XVI sanctioned the decree in July 1790.[7] The clerics, however, were hesitant to act without the critical vote of approval from Rome. By 27 November 1790 the National Assembly grew tired of waiting for the pope's acceptance and passed the fateful law that required "all bishops, former archbishops, parish priests, and other public officials" to take an oath to "be loyal to the Nation, to the Law, and to the King, and to uphold with all their power the Constitution decreed by the National Assembly and accepted by the King." In France as a whole only seven bishops took the oath, but about half the lower clergymen swore their loyalty, although many of these added restrictions or retracted their oaths several months later when the pope formally condemned the Civil Constitution. The choice of the clergy varied greatly according to region. The incidence of oath taking was highest in the center, the Ile-de-France, and the southeast. In those regions later known for a high level of religious practice—the northwest, northeast/east, and the Massif Central—well over half the clergy refused the oath.[8] Historians have frequently seen the requirement of the oath as one of the critical errors of the Revolution, for it provoked unending controversies among the clergy and laity alike and persuaded many villagers to oppose the Revolution.

Despite the disputes over the oath, the Constitutional Church began to organize and function as a state church. Initially, the national deputies intended to use Christianity as a national religion to support the authority of the new nation. For example, at the festival of the Federation in 1790, Talleyrand said mass on the "altar of the nation" to commemorate the taking of the Bastille and the unity of the Revo-

[7]McManners, *French Revolution*, pp. 43–45.
[8]Timothy Tackett, *Religion, Revolution, and Regional Culture in Eighteenth-Century France: The Ecclesiastical Oath of 1791* (Princeton, N.J., 1986), pp. 52–57, 307–63.

lution. Ceremonies throughout France fused patriotic and Christian symbolism as priests baptized babies with both the sign of the cross and the cockade and sang the Te Deum to honor the unity of the nation or, later, to rejoice in its war victories.

In the early 1790s, many clergymen hoped that Christianity and the Revolution might work together to reform both religion and society. They anticipated an end to the corrupt practices of the church, the institution of Richerist reforms to benefit the lower clergy, and perhaps even a return to the presumed purity and simplicity of early Christianity. Some Catholic revolutionaries, most notably Bishop Claude Fauchet, editor of the left-wing journal *La bouche de fer* and founder of the patriotic Cercle Social, envisioned the creation of an evangelical socialism rooted in the egalitarian and fraternal notions of the Gospels and the Revolution.[9] A radical fringe of millenarians, inspired by revolutionary fervor and popular piety, even awaited the total regeneration of mankind.[10] But by the fall of 1792 the hopes for syncretism between revolutionary and Christian symbols and ideals were fading fast. The institutional breaches between church and state widened in the aftermath of the 10 August insurrection as the national legislature demanded new oaths of clerical loyalty, laicized the *état civil,* and voted to deport refractory priests.

With the overthrow of the constitutional monarchy and the creation of a republic, the relationship between the old church and the fledgling state entered a new phase. The radical builders of the new Republic no longer viewed the church as a potential ally or a viable institution in need of economic and structural reform. In the first place, the religious policies of the early 1790s had awakened violent opposition to the central government in large regions of France; republican deputies had little patience with Catholic clergy and laity who supported counterrevolution or royalism. Second, and perhaps even more important, Christianity as a whole came to be seen as a rival cultural system that prevented people from becoming true citizens of the new Republic. To build a unified republican nation of

[9]Norman Ravitch, "Abbé Fauchet: Romantic Religion during the French Revolution," *Journal of the American Academy of Religion* 42 (1974): 247–62; Gary Kates, *The Cercle Social, the Girondins, and the French Revolution* (Princeton, N.J., 1985).

[10]Clark Garrett, *Respectable Folly: Millenarians and the French Revolution in France and England* (Baltimore, Md., 1975), esp. chaps. 2–5, on millenarian visionaries Suzanne Labrousse, Catherine Théot, and the mystical Avignon Society. On Catherine Théot, see also Albert Mathiez,*Contributions à l'histoire religieuse de la Révolution française* (Paris, 1907), chap. 3.

rational and virtuous citizens was a cultural as well as a political task: the Republic had to do away with the religious beliefs and practices that had underpinned monarchy, hierarchy, privilege, and superstition, and instead had to reeducate the French people according to the rational and largely secular ideals of the Enlightenment. As the administrators of the department of the Yonne put it, Catholicism was "a cult which had as its only goal to make men into beasts," whereas revolutionary festivals and institutions sought "to cultivate attachment to the rights and duties of man and to excite in their hearts the emulation of all the civic virtues."[11] Indeed, the revolutionaries despised the very tenets of Christianity, especially its emphasis on mystery, faith, and human dependence on God. The most radical revolutionaries believed that the conflict between Christianity and Revolution was inevitable. They created a rhetoric of opposition in which superstition and corruption, hierarchy and counterrevolutionary conspiracy were contrasted to reason and virtue, equality and revolutionary transparency.[12]

These theoretical convictions took more concrete form in the "dechristianization" campaign of 1793–1794, aimed at the intellectual and moral regeneration of the French people. The revolutionary leadership embarked on a massive campaign to eradicate Christian practices and to institute revolutionary festivals, symbols, and calendar in place of Catholic ones. The dechristianization movement began in a few scattered provinces, such as the Nièvre, Somme, Cher, and Haute-Marne, early in the fall of 1793 with attacks on churches and with the institution of explicitly nonreligious patriotic ceremonies. For example, in Nevers in early October the *représentant en mission* Joseph Fouché decreed that civic funerals would replace Catholic ones; over the new civic cemetery, he placed the famous inscription "Death is an eternal sleep." Dechristianization followed no set program or organized form, but its manifestations, whether burlesque, creative, or destructive, were always controversial. The festivities, vandalism, and mockeries were sometimes indigenous and spontaneous and sometimes imposed by outsiders. Typically, various représentants en mission, soldiers in the *armée révolutionnaire*, and local

[11]Arrêté du département de l'Yonne, n.d., [c. brumaire an VII/October 1798], as reprinted in BN, *Observateur de l'Yonne*, 15 brumaire an VII (5 November 1798).

[12]See Lynn Hunt, *Politics, Culture, and Class in the French Revolution* (Berkeley, Calif., 1984), esp. pp. 44–46, on the importance in politics of "transparency," i.e., openness and authenticity.

Popular Societies pushed for drastic measures such as the closing of churches; the destruction or confiscation of sacred objects, bells, and statues; the resignation of priests; the renaming of towns and streets; and the performance of burlesques of Catholic practice.[13]

The movement gained momentum in the winter of 1793–1794 and spread in waves throughout France. Most far-reaching in the Paris Basin, the north, the center, and in parts of the southeast, dechristianizing activity peaked in the spring of 1794, though it continued to gain strength in some areas even after the fall of Robespierre. While it is virtually impossible to measure the exact extent of dechristianization, it is clear that most churches in France were closed or transformed into revolutionary temples by about March 1794; likewise, priests in many areas of France had abdicated, fled, or gone into hiding. In short, despite extensive resistance, by the spring of 1794 the public practice of Catholicism had come to a standstill in most of France.[14]

In place of Catholicism the revolutionaries in Paris and the provinces created various ceremonies to cultivate revolutionary ideals, stimulate patriotic fervor, and proclaim the unity of the Revolution.[15] The festival of Reason, celebrated in the cathedral of Notre Dame in Paris in November 1793, inspired similar festivals in the provinces. Throughout France fervent revolutionaries planted liberty trees, chose young women to represent Liberty or Reason in outdoor processions, enacted ceremonies to glorify revolutionary heroes such as Jean-Paul Marat and Louis-Michel Lepeletier, and danced a macabre burlesque to commemorate the death of the king.[16] Meanwhile in Paris,

[13]Michel Vovelle, *Religion et Révolution: La déchristianisation de l'an II* (Paris, 1976), and *La Révolution contre l'église: De la Raison à l'Etre Suprême* (Paris, 1988); Maurice Dommanget, *La déchristianisation à Beauvais et dans l'Oise (1790–1801)* (Paris, 1918–22); McManners, *French Revolution*, pp. 86–97.

[14]Vovelle, *Révolution contre l'église*, pp. 47–51, 78–81. Church closing varied considerably within each region. In the Yonne almost all churches appear to have been closed (to Catholic worship) by about March 1794. On 4 nivôse an III (24 December 1794), représentant en mission Maure issued a decree declaring that churches not being used "for the general good" (as arsenals, meeting halls, etc.) be definitively closed or reclosed (AN AFII 146B). See also Jean Viguerie, *Christianisme et Révolution: Cinq leçons d'histoire de la Révolution française* (Paris, 1986), p. 227.

[15]Mona Ozouf, *La fête révolutionnaire, 1789–1799* (Paris, 1976), pp. 112–24, 240; Francesco Pitocco, "La costruzione del consenso rivoluzionario: La festa," in *La Rivoluzione francese: Problemi storici e metodologii* (Milan, 1979), pp. 159–210, esp. 166–69.

[16]Hunt, *Politics, Culture, and Class*, pp. 64–65, points out that the revolutionaries chose living goddesses because they sought transparent representations of revolution-

Robespierre, wary of the effect of dechristianization on popular attitudes toward the Revolution, sought to temper these radical manifestations and in 1794 proposed the cult of the Supreme Being to
replace that of Reason.

In the hope of regenerating humankind and creating a "republic of
virtue," zealous revolutionaries left no stone unturned. They developed a vast symbolic system touching every aspect of human life. In
October 1793 the National Convention instituted a new calendar,
which marked out time in "rational" units of ten days (*décades*) rather
than seven-day weeks, substituted a secular commemoration of the
seasons for Christian festivals, and used the proclamation of the
Republic, rather than the birth of Jesus, as the starting point of
measured time.[17] Furthermore, revolutionary leaders, like other
iconoclasts, relied heavily on the power of the *word* to clarify the ever-
changing meaning of revolutionary symbols. Songs, almanacs, newspapers, plays, and slogans all vied with one another in the race to
define and reinforce revolutionary allegiances.[18] Even objects of daily
use—such as coins, clothing, and playing cards—bore the stamp of
this all-encompassing new culture.

One crucial characteristic of this revolutionary refashioning was
that it grew up piece by piece amid an atmosphere of great uncertainty and intense politicization. In their fervor to build the world anew,
the revolutionaries intended this new political culture to take over the
didactic, ceremonial, and spiritual functions of Christianity and to
become in essence a new form of the *sacred,* albeit an essentially *secular*
form of sacrality.[19] Yet the various republicans who molded the sym-

---

ary principles which did not evoke the "old fanatical strivings after false images." Albert
Soboul, "Sentiment religieux et cultes populaires pendant la Révolution: Saints patriotes et martyrs de la liberté," *AHRF* 148 (1957): 193–213.

[17]Serge Bianchi, *La révolution culturelle de l'an II: Elites et peuple (1789–1799)* (Paris,
1982), chaps. 5 and 6; James Friguglietti, "The Social and Religious Consequences of
the French Revolutionary Calendar" (Ph.D. diss., Harvard University, 1966).

[18]Victor and Edith Turner, *Image and Pilgrimage in Christian Culture* (New York,
1978), pp. 28, 144. Turner suggests that iconoclasts may succeed in destroying the
social and cultural integration provided by a rival world view but have the "problem of
devising a religion with visible, tactile signifiers, or of developing signifiers of an imper-
sonal, neutral, or abstract type." Consequently iconoclasts rely heavily on the power of
the word and benefit from the development of mass literacy. On the power of the word
in the Revolution, see Hunt, *Politics, Culture, and Class,* pp. 19–26.

[19]On the "transfer of sacrality" from Catholicism to revolutionary cults, see Ozouf,
Fête révolutionnaire, p. 336. The revolutionaries' goals of cultural reform were so pervasive and their fervor was so great that many historians have remarked on the "religious" nature of the Revolution, though ultimately most stress its peculiarly secular

bols, rituals, and rhetoric of the new political culture were constantly debating the nature of the Republic and its representation. They threw open the debate on politics and the sacred and created a situation that charged symbols with additional power.[20] In addition, they generated and disseminated a whole language of political demands which Catholic citizens could learn, reinterpret, and turn to their own advantage. The program of cultural reform included education in the techniques of popular politics as well. The cultural fluidity of the revolutionary era created not only the need but also the possibility and some of the tools for political and religious creativity in the Catholic response.

Although dechristianization met with deep-rooted popular resistance, which intensified in the Thermidorean period, the attempt to formulate a new secular political culture certainly did not die with Robespierre. The national religious policy of the late 1790s followed the *jeu de bascule* of national politics. But two distinct phases characterized these years: first, a gradual return to limited freedom of worship from February 1795 to autumn 1797; second, a thorough two-year dechristianization campaign in the aftermath of the left-wing coup d'état of September 1797 until the coming of Napoleon in December 1799. At the outset, the Thermidorean Convention tried to relegate religion to the private sphere as much as possible by literally separating church from state: the 3 ventôse an III (21 February 1795) law reiterated a slightly earlier law ending clerical salaries and decreed that the state would neither recognize nor fund any cult.[21] But this

PRIVATE RELIGIOUS LAW

quality. For example, Mathiez emphasizes the Durkheimian capacity of revolutionary cults to form religious social bonds but notes that the "religious sentiment" of revolutionary patriotism stirred up faith "not in a supernatural object, but in the political institution itself." Mathiez, *Contributions à l'histoire religieuse*, pp. 21–22, 29–38. See also Alexis de Tocqueville, *The Old Regime and the French Revolution*, trans. Stuart Gilbert (New York, 1955), pp. 10–13; Jules Michelet, *Histoire de la Révolution française*, 2 vols., 2d ed. (Paris, 1868), vol. 1: part 1: chaps. 1 and 2, esp. p. 23; Georges Lefebvre, "Les foules révolutionnaires," in *Etudes sur la Révolution française* (Paris, 1954), 283, as quoted in Bernard Plongeron, "Le fait religieux dans l'histoire de la Révolution: Objets, méthodes, voies nouvelles," in *Voies nouvelles pour l'histoire de la Révolution française* (Paris, 1978), p. 254; Crane Brinton, *The Jacobins: An Essay in New History* (New York, 1930), esp. pp. 218–22, 231–42; Soboul, "Sentiment religieux et cultes populaires."

[20]François Furet, *Interpreting the French Revolution*, trans. Elborg Forster (Cambridge, Eng., 1981), p. 25; Hunt, *Politics, Culture, and Class*, pp. 53–56; Mona Ozouf, "De thermidor à brumaire: Le discours de la Révolution sur elle-même," *Revue historique* 243 (1970): 31–66, esp. 33–40.

[21]On 18 September 1794 the National Convention ended clerical salaries, which were not being consistently paid anyway. McManners, *French Revolution*, pp. 118–19.

same law allowed small religious assemblies in private homes and promised religious freedom in theory if not in fact. Further laws in May and September 1795 gradually allowed Catholics to return to partial public practice: villagers could make legal declarations to reclaim certain churches within strict limitations; clergy who swore loyalty to national laws and to popular sovereignty could practice again. But by and large, the republican leadership continued to promote republican festivals and to curtail Catholic practice. Refractory priests, outdoor processions, habits, inscriptions, bells, and religious foundations were still outlawed.[22]

The electoral victory of moderate and right-wing candidates in April 1797 fired hopes for freer religious practice as pro-Catholic deputies moved toward gradual relaxation of laws limiting public worship and hindering nonjuring priests. It was even briefly legal for refractory priests to return to France. But the left-wing fructidorean coup d'état in September 1797 led to an immediate crackdown on public practice. The newly purged legislature required all priests to take a new oath of "hatred of royalty and anarchy," reactivated the 1792 and 1793 laws against refractory clergy, and purged local governments of "counterrevolutionary or pro-Catholic" officials. Several thousand priests were outlawed or imprisoned, and 256 were deported to French Guiana. In addition, the second dechristianization campaign of 1797–1799 strove once again to close churches definitively, to institute the republican calendar more decisively, and to encourage revolutionary festivals as well as a new deist cult known as Theophilanthropy. In some regions, including the Yonne, this second dechristianization was more penetrating than the first, particularly in its treatment of the clergy.[23]

---

[22]According to the 7 vendémiaire an IV (29 September 1795) law, priests had to declare where they wished to practice and had to make the declaration: "I recognize the universality of French citizens as sovereign and I promise submission and obedience to the laws of the Republic." Gustave Bonneau, *La clergé de l'Yonne pendant la Révolution, 1790–1800* (Sens, 1900), p. 2. The law also codified and tightened police surveillance of public worship and reactivated the laws passed in fall 1792 and spring 1793 which decreed the deportation of all priests who had not taken or had retracted the oath to the Civil Constitution of the Clergy as well as the deportation or imprisonment of any priest denounced by six or more citizens.

[23]According to the new oath of 19 fructidor an v (5 September 1797), priests had to declare "hatred of royalty and anarchy, and attachment and fidelity to the Republic and to the Constitution of the Year III." Bonneau, *Clergé de l'Yonne*, p. 3; Henri Daniel-Rops, *L'église des révolutions* (Paris, 1960), p. 105; Jean-Pierre Rocher, "Aspects de l'histoire religieuse du département de l'Yonne pendant la Révolution," in *La Révolution dans le département de l'Yonne*, ed. Léo Hamon (Paris, forthcoming).

Nonetheless, neither Theophilanthropy nor the *fêtes décadaires* met with much success in rural areas, and the republican calendar faced continual resistance. Catholic activists only redoubled their efforts, legal or not, to restore public worship. Revolutionary cults were no more satisfying to the majority of the French people in 1798 than they had been in 1794. In 1799 Napoleon recognized what the Directorials had refused to admit: only a religion that held sway in the hearts of the people, in effect only Catholicism, could effectively bind the state back together, provide a basis for morality, and support the authority of the state. Within two months after his 18 brumaire an VIII (9 November 1799) coup d'état, Napoleon allowed nonalienated churches to reopen, suppressed all but two national festivals, and began to grant amnesty to deported priests. Within two years his ministers had negotiated the Concordat with the pope, and French Catholicism entered a new, completely legal phase as the "religion of the majority of the French people."[24]

From 1793 to 1799, then, national religious policy followed the political fluctuations of the national leadership. The cultural crusade of the radical Revolution flagged slightly after the fall of Robespierre: the years 1795–1797 in particular saw a partial relaxation of laws limiting Catholic worship. But despite the variations in religious policy, throughout the later 1790s the revolutionary leadership continually fostered revolutionary cults, symbols, and belief structures to replace traditional Catholic ones. This cultural agenda brought the Revolution and Catholicism into violent confrontation.

Yet, even in the conflict of these two very different world views they influenced each other. Neither Catholicism nor the Revolution was a cultural monolith. Indeed, the character of the religious resurgence after Thermidor was defined not only by Catholic beliefs and customs but also by the constant interaction with revolutionary political culture within this era of great political and cultural flux. While revolutionary political culture launched a massive attack on Catholic beliefs and practices, it also generated specific political techniques and an ideology of ambiguous and powerful concepts that Catholics could and did use to reclaim their religious rights and to justify their religious innovations. Moreover, by destroying the institutional and

[24]As quoted in Claude Langlois and Timothy Tackett, "A l'épreuve de la Révolution, 1770–1830," in *Histoire des Catholiques en France du XVe siècle à nos jours,* ed. François Lebrun (Paris, 1980), p. 276.

clerical structure of the church, the revolutionaries inadvertently encouraged lay religious initiative and zeal. Finally, the intense politicization of religious expression and the crisis of cultural authority
during the Revolution created the opportunity for local religious activists to achieve spiritual and political power.

The revival of Catholicism after the fall of Robespierre was a popular movement throughout France, largely led by the laity, to defend a
way of life and a belief system that the new republican institutions
seemed to threaten. The resurgence was influenced both by the revolutionary setting and by Old Regime Catholicism in the Yonne as in
the rest of France. In the late 1790s Bishop Henri Grégoire's weak
Constitutional Church and the stronger, refractory Roman Church
each strove to provide clerical leadership for the restoration of religion, but these institutional efforts succeeded only insofar as they
found support from local lay people. In most instances the laity, especially women, provided the initiative for the religious movement.

The Revolution profoundly influenced the political aspects of the
religious movement not only by making the political struggle for freedom of worship necessary in the first place but also by providing
certain specific techniques for conducting that struggle. The creation
of a rival revolutionary culture made public religious expression into
a political matter. The choice to attend mass, wear finer clothes on
Sunday, or baptize one's child with a saint's name suddenly became a
political issue. Religious allegiances and practices became means of
playing out political or social conflicts within towns and villages. But
this politicization of religion had some varied and paradoxical effects
that differed according to region. In much of France, dechristianization fueled counterrevolutionary movements; these were particularly
violent and pervasive in the west and parts of the southeast.[25] And

[25]On the links between religious sentiment and counterrevolution, see Nadine-
Josette Chaline, Michel Legrée, and Serge Chassagne, *L'eglise de France et la Révolution:
Histoire régionale, l'ouest* (Paris, 1983); T. J. A. Le Goff and Donald Sutherland, "Re-
ligion and Rural Revolt in the French Revolution: An Overview," in *Religion and Rural
Revolt*, ed. Janos M. Bak and Gerhard Beneche (Dover, N.H., 1984), pp. 123–45;
Gwynne Lewis, *The Second Vendée: The Continuity of Counter-revolution in the Department of
the Gard, 1789–1815* (Oxford, 1978); Raoul Patry, *Le régime de la liberté des cultes dans le
département du Calvados pendant la première séparation, 1795 à 1802* (Paris, 1921); Hervé
Pommeret, *L'esprit public dans le département des Côtes-du-Nord pendant la Révolution,
1789–1799* (Saint-Brieuc, 1921); Marcel Reinhard, *Le département de la Sarthe sous le
régime directorial* (Le Mans, 1936); Donald Sutherland, *The Chouans: The Social Origins of
Popular Counter-revolution in Upper Brittany, 1770–96* (Oxford, 1982).

throughout France, Catholics had to develop political methods of reclaiming and maintaining their right to practice publicly.

But whereas the revolutionaries had created a political language, ideology, and techniques to further their own goals, religious activists, especially in prerevolutionary regions, quickly took their new political education to heart and adapted these same tools for very different purposes. Just as the revolutionaries themselves were constantly re-defining the meaning of revolutionary political concepts, so, too, could less powerful groups, including Catholic peasants and towns-people, assimilate and redefine the discourse and politics of the revo-lution. They could graft the new tools of revolutionary culture and politics onto forms of protest which they had long used for various purposes, ranging from tax riots against central government officials to charivari protests against local transgressors. This fusion of tradi-tional forms of protest with the Revolution's validation of popular politics lent strength to the revival. To demand the right to worship, Catholic villagers made use of new means of political expression as well as traditional ones given greater legitimacy by the Revolution: the petition, the vote, the general assembly, the riot. They coupled all these methods with the ideologies of popular sovereignty and re-ligious liberty. Religious protesters drew a direct correlation between the revolutionary promise of liberty and their own freedom of prac-tice, for although Catholics could not accept the revolutionary cults, they were deeply influenced by revolutionary discourse and by the possibilities of participatory politics.

Paradoxically, the late 1790s were in some ways a moment of great creativity and opportunity for lay Catholics. The dispute over the Civil Constitution of the Clergy and the intensely anticlerical dechris-tianization campaign wrought havoc among the Catholic clergy and disrupted the regular practice of Catholicism. But the context of Rev-olution and the dissolution of a clearly defined clerical hierarchy left the laity free to experiment with new forms of worship. The revival of Catholicism was not, and could not be, solely a direct reaction to the Revolution, nor could it be a simple return to past practices. Catholic activists were more than willing to make changes to adapt to the new situation: they created new rites or transformed old ones to incorpo-rate their changing religious beliefs and their own response to the revolutionary social and political reforms. Sometimes the ideology of Revolution itself influenced their innovations. These devotional re-sponses to the revolutionary attack on Christianity would influence nineteenth-century Catholicism. In sum, while the devastating and dechristianizing impact of the Revolution on religious expression is undeniable, the Directory was in some ways an extremely fertile and creative period for lay religiosity.

Moreover, on the local level the struggle over public religious expression affected community dynamics. Certain groups formerly without power gained authority or identity within the village by fusing powerful political activism and innovative religious ritual. Two groups in particular—the lay men who said "white masses" without priests and the women who led religious riots and female worship services—won spiritual and even political power within the community.

The lay religious movement of the late 1790s was above all a struggle to make religion public and official. Under the Old Regime villagers found reminders of the spiritual power and official authority of Catholicism everywhere: in the crosses along the roadside, in the sound of bells ringing out the Angelus, in the annual processions and festivals, and above all in the parish church building itself. Many Catholics conceived of the sacred in a very concrete and localized sense: certain material symbols, specific places, and sacred moments best focused their beliefs, enabled them to reach the divine, and helped to protect them from misfortune.[26] For the believer, crosses, bells, statues of saints, relics, tombstones, and church objects all embodied many layers of powerful and, often, ambiguous meaning. Thus, a cross by the roadside, for example, might convey to one passerby the vast cosmology of Christ's sacrifice as the hope for human salvation, suggest to another the fragility and incomprehensibility of human existence, inspire a third passerby to appreciate the aesthetic quality of the sculpture, and prompt a fourth to rejoice at being only one short kilometer from home. In some cases, a cross was endowed with thaumaturgical power as well. The Revolution added layers of political significance; the cross frequently became an emblem of village conflict or bitter resentment. Its defense suddenly

---

[26]William Christian, *Local Religion in Sixteenth-Century Spain* (Princeton, N.J., 1981), esp. chap. 4 and pp. 177–79, offers a useful discussion of rural religious belief rooted in attachment to specific, localized places of sacred power. He suggests replacing the term "popular religion" with "rural religious belief" or "local religion." See also his *Person and God in a Spanish Valley* (New York, 1972). François André Isambert, *Le sens du sacré: Fête et religion populaire* (Paris, 1982), p. 225. See also Ozouf, *Fête révolutionnaire*, pp. 150–53, on revolutionary challenges to traditional sacred space.

became pivotal in the battle against the institution of a rival revolutionary symbolic system.[27]

But above all, when Catholics rioted or petitioned for the right to practice, they most often sought to reclaim the parish church and to reestablish the celebration of public rituals. Although the Catholic Reformation had partially succeeded in cultivating private forms of Christian spirituality, for many rural Catholics under the Old Regime, collective ritual was still the most forceful form of religious expression. As the parishioners of Villeneuve-sur-Yonne pointed out in 1800 in an eloquent petition for their church: "Christianity is all interior and spiritual; but it is in churches that we meet and these assemblies are for us the source of all the advantages that Christianity offers: it is there that are opened the channels through which God condescends to communicate with man; it is there that we animate one another toward the love of order and of virtue. . . . And by offering our homages to the Very High in common, our piety is made more fervent, our faith more active."[28]

Catholics adapted as well as they could to the prohibition against public worship and symbols. Many welcomed priests into their homes for clandestine masses, taught their children catechism at home, or assembled privately to recite the rosary or other prayers in common. But Catholics essentially viewed these private and clandestine forms of devotion as temporary practices. They did not stop believing that religion should be public and communal to carry full authority and sacrality. In 1795 many French villagers shared the fear of the pastor of Mauges in the Vendée: "What they promise as religion is in reality like nothing, because there will be no solemn and public cult, no bells, no processions, not even religious vestments outside of church."[29]

Furthermore, Catholics were defending a whole mode of existence

[27]On the ambiguity and multivocality of symbols, see T. O. Beidelman, *Moral Imagination in Kaguru Modes of Thought* (Bloomington, Ind., 1986), pp. 6–7, 45–46; Caroline Walker Bynum, "The Complexity of Symbols," in *Gender and Religion: On the Complexity of Symbols*, ed. Bynum, Stevan Harrell, and Paula Richman (Boston, 1986), pp. 1–20, esp. 9–10; Paul Ricoeur, "The Symbol Gives Rise to Thought," in *Ways of Understanding Religion*, ed. Walter H. Capps (New York, 1972), pp. 309–17; Victor Turner, *Dramas, Fields, and Metaphors: Symbolic Action in Human Society* (Ithaca, N.Y., 1974), pp. 55–57, and his Introduction to *Forms of Symbolic Action*, ed. R. Spencer (Seattle, 1970).

[28]Bibliothèque municipale d'Auxerre, "Invitation de quelques habitants de la commune de Villeneuve-sur-Yonne à leurs concitoyens, sur les réparations à faire sur leur église," printed, an XI (1800–1), Receuil Tarbé, vol. 8.

[29]As quoted in Langlois and Tackett, "A l'épreuve de la Révolution," p. 265.

as well as a set of religious beliefs and practices. As the revolutionaries strove to endow their own festivals and symbols with public, sacred power, they forced Catholicism to become more private and contained, but religious activists consistently resisted the revolutionary attempt to separate sacred and profane elements of everyday life. Under the Old Regime sacred moments and places held their own special mystique and "otherness"; yet the sacred pervaded more routine existence as well. Believers filtered everyday life through an awareness and expectation that the holy was ever near at hand. Church bells rang to prompt a moment of prayer and contemplation and also to mark the rhythms of the workday. The patron saint's festival included a mass and religious procession as well as a market, dances, and perhaps a harvest feast. This pervasive intermingling of the sacred and profane makes it impossible to interpret the causes of the Catholic revival without oversimplifying the activists' motivations. Defenders of the Catholic calendar, for example, might act out of deep-rooted religious conviction or a less religious attachment to their habitual way of life and patterns of work and celebration, or both. Just as traditional Catholicism took the linking of the sacred and profane as a given, Catholic activists were often motivated not solely by spirituality but also by habit, politics, sociability, or fear of change. The defense of Catholicism went beyond adherence to specific beliefs and forms of devotion; for many, it meant the defense of a way of life and a vast frame of cultural reference.

Approaches to Religion and the Revolution

In the past, historians have generally chosen to emphasize one of two main interpretations of the resurgence of Catholicism during the Revolution. Many have portrayed Catholic activism primarily as political reaction against the central government and the social and political changes of the Revolution. In short, these historians have seen Catholicism as invariably allied with counterrevolution. A second group of historians, primarily clergymen, has been more interested in religion per se. These authors have depicted the Catholic revival as an attempt to return directly to the religious practices and structures of the Old Regime and have concentrated mainly on the fate of the clergy and the institutional church. Religious issues and sentiments were clearly major motivating factors in the counterrevolutionary movements that tore France apart between 1793 and 1799; and Catholic activists certainly sought to revive Old Regime practices. But both of these interpretations, whether political or religious in emphasis, have exaggerated and reified the opposition between the Revolution and Catholicism as the major point of focus. This historiography, whether written by the left or the right, has essentially adopted the language and the categorizations, if not always the value judgments, of the early revolutionaries. The political and religious debates of nineteenth-century France, and especially the debates over separation of church and state during the Third Republic, further ossified these categories. Historians tended to view the Revolution as a monolith, which, depending on the particular historian's viewpoint, either freed the French people from the bonds of superstition and priestcraft or destroyed social bonds and stability and cast terror into the hearts of all. Along these same lines, Catholicism has usually been seen as a static, single entity. Rarely did early histories of religion during the Revolution focus on the laity as an autonomous religious force or examine the innovations and transformations of religious practice following dechristianization. Above all, they did not take into account the profound and complex impact of revolutionary ideology and discourse on religious practice and on the political techniques and ideas of Catholic activists.[30]

In the aftermath of the debate over the separation of church and state in France, interest in religion during the Revolution faded. More recently, however, two trends in religious studies have led historians to focus anew on religion. Gabriel Le Bras and Fernand Boulard stimulated research on religion by illustrating the potential of quantitative, sociological methods to gauge levels of religious practice.[31]

[30]At the turn of the century several important works on religion during the Revolution were written from a Catholic point of view, including Pierre de la Gorce, *Histoire religieuse de la Révolution française*, 5 vols. (Paris, 1909–23), useful despite its Catholic bias; Victor Pierre, *La déportation ecclésiastique sous le Directoire* (Paris, 1896); M. Sciout, *Histoire de la Constitution civile du clergé* (Paris, 1891); and Augustin Sicard, *Le clergé de France pendant la Révolution*, 3 vols. (Paris, 1912–17). Many works trace the fate of the clergy in various regions. For the Yonne, see Bonneau, *Clergé de l'Yonne*. The principal works written in this era on religion from the revolutionary point of view are F. A. Aulard, *Le christianisme et la Révolution française* (Paris, 1924), and *Le culte de la Raison et le culte de l'Etre Suprême* (Paris, 1892); and Albert Mathiez, *Contributions à l'histoire religieuse*, and *La Révolution et l'église* (Paris, 1910). Mathiez's books are collections of essays that appeared in article form between 1900 and 1910.

[31]Gabriel Le Bras, *Introduction à l'histoire de la pratique religieuse en France*, 2 vols. (Paris, 1942–45, and *Etudes de sociologie religieuse*, 2 vols. (Paris, 1955–56); Fernand

Then, in the 1960s and 1970s many historians began to combine the new techniques of the "histoire des mentalités" with religious sociology to reexamine the effects of the Catholic Reformation on popular religious practice.[32] These studies also generated debate on the level of "christianization" or "dechristianization" in prerevolutionary France.[33] This renewed interest in religion produced works that have greatly increased our knowledge about Catholicism during the Revolution. Although this more recent historiography no longer wages the battles of the clericals and the anticlericals of the Third Republic, for the most part the points of emphasis and choices of topic still fall within the established categories: the creation of revolutionary cults, clerical attitudes, the conflicts between the refractory and Constitutional churches, and lay practices in counterrevolutionary areas known for their piety.

The whole discussion of Old Regime dechristianization is still crucial to the history of religious practice during the Revolution, as historians have sought to put the short-term dechristianization campaign of 1793–1794 within the context of the *longue durée* of the eighteenth-century decline in practice.[34] In recent years several historians have looked closely at the mechanisms of dechristianization on the local level: they have provided detailed and necessary information on the identity and techniques of the dechristianizers, the sociology of clerical abdications, and the nature of dechristianizing discourse and festivals.[35] Ultimately, these historians of dechristianization, led pri-

---

Boulard, *Premiers itinéraires en sociologie religieuse*, 2d ed. (Paris, 1954), *Pratique religieuse urbaine et régions culturelles* (Paris, 1968), and *Matériaux pour l'histoire religieuse du peuple français, XIXe–XXe siècles* (Paris, 1982).

[32]Particularly helpful is Jean Quéniart, *Les hommes, l'église, et Dieu dans la France du XVIIIe siècle* (Paris, 1978). For reviews of the literature, see Keith Lurai, *Territories of Grace: Cultural Change in the Seventeenth-Century Diocese of Grenoble* (Berkeley, Calif., forthcoming), chap. 1; R. W. Scribner, "Interpreting Religion in Early Modern Europe," *European Studies Review* 13.1 (1983): 89–105.

[33]Jean Delumeau, *Le catholicisme entre Luther et Voltaire* (Paris, 1971).

[34]Vovelle, *Religion et Révolution*. For a more general overview, see his *Révolution contre l'église*. Vovelle had previously examined dechristianization of the *longue durée* in his analysis of wills in eighteenth-century Provence: *Piété baroque et déchristianisation en Provence au XVIIIe siècle* (Paris, 1973).

[35]Jacques Bernet, "Recherches sur la déchristianisation dans le district de Compiègne (1789–1795)" (Thèse de troisième cycle, Université de Paris I, 1982), and "La déchristianisation dans le district de Compiègne (1789–1795)," *AHRF* 248 (1982): 299–305; Serge Bianchi, "Essai d'interprétation de la déchristianisation de l'an II," *AHRF* 233 (1978): 341–72, and *Révolution culturelle*.

marily by Michel Vovelle, have argued that the gradual dechristianization of the eighteenth century prepared the way for the radical
dechristianizing burst of the year II, which in turn accelerated "the
evolutions of the *longue durée*" and became one of "the major turning
points in the collective sensibility of France."[36] Since these studies
have focused on the dechristianizing or revolutionary side of this
"collective sensibility," however, they understandably have left the
issue of Catholic lay reaction to the revolutionary cults largely
unexplored.

Recent historians have also concentrated on a second major topic:
the response of the clergy to the Revolution. Since the clergy were
required to take a whole series of oaths over the course of the Revolution and were often asked or pressured to abdicate entirely in the year
II (1793–1794), the records of clerical oath taking, abdication, and
emigration have enabled historians to trace clerical attitudes and to
discover regional patterns. Clergymen were least likely to take the
oath to the Civil Constitution in those regions of France later known
for their piety and, in most cases, for their political conservativism,
such as the west, the Massif Central, and parts of the north and
northeast. Timothy Tackett's work, in particular, has helped us to
understand how regional variations in the Old Regime religiosity of
clergy and laity in turn had an impact on the geography of the oath in
1791 and of French religion and politics over the next two centuries.[37] Scholars have also continued to analyze the conflicts between
the nonjuring and Constitutional clergy as well as their attempts to
reestablish Catholicism in France after 1794.[38]

Finally, some attention has recently been given to lay spirituality
during the Revolution. Historians have begun to show the critical

[36]Vovelle, *Religion et Révolution*, p. 300.
[37]Tackett, *Religion and Revolution;* "The West in France in 1789: The Religious
Factor in the Origins of the Counterrevolution," *Journal of Modern History* 54 (1982):
715–45; Tackett and Claude Langlois, "Ecclesiastical Structures and Clerical Geography on the Eve of the French Revolution," *French Historical Studies* 11 (1980): 352–70.
Bernard Plongeron is currently heading a vast quantitative study of oath taking in the
later years of the Revolution. Of the more "pious" regions of France, the north tended
to be notably less conservative in modern politics than other regions of high practice.
[38]J. Boussolade, *L'église de Paris du 9 thermidor au Concordat* (Paris, 1950), and "Le
presbytérianisme dans les Conciles de 1797 et 1801," *AHRF* 121 (1951): 17–37. See also
Olwen Hufton, "The Reconstruction of a Church, 1796–1801," in *Beyond the Terror:
Essays in French Regional History, 1794–1815*, ed. Gwynne Lewis and Colin Lucas
(Cambridge, Eng., 1983), pp. 21–52, esp. 43–48; Langlois and Tackett, "A l'épreuve
de la Révolution," pp. 247–52, 268–72.

links between Old Regime popular culture and lay religious practice
in the 1790s.[39] The Revolution freed popular culture from clerical
control and gave the laity the opportunity to revive traditional popular religious practices that the Catholic Reformation had tried to suppress.[40] Religious activists used traditional forms of devotion either to
support or to oppose the Revolution.[41] Historians, notably Olwen
Hufton, have begun to ask why women were such leading figures in
the religious revival.[42] Nevertheless, female activism and, above all, its
crucial links to the long-term feminization of religion remain under-
explored. Although scholars have recently expanded the study of lay
religiosity during the Revolution, most of the study of Catholicism
during the Revolution has centered on regions of France that were
known for their piety and were predominantly counterrevolutionary.[43]

These recent examinations have increased our knowledge about
religion during the Revolution, particularly regarding the mechanisms of dechristianization, the responses of the clergy, and lay religious practice in certain regions. But these studies have left some
critical questions unasked. Few have looked closely at lay religious
activity in areas of France that were neither counterrevolutionary nor
known for their piety. Moreover, the religious and political activism
of women in these prorevolutionary areas needs further considera-
tion. Most aspects of the *means* of lay revival remain unexplored as
well. Little, if any, attention has been paid to the political and rhetorical techniques of Catholic villagers. Nor have even the most recent
works examined the influence of revolutionary discourse and ideology on traditional devotion and political activism.

The impact of the Revolution on lay religious practice and on popular political activism lies at the heart of this book. By studying a
region that was both prorevolutionary and religious in the 1790s, yet

[39]Bernard Plongeron, *Conscience religieuse en révolution: Regards sur l'historiographie
religieuse de la Révolution française* (Paris, 1969), and "Le fait religieux." See also Hufton,
"The Reconstruction of a Church."

[40]Hufton, "The Reconstruction of a Church," pp. 30–31, 50–51; Langlois and Tackett, "A l'épreuve de la Révolution," pp. 267–68.

[41]Michel Lagrée, "Piété populaire et Révolution en Bretagne: L'exemple des canonisations spontanées (1793–1815)," in *Voies nouvelles*, pp. 265–79.

[42]Olwen Hufton, "Women in Revolution, 1789–1796," *Past and Present* 53 (1971):
90–108.

[43]An exception is Louis Pérouas and Paul d'Hollander, *La Révolution française: Une
rupture dans le christianisme? Le cas du Limousin (1775–1822)* (Treignac, 1989).

became dechristianized in modern times, I am able to shift the focus away from traditional counterrevolutionary regions of study and to uncover distinctly different forms of political activism and religious change. Second, by focusing on the laity, I hope to carry forward the examination of local lay devotion and religiosity and to probe the impact of the Revolution on popular culture and political consciousness. Finally, by paying particular attention to the role of women in the religious resurgence, I seek to understand the effect of gender on religious expression, the leadership role of women in religious riots, and the long-term influence of the revival movement on the feminization of religion.

The Department of the Yonne

The department of the Yonne, located about a hundred kilometers to the southeast of Paris (see Map 1), well represents the post-Thermidorean religious revival in prorevolutionary regions. The northern and eastern portions of the newly formed department lay in the grain-rich fields of Champagne and the Ile-de-France; its southern and eastern parts had belonged to the wine-producing province of Burgundy. The Yonne also contained portions of four different pre-revolutionary dioceses: Auxerre, Sens, Autun, and Langres.[44]

This diverse department is ideal for the analysis of the Catholic resurgence after Thermidor for several reasons. First, the archives of the Yonne have preserved an exceptionally rich body of sources and documentation on the revival, including police records, court cases, religious petitions, reports by local *commissaires*, municipal and departmental deliberations, some local newspapers, and even some diaries and memoirs. More important, this department can be taken as representative of a larger region, for it shared many of the religious and political characteristics of northern and central France, including the Bourbonnais, Bourgogne, Champagne, Orléanais, Ile-de-France, the Loire Valley, and the eastern parts of Picardy and Normandy. Broadly speaking, this central corridor of northern France either accepted the Revolution peacefully or, in many cases, welcomed it actively.

[44]Jean-Luc Dauphin, "La création d'un département: Emergence d'une nouvelle collectivité," in *La Révolution dans le département de l'Yonne*, ed., Léo Hamon (Paris, forthcoming).

Map 1

Acceptance of the Civil Constitution was high. At the same time, Catholics in these areas fought hard to restore religious worship in the later 1790s, though their descendants would be strikingly less pious than their neighbors in western, eastern, and parts of southern France.[45] Of course, each canton or department had its own particular political and religious history, and this general assessment is not meant to discount these local variations. Nevertheless, the center, Paris Basin, and Burgundy stand together in sharp contrast to the regions of low oath taking or extensive counterrevolutionary activity: they shared certain broad religious and political configurations during the 1790s and experienced a similar form of religious revival after Thermidor.

The departments in these areas did not witness large-scale, violent resistance to the Revolution. Most of the population of the Yonne welcomed its early phases. The department proudly claimed to have offered the Revolution one of its most popular early leaders, Louis Lepeletier of Saint-Fargeau.[46] Although Avallon briefly supported the federalists, the rest of the Yonne remained loyal to the leadership of the Mountain until the fall of Robespierre. During the Thermidorean period moderates in most towns and villages in the Yonne worked hard to demolish any vestiges of the Jacobins' former power, but the Thermidorean reaction never reached the terrifying or violent proportions of the White Terror in the southeast or the *chouannerie* in the west. Although the Yonne, like most departments in central and northern France, elected moderate or right-wing candidates to the national legislature in the late 1790s, there was never any serious counterrevolutionary movement in Burgundy.[47] In the year VIII

[45]On the geography of the oath, see Tackett, *Religion and Revolution*, pp. 52–54, 307–66. On the modern geography of religious practice, see Boulard, *Matériaux pour l'histoire religieuse*, pp. 88–91, 552–53, and *Premiers itinéraires*, Carte de la France religieuse en trois grandes régions and Carte religieuse: France urbaine. See also François-André Isambert and Jean-Paul Terrenoire, *Atlas de la pratique religieuse des Catholiques en France* (Paris, 1980), pp. 34–36, 57.

[46]Though Lepeletier held land in the Yonne, he was in essence a Parisian by education and life-style.

[47]Hunt, *Politics, Culture, and Class*, chap. 4, esp. p. 131. Hunt's research on the political geography of the Revolution, based on election results, has shown that virtually all the departments in northern and central France supported conservative candidates after 1795. Some of these departments, including the Yonne, voted on the left in the early years of the Revolution, and others, particularly in Normandy and Ile-de-France, voted on the right early in the Revolution, although they did not offer counterrevolutionary resistance.

(1799–1800) a report by the Ministry of the Police listed the Yonne among those "peaceful departments where so far no major troubles have broken out."[48] In the nineteenth century the left in the Yonne gradually increased in strength and flourished, especially during the early Third Republic. After World War I the left divided and grew weaker; by the 1940s the Yonne's politics tended toward the center rather than the left. Emmanuel Todd and Hervé Le Bras include the modern department of their general category of "geographically central and politically centrist . . . neither very revolutionary, nor very reactionary."[49]

The Old Regime religiosity of the Yonne also resembled that of other parts of central and north-central France. Exactly what the average peasant of the Yonne believed about God and the heavens in the days before the Revolution will always remain a mystery; yet three important influences on the Yonne's religiosity stand out: the Catho-

---

[48]AN F7 3820, Tableaux des départements qu'on doit considérer comme en état de troubles, et des départements paisibles ou dans lesquels il n'a pas éclaté jusqu'ici des troubles essentiels, ministre de la police, vendémiaire an VIII (September–October 1799). This report includes fifty departments, primarily in the northern half of France. The "troubled" departments are mainly in the west, with a few listed in the southeast. "Peaceful" departments are concentrated in the central and northern part of France: Allier, Aube, Cher, Creuse, Indre, Loiret, Marne, Nièvre, Oise, Seine (Paris), Seine-et-Oise, Seine-et-Marne, Yonne, Aisne, Meuse, and Moselle. A third group of departments, listed as partially troubled, lies primarily in a band between the west and center, including Seine-Inférieure, Indre-et-Loire, Loir-et-Cher, Pas-de-Calais, Ardennes, Nord, and Somme, among others. The political geography of peaceful departments coincides quite well with the geography of clerical loyalty to the Revolution. In all but Moselle more than half the clergy took the oath. Oath taking was low in Brittany, Normandy, the rest of the west, the far north and northeast, the Massif Central, and the southwest corner of France. Tackett, *Religion and Revolution*, pp. 52–54, 307–66.

[49]Hervé Le Bras and Emmanuel Todd, *L'invention de la France: Atlas anthropologique et politique* (Paris, 1981), p. 376. The Yonne witnessed large armed uprisings against Napoleon III in 1851, but Democratic Socialists had not received a majority of the vote in 1849. Maurice Agulhon, *1848, ou L'apprentissage de la République (1848–1852)* (Paris, 1973), pp. 174–77; Ted W. Margadant, *French Peasants in Revolt: The Insurrection of 1851* (Princeton, N.J., 1979), pp. 3–40, 256–63; Jean-Pierre Rocher, "L'évolution politique et religieuse du département de l'Yonne pendant la Révolution," and "L'évolution politique et religieuse du département de l'Yonne pendant la première moitié du XIXe siècle," both in *Du jansénisme à la laïcité: Le jansénisme et les origines de la déchristianisation,* ed. Léo Hamon (Paris, 1987), pp. 89–109, 111–37; François Goguel, "Un siècle d'élections législatives dans l'Yonne (1848–1946)," in *Du jansénisme à la laïcité,* pp. 191–216. Goguel points out that the left in the Yonne peaked from 1869 to 1910, when anticlericalism was a central issue, but grew weaker as social issues came to the fore in the left-wing agenda.

lic Reformation, Jansenism, and popular devotional practices. In the late seventeenth and early eighteenth centuries several Catholic Reformation bishops, as well as Jansenist clergy in the Senonais and Auxerrois, did their best to suppress any "superstitious" or "magical" practices of the laity. Although the peasantry often resisted these reforms and persisted in various local, popular devotions, the Catholic Reformation and Jansenism left the Yonne with a more subdued form of religiosity by the late 1700s. Clerical vocations had also declined throughout the department in the eighteenth century. I discuss the implications of Old Regime religiosity in the Yonne at greater length in Chapters 2 and 3; but the significant point here is that the spirituality of the Yonne on the eve of Revolution was the product of partially successful reform attempts and persistent popular religious practices.[50]

Though not all subject to Jansenist spirituality, many other Old Regime dioceses of the center, north-center, and parts of the southeast shared this mixed influence of the Catholic Reformation, which seemed to kindle devotion with one hand and suppress it with the other. This ambiguous heritage would leave its mark on the religious revival during Thermidor and the Directory. In contrast, in those regions of intense resistance to the oath—regions such as the west, the Massif Central, and the northeast, all known for their piety in more modern times—the clergy of the late seventeenth and early eighteenth centuries seem to have done a better job of tempering the most austere reforms, respecting their parishioners' attachment to the localized sacred and creating good rapport with lay villagers.[51] Partly

[50]Jean-Pierre Locatelli, "La vie matérielle et l'enseignement dans le diocèse d'Auxerre de 1672 à 1712" (Mémoire de maîtrise, Université de Paris I, 1970); Pierre Roudil, "La vie religieuse et mentalité collective dans le diocèse d'Auxerre de 1672 à 1712" (Mémoire de maîtrise, Université de Paris I, 1970); Dominique Dinet, "Les ordinations sacerdotales dans les diocèses d'Auxerre, Langres, et Dijon (XVIIe–XVIIIe siècles)," Revue d'histoire de l'église de France 66 (1980): 211–41, esp. 221–29; Le Bras, Etudes de sociologie 1:39–51. For recruitment and density in a national context, see Tackett, "The West in France," pp. 722–27.

[51]Alain Croix, La Bretagne au 16e et 17e siècles: La vie, la mort, la foi, 2 vols. (Paris, 1981), 2:1241–42, and Les Bretons, la mort, et dieu (Paris, 1984), pp. 150–51, 220–25; Charles Berthelot du Chesnay, Les missions de Saint Eudes (Paris, 1967), pp. 241–44, and Les prêtres séculiers en Haute-Bretagne au XVIIIe siècle (Rennes, 1984), p. 514; Tackett, Religion and Revolution, pp. 233–46; Alain Lottin, "Contre-réforme et religion populaire: Un mariage difficile mais réussi au XVIe et XVIIe siècles en Flandre et en Hainaut," in La religion populaire (Paris, 1979), pp. 53–63.

because of different patterns in Old Regime religiosity, in these areas the religious movement of the 1790s would take a different form: illegal clerical leadership would play a larger role and the lay assimilation of revolutionary politics a smaller one. Over the longer term here, the Catholic Church had greater success in encouraging religious practice.

At the outset of the Revolution, the priests and people of the Yonne and the surrounding regions seemed willing to accept the religious reforms of the new government. The *cahiers* of the Third Estate had requested reductions of clerical wealth and privilege along the lines that the national legislature soon decreed.[52] In contrast to the west, the far north, the northeast, and parts of the south, clergy in most of central and northern France took the oath to the Civil Constitution. Over 85 percent of the clergy of the Yonne took the oath without invalidating clauses or conditions and without retracting it in 1791.[53] The Yonne also shared with the center and Paris Basin the experience of an intense and widespread dechristianization campaign. Although dechristianization provoked local popular resistance, especially in the countryside, clerical abdications were high in the Yonne (taking place in at least 76 percent of the communes), many churches were closed, and the new revolutionary festivals initially drew large crowds, especially in the populous towns of Sens and Auxerre.[54] When the fall of Robespierre seemed to lend hope for a return to the public practice of Catholicism, however, villagers in the Yonne, as in most other regions of France, demanded en masse the right to public worship. Throughout the department, Catholics broke into churches, led illegal processions, and avidly petitioned for religious liberty. Between the fall of Robespierre and the coming of Napoleon, police recorded

[52]M. Courtaut, "Etudes sur l'esprit public du Tiers Etat du bailliage d'Auxerre en 1789," *BSSY* 4 (1850): 265–368, esp. 312–15; Charles Demay, "Cahiers des paroisses du bailliage d'Auxerre pour les Etats-généraux de 1789," *BSSY* 38 (1884): 65–400, esp. 66, 72–76, 116–17, and 39 (1885): 5–150. Demay reprints the original texts of the parish cahiers, offering many specific examples of resentment of clerical wealth. The parishioners are generally sympathetic to the poverty of local curés and some suggest that the *casuel* be replaced with a regular clerical salary.

[53]Rocher, "Aspects de l'histoire religieuse."

[54]Vovelle, *Révolution contre l'église*, esp. maps pp. 277–88; AD Yonne L705, Etats nominatifs des ecclésiastiques qui ont abdiqué leurs fonctions, tableaux par district (dated in various months in the spring and summer of 1794); Henri Forestier, "Les campagnes de l'Auxerrois et la déchristianisation, d'après la correspondance d'E. A. Rathier," *AB* 24 (1947): 185–206.

some violation of the laws restricting public worship in every one of the sixty-nine cantons of the Yonne.[55] Yet, despite this zealous revival of Catholicism in the 1790s, the Yonne, like much of central and northern France, underwent a serious decline in religious observance in the nineteenth and twentieth centuries.[56]

In short, the Yonne shared many religious and political characteristics with the vast heartland of France, stretching from the eastern Loire Valley, Bourbonnais, and Burgundy up through the Ile-de-France to Champagne and parts of Picardy and Normandy in the north. Examining the lay religious movements in the Yonne during the crucial period of the late 1790s can give us a close-up view of the charged interaction between revolutionary and traditional culture on the local level and can contribute to our understanding of the religious and political geography of France as a whole.

 The next chapter will examine the Old Regime religiosity of the Yonne and explore certain basic political and religious tendencies within its varying geography during the Thermidorean revival. Chapter 3 will probe the impact of the Revolution on religious practice as lay activists adapted their rituals and took advantage of the void left by the clergy to transform their modes of religious expression. Next, I turn to the *means* of defending Catholicism, from peaceful politics to violent activism. Chapter 4 will analyze Catholics' assimilation of revolutionary rhetoric and politics to defend their right to practice and will also illustrate certain effects of the Revolution on popular mentality and activism at the local level. Chapter 5 will explore religious violence as a fusion of traditional and revolutionary techniques and question the impact of rioting on communal power struggles and on

[55]On violation of religious laws, see AD Yonne, *police des cultes* and court records, departmental, district, and municipal deliberations; AN, esp. F7 (police) and F19 (cultes) series; BN, newspapers; and various archives communales in the Yonne. Particularly useful are two reports on religious practice in each canton of the department in spring 1797 and fall 1798: AN F7 7237, Enquête sur l'exercice et la police intérieure des cultes dans le département de l'Yonne, ventôse an v (February–March 1797); AN AFiii 280, Situation du département de l'Yonne, germinal an vii (March-April 1799). Both were written by Etienne Housset, commissaire près les tribunaux civils et criminaux du département de l'Yonne.

[56]Boulard, *Matériaux pour l'histoire religieuse*, pp. 88–91, 552–53, and *Premiers itinéraires*, Carte de la France religieuse en trois grandes régions and Carte religieuse: France urbaine; Isambert and Terrenoire, *Atlas de la pratique religieuse*, pp. 34–36, 57.

religious practice. In particular, it will probe the roots of the strong devotion and activism among women and ask how female religious leadership during the Revolution influenced nineteenth-century Catholicism. The last chapter will draw some conclusions about cultural change during the Revolution and suggest how these transformations affected religious expression as well as the interaction of religion and politics in the postrevolutionary era.

CHAPTER TWO

Religious and Political
Landscapes of the Yonne

I n the spring of 1797, Etienne Housset, the commissaire of the
department of the Yonne, conducted a systematic survey of the
religious habits and practices of the citizens under his responsibility.
He concluded ruefully, "first, that the Catholic, apostolic and Roman
religion is the only one practiced in the department of the Yonne;
second, that the people are very attached to the ceremonies of their
religion and that in some communes this attachment becomes superstition." He went on to bemoan lenient local officials, to recount uprisings by Catholic citizens, and to note in great detail the presence of
outlawed clergymen, of illegal bell-ringing, and of crosses and other
"exterior signs of cult."[1] Indeed, throughout the department of the
Yonne there was a resurgence of Catholic practice after the fall of
Robespierre. Yet the religious movement varied in intensity, form,
and political style in the different geographic regions of the Yonne.
As Housset himself commented, certain places were marked by a
"furious fanaticism." Conflicts between Catholics and supporters of
republican cults were most common in large towns, and the Auxerrois
region in south-central Yonne was by far the most religiously active.
The Northern Senonais area was the least active, and the officials in
the district of Avallon in the far south did little to repress or even
report illegal Catholic worship.

Like many of the newly formed departments, the Yonne was in

---

[1]AN F7 7237, Enquête sur l'exercice et la police intérieure des cultes dans le département de l'Yonne, ventôse an v (February–March 1797).

many ways a piecemeal creation. United primarily by the river that
offered the department its name, the Yonne consisted of odds and
ends of "five different provinces, four dioceses, fourteen Old Regime
bailliages, and fourteen *élections*."[2] Vineyards, bocage country, and
wheat fields lay within its boundaries. Levels of literacy, land-tenure
systems, density of population, contact with Paris—all varied according to region, and all influenced Catholic activism during the Thermidorean and Directorial periods. But two factors seemed most
important in defining the regional character of the religious movement. First, the nature of Old Regime religiosity differed in the four
dioceses that contributed parishes to the Yonne. The varying intensity
of the Catholic Reformation and the presence or absence of Jansenism particularly influenced lay spirituality. Second, the attitude of
local authorities and revolutionaries toward promoting dechristianization in the year II and enforcing religious laws in the later
1790s affected the nature of Catholic response. Forceful dechristianization and stringent enforcement of the new calendar and festivals tended to provoke high levels of religious reaction but also
politicized Catholics and exposed them to political techniques and
language that they could turn to their own advantage. On the other
hand, the silence and toleration of pro-Catholic officials in some regions made the revival of public Catholic practice smoother and less
eventful.

The Geography and Religiosity of the Yonne

The department of the Yonne encompassed four main agricultural
regions: the fertile wheat fields of the Senonais to the north; the
rolling vineyards and cereal fields of the Auxerrois and Tonnerrois in
the south; the poorer and sparsely populated bocage country of the
Puisaye in the southwest; and finally, in the southern tip of the department, the vineyards of the Avallonais and the mountains of the
Morvan (see Map 2).

In the north lay the Senonais and part of the Gâtinais. Formerly
part of Champagne and Ile-de-France, this region included the dis-

---

[2]Gaston David, "Tableaux de l'histoire d'Auxerre de 1789 à 1817," *Echo d'Auxerre* 71
(1967): 37, as quoted in Alype-Jean Noirot, *Le département de l'Yonne comme diocèse*, 2
vols. (Auxerre, 1979), 1:3. The Yonne contained parts of the Old Regime provinces of
Bourgogne, Champagne, Ile-de-France, Orléanais, and Nivernais.

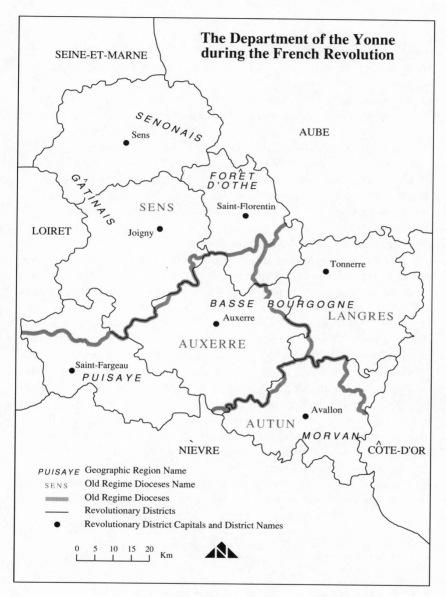

The Department of the Yonne during the French Revolution

SEINE-ET-MARNE

SENONAIS

Sens

AUBE

GÂTINAIS

FORÊT D'OTHE

SENS

Saint-Florentin

LOIRET

Joigny

Tonnerre

BASSE BOURGOGNE

Auxerre

LANGRES

AUXERRE

Saint-Fargeau

PUISAYE

Avallon

AUTUN

MORVAN

NIÈVRE

CÔTE-D'OR

PUISAYE	Geographic Region Name
SENS	Old Regime Dioceses Name
	Old Regime Dioceses
	Revolutionary Districts
●	Revolutionary District Capitals and District Names

0 5 10 15 20 Km

Map 2

trict of Sens and the northern parts of the districts of Joigny and Saint-Florentin. In this rich grain-producing region of fertile alluvial soil and open-field agriculture, peasants owned a little over half the land, nobles owned about 16 percent, bourgeois landholders another 16 percent, and the clergy about 13 percent.[3] Sens, an important commercial and ecclesiastical center, was the second largest town of the department and became the seat of the newly formed diocese of the Yonne. The Senonais was the most literate region within the Yonne: 64 percent of the men and 35 percent of the women signed their marriage contracts in the late eighteenth century.[4]

A heavily wooded region, known as the Forêt d'Othe (or Pays-d'Othe), separated the Senonais from the Basse Bourgogne to the south. This area comprised the districts of Auxerre and Tonnerre and the southern parts of the districts of Saint-Florentin and Joigny. The Auxerrois and Tonnerrois produced wine and some cereal, and the inhabitants of the Joigny and Saint-Florentin regions made their livings mainly from cereal and wood. As the commissaire Collet noted in 1798, aside from the shipment of wood and charcoal, "there was little industry; no great manufacturers or factories with big works," only some smaller producers of "leather, pottery, and tile . . . and a few of iron and paper." The villages of the Basse Bourgogne tended to be densely concentrated and to have relatively large communal landholdings. Small proprietors owned a good 75 percent of the land here; the church held about 10 percent; and noble landholdings fell well below the national average of 20 percent in most cantons. Where the Yonne River met the road from Paris to Dijon and Lyon, at the heart of a vast *vignoble* lay Auxerre, a former diocesan seat, the largest town in the department, and the home of its new administration. The male inhabitants of the Basse Bourgogne were fairly literate by the end of the eighteenth century. In the Auxerrois in the 1780s a striking 87 percent of parishes had schools. Over 40 percent of the men and about 21 percent of their wives could sign their marriage certifi-

[3]Charles Porée, *Documents relatifs à la vente des biens nationaux dans le district de Sens* (Auxerre, 1912), p. xviii; P. Dupéron, *La question du pain dans l'Yonne sous le règne du maximum* (Paris, 1910), pp. xi, 3–5. See also AN F20 273, Statistique du département de l'Yonne, signée du préfet Rougier-Labergerie, an ix (1800–1).

[4]Marie-Laurence Netter, "Alphabétisation et scolarisation dans l'Yonne et dans la Haute-Garonne de la fin du XVIIIe siècle à 1833" (Thèse du troisième cycle, Université de Paris i et l'Ecole Pratique des Hautes Etudes en Sciences Sociales, 1980), pp. 33–34, 39. I am grateful to Marie-Laurence Netter for discussing education in the Yonne with me.

cates. Slightly fewer could sign in the forested region of the Forêt d'Othe.[5]

To the east of the relatively rich area of the Basse Bourgogne lay the Puisaye, the district of Saint-Fargeau. A poor area of marshes, ponds, and forests, the Puisaye was a bocage country, dominated by wealthy landowners and farmed mainly by sharecroppers. Communes tended to be large and sparsely populated with widespread hamlets. No town boasted over two thousand inhabitants. Communal land was scarce. Most farms raised poultry, dairy cows, or horses, or grew apples for cider in this humid and rugged land whose clay soil was too infertile for large-scale cereal production or grape growing. The Puisaye also shipped wood and charcoal down the rivers to provide fuel for Paris and produced a small amount of iron, pottery, and cloth. Not surprisingly, this isolated and impoverished region had the lowest literacy rate of the department: on the eve of the Revolution schools were few and only 19 percent of the men and 10 percent of the women were able to sign their names.[6]

In the southeast corner of the department, the district of Avallon had yet another set of geographic characteristics. The northern part of the district lay at the edge of the Basse Bourgogne and shared its fertile soil. Avallon, the district capital, was a center of trade for the wine, wood, cereals, livestock, and cloth produced in the area. To the south of Avallon, the countryside grew poorer and much hillier. This southernmost part of the Yonne formed the upper corner of the Morvan, a mountainous region whose forested and rocky slopes were suitable only for subsistence agriculture, livestock raising, and logging. Many of the workers were migrants, including loggers, day laborers, artisans, and wet nurses. The commissaire of Quarré-les-Tombes in the Morvan reported in 1795 that his canton could not produce wheat or grapes; in contrast to the inhabitants of the more productive valley to the north, the people lived in "perpetual scarcity," subsisting largely on "buckwheat bread, heavily salted potatoes,

[5]Jean-Paul Moreau, *La vie rurale dans le sud-est du bassin parisien* (Paris, 1958), pp. 81–103; AN F1cIII Yonne 5, Rapport par Commissaire Collet aux directeurs, thermidor an VI (July–August 1798); AN F1c III Yonne 7, Rapport par Collet au ministre de la police, 21 frimaire an VI (11 December 1797); AN F20 273, Statistique du département de l'Yonne, signée du préfet Rougier-Labergerie, an IX (1800–1); Netter, "Alphabétisation," pp. 34, 43–44, 92, 176–80.
[6]Moreau, *Vie rurale*, pp. 9–10, 43–46, 238–48; Dupéron, *Question du pain*, p. 16; Netter, "Alphabétisation," pp. 34, 47–48, 180.

and milk products. . . . Living far from towns and big roads, the inhabitants are a little savage but good and honest; the forest air endows
them with a great character of liberty, loyalty, and hospitality." Literacy was low in this isolated Morvan region, though the northern part
of the Avallonais had schools in about half its parishes. In the district
as a whole, only one man in three and one woman in ten signed their
marriage contracts.[7]

Before the Revolution the various regions of the future department
of the Yonne made up portions of four different dioceses. Most of the
communes of the new districts of Sens, Saint-Florentin, and Joigny
had belonged to the diocese of Sens. The former diocese of Auxerre
had contributed the parishes in the Auxerrois and Puisaye. The Tonnerrois once had been part of the diocese of Langres, and the Avallonais part of the diocese of Autun. The impact of the Catholic Reformation on lay spirituality has been studied more thoroughly in the
dioceses of Auxerre and Autun than in the Senonais and Tonnerrois.[8] It is beyond the scope of this book to supplement this work with
a scrutiny of the prerevolutionary religiosity of these and the other
two dioceses. Yet some exploration of salient differences and sim-
ilarities in Old Regime region will provide useful background for
understanding the religious resurgence during the Revolution.

The dioceses that contributed to the Yonne shared certain major
religious experiences. They all witnessed the flowering of Catholic
Reformation orders in the early seventeenth century, for example.
Particularly in the major ecclesiastical centers of Sens, Auxerre, and
Avallon, new active orders, such as the Oratorians, Doctrinaires,
Jesuits, Visitandines, Sisters of Charity, Ursulines, and Providenciennes joined the refurbished traditional monastic communities.
Seminaries were founded in Sens and Auxerre in 1653 and 1672
respectively, and in smaller ecclesiastical centers—such as Joigny in
the Gâtinais, Saint-Fargeau in the Puisaye, Tonnerre and Noyers in
the Tonnerrois, and Vézelay and Montréal in the Avallonais—hospi-

[7]Jean B. Baudiau, *Le Morvan, ou Essai géographique, topographique, et historique sur cette contrée*, 3 vols., 3d ed., (Paris, 1965, orig. ed., Nevers, 1865), p. 52; AN F7 7129, Rapport sur le canton de Quarré-les-Tombes, 19 nivôse an IV (9 January 1796); Netter, "Alphabétisation," pp. 36, 45–46, 176–80.

[8]On Auxerre, see esp. Roudil, "Vie religieuse"; Locatelli, "Vie matérielle"; Le Bras, *Etudes de sociologie* 1:39–51. For Autun, see André Lanfrey, "L'évolution de la vie religieuse dans le nord de l'évêché d'Autun de 1667 à 1710" (Mémoire de mâitrise, Université de Lyon II, 1971); Thérèse-Jean Schmitt, *L'organisation ecclésiastique et la pratique religieuse dans l'archidiaconé d'Autun de 1650 à 1750* (Autun, 1957).

tals, *collèges,* and foundations were also started or reformed. The proliferation of new orders was primarily a phenomenon of large towns, however; the region as a whole maintained relatively low clerical density, typical of the center and Paris Basin. Especially in the countryside, vicars and nonparish clergy were few; a survey at the beginning of the Revolution discovered that only 75 vicars and chaplains aided the 468 parish curés.[9]

All the dioceses also participated in Tridentine reforms of rural religiosity. During the reign of Louis XIV, bishops in all four dioceses embarked on serious campaigns to stamp out "superstitious" practices among the laity, encourage a more abstract, Christocentric spirituality, and train a cadre of upright, well-educated clergymen. According to Catholic Reformation ideals, the priest should receive thorough theological training and be a moral and spiritual leader within the parish; there should be much less emphasis on his traditional role as a potential miracle worker. Parishioners should learn the basic tenets of Christianity; faith in Christ as the road to salvation should replace medieval devotion to assorted saints, relics, shrines, and fountains. The reformers sought to endow Catholicism with a new dignity and solemnity and a sharper separation between the sacred and the profane. Central to Tridentine spirituality was the uniform and solemn celebration of the mass and reception of the Eucharist in a well-maintained church building. Live animals and "indecent" or "grotesque" statues were chased from the church and cemetery. Raucous religious festivals and long pilgrimages without clerical supervision had little place in the Tridentine vision.

Strong clerical leadership, proper rituals, catechism, and a balance between active charity and contemplative, Christocentric spirituality—these were the hallmarks of the Catholic Reformation, but its

---

[9]AD Yonne L667, Tableau de maisons religieuses, prieurés, cures, collèges, et séminaires du département; Claude Hohl, *Le jansénisme dans l'Yonne* (Auxerre, 1986), pp. 35–37, 61–68; Jean-Pierre Rocher, "La vie religieuse aux XVIIe et XVIIIe siècles," in *L'histoire d'Auxerre à nos jours,* ed. Rocher (Auxerre, 1984), pp. 253–57; Tackett and Langlois, "Ecclesiastical Structures," p. 358. Their study places the Yonne in the second lowest category of vicar-to-curé ratios (between .41 and .69) according to a Ministry of Finance report on surviving pensioners in 1817. In some areas of high clerical density in the west and the far southeast, for example, vicars outnumbered curés by as much as three or four to one. On clerical structures, see also Dominique Julia, "La réforme post-tridentine en France d'après les procès-verbaux de visites pastorales: Ordre et résistances," *La società religiosa nell'eta moderna: Atti del convegno studi di storia sociale e religiosa, Cupaccio-Paestum, 18–21 maggio 1972* (Naples, 1973), pp. 341–44.

impact was ambiguous. Lay Catholics clung tenaciously to traditional forms of popular devotion and often were dismayed when their newly trained priests were reluctant to ring bells to ward off storms or sprinkle holy water over the fields to guarantee the harvest. In the eyes of some villagers, the curé's new role seemed to make him less spiritually powerful than his pre-Trindentine predecessors; yet his parishioners still wanted a religion concretely based on the sacred power of objects and places. In fact, the Yonne forms an interesting test case for the prevalent theory that the Catholic Reformation, *over the long run,* sometimes weakened Catholic devotion, especially in those areas where clergy were not so numerous.[10] Within the Yonne this general pattern varied according to region. Bishops were zealous and successful reformers to different degrees, and in some cases disputes over Jansenism accompanied and complicated reform attempts.

The Catholic Reformation also had a mixed impact on female spirituality. On the one hand, women seemed to cling with particular tenacity to certain customs the Catholic Reformers sought to suppress. Not surprisingly, women were notably unwilling to surrender certain "superstitious" practices having to do with pregnancy, childbirth, and healing, such as devotion to fountains that promoted fertility or statues that had the miraculous power to resuscitate stillborn infants, if only for a moment. On the other hand, the Catholic Reformation led to the creation of numerous female religious orders and female confraternities, often devoted to Mary or to Christ. Women were thus able to play a much more active and public role in charitable and devotional organizations than before the Catholic Reformation, even in small villages. In 1682, for example, Bishop André Colbert was pleased to discover and encourage a small, spontaneous female confraternity of the Virgin in the tiny village of Arrablay in the diocese of Auxerre. Of Coulanges-la-Vineuse in the same period, he noted that "the women, following the inclination of their sex toward devotion, take the sacrament fairly frequently." Hoping to en-

---

[10]Delumeau, *Catholicisme,* chaps. 4 and 5; Hoffman, *Church and Community,* chaps. 4 and 5; Julia, "La réforme post-tridentine," esp. pp. 379–97; Quéniart, *Les hommes, l'église,* esp. pp. 277, 317; Tackett, *Religion, Revolution,* pp. 233–46, and *Priest and Parish,* chap. 6; Nicole Perin, "La religion populaire: Mythes et réalités. L'exemple du diocèse de Reims sous l'ancien régime," in *La religion populaire* Paris, 17–19 octobre 1977 (Paris, 1979), pp. 221–28; Jeanne Ferté, *La vie religieuse dans les campagnes parisiennes (1622–1695)* (Paris, 1962); R. Sauzet, *Les visites pastorales dans le diocèse de Chartres pendant la première moitié du XVIIe siècle* (Rome, 1975).

courage this apparent female bent toward piety, the reformers allowed some clerically controlled forms of traditional female devotion to flourish. Restif de la Bretonne gleefully reports that young girls from around Sacy in the 1740s made a pilgrimage on 29 June each year to a chapel in Cravant devoted to "la Vierge-d'Harbeaux."[11]

In some parts of the Yonne Jansenism influenced the effects of the Catholic Reformation on lay religiosity and left a crucial mark on Old Regime spirituality. Jansenism was most influential in the diocese of Auxerre. Likewise, the Senonais witnessed a strong Jansenist movement in the late seventeenth century, though opponents of Jansenism somewhat curtailed this theological movement in the eighteenth century. The Tonnerrois never had a truly Jansenist bishop but was nonetheless the most Jansenist region of the diocese of Langres. Only the Avallonais remained largely immune, though the town of Avallon itself held Jansenist enclaves.[12]

Jansenism had many faces, but the Jansenist clergy of the Paris Basin shared certain key goals.[13] First, in opposition to their theological rivals, the Jesuits, the Jansenists encouraged rigorous moral standards for laity and clergy alike. Believers were expected to undergo intense soul searching and sincere conversion before receiving the sacraments. Second, even more than non-Jansenist Catholic Reformers, Jansenists aimed at inculcating an interior spirituality stripped of unnecessary ceremony, superstition, or frivolity. They favored subdued religious rituals that appealed to the spirit and the mind rather than the senses, and they wanted parishioners to understand and participate in them. In the 1740s and 1750s Charles de Caylus (1704–

[11]Natalie Zemon Davis, "City Women and Religious Change," in her *Society and Culture in Early Modern France* (Stanford, Calif., 1975), pp. 65–96; Hoffman, *Church and Community*, pp. 126–28, 144–46; R. Sauzet, "Présence rénovée du catholicisme (1520–1670)," in *Histoire des catholiques*, ed. Lebrun, chap. 2; AD Yonne G1651, Visite pastorale à Arrablay, 1683, as cited by Roudil, "Vie religieuse," p. 69. Roudil emphasizes the reluctance of women as "gardiennes de tradition" to give up those "superstitions" that have to do with sorcery or thaumaturgy (pp. 92–94). Restif de la Bretonne, *L'enfance de Monsieur Nicolas*, ed. Gilbert Rouger (Paris, 1955, orig., 1794–97), pp. 54–55, 73–74.

[12]Hohl, *Jansénisme;* Schmitt, *L'organisation ecclésiastique*, pp. 236–37.

[13]On the multiple versions of Jansenism in different regions, see Pierre Chaunu, "Jansénisme et frontière de catholicité (XVIIe–XVIIIe siècles): A propos du jansénisme lorrain," *Revue historique* 227 (1962): 115–38; René Taveneaux, *La vie quotidienne des jansénistes aux XVIIe et XVIIIe siècles* (Paris, 1973), pp. 9–13; Bernard Plongeron, "Une image de l'église d'après les *Nouvelles ecclésiastiques* (1728–1789)," *Revue historique de l'église de France* 53 (1967): 241–68, esp. 241–43.

1754) the Jansenist bishop of Auxerre, encouraged the laity to follow
the words of the mass in their missals and even urged priests to read
certain parts aloud in French. In their desire to stimulate inner faith,
the Jansenists, like the Protestants before them, advocated greater lay
education. The Tabourin Brothers founded six primary schools in
Auxerre, for example, to prepare children for a contemplative, intellectual spirituality and upright life. Parents and children were urged
to pray together and to study the Bible and devotional manuals at
home. Jansenists had little use for many traditional, less intellectual
types of worship, such as saints' cults or outdoor pilgrimages. Even
new forms of devotion, including the cult of the Sacred Heart of
Jesus, came under virulent attack by purist Jansenists.[14]

Though Jansenists often disputed with other Catholic reformers
over such issues as the frequency of communion, the theological content of diocesan catechisms, and the establishment of certain confraternities, Jansenism echoed and reinforced the Catholic Reformation in suppressing quasi-superstitious beliefs and customs. Even
more than the Catholic Reformation, Jansenist severity in both personal morality and religious practice often seemed to drain traditional
spirituality of its vitality and to distance the priest from his parishioners.[15] The priest lost some of his sacerdotal power and sometimes his moral austerity brought him into head-on conflict with villagers. In 1723, for example, the new young Jansenist curé of Celle-

[14]Taveneaux, *Vie quotidienne*, chap. 7; Pierre Ordioni, *La résistance gallicane et janséniste dans le diocèse d'Auxerre (1704–1760)* (Auxerre, 1932), esp. pt. 1, chaps. 2 and 3,
La survivance des idées gallicanes et jansénistes en Auxerrois de 1760 à nos jours (Auxerre,
1933), esp. pt. 1, chap. 3, and "Les origines gallicanes de l'anticléricalisme en Auxerrois," in *Du jansénisme à la laïcité*, pp. 167–88, esp. 168–70. On Jansenist attitudes to the
liturgy, see also Edmond Préclin, *Les jansénistes du XVIIIe siècle et la Constitution civile du
clergé* (Paris, 1929), pp. 179–97. Bishop Caylus's own *Rituel d'Auxerre* also encouraged
lay participation. André Gazier, *Les écoles de charité du Faubourg Saint-Antoine: Ecole
normale et groupes scolaires (1713–1887)* (Paris, 1906), pp. 9–25. These Jansenist schools
were founded by the Jansenist Charles Tabourin in 1713 and run by lay brothers.
There were thirty-two in Paris and six in Auxerre until the French Revolution. On the
attack of Jansenists against the cult of the Sacred Heart, see Dominique Dinet, "Jansénisme et les origines de la déchristianisation au XVIIIe siècle: L'exemple des pays de
l'Yonne," in *Du jansénisme à la laïcité*, pp. 1–34, esp. p. 16.

[15]Dinet, "Jansénisme et déchristianisation," esp. pp. 26–28, and pp. 1–4 for a review
of the literature on the secularizing impact of Jansenism; Boulard, *Matériaux pour
l'histoire religieuse*, pp. 88–89; Hoffman, *Church and Community*, pp. 160–61; Quéniart,
Hommes et l'église, p. 275; Tackett, *Religion, Revolution*, pp. 235–36. On the Jansenist
attitude toward festivals, see also Antoine Arnauld, "Eclaircissement sur la défense des
danses et de la profanation des fêtes," *Oeuvres* (Paris, 1780), 36:471–79.

Saint-Cyr barricaded the main entrance to the village church and told his congregation, "You are not worthy to use the main door." His parishioners protested, drew up a petition, and took him to court in good Old Regime fashion before the *juge ordinaire* from Sens. In 1741 the inhabitants of Bernouil near Tonnerre reported that their Jansenist curé was "too severe about confession; he postpones some people's penance many times and that rebuffs and disheartens them. Very few took Easter communion." In 1733 Bishop Caylus forbade the parish priests in one part of his diocese to marry "people who were ill informed about the principal mysteries of their religion." He repeatedly refused to confirm young people (in Lainsecq and Sainte-Colombe in the Puisaye in the 1730s, for example) because they did not know their catechism well enough.[16]

Jansenism also affected religious vocations. Dominique Dinet has argued convincingly that Jansenist rigorism and theological quarrels contributed seriously to the decline of clerical recruitment in the Jansenist regions of the Yonne from the 1730s on. Jansenist theology discouraged many young men from the priesthood by demystifying the role of the priest, yet demanding an inordinately high standard of vocation and morality in the young novice. During the episcopate of Caylus, for example, Restif de la Bretonne's half brother, Thomas Restif, remained a tonsured cleric and never became an ordained priest because of doubts about his own worthiness. The continual disputes over theology and liturgy in Jansenist regions only exacerbated the situation. The diocese of Auxerre provided 71 percent of its own clergy in the early part of Louis XIV's reign, but under the episcopate of Caylus local clerical recruitment dropped drastically from about 1720, and the diocese had to rely increasingly on clergy from other regions, especially Lorraine and Normandy. Despite a brief upswing in vocations in the 1760s, by 1789 only 31 percent of the clergy were indigenous to the diocese. Likewise, in the Senonais recruitment of secular and religious clergy decreased at midcentury, especially in the larger towns. Finally, the Tonnerrois experienced a larger decline than the rest of the diocese of Langres from about 1730 to 1760, primarily because its proximity to the diocese of Auxerre

---

[16]Edmond Franjou, "Histoire d'un conflit entre le jeune curé janséniste Jazu de la Celle-Saint-Cyr et ses paroissiens au début de XVIIIe siècle," *L'echo d'Auxerre* 57 (1965): 19–21; AD Yonne 1 J 83: 79, 219, 223, and *Nouvelles ecclésiastiques* (1741), p. 201, both as quoted in Dinet, "Jansénisme et déchristianisation," pp. 19–21.

made it prey to the negative influence of Jansenism and to the disputes it provoked.[17] The necessary recruitment of additional clergy from distant parts of France may have increased the gap between priest and parishioners; villagers often distrusted these outsiders and were slow to form spiritual and social ties with them.

Though historians of Old Regime religion in the Yonne have noted the long-term secularizing effects of Jansenism and the Catholic Reformation, this interpretation needs to be counterbalanced and its nuances brought out. In the first place, despite the vigorous attempts of Jansenists and Catholic Reformers to suppress saints' cults, fertility rites, and devotion to thaumaturgical shrines and statues, the laity resisted fiercely. Even in the late 1700s bishops still faced the challenge of suppressing or altering popular practices. In 1770, for example, Bishop Albert de Luynes of Sens persuaded the Catholics of Saint-Florentin to replace their traditional procession to Butteaux on Saint Madeleine's day with a shorter one to a closer chapel "to avoid the scandals which occur." During the Revolution republican authorities remarked upon the resilient popular attachment to "pagan institutions," such as saints' cults and festivals, which their official religion had "outlawed" long ago. In 1792, for example, the inhabitants of Tonnerre begged for the return of their "antique and venerable vase containing a piece of the true cross" and proclaimed its sacred power, noting that "especially in moments of calamity or in the last moments of life, many have had recourse to it, and . . . [those] touching clothes to the vase have found relief from their afflictions and often even a complete cure."[18] These petitioners bore testimony to the persistence of age-old forms of devotion.

Second, the Catholic Reformation and Jansenism stimulated religious faith even as they remolded it. In the Senonais and Tonnerrois, for example, in the mid-eighteenth century new or reestablished

---

[17]Dinet, "Ordinations sacerdotales," pp. 221–29, "Les visites pastorales du diocèse de Sens aux XVIIe et XVIIIe siècles," *AB* 49 (1987): 20–55, esp. 28–29, "Jansénisme et déchristianisation," pp. 6–13, and "Administration épiscopale et vie religieuse au milieu du XVIIIe siècle: Le bureau pour le gouvernement du diocèse de Langres de Gilbert de Montmorin," *Revue d'histoire ecclésiastique* 78 (1983): 721–74, esp. 742–43; Restif de la Bretonne, *La vie de mon père* (Paris, 1970, orig. 1778), p. 168.

[18]M. Moiset, "Vieux us et coutumes en l'église de Saint-Florentin," *BSSY* 49 (1895): 199–210, esp. 203–5; BN, *Observateur de l'Yonne*, 15 pluviôse an VIII (4 February 1800); AD Yonne L707, Pétition des habitants de Tonnerre à l'administration du district de Tonnerre, October 1792.

Tridentine confraternities devoted to Mary or Christ flowered. In the diocese of Sens, Bishop Luynes approved the founding of forty-six new confraternities during his episcopate (1753–1788). In more Jansenist regions, the clergy also succeeded in creating a substantial and powerful following, particularly in the town of Auxerre. Here, for example, Jansenist theological disputes became deeply embroiled in municipal politics as lay Jansenists fought hard in the 1760s to control the literary society and the collège (after the Jesuit expulsion).[19] Indeed, during the Revolution the most heavily Jansenist region of the Yonne, the Auxerrois, was the most zealous in fighting for the right to practice in public. In short, the impact of religious reform was ambiguous: while it suppressed certain forms of religiosity, it generated others.

Third, it seems that the gradual secularizing influence of the reforms, and especially of Jansenism, took on a particular character. It seemed to distance the people from the clergy first, and then only more gradually to detach them from a religious world view, symbols, and rituals. The religious activism of the Revolution would bear witness to this progression. With this general background on Old Regime religiosity in mind, let us turn more specifically to the four regions.

The Avallonais in the old diocese of Autun was the only area in the future department of the Yonne to remain largely free of the influence of Jansenism. The late seventeenth-century attempt to wipe out questionable or "pagan" forms of devotion was least successful here, especially in the Morvan. Gabriel de Roquette, the energetic bishop of Autun in the 1670s–1680s, had more difficulty, for example, suppressing lengthy, nighttime processions, organizing charitable foundations and new confraternities, and establishing properly trained priests in the archdeaconry of Avallon than in that of Flavigny (Côte-d'Or) to the east. The distance from Autun and, above all, the isolated, mountainous nature of the Morvan hindered reform and enabled the persistence of forms of devotion dating back to medieval or even pre-Christian times, such as belief in the healing power of cer-

[19]Dinet, "Visites pastorales," p. 41, and "Administration épiscopale," pp. 672–77. In Auxerre membership in the confraternity of the Blessed Sacrament in the parish of Saint-Loup increased from 39 in 1775 to 185 in 1789. Charles Demay, "Confréries de métier, de charité, et autres établies à Auxerre avant 1789," BSSY 56 (1902): 197–243, esp. 222; Ordioni, Survivance des idées, pp. 86–130.

tain fountains, reliance on sorcery, and attachment to powerful, back-woods sites of pilgrimage.[20] In the mid-nineteenth century, Abbé Jean Baudiau commented that the inhabitants of the Morvan were "naturally religious" but that "a thousand causes in these mountains have inspired in them strange beliefs and . . . superstitions." Noting that persistent belief in witchcraft and werewolves, he added that Druidism had left the roots of strong devotion to miraculous foun-tains: "Even today it is not unusual, early in the morning before sunrise, to see women in their Sunday best kneeling near certain fountains, devoutly praying for the cure of a fever or other illness; then, they draw water for the sick . . . or dip their bedclothes into the fountain." Baudiau denounced the continuing belief in black sabbaths as an "odious mixture of Christian practices and pagan beliefs."[21] In the Revolution the Morvan would not witness much religious con-frontation, for the dechristianization campaign made few inroads in this distant and pious region and local authorities made scant effort to enforce antireligious laws.

To the north in the diocese of Auxerre the reforming bishops Nicolas Colbert (1672–1676) and his cousin André Colbert (1676–1704), found regional variations in religious practice which would affect revolutionary religious activism over a hundred years later. Unacceptable habits and beliefs were universal. The Colberts felt compelled to remove "indecent, malformed, or useless" statues or tableaux from over one-third of the parishes throughout the diocese. Everywhere Catholics believed in pragmatic uses of the holy and mingled the sacred and the profane in ways that did not accord with the new Tridentine spirituality. Hardly unusual were the villagers of Villefargeau who put "blessed palm fronds among their strawberry plants" to protect them from snakes. The curé of Pourrain echoed many of his colleagues when he complained that after his parishion-ers went on pilgrimage to Saint-Georges-d'Escamps, they usually "went to the cabaret to take part in debauchery and returned only late at night or even spent the night out."[22]

---

[20]Lanfrey, "Evolution de la vie religieuse," pp. 33–34, 64–72, 94–96; Schmitt, *Organisation ecclésiastique*, pp. 165–220, 240–46.

[21]Baudiau, *Le Morvan*, pp. 42–48.

[22]Le Bras, *Etudes de sociologie* 1:44; Roudil, "Vie religieuse," p. 10; AD Yonne G1687, Visite pastorale d'André Colbert, 1687, and G1668, Visite pastorale d'André Colbert, 1679, both quoted by Roudil, pp. 92, 78. Pierre Roudil was kind enough to lend me his *mémoire* and provide me with much useful information on religious practice in the

Yet distinct regional patterns emerged within the diocese of Auxerre. Rural regions tended to be more devout than towns, where more parishioners skipped their Easter duty. The reformers considered the villagers distinctly more "pious" and more willing to reform in the Auxerrois than in the Puisaye (the future district of Saint-Fargeau). In the 1670s virtually all parishioners in the diocese of Auxerre took Easter communion, but when André Colbert cited rural parishes for lack of devotion, they were almost all in the Puisaye or in the equally poor Varzy region (in the Nièvre).[23] Likewise, the Puisaye stood out for its lack of schoolteachers and for its parishioners' recalcitrance toward catechism. Attachment to thaumaturgical or magical practices was more prevalent in the Auxerrois region, however, than in the Puisaye: a third of the parish priests in the Saint-Bris *archiprêtré* (wine-producing region to the south of Auxerre) and slightly fewer in the Auxerre and Puisaye regions complained of their parishioners' "superstitious" ideas, such as the belief in white and black magic, miraculous cures for animals, and fountains with power to resuscitate stillborn infants just long enough to be baptized. Villages in the richer Auxerrois region were more likely to have confraternities and *fabriques* and to maintain their rectories, church furniture, and ornaments in better condition. Finally, Colbert found the parishes of the Auxerrois most willing to accept his new Blessed Sacrament confraternities or to found "spontaneous" confraternities without his initiative or approval.[24]

Yonne during the Old Regime. Delphin Delagneau, "Associations corporatives d'ouvriers de bois," *Annuaire de l'Yonne* 65 (1901): 63–71.

[23]Roudil, "Vie religieuse," pp. 39, 43. He reported that of the 110 parishes (out of 207 total) which provided information on Easter communicants in the 1670s, 92 percent had less than 1 percent *non-pascalisants;* 13 percent had 1–3 percent; 4 percent had 3–4.5 percent; and only one of the parishes had 12.5 percent *non-pascalisants.* See also Le Bras, *Etudes de sociologie* 1:45, 51.

[24]Locatelli, "Vie matérielle," pp. 40ff., 72, 79ff.; Roudil, "Vie religieuse," pp. 61, 68, 79–80, 90–96. In the archiprêtré of Puisaye 42 percent of the curés complained about parents who did not send their children to catechism, compared to 35 percent in Auxerre and only 22 percent in Saint-Bris. The archiprêtré of Saint-Bris had confraternities in 81 percent of its towns, as opposed to only 71 percent in the Puisaye and 67 percent in Auxerre, but Auxerre nonetheless had the wealthiest *fabriques.* On the persistence of certain customs in the Auxerrois, see Ernest Cherest, "Jardinville, ou Croyances, coutumes, et superstitions qui existent encore à la fin du XIXe siècle dans un coin des départements de l'Yonne, du Loiret, et de Seine-et-Marne," *Annuaire de l'Yonne* 51 (1887): 320–54; E. Lorin, "Chants populaires de l'Auxerrois," *BSSY* 13 (1859): 225–74, esp. 240–52. Local histories often refer to the continuation of suppressed practices. For example, Bénoni Duranton, "Les sorciers de la Puisaye," *An-*

In short, the Auxerrois region, particularly the archiprêtré of Saint-Bris, seems to have been more attached than the Puisaye both to traditional popular devotion and to more institutional Catholicism. The Auxerrois was also more open to the Tridentine reforms. Amid their vineyards and grain fields, these villagers enjoyed relative stability and at least the hope of a productive harvest in good years. In contrast, the people of the Puisaye were poverty-stricken; in part because they lived in scattered hamlets, they were less tied to local parish devotions and less likely to observe the formal obligations of Catholic practice. Many of the men were woodcutters whose itinerant life-style worsened this tendency toward nonpractice. The reform attempts only exacerbated these existing problems, for poverty and itinerancy were ill suited to late seventeenth-century Catholicism, which required at least a minimum of revenue as well as time to participate.[25] Both the Puisaye and the Auxerrois would be known for their anticlericalism in modern times, but in the 1790s Auxerrois Catholics were more avid and more politically informed than their Puisaye neighbors in the struggle to restore Catholicism.

The diocese of Auxerre as a whole also bore the strong imprint of Jansenism, encouraged above all by Bishop Charles de Caylus. Particularly after his 1717 refusal of the Bull Unigenitus, Caylus worked tirelessly to transform Auxerre into a bastion of Jansenism. He created a Jansenist seminary and collège to rival the existing ones run by the Lazarists and Jesuits. He forbade Jesuits from preaching or confessing in 1725 and opened the diocese to Jansenist refugees from across the kingdom. He and his followers produced a new missal, breviary, set of rites, and a hotly contested catechism. Gradually, despite countless battles both inside and outside his diocese, Caylus succeeded in imprinting clerical and lay spirituality with Jansenist and Gallican traits. Thus, when Caylus's harshly anti-Jansenist successor, Jacques-Marie de Condorcet (1756–1760) sought to bring the diocese back to orthodoxy, he found that many clergymen and lay people believed communion should be received only infrequently, that God was decidedly distant and severe, and that the pope could not rightfully claim much power over his bishops. During pastoral visits, Con-

---

nuaire de l'Yonne 28 (1864): 161–216, esp. 166–70; "Recherches sur l'histoire et les institutions de la ville de Vermenton," BSSY 30 (1876): 53–58.

25Le Bras, Etudes de sociologie 1:50; Locatelli, "Vie matérielle," pp. 108ff.; Roudil, "Vie religieuse," pp. 39, 64, 68–71, and "Conclusion."

dorcet was appalled to discover masses said aloud, the postponement of first communion until age sixteen, and a pervasive hostility to his reforms among parishioners and priests alike. Aided by the passage of time and the gradual dying off of many Jansenists, Bishop Jean-Marie Champion de Cicé (1760–1791) had better luck than the antagonistic Condorcet in methodically purging the Jansenist influence in his diocese. The surviving Jansenists in Auxerre bemoaned the resurgence of carnival, charivari, and theater in the 1770s as their influence waned. By 1789 the aged Jansenist priests were in a minority, but the movement's influence lingered and may well have contributed to the declining performance of Easter duty in some parishes of the diocese.[26]

In the diocese of Sens, Jansenism took root even earlier, during the episcopate of Louis-Henri de Gondrin (1646–1674). This bishop's Jansenist sympathies colored the first serious attempts at carrying the Catholic Reformation to the Senonais countryside in the 1660s and 1670s. By founding a new seminary, promoting a Jansenist catechism (1669), holding diocesan conferences for parish priests, and spreading his ideas in pastoral visits, Gondrin sought to influence clergy and laity. The severe bishop encouraged parish priests to be rigorous against quasi-magical customs or moral laxity and to assign public penance when necessary; this policy ignited confrontation with humiliated and recalcitrant parishioners. One woman in Vitry aligned the village leadership against the curé and very nearly took him to court when he imposed public penance on her for starting a fistfight

[26]AD Yonne 1J183, Registre de PVs de visites pastorales de Caylus, 1728–36; Abbé Jean Lebeuf, *Mémoires concernant l'histoire civile et ecclésiastique d'Auxerre . . . continués jusqu'à nos jours*, ed. A. Challe and Max Quantin, 4 vols. (Auxerre, 1848–55), 2:350–65; Ordioni, *Résistance gallicane et janséniste*, esp. pp. 30–40, 57–73, 102–5, and *Survivance des idées*, pp. 128–32; Hohl, *Jansénisme*, pp. 38–55; Rocher, "Vie religieuse aux XVIIe et XVIIIe siècles," pp. 257–69; Dinet, "Ordinations sacerdotales," pp. 224–27; Abbé Leboeuf, "Etat des travaux sur le jansénisme dans l'Yonne," in *Du jansénisme à la laïcité*, pp. 35–87; Taveneaux, *Vie quotidienne*, pp. 129, 137–43; Le Bras, *Etudes de sociologie* 1:51, n. 2; Ambroise Challe, "Le chanoine Blonde," *BSSY* 36 (1882): 5–19; A. J. Rance, "Contributions à l'histoire de l'épiscopat de Condorcet," *BSSY* 44 (1890): 319–52, esp. 335–45; *Relation de la visite générale faite par Monsieur de Condorcet, évêque d'Auxerre, dans son diocèse* (n.p., n.d. [c. 1760]). See also AD Yonne G1619, PVs de visites pastorales de Jacques de Hey (1760–64 dans la Puisaye) et de Charles Huet (1761 en Auxerrois). AD Yonne 1J184, Registre de PVs de visites pastorales de Cicé, 1767–86, gives brief examples of concern at declining practice, for example, for Coulanges-la-Vineuse in 1785: "Easter duty is very neglected." AD Yonne 1J231, Jacob-Nicolas-Edme Duplessis, "Mémoire historique pour continuer l'histoire de l'église d'Auxerre: L'épiscopat de Monseigneur Champion de Cicé (1761–1805)," pp. 5–16.

in church. In the Senonais the repression of raucous festivals, wedding charivaris, and excessive dancing met with the usual resistance, but the Catholic Reformation seems to have achieved greater early success here than in neighboring dioceses. In cleansing churches of "inappropriate" statues, for example, Gondrin faced less opposition than did his neighbors in the dioceses of Auxerre and Langres; by the eighteenth century, Tridentine images were more securely in place.[27]

With the exception of Hardouin de la Hoguette (1685–1715), Gondrin's successors did not share his theology. Nonetheless, at the outset of his episcopate, the virulently anti-Jansenist Languet de Gergy (1730–1753) faced the dogged opposition of a staunch minority of Jansenist priests, nuns, and monks. Anxious to promote more frequent sacraments, a less severe theology of salvation by good works, and devotion to the Sacred Heart of Jesus, Languet made the diocese a battleground against Jansenism. Several convents of Ursulines and of Sisters of Notre-Dame, for example, became particular objects of the bishop's purifying zeal. For lay parishioners his most disturbing technique was to forbid parish priests to give the sacraments of Penance, the Eucharist, or Extreme Unction to Jansenist laity. Although Languet was quite successful in purging Jansenism, the diocese paid a price for its years of conflict. Unfortunately, late eighteenth-century pastoral visits in the Senonais (and the other dioceses) are notably less informative than those of a century earlier, but they do offer multiple examples of declining performance of Easter duty (in Saint-Martin-du-Tertre, Bussy-le-Repos, Voisines, Saint-Denis, Villefolle, Nailly, and Saint-Clément, for example.) Bishop Albert de Luynes (1753–1788) faced the secularizing spread of Enlightenment thought, decline in clerical recruitment, and according to some accounts, a certain spiritual laxness among his clergy, but his episcopate was much less conflict ridden.[28] The age of the-

[27]Henri Bouvier, *Histoire de l'église et de l'ancien archdiocèse de Sens*, 3 vols. (Paris, 1906–11), vol. 3, chap. 2, sec. 4; M. Cherest, "Recherches sur la fête des innocents et de fous," *BSSY* 7 (1853): 7–82, esp. 75–82; Dinet, "Visites pastorales," pp. 24–37; Hohl, *Jansénisme*, pp. 61–70; Taveneaux, *Vie quotidienne*, pp. 137–39.

[28]Hoguette was a Jansenist sympathizer, but he approved the Bull Unigenitus. His hesitant successor, Louis de Chavigny (1718–30), did not pursue a constant anti-Jansenist policy. For examples of decline in communion going, see AD Yonne G56, PVs de visites pastorales de l'archevêché de Sens par J. J. de Gabriac, (1757–59). The pastoral visits also illustrate the archdeacons' intent interest in promoting the cult of the Blessed Sacrament and the ceremony of the Benediction to counter the Jansenist tendency toward infrequent communion. See, for example, AD Yonne G56, pièce 17, PV de la

ological warfare gave way to a period of peace but of declining zeal in this region, which would least ardently defend Catholicism in the revolutionary era.

Unfortunately, the shortage of surviving accounts of pastoral visits for the diocese of Langres in the late seventeenth and eighteenth centuries makes it difficult to gauge the impact of the Catholic Reformation on the Tonnerrois. Although the reformer Sébastien Zamet (1615–1655) founded an early seminary and encouraged the growth of new orders, the diocese of Langres had no zealous late seventeenth-century bishop comparable to a Colbert or a Gondrin. The fluctuating policies of successive bishops allowed Jansenism to take hold in the Tonnerrois, especially in the early 1700s. Bishop Gilbert de Montmorin (1734–1770) stood out for his unyielding battle against Jansenism and for his Tridentine reforms. Responding in part to lay complaints about the rigorism of Jansenist curés, Montmorin relentlessly demanded that his clergy align themselves against this "heresy." To be appointed or promoted clergymen must formally accept the Bull Unigenitus, and a few faced public ceremonies of retraction or even expulsion for their Jansenist beliefs.[29]

In his attempt to implement Catholic Reformation spirituality, Montmorin discovered stronger, or at least longer lasting, attachment to traditional forms of devotion than was the case in the Senonais. While he waged the usual Tridentine combats, this bishop seems to have recognized the need to be somewhat patient toward the lay desire for thaumaturgical use of the sacred. He sometimes criticized priests for their rigorism and tempered his own restrictions on festivals and other devotional customs. For example, in 1744 when an animal epidemic was ravaging the diocese, he allowed public outdoor prayers and blessings but not processions to bless the animals. Finally, Montmorin successfully encouraged the founding and growth of

visite pastorale de Louis Chambertrand à Beton-Bazoches, 13 september 1766. Bouvier, *Histoire de l'église*, vol. 3, chap. 3, secs. 1–3; Dinet, "Visites pastorales," pp. 46–55, and "Jansénisme et déchristianisation," pp. 24–26; Hohl, *Jansénisme*, pp. 70–80. For an account of the decline of certain religious festivals in the 1700s and the persistence of others into the 1800s, see Pierre Cornat, "Notice historique et religieuse sur le Mont-Saint-Sulpice," *BSSY* 2 (1848): 379–410, esp. 397–401.

[29]Dinet, "Administration épiscopale," pp. 724–33; Hohl, *Jansénisme*, pp. 84–89; Charles-François Roussel, *Le diocèse de Langres: Histoire et statistique*, 4 vols. (Langres, 1873–79), vol. 1, esp. pp. 73–80; Georges Viard, "Les visites pastorales dans l'ancien diocèse de Langres," *Revue d'histoire de l'église de France* 68 (1977): 235–72, esp. 256–66.

Marian and Christocentric confraternities, especially in rural areas in the 1740s and 1750s.[30] Despite Montmorin's efforts, the episcopate of César-Guillaume de la Luzerne (1771–1802) seems to have witnessed a decline in zeal—a certain "laziness and passivity of the faithful," according to one historian's reading of the pastoral visits of this era.[31]

We are left, then, with a complex picture of religiosity in the future department of the Yonne on the eve of the Revolution. The Avallonais stood out as unscathed by Jansenist disputes and less marked by the Tridentine suppression of popular forms of devotion. In the Auxerrois and Puisaye, and to a lesser extent the Senonais and Tonnerrois, Jansenism had left its ambiguous legacy—years of clerical conflict, decline in clerical recruitment, a potential distancing of priest and people, and a deemphasis on the Eucharist, but also in some instances a deepening of interior spirituality. The Catholic Reformation attempt to do away with "superstitions" seems to have been most thoroughgoing in the Senonais, followed by the diocese of Auxerre. Yet, everywhere, the majority of the people clung to their traditional saints, symbols, and outdoor processions—in short, to a strong belief in the power of sacred objects, places, and rituals. This attachment is hard to measure; yet the revolutionary challenge to Christianity would bring it to the fore in tangible ways.

The Geography of Religion and Revolution

These religious variations within the area of the Yonne during the Old Regime, would eventually affect the religious activism and attitudes of clergy and laity during the Revolution. In turn, the religious experiences and decisions of the first years of the Revolution—particularly in response to the oath to the Civil Constitution in 1791 and the dechristianization campaign in the year II—would have a further influence on the geography of the religious resurgence following the fall of Robespierre.

While allegiance to the Civil Constitution of the Clergy was strikingly high throughout the Yonne, the priests in certain regions were

---

[30]Dinet, "Administration épiscopale," pp. 744–69; Viard, "Visites pastorales," pp. 266–72. Dinet emphasizes the moderation of Montmorin's reforms; Viard stresses their repressive side and the increase in centralized clerical control.
[31]Viard, "Visites pastorales," p. 270.

more likely to agree to the oath. In the district of Saint-Fargeau an astounding 98 percent of the clergy took the oath without retracting it, and the districts of Sens, Saint-Florentin, and Joigny were not far behind, with 91, 87, and 86 percent Constitutional clergy respectively. Oath taking (without retraction or invalidation) was lowest in the Tonnerrois (75 percent) and Avallonais (81 percent) and only slightly higher in the district of Auxerre (83 percent).[32] In the next chapter I will discuss the fate of the clergy over the course of the Revolution in more depth, but the important point here is that in the Tonnerrois and Avallonais, where there were more nonjuring clergy early in the Revolution, returning refractories would play a larger role in the religious resurgence after Thermidor.

As in much of the center and Paris Basin, the department of the Yonne experienced a particularly ambitious and far-reaching dechristianization campaign in the year ii. In fact, when Michel Vovelle compiled statistics on dechristianizing speeches, clerical abdications, and the celebration of revolutionary festivals in order to map dechristianization across France, he placed the Yonne within the second highest level of "intensity of dechristianization."[33] Although authorities in the department began late in 1792 to imprison refractory clergy and to collect church bells and ornaments, it was in fall 1793 that the first wave of dechristianization hit the region full force. Early in November 1793 the *armée révolutionnaire* passed through the Yonne en route to Lyon. In many towns along the Paris-Lyon road, including Sens, Villeneuve-sur-Yonne, Joigny, Auxerre, and Vermenton, the soldiers elicited the support of local revolutionaries and Popular Societies to smash saints' statues, chop down crosses, and build bonfires of religious images and relics.[34] On 15 November Constitutional Bishop Etienne-Charles de Loménie de Brienne abdicated, only six

[32]These percentages refer to those oaths still valid after the wave of retractions in summer 1791 and after government authorities invalidated some oaths because of conditional language. Jean-Pierre Rocher has kindly allowed me to use his statistics, soon to be published in "Aspects de l'histoire religieuse."

[33]Vovelle, *Révolution contre l'église*, pp. 58–61, 161, 277–86.

[34]AD Yonne 37J5, "Mémorial d'un Auxerrois," vol. 2 (1793–96), typed version of original manuscript, pp. 245–65; AN AFii 151, Lettre de Maure, représentant en mission, au Comité de salut public, 14 brumaire an ii (4 November 1793); Richard Cobb, *Les armées révolutionnaires: Instrument de la Terreur dans les départements*, 2 vols. (Paris, 1961–63), 2:661–64, 690; Rapport de Laire au district de Sens, 18 brumaire an iii (8 November 1794), as reprinted in *Annuaire de l'Yonne* (1858): 25; M. G. Fenouillet, "Les mémoires de Lombard de Langres et l'histoire de Villeneuve-sur-Yonne pendant la Terreur," *BSSY* 77 (1923): 142–61, esp. 151–53.

Villagers receiving the Decree of the Supreme Being. Courtesy of the
Bibliothèque nationale.

days after Bishop Jean-Baptiste Gobel set the first example at the bar
of the National Convention. On 27 November the departmental administration decreed that only one church per canton could remain
open and ordered all statues, gold or silver church ornaments, and
other sacred objects to be deposited at district administrations.[35]

After this initial burst of dechristianizing zeal, in the Yonne as
elsewhere the dechristianization movement took place in waves, ema-

[35]Forestier, "Campagnes de l'Auxerrois," p. 189; Rocher, "Aspects de l'histoire religieuse," pp. 15–16.

nating from large towns where représentant en mission Nicolas Maure, local revolutionary committees, Jacobin clubs, and national agents acted as catalysts. The coldest winter months saw a temporary lull before the movement culminated in early spring in widespread church closings, clerical abdications, and belated celebrations of the festival of Reason. Events in the tiny village of Taingy in the Puisaye followed a typical pattern. Here, the district commissaire came in late November 1793 to collect church goods and seal the tabernacle and sanctuary. Four months later on 3 germinal an II (23 March 1794) the church was locked; the Constitutional curé abdicated and soon headed to his childhood home after narrowly escaping arrest. On 30 germinal an II (19 April 1794), the commune celebrated the festival of Reason. By November 1794, however, illegal Catholic assemblies had become increasingly frequent, and the hapless mayor complained, "The progress of Reason will soon be destroyed."[36]

Despite the official uniformity of departmental policies and decrees, dechristianization in fact affected the various regions of the Yonne very unevenly. In the first place, according to contemporaries of all political positions, virtually every manifestation of the movement, from iconoclasm to revolutionary festivals, achieved greater proportions in the towns than in the countryside. The mayor of the village of Courgis provided a typical account of rural dechristianization when he recorded that in the spring of 1794 "they closed the churches. On Easter the villagers all went to the woods and sang offices. That same day, some people from Chablis came to preach revolutionary doctrine in the church, but not even ten men went. . . . When two commissaires [of the Jacobin club of Chablis] came to Courgis to cut down the crosses, a group of women armed with stones

---

[36]Churches closed in February or March in much of the department (e.g., in the Tonnerrois and Auxerrois, in Saint-Florentin and some of its surrounding communes). In the town of Auxerre the cathedral Saint-Etienne was the last church to close, on 2 February 1794. AD Yonne 37J5, "Mémorial d'un Auxerrois"; Rocher, "Aspects de l'histoire religieuse," p. 16. In rural areas church closings often coincided with the abdication of the priest. See AD Yonne L705, Etats nominatifs des ecclésiastiques qui ont abdiqué leurs fonctions, tableaux par district (dated in various months from late winter to the summer of 1794). Additional information on church closings in individual communes exists in AD Yonne L203–7 (Esprit public, an II) and L1406–10 (Copies de pièces sur la Révolution dans l'Yonne, Don Lorin): e.g., L1410, Lettre de l'agent national de Truchy au comité révolutionnaire d'Auxerre, 16 vendémiaire an III (7 October 1794), reporting that the church had closed and the priest had abdicated on 15 February 1794. On Taingy, see G. Rouillé, "Taingy: Une commune sous la Révolution," *Annuaire de l'Yonne* 49 (1885): 81–84.

persuaded them to take the road back to Chablis much more quickly than they had come, and the crosses stayed." In contrast, in the towns, especially Auxerre, Sens, Saint-Florentin, Joigny, Chablis, and Avallon, such revolutionary festivals as those of Reason, of Martyrs to Liberty, and of the Supreme Being met with much greater initial success. In Auxerre, for example, public interest in the thirty-five different fêtes décadaires waxed and waned, but certain ceremonies such as the building of an artificial mountain in honor of the Jacobins in May 1794 attracted many participants.[37]

Second, in rural areas, dechristianization made greater headway in the Senonais and Auxerrois than in the Avallonais or Tonnerrois. For example, clergy abdicated in 76 percent of the Yonne's communes, but in the Tonnerrois abdications occurred in only 58 percent and in just under half the communes of the Avallonais.[38] Moreover, the Tonnerrois and Avallonais had fewer Popular Societies than the district of Auxerre, for example, which claimed seventeen. The more peripheral districts of Avallon, Tonnerre, and Saint-Fargeau were not as closely connected to Parisian commerce and politics or to the dechristianizing efforts of the représentants en mission. Federalist tendencies and a political purge in Avallon and heated internecine battles in the municipal politics of Tonnerre may have diverted key potential leaders of dechristianization in these district capitals. For in many cases, pivotal figures, such as National Agent Edme-Antoine Rathier for the Auxerrois or représentant en mission Maure for the Senonais and Auxerrois, provided the crucial impetus behind organizing revolutionary celebrations or inducing priests to resign.[39]

[37]"Souvenirs d'un maire de village, Droin, maire de Courgis," as reprinted in Claude Delasselle, *L'Yonne pendant la Révolution, 1789–1799* (Auxerre, 1987), folio 43. For contemporary accounts of dechristianization in Auxerre, see esp. AD Yonne 37J5, "Mémorial d'un Auxerrois," and 1J231, Duplessis, "Mémoire," pp. 40–75; Forestier, "Campagnes de l'Auxerrois"; Camille Hermelin, "Histoire de la ville de Saint-Florentin (seconde partie, 1789–1816)," *BSSY* 92 bis (1938): whole vol., esp. pp. 120–74; Claude Hohl, "Les fêtes à Auxerre durant la Révolution," *BSSY* 106 (1974): 125–58, and 107 (1975): 127–45; Rocher, "Aspects de l'histoire religieuse," pp. 14–19; Pierre Tartat, *Avallon au XVIIIe siècle—la Révolution, 1789–1799* (Auxerre, 1953).

[38]AD Yonne L705, Etats nominatifs des ecclésiastiques qui ont abdiqué leurs fonctions, tableaux par district. Avallon's report is dated April 1794; more priests may have abdicated after this date.

[39]AD Yonne L202, Réponses des communes au questionnaire de l'administration du district d'Avallon, envoyé juillet 1793, L205, Réponses des municipalités au questionnaire de l'administration du district de Sens, envoyé 24 nivôse an II (13 January 1794), L207, Réponses par agents nationaux au questionnaire du comité révolutionnaire d'Auxerre, envoyé 7 fructidor an II (24 August 1794), L782, Lettre de Rathier, agent

Finally, by late spring 1794 proponents of dechristianization could make many tangible claims to success: public Catholic practice had come to a virtual halt, most churches in the Yonne were closed, and almost all priests had abdicated, been imprisoned, gone into hiding, married, or fled. Nowhere, however, least of all in the rural areas, had the movement succeeded in truly destroying the Catholic allegiance of the majority of the population. The most optimistic republican officials expressed grave doubts about the power of "reason over fanaticism," and many municipal authorities reported the coexistence of revolutionary cults and Catholic beliefs. As the national agent of Champs commented in response to a questionnaire in the summer of 1794, the public celebration of Catholicism had duly stopped as ordered, but "religious ideas are the same as before." The inhabitants of Diges and Coulanges-la-Vineuse expressed a pervasive popular sentiment when they "attacked the popular society and municipal officers" after a hailstorm destroyed their vines in April 1794. The angry crowd "attributed the disaster to the disappearance of their priests and saints of stone."[40]

The dechristianization campaign did not come to an immediate halt after the fall of Robespierre. In the Yonne the new représentant en mission Ferdinand Guillemardet on Christmas Eve 1794 renewed the decree closing churches and required all priests to move to the nearest town with over five thousand inhabitants for surveillance. But the National Convention annulled this law within a few months, before it was enforced, and even as Guillemardet promulgated the decree, parishioners broke into churches in many communes to celebrate Christmas. As National Agent Rathier had reported in late October 1794, "Although there are no priests and the churches have been

national d'Auxerre, au comité de législation, 14 nivôse an II (3 January 1794); Delasselle, *Yonne pendant la Révolution,* folio 56; Abbé Giraud, "La ville d'Avallon pendant la période révolutionnaire d'après les procès-verbaux de l'administration municipale," *Bulletin de la Société d'études d'Avallon* 52–53 (1910–11): 166–70; AD Yonne L199, "Mémoire historique des événements qui se sont passés à Tonnerre pendant le cours de la Révolution" (Paris, n.d., 19 pp., quarto); Jean Pimoule, "Le conventionnel Nicolas Maure (1743–1795)" (Thèse inédite, Université de Lille, 1949). According to Chanoine Frappier, Maure was a more gentle dechristianizer in his native Auxerrois than in the Senonais. Charles Porée, ed., "Mémoires du chanoine Frappier sur le clergé d'Auxerre pendant la Révolution (de 1789 à l'an IV)," *BSSY* 77 (1923): 126–28, as cited in Rocher, "Aspects de l'histoire religieuse," p. 18.
[40]AD Yonne L207, Réponse de l'agent national de Champs au questionnaire du comité révolutionnaire d'Auxerre, 11 vendémiaire an III (2 October 1794), L782, Rapport de Rathier, agent national du district d'Auxerre, 9 floréal an II (28 April 1794).

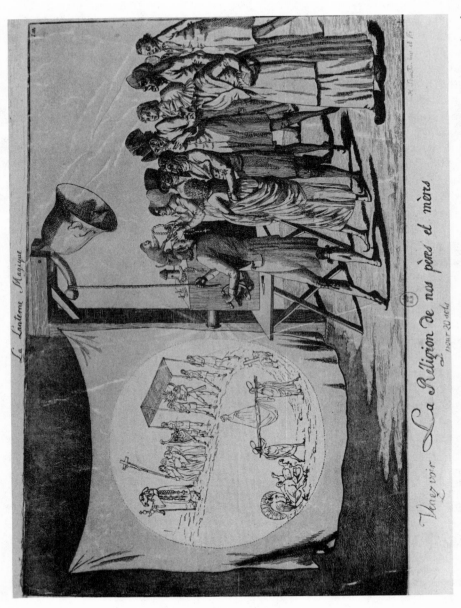

The magic lantern: "Come and see the religion of our fathers and mothers." Courtesy of the Bibliothèque nationale.

stripped bare, fanaticism breathes once again in the countryside. (One could almost say it is regenerating itself.)"[41]

How did this resurgence of Catholic practice in the aftermath of Thermidor vary in form, intensity, and style in the different regions of the Yonne? Various manifestations of the revival between Thermidor and the Concordat—such as riots, petitions, illegal festivals, bell ringing, violations of calendar laws, and the celebration of lay-led masses—all provide indexes of regional variations. Government reports, particularly the two surveys of religious practice written by the departmental commissaire Etienne Housset in early 1797 and late 1798 complement this picture.[42] Admittedly, religious activism is not always the best indicator of piety or devotion. Particularly in rural communes in a region such as the Avallonais, by far the majority of villagers supported the return to Catholicism; so religious conflict did not attract the attention of departmental authorities. Above all, pro-Catholic local officials failed to report violations of laws concerning public practice. Nonetheless, the analysis of various kinds of religious activism, whether legal or illegal, allows us to discover the hottest areas of Catholic resistance and to explore regional differences of method and style.

Three major patterns of religious revival appear during the Thermidorean and Directorial periods. First, the inhabitants of the southern part of the Yonne tended to defend their prerevolutionary traditions more fervently than the inhabitants in the northern part of the department. Second, certain specific areas were especially zealous and vocal. In particular, villages with a special source of devotion, a high concentration of clergy, or a proximity to the borders of the depart-

[41] AN AFII 146B, Arrêté du représentant en mission Guillemardet, 4 nivôse an III (24 December 1794); AD Yonne L702–4, Exécution de l'arrêté de Guillemardet du 4 nivôse an III. These *liasses* contain many requests by priests for exceptions from Guillemardet's decree. Forestier, "Campagnes de l'Auxerrois," pp. 196–98; AD Yonne L782, Rapport de Rathier, agent national du district d'Auxerre, 7 brumaire an III (28 October 1794).

[42] Evidence of petitions, violations of religious laws, the celebration of lay-led masses, etc., can be found in AD Yonne, series L, esp. the police des cultes and court records and departmental, district, and municipal deliberations; AN, esp. the F7 (police) and F19 (cults) series; various communal archives in the Yonne; and BN, newspapers. See also AN F7 7237, Enquête sur l'exercice et la police intérieure des cultes dans le département de l'Yonne, ventôse an v (February–March 1797); AN AFIII 280, Situation du département de l'Yonne, germinal an vII (March–April 1799). Both were written by Etienne Housset, commissaire près les tribunaux civils et criminaux du département de l'Yonne.

Table 1. Religious activism in the department of the Yonne,
August 1794–April 1802: Percentages of departmental totals

District	Population		Petitions[a]		Riots[b]		Illegal festivals[c]	
	N	%	N	%	N	%	N	%
Auxerre	66,755	(21)	48	(45)	52	(35)	31	(28)
Avallon	40,098	(12.5)	11	(10)	11	(7)	6	(5.5)
Joigny	50,728	(16)	9	(8.5)	8	(5)	17	(15.5)
Saint-Fargeau	28,361	(9)	4	(3.5)	20	(13)	10	(9)
Saint-Florentin	36,884	(11.5)	15	(14)	28	(19)	13	(12)
Sens	56,201	(18)	10	(9.5)	16	(11)	18	(17)
Tonnerre	37,689	(12)	10	(9.5)	15	(10)	14	(13)
Departmental totals	316,716	(100)	107	(100)	150	(100)	109	(100)

Sources: (1) AD Yonne police des cultes and court records, departmental, district, and municipal deliberations; AN F7 (police) and F19 (cults) series; BN newspapers. Population figures are from AN F20 * 20, Denombrement et population du département de l'Yonne, an III (1794–95).

[a] Includes any written petitions sent by groups of citizens making any type of request in favor of the practice of Catholicism. This table does not include petitions sent by priests, lay individuals, or municipal councils.

[b] Includes illegal religious gatherings of large groups of people who took violent or highly threatening actions.

[c] Includes illegal religious gatherings in violation of the republican calendar on specific Catholic holy days, such as Christmas or a patron saint's day. I have not included routine Sunday assemblies, which also violated the calendar laws.

ment became hotbeds of religious activism in the Yonne. Finally, rural Catholics returned more easily and more numerously to public practice, whereas in the larger towns religious conflict was persistent, and Catholics were more likely to find serious competition from the followers of revolutionary cults or Theophilanthropy.

The Catholics of the Auxerrois led the department in virtually every possible form of religious activism: they rioted, petitioned, rang bells, and celebrated illegally more than the Catholics of any other district. Even when one takes into account the large size of the district and the possibility that local officials in this district, as in Sens and Saint-Florentin, were especially conscientious in reporting violations of religious laws, the Auxerrois stands out as the most religiously active region of the Yonne.[43] As Table 1 illustrates, the district of

[43] As one indicator of local authorities' reliability regarding violations of religious laws, see AN F7 7237, Enquête sur l'exercice des cultes, March 1797. When Housset conducted this survey to determine how many communes had made the declaration to use their churches, he in effect also measured the willingness of authorities in each

Table 2. Religiously active communes in the Yonne,
August 1794–April 1802: Percentages of departmental totals

District	Total communes in district		Petitioning communes		Rioting communes		Communes holding illegal festivals	
	N	%	N	%	N	%	N	%
Auxerre	86	(17.5)	19	(29)	29	(30)	20	(28)
Avallon	71	(14.5)	8	(12.5)	9	(9)	4	(6)
Joigny	72	(15)	8	(12.5)	8	(8)	11	(15)
Saint-Fargeau	36	(7)	4	(6)	13	(13.5)	8	(11)
Saint-Florentin	57	(12)	11	(17)	18	(18.5)	11	(15)
Sens	91	(19)	6	(9)	11	(11.5)	8	(11)
Tonnerre	74	(15)	9	(14)	9	(9)	10	(14)
Departmental totals	487	(100)	65	(100)	97	(99.5)	72	(100)

Sources and definitions: Same as for Table 1.

Auxerre had 21 percent of the departmental population but addressed 45 percent of its petitions, had 35 percent of its riots, and held 28 percent of its illegal festivals. Table 2 shows, moreover, that although the Auxerrois had only 17.5 percent of the district communes, it had nearly 30 percent of those that rioted, petitioned, or celebrated illegal festivals. (South of the Forêt d'Othe, the district of Saint-Florentin shared the geographic features of the Auxerrois as well as its religious activism.) This active desire to restore Catholicism seems to have grown in part out of Old Regime religious tendencies: just as the inhabitants of the Auxerrois seemed more attached to Catholic practice than their neighbors in the Puisaye or Senonais in the days of the Catholic Reformation, so too they clung more tightly to public practice in the 1790s (see Map 3). But the intensity of Auxerrois Catholic activism had multiple causes and characteristics.

For one thing, Auxerre became a center for both the Constitutional and the Roman clergy as they sought to reorganize in 1795. Pierre-François Viart, the vicar-general of the refractory Bishop Cicé of the Old Regime diocese of Auxerre, concentrated his campaign to revive Roman Catholicism in the Auxerrois. Viart was highly successful both in stirring up lay support for the revival and in persuading former

district to provide information. Local officials in the districts of Saint-Florentin, Auxerre, and Sens (in that order) responded most zealously to Housset's inquiries. The authorities in these regions also generally were more thoroughgoing in reporting violations of the laws.

Religious Petitions in the Yonne
(August 1794 – April 1802)

SEINE-ET-MARNE

Courlon
Villeneuve-
la-Guyard
Pont-sur-
Yonne
Courgenay

AUBE

SENS   SENS

Vernoy

ST.-
FLORENTIN
Sormery   *Neuvy-*
Sautour

Villeneuve-
sur-Yonne   Beugnon
Avrolles   ST.-FLORENTIN
Saint-Julien-   Brienon   Germigny
du-Sault   Flogny

LOIRET   Mont-St.-
JOIGNY   Sulpice   Ligny   Molosmes
Volgré   Fleury   Valichères   Saint-Martin
Perreux   Aillant   *Maligny*   Tonnerre   Baon
Sommecaise   Saint-
Merry-la-   Georges   Beine   CHABLIS   Lézinnes
Vallée   Quenne
AUXERRE   *Courgis*   *TONNERRE*
Pourrain   St.-Bris   St.-Cyr-les-
SAINT-   *Diges*   Coulanges-   Colons   *Noyers*
FARGEAU   la-Vineuse   IRANCY
Coulangeron   *Val-de-*   Nitry   Grimault
Saint-   Levis   *Merci*   Vermenton
Fargeau   Sementron   *AUXERRE*   Précy-le-Sec
Lavau   Thury   Courson   Merry-sur-   *AVALLON*
Yonne   Sauvigny-
Druyes   le-Bois
Lichères   AVALLON
Vézelay   Asquins   Magny
Saint-Père

NIÈVRE   CÔTE-D'OR

- 1 Petition
- *2 Petitions*
- 3 PETITIONS OR MORE

0   5   10   15   20   Km

Map 3

Constitutional clergy to retract their oaths in the spring and summer of 1795. Likewise, the core of juring clergy in the Yonne who sought to promote Bishop Grégoire's national effort to rebuild the faltering Constitutional Church were also centered in Auxerre. While many believers needed little encouragement, they benefited from their proximity to a former diocesan seat and a group of well-organized clergy in the Auxerrois.[44]

But what is most striking in the Auxerrois is the extent to which the laity seized the initiative in both religious worship and political action. In many parts of the Yonne, when priests were scarce, the laity led worship services on their own, even going so far as to say mass without the consecration. Despite the strength of its capital as a clerical center, lay masses were far more prevalent in the district of Auxerre than elsewhere: 46 of the 100 incidents of lay-led masses reported in the Yonne between Thermidor and the Concordat occurred in the district of Auxerre, and most of the reports referred to an on-going practice, rather than a single occurrence. Here, Auxerrois Catholics reflected their strong Jansenist heritage. For as the next chapter will explore, Jansenism paved the way for lay cults by desanctifying the role of the priest, encouraging the laity to participate in the mass, and inadvertently making the Eucharist a less central part of religious experience.

Just as the laity in the Auxerrois took the initiative in worship more forcefully than elsewhere, so too were they particularly astute at using peaceful political and legal methods to their own advantage. They were quick to petition for religious rights, to make church declarations, and to use the vote to elect pro-Catholic local officials. According to the survey on religious worship written by the departmental commissaire Etienne Housset in 1797, parishioners in the district of Auxerre had made declarations to use their churches in *all* the communes he knew about (seventy of eighty-six communes had reported).[45] Catholics in at least nineteen communes, that is, in about

---

[44]Porée, "Mémoires du chanoine Frappier," pp. 139–41; AD Yonne 1J231, Duplessis, "Mémoire," p. 89; AN F7 7237, Enquête sur l'exercice des cultes, March 1797; Ordioni, *Survivance des idées,* pp. 201–7; Bibliothèque de la Société du Port Royal, Carton Yonne, Lettres du presbytère d'Auxerre à Grégoire, mostly dated in 1797.

[45]AN F7 7237, Enquête sur l'exercice des cultes, March 1797. In Saint-Florentin, fifty of fifty-one reporting communes had also made church declarations. These two districts were quickest to conform to the law, and the districts of Avallon and Tonnerre were the most remiss.

Table 3. Religiously active communes in the Yonne,
August 1794–April 1802: Percentages of total communes in each district

District	Total communes	Petitioning communes		Rioting communes		Communes holding illegal festivals	
		N	%	N	%	N	%
Auxerre	86	19	(22)	29	(34)	20	(23)
Avallon	71	8	(11)	9	(13)	4	(6)
Joigny	72	8	(11)	8	(11)	11	(15)
Saint-Fargeau	36	4	(11)	13	(36)	8	(22)
Saint-Florentin	57	11	(19)	18	(32)	11	(19)
Sens	91	6	(7)	11	(12)	8	(9)
Tonnerre	74	9	(12)	9	(12)	10	(14)
Departmental totals	487	65		97		72	

Sources and definitions: Same as for Table 1.

22 percent of the district's communes, composed 48 petitions to demand religious rights (see Tables 1 and 3). Relatively high literacy
rates and the web of roads and commerce connecting Auxerre to
outlying wine-growing villages facilitated political education and contact with new ideas. Moreover, the relative economic independence of
vignerons who were small property owners may have made them
more willing and better able to take political action on behalf of their
religion.[46] The especially zealous dechristianization campaign politicized the countryside and taught villagers revolutionary ideology
and political techniques that Catholics would turn against the dechristianizers. Dechristianization also awakened a strong reaction, particularly in villages that had some special cause for devotion.[47] In short,
whereas the legacy of Jansenism made lay Catholics in the district of
Auxerre particularly apt to lead worship on their own, the particular

[46]As mentioned before, small property owners were more common in the wine-
producing district than elsewhere in the Yonne, though of course some vignerons were
tenants or day laborers. On the multiple possible correlations between political and
religious positions of vignerons in the postrevolutionary period, see Pierre Lévêque,
"Vigne, religion, et politique en France aux XIXe et XXe siècles," in *Du jansénisme à la
laïcité*, pp. 139–66. On commerce routes, see Dupéron, *Question du pain*, pp. 17–18.
[47]For example, the Catholics of Saint-Bris were especially proud of their relics of
Saint Prix, and the rebellious town of Irancy clung fiercely to its festival of Saint
Germain; these two villages were especially active in demanding their religion. AD
Yonne 1J231, Duplessis, "Mémoire," p. 89, L213, Lettre de l'agent national d'Irancy au
département de l'Yonne, 3 thermidor an VI (21 July 1798). See, for Saint-Bris, AC
Saint-Bris, Dépôt 583, D2; AD Yonne L215, 216; for Irancy, see esp. AD Yonne L214,
992.

configuration of education, proximity to roads and cities, and contact with revolutionary ideas encouraged the Auxerrois to be particularly politically active in their demands for religious rights.

The religious resurgence in the bocage country in the district of Saint-Fargeau provides an interesting point of comparison. In general, the inhabitants of the Puisaye were less religiously active than the Auxerrois, just as the Colbert bishops had found the Puisaye less zealous a century earlier. When Catholics in this poor district took action on behalf of their religion, they were much more likely to break into a church or hold an illegal festival than to petition. Except in the northernmost canton of Champignelles, largely outside the bocage country, the Catholics of the Puisaye were strikingly quick to resort to illegal religious activism. As Table 3 shows, riots took place in one-third of the communes in the district, and over one-fifth of them were caught holding illegal festivals (see also Maps 4 and 5). If one considers festivals, bell ringing, riots, and illegal, dangerous gatherings, over two-thirds of the communes were denounced by name for some violation. In some cases police reported violations in a canton as a whole, and so some of the tiny communes escaped mention by name. On the other hand, the inhabitants of the isolated and scattered hamlets of the Puisaye were far less literate and less exposed to revolutionary political culture than the Auxerrois. This less-politicized district produced only 3.5 percent of the total religious petitions in the department (see Table 1). The Puisaye had no strong ecclesiastical center comparable to Auxerre, nor did it manifest the same high number of lay-led masses. In short, the religious resurgence in the Puisaye was not as well organized or as politically sophisticated as that of the Auxerrois. But the Catholics of the Puisaye relied on direct and defiant forms of activism almost as often as the Auxerrois; and taking into account the smaller number of communes, direct activism was more widespread in the district of Saint-Fargeau than in the Senonais to the north.

In contrast to the activist villagers of the Auxerrois, Puisaye, and the southern part of the Saint-Florentin district, Catholics in the Avallonais and Tonnerrois districts clung to their traditions through a quieter, more clandestine, and less flamboyant means. The resurgence here is difficult to interpret. For while lenient authorities existed throughout the Yonne, officials in the districts of Tonnerre and Avallon were especially remiss in executing laws and recording infractions. For example, Commissaire Housset bemoaned the "favoritism"

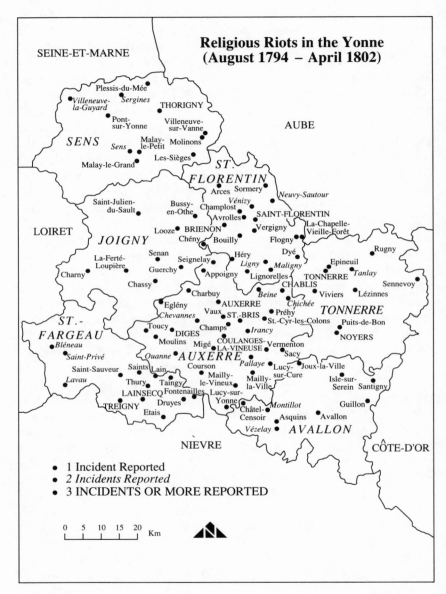

Map 4

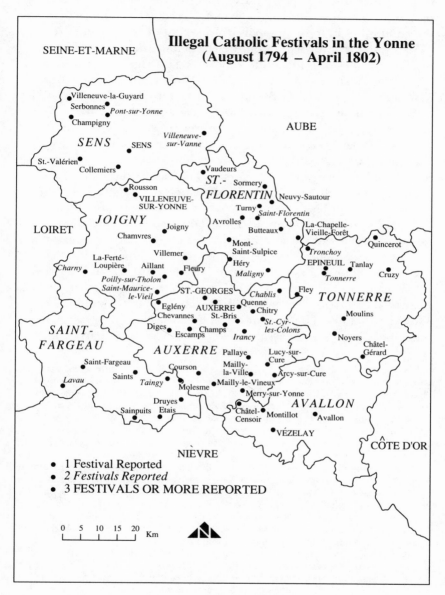

**Illegal Catholic Festivals in the Yonne
(August 1794 – April 1802)**

SEINE-ET-MARNE

Villeneuve-la-Guyard
Serbonnes
Pont-sur-Yonne
Champigny

AUBE

SENS
SENS
Villeneuve-
sur-Vanne

St.-Valérien
Collemiers

Vaudeurs
ST.-   Sormery
Rousson   *FLORENTIN* Neuvy-Sautour
VILLENEUVE-
SUR-YONNE   Turny
                   Saint-Florentin

JOIGNY   Avrolles
Joigny   Butteaux   La-Chapelle-
Chamvres   Mont-   Vieille-Forêt
                 Saint-Sulpice   Quincerot
LOIRET   *Tronchoy*
La-Ferté- Villemer   Héry   EPINEUIL Tanlay
Charny   Loupière Aillant *Maligny*   Cruzy
          Fleury   *Tonnerre*
Poilly-sur-Tholon
Saint-Maurice-   ST.-GEORGES *Chablis* Fley
le-Vieil   Quenne   *TONNERRE*
         Eglény AUXERRE *Chitry*
         Chevannes St.-Bris   Moulins
SAINT- Diges   *St.-Cyr-*
FARGEAU Escamps Champs *les-Colons*
                Irancy   Noyers
         AUXERRE Pallaye Lucy-sur- Châtel-
                          Cure   Gérard
Saint-Fargeau   Mailly-
Lavau Saints Courson la-Ville Arcy-sur-Cure
        Taingy Molesme Mailly-le-Vineux
                       Merry-sur-Yonne
         Druyes   *AVALLON*
Sainpuits Etais Châtel- Montillot Avallon
                 Censoir
                 VÉZELAY

NIÈVRE   CÔTE D'OR

- 1 Festival Reported
- *2 Festivals Reported*
- **3 FESTIVALS OR MORE REPORTED**

0   5   10   15   20   Km

Map 5

of local authorities toward "fanaticism"; in fact, when he conducted his survey on church use in the winter of 1796–1797, more than half the communes in the Avallonais (thirty-eight of seventy-one) refused to provide any information on their religious practice. Even though local authorities often failed to report illegal religious activism in the districts of Avallon and Tonnerre, departmental government officials describing the *esprit public* frequently pointed to these areas, especially the mountainous and secluded Morvan, as cradles of furtive religious activism. In 1797, for example, Housset wrote of the commune of Guillon in the Avallonais: "No special information has come to me about the priests in this canton. I know only that they are fanatic and intolerant, and that some members of the administration favor them." He then noted a threatening band of women at Santigny who held the "laws policing public worship in contempt." Likewise, two years later he complained about Vézinnes in the Tonnerrois, where "the spirit of fanaticism wins out over republican spirit, and the new institutions cannot make any headway against the mass of superstition."[48]

In short, though local officials in these two districts did not report many incidents of violent or illegal activism, authorities at the departmental and district level worried constantly about clandestine worship, and neither Theophilanthropy nor the fêtes décadaires made much headway in these areas.[49] For the Avallonais in particular, one

[48]AN F7 7237, Enquête sur l'exercice des cultes, March 1797. Cantons that refused to provide information on church declarations included several of the hottest centers of clandestine practice and religious activism, such as Saint-Fargeau and Mézilles in the Puisaye, several towns in the Morvan, and Brienon in the district of Saint-Florentin. In many communes Catholic devotion flourished without receiving much attention from the authorities. The canton of Yrouerre in the Tonnerrois, for example, was scarcely mentioned in the various police accounts of cult violations and suspicious areas; yet when the communes in Yrouerre canton made their church declarations in ventôse an IV (February–March 1796), in each village virtually all the male heads of household, and in some cases the women as well, signed or were named as supporters on the declarations. In the commune of Viviers, in fact, the number of subscribers to the declaration exceeded the population estimate of the year III census! AD Yonne L706, Extraits des registres des communes de Béru, Chémilly, Poilly-sur-Serein, Sainte-Vertu, Viviers, and Yrouerre, all in ventôse an IV (February–March 1796), and AN F20*20 Yonne, Dénombrement et population du département de l'Yonne, an III (1794–95).

[49]Additional reports on *esprit public* include the *comptes décadaires* written by the departmental commissaire Collet and other officials in AN F1cIII Yonne 5 and 7; AN AFIII 280, Situation du département de l'Yonne, germinal an VII (March–April 1799); AN F7 7377, Rapport du commissaire près l'administration départementale de l'Yonne, Collet, au ministre de la police, 5 pluviôse an V (24 January 1797). Châtel-Censoir was apparently the only town in the district of Avallon with Theophilanthropists. E. Pallier, "Recherches historiques sur l'histoire de Châtel-Censoir," *BSSY* 34 (1880): 103.

gains the qualitative impression that Catholic villagers still clung quietly to the customs the Catholic Reformation had failed one hundred years earlier to suppress. In this southeastern corner of the Yonne, attendance at mass and the performance of Easter duty remained the strongest in the department into modern times.[50]

Returning refractory clergy played an especially important role in promoting the revival in the districts of Avallon and Tonnere. Despite the massive oath taking by clergy in the rest of the Yonne in 1791, 20 to 25 percent of the clergy in these two districts had refused to take the oath or had retracted it. In the late 1790s vigilant departmental authorities reported cases of nonjurors in other parts of the Yonne, especially in large towns and in the Forêt d'Othe in the district of Saint-Florentin. But refractories were most active in the southeastern part of the department, particularly in the former ecclesiastical centers of Vézelay, Tonnerre, and Montréal and in heavily wooded areas, such as the hilly Quarré canton of the Morvan and the easternmost parts of the Tonnerrois. (Government authorities were more wary of these longtime nonjurors than of recent retractors, such as Viart's followers in the Auxerrois, who nonetheless agreed to new oaths.) In the Yonne secretive nonjurors did not pose so much a political threat to the Revolution as a cultural or symbolic one: in this relatively peaceful area they did little to ignite counterrevolution but much to encourage cultural resistance to revolutionary cults by kindling Catholic faith and practice.[51]

The refractory clergymen particularly concentrated their clandestine pursuits along the borders between the Yonne and the Côte-d'Or or the Nièvre. Borders were liminal areas of intense activism: clergy and laity alike could play with the boundaries of jurisdiction and turn various interpretations of laws to their own advantage. Catholics in villages bordering the Aube, the Nièvre, and the Côte-d'Or were energetic supporters of the revival. For example, in spring 1799 inhabitants of the cantons of Neuvy-Sautour and Saint-Florentin crossed into the Aube to Courson to attend mass and have their babies baptized, especially on Easter. People claimed, "There is no law

[50]Boulard, *Matériaux pour l'histoire religieuse*, pp. 88–91, 552–53.
[51]AN F19 1017, Liasse "prêtres séditieux de l'Yonne"; AD Yonne L691–99, Affaires ecclésiastiques: Serments et dossiers personnels des ecclésiastiques. Many AN F7 folders; Bonneau, *Clergé de l'Yonne;* and Michel Gally, "Notices sur les prêtres et religieux de l'ancien archdiaconé d'Avallon," *Bulletin de la Société d'études d'Avallon* (1898): 13–177, offer information on various specific individuals.

[against mass], and if the law they tell us about existed, it would be enforced in the Aube as well." On the other side of the department, inhabitants of the Nièvre stole into the Yonne to attend Easter mass in Treigny and to take part in the age-old outlawed festival of Saint Eloi at Lavau in the Puisaye. Commissaires of the Yonne frequently complained to the minister of the police or the departmental administration that the departments of Nièvre, the Aube, the Loiret, and the Côte-d'Or were not zealous enough in enforcing the laws.[52]

While clandestine worship, complicity of local officials, and the aid of refractory clergy characterized the religious movement in the southern corner of the Yonne, the northern third of the department offered a marked contrast in political and religious style. In the district of Sens and the northern parts of the Saint-Florentin and Joigny districts, the inhabitants were decidedly less active in defense of their Old Regime traditions. More specifically, as the Catholics in the districts of Sens and Joigny and in the far northern part of the district of Saint-Florentin were much less likely to petition, riot, or hold illegal festivals (see Maps 3–5). Officials in these regions were much more thorough in recording infractions than those in the southeast; yet they reported illegal festivals in only 9 percent of the communes of the district of Sens and in only 15 percent of those of Joigny (see Table 3). Together, these two districts held about one-third of the communes and population of the department but produced well under one-fifth of the religious petitions and riots in the late 1790s (see Table 1). Despite its large population, the district of Sens in particular lagged behind in virtually every form of religious activism. Although officials complained of Catholic resistance in these areas, as in all parts of the Yonne, one does not discover the same repeated expressions of hopelessness about stamping out "fanaticism" as one finds for the southeastern part of the department or even for the Auxerrois.

Several factors help to explain this lower level of zeal and religious activism in the northern third of the department. First, the Catholic Reformation had been most successful in the former diocese of Sens

<hr>

[52]AD Yonne L217, Lettre du commissaire de Neuvy-Sautour au commissaire de l'Yonne, 26 germinal an VII (15 April 1799); AN F7 7237, Enquête sur l'exercice des cultes, March 1797. On the use of border jurisdictions by villagers in the Old Regime, see Mary Ann Quinn, "Pratiques et théories de la coutume: Allodialité et conflits de droits dans la seigneurie de L'Isle-sous-Montréal au XVIIIe siècle," *Etudes rurales* 103–4 (1986): 71–104.

at supressing popular forms of devotion, and in the mid–eighteenth century the continual conflicts over Jansenism no doubt wearied the laity. (The same might be said of the diocese of Auxerre, but at least there the Jansenists held out longer and succeeded in cultivating the internalized lay devotion of a significant part of the population. The district of Sens ran a distant second to the Auxerrois in recorded numbers of lay-led masses.) It is possible, moreover, that the inhabitants of the Senonais, as the best-educated of the department and the most closely connected to Paris and its Enlightenment circles, were consequently more exposed than the people of the Puisaye or the Morvan to the questioning of superstition by eighteenth-century thinkers.

In addition, the Senonais had less vigorous clerical leadership than other regions. Nonjurors and retractors were rare in the districts of Sens and Joigny. Moreover, the Constitutional clergy, almost all of whom had abdicated, lost their potential leader when Loménie de Brienne, the Constitutional bishop and former bishop of the Sens diocese, died in 1794. The Vicar-General Pierre-Jacques de Condé, who led the nonjurors and retractors in Sens, had more difficulty than his colleague Viart in Auxerre in getting former Constitutional priests to return to practice. Fewer of those priests who had abdicated were willing to make the declaration of submission and of church use in the year IV (1795–1796).[53]

Furthermore, the Senonais had a closer relationship to revolutionary culture. While many villagers throughout the Yonne favored revolutionary reforms, the district of Sens seemed to welcome the Revolution with exceptional enthusiasm. Unlike the local governments of the other district capitals, the municipal government of Sens remained Jacobin for most of the Thermidorean and Directorial periods. Although revolutionary officials had difficulty promoting revolutionary institutions everywhere in the Yonne, they seemed to be more successful in the Senonais than elsewhere. When the Theophilanthropists struggled to spread their deist cult into rural areas of France, the districts of Sens, Auxerre, and Saint-Florentin were among the few regions where the cult caught on in quite a few small villages.[54] Catholics in these regions inevitably found themselves com-

[53]Rocher, "Aspects de l'histoire religieuse," pp. 20, 25–26; AN F7 7237, Enquête sur l'exercice des cultes, March 1797.

[54]AD Yonne L series, esp. L734, offers information on the location of Theophilanthropists in the Yonne. See also Charles Moiset, "La théophilanthropie dans le départe-

ing into conflict with Theophilanthropists and supporters of revolutionary cults. The presence of Theophilanthropists seemed to stimulate greater Catholic devotion in response. Indeed, disagreements
over shared church space between Catholics and Theophilanthropists
provoked some of the more heated religious confrontations in the
Senonais, erupting into violent disputes in Malay-le-Grand, Malay-le-
Petit, and Vénizy, for example, in the late 1790s.[55]

In summary, Catholicism was practiced throughout the Yonne but
religious activism took on particular characteristics in certain areas
and certain situations. Catholics in the Auxerrois were particularly
prone both to take illegal action and to adopt revolutionary political
methods, such as petitions, assemblies, and revolutionary rhetoric, to
make their demands known. In the forested Puisaye, villagers relied
most heavily on persistent, flagrant, and sometimes violent violations
of the law: their defense may not have been eloquent, but they insisted on continued practice of old traditions. In the isolated Morvan and
parts of the Tonnerrois, refractory clergy stimulated the revival, villagers clung to their ancient devotions, and local authorities neglected
to report illicit religious activity. Farther north, the inhabitants of the
Senonais were the least active in the name of their religion: Catholics
there tended to defend their religious traditions most tenaciously
when they were challenged by local Theophilanthropists or by strong
promotion of the revolutionary cults and calendar.

Just as there were regional contrasts in method of revival, so too,
town and countryside experienced the Catholic resurgence differently. The larger towns, particularly Sens, Auxerre, Saint-Florentin,
and Tonnerre, invariably became arenas of religious conflict and activism. The open practice of Catholicism was an intensely politicized

---

ment de l'Yonne," *BSSY* 52 (1898): 235–59. Theophilanthropists initially were very
successful in Sens under the zealous leadership of Benoist-Lamothe, who edited the
republican paper in Sens, the *Observateur du département de l'Yonne*. From Sens, Theophilanthropy radiated out into the countryside and took hold in nearby communes.

[55]AD Yonne L734, Lettre des citoyens (théophilanthropes) de Malay-le-Petit au commissaire près le tribunal de Sens, 19 nivôse an VII (8 January 1799), Information faite
par le juge de paix de Véron, 27 nivôse an VII (16 January 1799), Lettre de l'agent
national de Malay-le-Petit au ministre de la justice, 27 pluviôse an VII (15 February
1799), Extrait du PV par le commissaire près le canton de Véron, 25 frimaire an VI (15
December 1797), L212, Lettre de l'instituteur de Malay-le-Grand à l'administration
départementale de l'Yonne, [c. early frimaire an VI (November 1797)], L217, Lettre du
commissaire près Vénizy au celui près l'Yonne, 2 germinal an VII (22 March 1799);
Henri Forestier, "Catholiques et théophilanthropes dans l'Yonne à la veille du Concordat," *Echo de Saint-Pierre d'Auxerre* 35 (1961): 3–5.

and controversial issue.[56] In contrast, although some small villages were riddled with religious conflict, in many cases Catholics outnumbered the few supporters of revolutionary cults. If religious disputes arose, they were often less deeply rooted or long lasting.

Various factors contributed to this urban-rural contrast. In rural areas public worship faced less police surveillance and less local opposition. Local officials were generally more detached from national or departmental policies and networks of authority and could more easily turn a blind eye to violations of laws. Rural local officials seem to have been more likely than urban ones to believe that Catholicism and the Republic were compatible. The municipal officer of Courtois, for example, commented in the year II that "superstition has never put any obstacle in the way of the sublime movement of the people."[57] Although revolutionary festivals were celebrated in all the major towns, rural authorities often did little to promote republican ceremonies. Most laws during the Directory mandated that they be celebrated at cantonal *chefs-lieux* but not necessarily in every tiny commune, and few rural inhabitants had the desire or motivation to travel to a major town to participate. The departmental commissaire summed up much of the problem when he wrote to the minister of the interior in 1798, "The man of the countryside says to you coldly, 'The laws! the laws! Do we know them?'" He argued that republican education, persistent promotion of the fêtes décadaires and national festivals, and stringent enforcement of the *police des cultes* laws offered the only solutions to the deep-rooted "fanaticism of the countryside."[58]

[56]The department of the Yonne had two major towns, Auxerre and Sens, with populations of 12,000 and 10,597 respectively, according to AN F20*20, "Dénombrement et population du département de l'Yonne, an III (1794–95)." Four other towns had populations over four thousand in the year III (Joigny: 5,357; Villeneuve-sur-Yonne: 4,605; Avallon: 4,166; Tonnerre: 4,012). Five more towns had a population just above two thousand (Saint-Florentin, Brienon, Vermenton, Chablis, and Saint-Julien-du-Sault).

[57]AD Yonne L205, Réponse de la municipalité de Courtois au questionnaire de l'administration du district de Sens, questionnaire envoyé 24 nivôse an II (13 January 1794).

[58]For administrative purposes communes in groups of about five to ten became part of "cantons" during the Directory. The communes would send their local agent and adjunct to form the cantonal administration. Chefs-lieux of cantons were meant to be the location for revolutionary festivals every *décade* in the countryside. AN F1cIII Yonne 9, Lettre de représentants du people de l'Yonne au ministre de l'intérieur, 7 nivôse an VII (27 December 1798); AN F7 7377, Compte décadaire du département de l'Yonne au ministre de la police, 14 germinal an VI (3 April 1798); AN F1cIII Yonne 7, Compte

In fact, in many villages most of the inhabitants seem to have considered themselves Catholic. Often, the majority of the heads of household signed the communal declaration for church use in fall 1795.[59] Those who did not wish to practice might well be reluctant to voice opposition in a small face-to-face community. When commissaires complained about the leniency of local *juges de paix* who failed to enforce the laws regulating public worship, they also deplored the hesitancy of witnesses to give testimony against their fellow villagers; in many cases, no witnesses at all could be found.[60] Villagers who failed to attend Catholic ceremonies and to observe the Catholic calendar might well face "threats and insults" from their neighbors. In Ligny, for example, Catholic villagers forced one servant to stop working on Sunday and told him, "You are the only who hinders the perfect triumph of religion." In the same village another woman faced mockery for taking care of the children of the commissaire: "Aren't you ashamed to care for those children. . . . Have you changed religion then?"[61]

In large towns, on the other hand, not only did officials and republicans promote revolutionary culture more avidly, but more inhabitants participated in revolutionary and Theophilanthropist festivals. After the fall of Robespierre, as Catholics struggled to return to public worship, republicans maintained their organizations and identity more successfully in towns than in rural areas. Particularly after the coup d'état of fructidor an v (September 1797), the Jacobin clubs closed by the Thermidoreans could resurface legally. In Auxerre longtime Jacobins reorganized the Cercle constitutionnel, supported by the newly appointed municipality. (The club had found its first attempt to organize suppressed a month earlier by the moderate mu-

analytique du commissaire de l'Yonne au ministre de l'intérieur, nivôse an VII (December 1798–January 1799).

[59]AD Yonne L706.

[60]AN F19 1017, Réponse du commissaire des tribunaux de l'Yonne au ministre de la justice, 11 floréal an IV (30 April 1796); AN F7 3699², Lettre de l'administration du département de l'Yonne au ministre de l'intérieur, 11 brumaire an V (1 November 1796); AN F1bII Yonne 1, Lettre anonyme au ministre de la police, 8 vendémiaire an V (29 September 1796); An F1cIII Yonne 7, Compte décadaire par le commissaire de l'Yonne pour le ministre de l'intérieur, 3 nivôse an VI (23 December 1797).

[61]AD Yonne L220, Rapport du commissaire de Ligny, 13 vendémiaire an VIII (5 October 1799). For further instances of menacing or pressuring non-Catholics, see, for example, AN F7 3699², Bulletin de la police de l'Yonne, 1–9 frimaire an VII (21–29 November 1798); AD Yonne L209, PV du canton de Saint-Georges, 3 floréal an IV (22 April 1796).

nicipal officers.)[62] In Sens republicans maintained control of the municipal government throughout most of the Directory and used the newspaper *L'Observateur du département de l'Yonne* to satirize Catholicism and to further republican institutions and ideology. Well-organized republicans in Sens, Auxerre, Joigny, Saint-Florentin, and Tonnerre championed the celebration of the *décadi* and of Theophilanthropy and had no qualms about mocking or hindering Catholic practice.

Just as supporters of revolutionary cults were more numerous and well organized, both lay and clerical religious groups tended to be better organized in towns than in villages. More clergymen lived in the towns and could provide clerical leadership for the revival. Former canons of urban collegiate churches frequently remained or returned after the Terror.[63] In addition, lay religious groups tended to have more structure and political consciousness in the towns than in the villages. Early attempts to suppress parishes in 1791 and 1793 threatened towns more than villages because the initial plan sought to limit each commune to one church. This confrontation provoked early politicization of urban parishioners. In the late 1790s parishes that had petitioned early for survival, such as Saint-Julien and Saint-Pierre in Avallon, Saint-Pierre in Auxerre, and Saint-Pierre in Chablis, were especially tenacious in demanding a return to public practice in their churches.[64] Some of the poorer villages lacked *fabriques,* but in the towns *fabriciens* and members of prerevolutionary confraternities often led the legal attempts to reestablish Catholicism. In Auxerre, for example, the boatmen from the confraternity of Saint Nic-

[62]AC Auxerre Dépôt 3 I2, Arrêté de l'administration municipale d'Auxerre, 7 thermidor an v (25 July 1797); Déclarations par le Cercle constitutionnel d'Auxerre, 25 messidor, 28 fructidor an v (13 July, 14 September 1797). See also Isser Woloch, *Jacobin Legacy: The Democratic Movement under the Directory* (Princeton, N.J., 1970), pp. 69, 93–94.

[63]There were fourteen chapters of canons in the Yonne before 1790, four in Sens, two in Auxerre, and one each in Avallon, Tonnerre, Vézelay, Chablis, Toucy, Appoigny, Châtel-Censoir, and Montréal.

[64]AD Yonne L711, Pétitions des habitants d'Avallon à la municipalité, 7 juin 1791, 12, 24 septembre 1791, and Pétition des marguilliers de Saint-Lazare d'Avallon à l'administration centrale de l'Yonne, 21 juillet 1792; AC Auxerre Dépôt 3 P5, Pétition des paroissiens de Saint-Pierre, Notre-Dame, et Saint-Eusèbe au conseil général d'Auxerre, 15 frimaire an II (5 December 1793); AD Yonne G2396, PV de l'assemblée paroissiale de Saint-Pierre, 24 octobre 1790. Parish suppression provoked a riot in Saint-Fargeau in 1793. Lettre de Maure au Comité de salut public, 2 nivôse an II (22 December 1793), in "Nouvelles lettres de Maure, député d'Auxerre," *Annuaire de l'Yonne* (1897): 115.

olas successfully petitioned the municipality for the return of their emblem and chapel, and the former *fabriciens* of Saint-Etienne, Saint-Pierre, and Saint-Eusèbe were critical leaders of the petitioning campaigns conducted by the sections and the parishes to regain these churches.[65]

Since religious revival in towns provoked more conflict and opposition, town-dwelling religious activists developed certain techniques of political activism more fully than did rural Catholics. For example, town Catholics were more likely to petition for their right to religion. Religious petitioning occurred in every town with a population of more than two thousand, except Joigny; 41 percent of religious petitions came from the eleven towns with more than two thousand inhabitants, and 25 percent from towns with one thousand to two thousand inhabitants, compared to 34 percent from villages of less than a thousand people.[66] It also seems likely that town Catholics had come into more contact than villagers with the revolutionary ideology of popular sovereignty and religious liberty and could more easily use the promises and language of the Revolution to make their claims for freedom of worship. In short, often faced with the organized opposition of republican reformers, Catholic groups in towns were better organized, better educated, and more highly politicized than their rural counterparts.

A complex set of factors helped to shape the geography of religious revival in the Yonne after the fall of Robespierre. Proximity to clerical centers, levels of literacy, the reception of the Civil Constitution in 1791, and isolation or contact with various outside forces all influenced forms of religious activism. Of crucial importance was the day-to-day experience of Revolution. Where republican leaders and officials challenged Catholicism most fiercely, they also often provoked

[65]AC Auxerre Dépôt 3 P5, Pétition des mariniers d'Auxerre à l'administration municipale d'Auxerre, n.d., granted by PV de l'administration municipale d'Auxerre, 27 messidor an III (15 July 1795); AD Yonne L710, PV du conseil général d'Auxerre, 9 germinal an III (29 March 1795); AD Yonne G2373, PV de l'assemblée paroissiale de Saint-Eusèbe, 17 février 1788; AC Auxerre Dépôt 3 P5, Pétition des citoyens de Saint-Eusèbe au conseil général d'Auxerre, n.d. [c. June 1795], Pétitions des paroissiens de Saint-Pierre au conseil général d'Auxerre, 1 ventôse an IV (20 February 1796), 7 messidor an V (25 June 1797), et 16 nivôse an VIII (6 January 1800); AD Yonne G2396, Comptes de fabrique de Saint-Pierre, 1774–92.

[66]For sources, see Table 1. In this case I included all religious petitions, including those written between 1790 and 1794.

the most active response, as in the Auxerrois and the large towns of the department. Most critical was the depth and nature of local devotion on the eve of the Revolution. In the Morvan deep-rooted attachment to traditional local religion made village officials reluctant—even more so than elsewhere—to enforce religious laws. The ambiguous Jansenist legacy in the Auxerrois helped to shape a highly activist and independent lay revival, but in the Senonais, already apparently less attached to regular practice by 1789, the resurgence was less forceful.

Throughout the Yonne the flexibility of religious and political tactics is striking. Catholic activists in the Yonne adapted their methods of revival to the particular concerns and conditions of each local situation. Whereas the educated editor of the *Journal politique et littéraire* in Sens used literary devices and religious propaganda to influence voters, a vigneron in Auxerre transformed a table in his home into an altar to celebrate a lay mass. The villagers in the hamlet of Puits-de-Bon in the Tonnerrois stole and hid their church bell; the women of Saints in the Puisaye used every possible means to drive the new schoolteacher from the parish rectory. One point stands out in clear relief: whatever the regional variations, after the fall of Robespierre the desire to return to Catholic practice was widespread and deeply rooted in the villages and towns of the Yonne. Lay Catholics in the Yonne willingly transformed their religious practices to deal with the hardships of the revolutionary context and to reflect their own changes in religious assumptions and priorities.

CHAPTER THREE

Recreating the Sacred:
The Emergence of Lay Cults

In January 1795 in the village of Courson, three women rang the
bells of the local church to call their fellow villagers to worship.
Then the Allard brothers and Grégoire Gautherot, two charcoal
workers and a cultivator, mounted the altar and sang the words of the
mass before a crowd of about sixty. Germain Bourguignon, a black-
smith, provided several prayer books and hymnals and the wife of the
local national agent brought the altar candles. No priest was present.
A group of parishioners had apparently broken into their church on
Christmas Eve, and since then several lay villagers had regularly taken
turns leading rituals normally performed by a priest, including the
mass, albeit without the consecration.[1] Similar enactments of "lay" or
"white masses" became widespread in the Yonne and elsewhere during the revolutionary years. By 1794 local priests, confronted with a
series of oaths and confusing laws, had often resigned from their
positions, endured deportation or imprisonment, fled to their homes,
left the country, disappeared into the countryside, or chosen to enter
secular life. Lay believers—deprived of their clergy, their customary
worship, and their sacred spaces—struggled to recreate public collective ritual as well as they could. Often, they took ritual matters into
their own hands, molding them into new patterns.

[1]AD Yonne L1118, PV du comité révolutionnaire d'Auxerre, 28 nivôse au 3 pluviôse
an III (17–22 January 1795), L207, PV de la municipalité de Courson, 22 nivôse an III
(11 January 1795), Certificat par les officiers de Courson, 4 pluviôse an III (23 January
1795), and Lettre de l'agent national de Courson à celui d'Auxerre, 14 nivôse an III (3
January 1795).

[76]

Historians have traditionally emphasized the secularizing impact of the Revolution. The revolutionary dechristianization campaign and the creation of a secular political culture undoubtedly undermined the strength of Catholic belief and institutions over both the short and long term. Yet the deeper process of secularization took place only slowly; it came about through a series of spiritual transformations and fluctuations. In fact, in many areas the Revolution first encouraged an upsurge of belief and a dynamism of lay practice and initiative. For while some inhabitants of the Yonne and of the rest of France willingly adopted the secular attitudes promoted by the radical revolutionaries, a large majority strove to resurrect and recreate their religion within the revolutionary context. Catholics clung to their old traditions and also forged new ones not only to deal with the hardships and limitations of worship in the 1790s but also to assimilate and express subtle shifts in cultural perceptions, born of the Revolution and the last years of the Old Regime.

The analysis of lay cults offers a window into just such a transformation, exemplifying the dynamic interaction among religion, tradition, and revolution. Faced with a loss of ritual and fearing a corollary loss of faith, the laity devised lay-led rituals, which, though firmly based on Old Regime traditions, incorporated antihierarchical, egalitarian, activist, and in some cases anticlerical elements of revolutionary ideology. This new means of worship not only shows lay religious creativity and regeneration in the late 1790s, it also provides clues to the more gradual metamorphosis of Catholic spirituality during the nineteenth century.

The Clergy Face the Revolution

On the eve of the Revolution most of the secular clergy of the future department of the Yonne seemed to fit the image of the "bon curé" of the eighteenth-century countryside. As educated representatives of church and crown, they said mass, taught catechism, recorded births and deaths, and provided moral leadership for their flocks. Trained in post-Tridentine seminaries, these men for the most part seem to have viewed themselves as "citizen priests," that is, as servants of society, spiritual educators, and moral exemplars, rather than as sacred intercessors with a direct line to God or as quasi-magical miracle workers blessing crops and animals. In the Yonne clerical recruitment was declining and clerical density was low; the clergy tended to be more poorly paid and perhaps less highly respected than their clerical colleagues in parts of the west, northeast, or southwest.[2]

In 1789 many priests in the Yonne expressed a desire for ecclesiastical reform. As their *cahiers de doléances* show, many parish priests were deeply concerned not only about their own status and political voice within ecclesiastical structures but also about signs of weakening lay devotion and morality. Imbued with the Richerist notion that the lower clergy should have a greater say in church affairs, many curés of the Yonne saw deep connections between their own lack of local prestige and ecclesiastical voice and their parishioners' tendency toward irreligion. As the curé of Gurgy commented in his cahier in 1789, "This degradation [of the lower clergy], which has gone on for more than a century, deprives them of full public esteem, is against the laws of the church, and does considerable harm to religion." He went on to appeal, like many of his colleagues in the bailliage of Auxerre, for structural changes within the church, including cantonal and provincial synods and a national council allowing representation for the lower clergy. Many curés seemed to feel that certain reforms of the French church would enhance their relationship with their parishioners and help improve the moral fiber and piety of laity as well as clergy. Some clergy combined these views with an appeal to return to the purity of the primitive church or with specifically Jansenist requests.[3]

In short, the attitudes and demands of the curés of the Yonne in 1789 favorably disposed many of them toward the attempts to create a national church. For their part, many of the laity were also open to

[2]Dinet, "Ordinations sacerdotales," pp. 221–29; Tackett and Langlois, "Ecclesiastical Structures," p. 358; Tackett, *Priest and Parish*, chaps. 5 and 6, and his *Religion, Revolution*, chap. 10. Summarizing much recent work on Old Regime rural religion and the clergy, Peter Jones notes that the priests in Brittany and parts of the southwest were the best paid. See Jones, *The Peasantry in the French Revolution* (Cambridge, Eng., 1988), p. 192.

[3]Charles Porée, *Cahiers des curés et des communautés ecclésiastiques du bailliage d'Auxerre pour les Etats-généraux de 1789* (Auxerre, 1927). Through the influence of Bishop Cicé, the final cahier for the First Estate of the diocese of Auxerre omitted the most radical opinions of the lower clergy. Ordioni, *Survivance des idées*, pp. 147–61, esp. quotation of the curé, p. 155; Rocher, "Evolution politique et religieuse," pp. 98–100, and his "Aspects de l'histoire religieuse," pp. 3–5. For a revealing biography of a "citizen" curé of this region (Gien in the diocese of Auxerre, but outside the Yonne), see P. Pinseau, *Un curé constitutionnel, l'abbé Vallet, député à l'Assemblée constituante (1754–1828)* (Orléans, 1947).

the promises of ecclesiastical reform; indeed, their cahiers had suggested the reduction of clerical wealth and privilege which the national legislature would soon put into effect. In contrast, the regular clergy were hardest hit by the restructuring of the church early in the Revolution. When the National Assembly closed convents and monasteries, nuns, in particular, had both spiritual and economic reasons to resist disbanding; most of them chose to live together in religious communities as long as possible (until 1792). Many former nuns would later participate quietly in the Thermidorean revival, by reopening and staffing hospitals, for example. The majority of the monks, on the other hand, elected to return to lay life. Some monks and canons returned to their native regions; others stayed in the Yonne and found work as teachers, civil servants, or *cultivateurs* or became Constitutional clergymen to replace parish priests who chose not to take the oath to the Civil Constitution of the Clergy in 1791.[4]

In fact, however, a very high percentage of the clergy—95 percent in the department as a whole—initially took the oath. Even after the wave of retractions and invalidations following the pope's condemnation of the Civil Constitution in March 1791, 86 percent remained jurors. Oath taking without retraction was highest in the northern and western parts of the department, whereas the southern and eastern districts of Avallon, Tonnerre, and Auxerre witnessed the highest percentages of refractories (see Table 4). The enthusiasm of priests

[4]Courtaut, "Etudes sur l'esprit public," 312–15; Charles Demay, "Cahiers des paroisses du bailliage d'Auxerre," 38:66, 72–76, 116–17; AD Yonne L669, Déclarations des religieux et religieuses des couvents d'Auxerre qui veulent quitter leurs maisons, décembre 1790, L667, Tableau des maisons religieuses, prieurés, cures, collèges, seminaires du département, février 1790. Initially, only 3 of the 108 nuns living in Auxerre in 1790 chose to leave their convents. Nuns throughout France tended to follow this pattern. Ruth Graham, "Nuns Who Broke the Vows of Poverty and Chastity," paper presented at International Congress on the French Revolution, Washington, D.C., May 1989; Viguerie, *Christianisme et Révolution*, p. 249ff. The Ursulines in Tonnerre continued to live together and teach young girls throughout the Revolution, alledgedly living as lay women, i.e., without wearing their habits. Charles Hardy, "Histoire de la congrégation des Ursulines de Tonnerre, 1672–1905," BSSY 70 (1916): 5–75, esp. 32–36. See also Noirot, *Le département de l'Yonne* 1:29–30 n. 15, for examples of the varied choices of former monks of the Yonne. AN F19 1127, Lettre de l'administration centrale de l'Yonne au ministre de la police, 19 septembre 1791, F19 481⁴⁻⁵, Lettre de l'administration du département de l'Yonne au ministre de l'intérieur, 2 octobre 1792. In 1790 of the twenty-five monks from the town of Auxerre who immediately chose to leave communal life, about a third declared that they would leave Auxerre for Paris or for their homes in northern or eastern France. By the spring of 1792 the departmental administration could report that its monasteries, like its chapters, had all been entirely disbanded.

Table 4. Oaths to the Civil Constitution by clergy in the Yonne, June 1791

| | Clergy subject to the oath | | | Clerical response | | | | | |
| | Parish clergy | Nonparish clergy | Total | Nonjurors or those with invalidated oaths | | Retractors | | Constitutional clergy | |
Districts				N	%	N	%	N	%
Auxerre	111	13	124	16	(13)	5	(4)	103	(83)
Avallon	69	5	74	8	(11)	6	(8)	60	(81)
Joigny	95	4	99	2	(2)	12	(12)	85	(86)
Saint-Fargeau	48	0	48	0	(0)	1	(2)	47	(98)
Saint-Florentin	70	1	71	2	(3)	7	(10)	62	(87)
Sens	126	11	137	2	(1)	11	(8)	124	(91)
Tonnerre	75	5	80	4	(5)	16	(20)	60	(75)
Totals	594	39	633	34	(5)	58	(9)	541	(86)

Source: Rocher, "Aspects de l'histoire religieuse."

and people about the possibilities of the Revolution was probably the major motivation for the high level of oath taking in the Yonne. The acceptance of the curé's role as "citizen-priest," the example of Loménie de Brienne, the juror bishop of the Yonne, and in some cases the influence of Jansenism encouraged priests of the Yonne to adhere to the Civil Constitution.[5]

Though compliance in the Yonne, with the rest of the Paris Basin, was exceptionally high, many individual priests nonetheless wrestled with divided loyalties. As Marcel Richard, the vicar of Chablis, wrote when he retracted his oath in June 1791: "Seen as an enemy of the Nation, . . . I will be forced to go far away . . . reduced to poverty and misery. . . . But I had no choice. So loud was the cry of my conscience." Some parishes found themselves torn apart by acrimonious disputes between their old nonjuror and a new Constitutional clergyman. These newcomers sometimes faced opposition from villagers or from rival refractory clergy who continued to say mass and administer sacraments clandestinely. Early in January 1792, for example, the Constitutional priest of Isle-sur-Serein narrowly escaped being dumped into the village fountain by an angry crowd, led by women who supported the local refractory. For the most part, however, the replacement of nonjurors went relatively smoothly, and the Yonne did not suffer the same intense factionalism as did regions of low oath taking.[6]

[5]On oath taking in the Yonne, see esp. Rocher, "Aspects de l'histoire religieuse," pp. 3–7 and tableau 1. Ordioni notes that most, but not all, Jansenists took the oath in the diocese of Auxerre (*Survivance des idées*, pp. 163–94). On Jansenism as a cause of oath taking throughout France, see Préclin, *Jansénistes du XVIIIe siècle*. For a discussion of the drawbacks of this argument, see William Williams, "Jansenism and the Pre-revolutionary Clergy," in *Studies in Eighteenth-Century Culture* 7 (1978): 289–302. On Loménie de Brienne, see Noirot, *Le département de l'Yonne* 1:6–11; and Joseph Perrin, *Le cardinal Loménie de Brienne, archevêque de Sens* (Sens, 1896). On citizen priests and Jansenism, see Tackett, *Religion, Revolution*, pp. 69–74, 127–33. Tackett hesitates to draw too strong a correlation between Jansenism and oath taking, but he argues forcefully that "citizen priests" who emphasized their moral, theological, and civic duties over sacerdotal leadership were more likely to take the oath throughout France.

[6]AD Yonne L1406, Lettre de Richard, vicaire à Chablis, au conseil municipal de Chablis, 4 juin 1791, L713, Lettre du curé de Dissangis aux administrateurs d'Avallon, 23 septembre 1791, PV de la commune d'Isle-sur-Serein, 27 décembre 1791, and Arrêté de l'administration du district d'Avallon, 5 janvier 1792. See also AD Yonne L713, Lettre de Perreau, Guilbert, et Letellier à Escamps à l'administration du district d'Auxerre, novembre 1791, Lettre du curé [Constitutional] LeCocq à Vézelay à "monsieur" [le maire?], 27 avril 1792; AN AFII 146B, Arrêté de représentants en mission Garnier et Turreau, 24 avril 1793; AN DIII 305, Lettre du citoyen Finot à l'Assemblée nationale, 8 novembre 1791; Bonneau, *Clergé de l'Yonne*, pp. 121–22; Noirot, *Le départe-*

In 1792, though, as the Revolution took a more radical turn, clergymen faced new difficulties. Although the majority (78 percent) of
the practicing clergy of the Yonne took the second required oath of
loyalty to "liberty and equality," by the fall of 1792 many priests,
particularly nonjurors, had already disappeared from their former
parishes. In the Auxerrois, for example, at least forty curés and vicars
from the ninety-seven original parishes of the district had fled to
Paris, returned to their native villages, left France entirely, or disappeared leaving no clue as to their destination. Laws passed in August
1792 and April 1793 required the deportation of all refractories. The
departmental administration would enforce such laws more strin-
gently during the second dechristianization campaign of 1797–1800,
but even in this first crackdown, about ninety clergymen from the
Yonne either were deported or emigrated, mainly to Switzerland or
Italy. In 1793–1794 only about ten priests were actually sent to Brest
or Rochefort to be deported to French Guiana; six of these died.[7] A
much larger number of priests faced imprisonment, especially since
the deputies Louis Turreau and Garnier decreed the imprisonment
in April 1793 of any priest, secular or religious, who was not employed as a Constitutional clergyman, civil servant, or teacher or who
was not married. For most of the year II (1793–1794) the prison at
Auxerre held sixty-three priests; they were gradually freed after the
fall of Robespierre.[8]

---

ment de l'Yonne 1:12; Rocher, "Aspects de l'histoire religieuse," pp. 9–10. For a discussion of the reception of the oath in parish communities throughout France, see Tackett,
Religion, Revolution, chaps. 7 and 8; Jones, Peasantry in the French Revolution, pp. 196–
204.

[7]AD Yonne L689, Etats des ecclésiastiques sujets à la déportation auxquels il a été
fourni des passeports pour se retirer à l'étranger, par les districts d'Auxerre, Avallon,
Mont-Armance [Saint-Florentin], et Tonnerre, septembre–décembre 1792; AN F19
481⁴⁻⁵, Etat nominatif des prêtres du département, réfractaires ou insermentés, sortis
du royaume ou déportés depuis le 7 septembre jusqu'au 15 octobre 1792; Bonneau,
Clergé de l'Yonne; Gally, "Notice sur les prêtres"; E. Audard, Actes des martyrs et des
confesseurs de la foi pendant la Révolution (Tours, 1916–20); AC Auxerre, Dépôt 3, I2,
Première liste supplétive, Emigrés sujets au sequestre, an II, (1793–94); AN F7 7237,
Enquête sur l'exercice et la police des cultes dans le département de l'Yonne par
Housset, le commissaire près les tribunaux civils et criminaux de l'Yonne, ventôse an v
(February–March 1797). As Vovelle notes, it is often difficult to determine which
priests were deported and which emigrated from France to avoid imprisonment or
deportation. Vovelle, Religion et Révolution, p. 77.

[8]AN AFii 146B, Arrêté de représentants en mission Turreau et Garnier, 9 avril
1793; AD Yonne L204, Arrêté du représentant en mission Maure, 20 floréal an II (9
May 1794); AN F7 4575, Arrêtés du Comité de sûreté générale, mises en liberté,
vendémiaire–frimaire an III (September–December 1794); AC Auxerre, Dépôt 3, I2,
Arrêté du représentant en mission Guillemardet, 6 nivôse an III (26 December 1794).

Table 5. Clerical abdications in the Yonne, 1793–1794

District	Curés	Vicars	Total abdicators	Number of communes in district[a]
Auxerre	55	9	64	86
Avallon	30	5	35	71
Joigny	51	17	68	72
Saint-Fargeau	32	0	32	36
Saint-Florentin	37	14	51	57
Sens	58	19	77	91
Tonnerre	35	8	43	74
Totals	298	72	370	487

Sources: AD Yonne L705, Etats nominatifs des ecclésiastiques qui ont abdiqué leurs fonctions, tableaux par district. The district administrations provided these lists at different dates during summer 1794 after the major waves of abdication in the spring of 1794. The report by the district of Avallon however is dated 28 germinal an II (17 April 1794); so more abdications may well have followed this date.

[a] The number of parishes exceeded the number of communes because some large communes had more than one parish, even after the parish suppressions of 1791 and 1793.

When the représentant en mission Maure joined with local Jacobins to bring the dechristianization campaign to the Yonne in the year II, many clergymen, mostly jurors, abdicated from the priesthood. Abdications occurred in at least three-quarters of the communes of the Yonne, primarily in the early spring of 1794 (see Table 5). In the district of Saint-Fargeau, for example, thirty-two (84 percent) of the thirty-eight remaining parish priests abdicated, and in the Auxerrois a slightly lower percentage (69 percent) or sixty-four of the ninety-three priests *still present* in the spring of 1794, made the same choice. (These sixty-four priests constituted only about 44 percent of the 147 Auxerrois secular clergy who served at some point between 1789 and 1794.)[9]

By the spring of 1794 one point stands out in clear relief: the ranks of the clergy had suffered massive decimation in the Yonne. A brief

[9] AD Yonne L705, Etats nominatifs des ecclésiastiques qui ont abdiqué leurs fonctions, tableaux par district (dated in various months in the spring and summer of 1794). Not all those who abdicated necessarily surrendered their "lettres de prêtrise," but they formally declared that they would not practice. Forestier, "Campagnes de l'Auxerrois"; Jean-Pierre Rocher, "Essai statistique sur les prêtres abdicataires du district de Saint-Fargeau," Actes du 39e congrès de l'Association bourguignonne des Sociétés savantes (Toucy, 1968), pp. 31–49. Cf. Vovelle, Religion et Révolution, pp. 38–42, 80. Vovelle also found that most abdicators had taken the 1791 oath and that a wave of abdications occurred in ventôse an II in many departments of southeastern France, though in Paris the wave of abdications came earlier, in late brumaire–frimaire an II (November–December 1793).

Table 6. Secular clergy of the district of Auxerre in the Year II

	Curés[a]	Vicars	Total priests	Percentage of all Auxerrois secular clergy
Abdicated	55	9	64	43.5
Imprisoned	30	2	32	22
Emigrated or deported	12	4	16	11
Disappeared	11	6	17	11.5
Died (by 1794)	7	0	7	5
Unknown	8	3	11	7
Total	123	24	147	100
Married (by 1794)	11	0	11	7

Sources: AD Yonne L685–706; AN F7, police dossiers on priests to be deported or imprisoned, F19 481⁴⁻⁵, (Yonne: Cultes), F19 1017, (Yonne: Prêtres refractaires); Abbé Bonneau, *Notes pour servir à l'histoire du clergé de l'Yonne pendant la Révolution, 1790–1800* (Sens, 1900); Jacques Leviste, "La régularisation de la situation des prêtres mariés durant la Révolution," *BSSY* 103 (1969–70): 241–263.

[a] Including the new Constitutional curés who came to replace priests who either were nonjurors or retractors or who died or disappeared in the first three years of the Revolution. Most of the replacements were former canons or monks.

glance at the plight of the clergy of the Auxerrois suggests the fate of the Yonne's parish clergy as a whole (see Table 6). There, the fate of eleven secular clergymen is unknown. All the rest either abdicated, died, disappeared, emigrated, or were imprisoned or deported.[10] Eleven curés married. (Over the course of the entire Revolution, sixty-three priests from the Yonne married; twenty-one of these were rehabilitated by Cardinal Jean-Baptiste Caprara as clergy after the Concordat, and the other forty-two chose to have their marriages validated.)[11]

By the fall of Robespierre, then, the clerical leadership of the church in the Yonne was virtually nonexistent. Although many of the abdicating or hidden priests remained in the area and would eventually return to religious practice in the later 1790s, initially their return was difficult, and many priests were understandably reluctant to face the dangers accompanying the open practice of Catholicism in the

[10]I focus on the Auxerrois because it was the largest district and has conserved good sources regarding the choices of its clergymen. AC Auxerre Dépôt 3, P5; AD Yonne series L686–706, esp. L687, Rapport sur les prestations de serment des ecclésiastiques dans le district d'Auxerre, mars 1791; AN F19 481⁴⁻⁵, F19 1017, and various police files in AN F7.

[11]Leviste, "La régularisation des prêtres mariés."

Table 7. Later oaths by secular clergy of the district of Auxerre, 1795–1798

Oath of	Curés	Vicars	Total	Number of communes
11 prairial an III (30 May 1795)	29	2	31	20
7 vendémiaire an IV (29 September 1795)	72	4	76	68
19 fructidor an v (5 September 1797)	25	3	28	24

Sources: Same as Table 6. Also AN F7 7237, Enquête sur l'exercice des cultes, ventôse an v (February–March 1797). For texts of oaths, see Appendix.

year III (1794–1795). Just when hopes for a return to Catholic practice grew during the early Thermidorean reaction, the représentant en mission Guillemardet decreed in December 1794 that all priests who were neither married nor employed in a profession "useful for the Republic" must reside in the chef-lieu of a district or in towns of over five thousand inhabitants. Although it was repealed before being thoroughly enforced, this decree left the priests of the Yonne with yet another reason for caution and bewilderment in the spring of 1795.[12] Relatively few priests declared their submission to the laws of the Republic as required by the law of 11 prairial an III (30 May 1795) to practice in public. Only thirty-one priests in the Auxerrois made the declaration, for example (see Table 7). More were willing to take the oath required by a law of 7 vendémiaire an IV, but again few swore the oath demanded on 19 fructidor an v. Often the continuity of clerical leadership within a town had been broken; one-third of the Auxerrois priests who made the declaration in the year III did so in a parish where they had not led worship in 1789. It would in fact be well into the nineteenth century before the region recovered from the loss of clergy and of new recruits.[13]

Despite the various difficulties, however, following the fall of Robespierre both the nonjurors and Constitutional priests began to work to kindle and direct the revival. During the Thermidorean and

[12]AN AFII 146B, Arrêté du représentant en mission Guillemardet, 4 nivôse an III (24 December 1794); AD Yonne L702–4, Exécution de l'arrêté de Guillemardet du 4 nivôse an III (24 December 1794).

[13]AN F7 3699², Rapport par le préfet de l'Yonne au ministre de la police, 16 juin 1808, F19 2381, Tableau d'ordination des prêtres dans le diocèse de Troyes, an x (1801–2) au 1810; Henri Forestier, "Le 'culte laïcal' et la crise des effectifs dans le clergé diocésain (1801–1821)," Echo de Saint-Pierre d'Auxerre 36 (1961): 3–6, and 37 (1962): 3–6; Rocher, "Aspects de l'histoire religieuse," pp. 38–40.

Directorial period the clergy of the Yonne fell into three groups. The returning nonjurors made up a relatively small group, most numerous in the Avallonnais and the Tonnerrois. They were joined by new retractors, who in 1795 renounced their earlier oaths and reconciled themselves with the Roman Church. This was the most significant group, and it grew rapidly in this period. Meanwhile, the third group, the hard-core Constitutional clergy who clung to the 1791 oath and supported Bishop Grégoire's Paris-based efforts to reorganize a national Constitutional Church, was dwindling.

Indeed, the most striking trend among the clergy in 1795 was their flight from the Constitutional Church and the pervasive desire to reconcile themselves with Rome. In the spring of 1795 the vicar-generals of the émigré Bishop Cicé of the former diocese of Auxerre came out of hiding to spearhead the reconciliation effort. Vicar-Generals Viart in Auxerre and Condé in Sens launched a highly successful campaign to persuade or pressure former Constitutionals to retract their 1791 oaths and undergo a public ceremony of repentance and purification.[14] In May the Committee on Legislation of the National Convention had invalidated the old 1791 oath; this decision encouraged a rash of retractions in the summer of 1795 and weakened the former legal advantage of jurors. Furthermore, Viart and Condé encouraged retractors and nonjurors to make the new promise of submission required by the 11 prairial an III (30 May 1795) law, to enable them to compete with jurors for parishioners' loyalty and help them to reclaim their churches. In 1795 Viart and his fellow priests also went out to the parishes around Auxerre to verify relics, purify churches, lead religious worship, and reawaken lay loyalty to the Roman Church. Likewise, in the Tonnerrois Abbé Maugras encouraged retractions on behalf of the nonjuror bishop of the old diocese of Langres, while Vicar-General Verdier of the former diocese of Autun administered a tightly organized missionary network of nonjurors and retractors in the Avallonais.[15]

---

[14]AN F7 7237, Enquête sur l'exercice des cultes, ventôse an v (February–March 1797); Porée, "Mémoires du chanoine Frappier," pp. 139–41. See also Noiret, Le département de l'Yonne 1:14.

[15]AD Yonne 1J231, Duplessis, "Mémoire," p. 89; AN DIII 306, Lettre au curé de Chigy au citoyen Laplaigne, représentant au comité de législation, 22 messidor an III (10 July 1795); AN F19 481⁴⁻⁵, Lettre du commissaire de l'Yonne au ministre de l'intérieur, 22 pluviôse an IV (11 February 1796); AC Auxerre, Dépôt 3, I2, Arrêté du représentant en mission Guillemardet, 6 nivôse an III (26 December 1794); Rocher,

Meanwhile, the Constitutional clergy also sought to consolidate their followers and to cooperate with Grégoire's attempt to revive and reorganize the Constitutional Church. In Paris, Grégoire and a handful of his fellow Constitutional bishops had formed a standing council and issued a profession of their faith in Catholicism and the Republic in March 1795. By December they had set forth a new system of church organization, based on presbyteries of clergymen meeting in episcopal towns to provide leadership for the resuscitated Constitutional Church and to elect new bishops if necessary. Despite stiff competition from the Roman Church and despite the loss of government backing, the Constitutional Church was able to hold a national council in 1797 with thirty bishops and many representatives of presbyteries.[16]

But out in the countryside of the Yonne, the Constitutional clergy faced myriad obstacles. By 1795 they had not only been denied their financial and legal status as civil servants and leaders of the short-lived national church, they had also lost spiritual legitimacy in the eyes of lay parishioners, who were often convinced of the greater purity and sacerdotal power of the nonjurors or the recent retractors. The *juge suppléant* at Avallon observed to Bishop Grégoire in 1795 that many Catholics viewed refractories as "good," returning deported or émigré clergymen as "excellent," and Constitutional clergy as "bad." During the Directory, especially during the anticlerical campaign of 1798 and 1799, departmental authorities treated jurors no better than nonjurors. In 1798 the Constitutional curé Claude-Isaac Lebrun, who wrote that he claimed "as his only motto 'God and the Nation,'" lamented to Bishop Grégoire, "How can I convey to you the cruel perplexity which we experience?" In their attempt to be loyal to both Catholicism and the Republic, the Constitutional priests found themselves spiritually demoted in the eyes of their own parishioners and threatened with imprisonment or deportation by government officials.[17]

"Aspects de l'histoire religieuse," pp. 20–27. The clandestine network of nonjurors in the Avallonais resembled the one in the Lyonnais. Charles Ledré, *Le culte caché sous la Révolution: Les missions de l'abbé Linsolas* (Paris, 1949), pp. 29–37, 80–110, 157–73.

[16]McManners, *French Revolution*, pp. 123–24; Boussolade, *L'église de Paris*, esp. chaps. 1–3.

[17]BSPR, Lettres de Grégoire, carton Yonne, Lettre du juge suppléant d'Avallon à Grégoire, 13 germinal an III (2 April 1795), Lettres de Lebrun, curé de Coulanges-la-Vineuse, à Grégoire, 26 pluviôse an VI/14 février 1798 and 9 floréal an VI/28 avril 1798.

LE CURÉ PATRIOTE.

Travaillez, mes enfans, obéißez aux loix,
Je veillerai pour vous et deffendrai vos droits.

The patriotic priest: "Work, my children, obey the laws. I will watch over you and defend your rights." Courtesy of the Bibliothèque nationale.

Furthermore, the death of the Constitutional bishop Loménie de Brienne in 1794 had left the juring clergy without leadership. In 1797 a handful of Jansenist former canons and curés of Auxerre and nearby communes met as a "presbytery" to elect a replacement bishop to send to the National Council of the Constitutional Church organized by Grégoire in Paris. These twelve jurors failed to recruit fellow members, although they sent out a twenty-three-page appeal for a return to the perceived purity of primitive Christianity, to be fostered by a national church dedicated to both the Republic and Catholicism. Despite their small number, the presbytery promised Grégoire their prayers for the Republic and the fledgling Constitutional Church.[18]

After the fall of Robespierre, then, the trickle of returning refractories, the growing band of retractors newly reconciled to Rome, and the leaders of the Constitutional faction all faced grave difficulties of recruitment and clerical participation, particularly at the earliest stages of the revival in the year III (1794–1795) and again following the coup d'état of 18 fructidor an V (4 September 1797). But the period from late 1795 to 1797 marked a brief hiatus in repression, a moment of hope when clergy and laity alike had relatively greater freedom of worship. During this period priests and people could reopen their local churches by making a new legal declaration of loyalty to the Republic, according to the law of 7 vendémiaire an IV (29 September 1795) (see Appendix). All priests, whether practicing or not, had to make such a declaration.[19]

Etienne Housset, the commissaire of the tribunals of the Yonne, reported in ventôse an V (February–March 1797) that at least 438 priests had made this promise of submission. Even more striking was his discovery that 332 of the 377 communes that responded to his survey, an impressive 88 percent, told of the presence of at least one priest who had made the declaration; 91 percent of the communes

---

(The Constitutional clergymen generally used both republican and traditional dates in their correspondence.)

[18]Bibliothèque municipale d'Auxerre, Collection Lorin, L138, 3d series, 50:31–54, Lettre pastorale du presbytère d'Auxerre, département de l'Yonne, aux prêtres et fidèles du diocèse, 16 décembre 1797/26 frimaire an VI; Ordioni, *Survivance des idées*, pp. 201–5; "Journal d'un Auxerrois du 19 novembre 1796 au 7 septembre 1797 (29 brumaire au 21 fructidor an V)," *Annuaire de l'Yonne* 30 (1866): 247–91, esp. 288–89; BSPR, Carton Yonne, Lettre de J. B. Villetard à Grégoire, 17 thermidor an V/4 août 1797, et Lettres du presbytére d'Auxerre au concile national, 3 vendémiaire an VI/24 septembre 1797, 21 bumaire an VI/11 novembre 1797.

[19]Bonneau, *Clergé de l'Yonne*, p. 2.

reported that Catholics had reopened the local church.[20] Since all clergy, regardless of religious activity, had to make the legal declaration, Housset's findings cannot tell us which priests were practicing or reveal any information on hiding refractory clergy. But it is clear that in the years 1796–1797 many priests were available and able to lead worship in the Yonne. They lacked rectories and faced legal limitations on public forms of practice, but they found huge numbers of Catholic villagers who urged them to return to religious duties. More priests emerged from hiding or returned to the Yonne in the late spring and summer of 1797 after the national electoral victory of right-wing and moderate deputies kindled hopes for a gradual return to more freedom of public practice and a loosening of the laws against refractories. From the fall of 1795 through the summer of 1797, then, Catholic villagers of the Yonne found it possible, albeit within limits, to return to the public practice of Catholicism; frequently, they were able to find a priest able to lead them in worship, although he often was not their parish priest from prerevolutionary days.

The left-wing coup d'état of 18 fructidor an v (4 September 1797) dealt a severe blow to the practice of Catholicism throughout France. Eager to purge the department of "counterrevolution and fanaticism," the new departmental administration of the Yonne was especially zealous in enforcing the law of 19 fructidor an v (5 September 1797), which promoted the republican calendar and festivals and subjected priests to a new oath of "hatred of royalty and of anarchy." Many priests in the Yonne, even among the non-retracting Constitutional clergy, refused to take the oath; others stopped practicing when the authorities closed their parish church or demanded that they shift their rituals to the *décadi*. In the Auxerrois only a third of those parish priests who agreed to the "submission" of the year IV were willing to submit to the more stringent oath of the year v (see Table 7). Government reports on the Yonne's sixty-nine cantons claimed that there were *no* priests practicing at all in five cantons, and that the number of priests had seriously diminished in twelve other cantons. This second dechristianization campaign struck the clergy of the Yonne harder than the first: many priests were deported or imprisoned. Eighty-four from the Yonne were condemned to deportation during the years VI

[20]AN F7 7237, Enquête sur l'exercice des cultes, ventôse an v (February–March 1797). More communes provided information about priests than about churches. Of the 351 communes for which Housset had information about church use, Catholics in 320 had legally declared their intent to use the church.

and VII (1797–1799), and half of these were in fact deported, primarily to the Ile-de-Ré off the coast of Rochefort, but eight were sent to French Guiana. (Four of these never returned.)[21]

The persecution of clergy, the enforcement of the republican calendar, and above all the closing of churches left the Catholic laity frustrated and angry. Stanislaus Copin, a wandering shoemaker from Nancy, wrote to the Council of Five Hundred in pluviôse an VII (February 1799) to warn them of popular discontent in the Yonne. "People don't dare to speak. . . . The administrators send spies to see if people work on Sundays; they force the people to attend their [republican] festivals. . . . Especially the administrators of Neuvy-Sautour near Saint-Florentin are all like devils."[22]

On the eve of Napoleon's coup d'état the clergy of the Yonne, even those who were the most well-meaning in their desire to support the Republic, found themselves in a difficult situation. Yves-Joseph Malary, the curé of Argenteuil, expressed the dilemma well when he wrote to the minister of the police in the spring of 1799. Malary commented that his parishioners were urging him to begin to lead worship once again, but he dared not do it without consulting the authorities. He begged the minister to tell him "with the frankness of a true republican whether one can practice the Catholic religion with impunity. . . . I predict that you will refer me to article 354 of the Constitution [which guaranteed the freedom of religious practice]. But despite the clarity of this article, those who execute the laws here want to set up hindrances, either by saying we won't be paid our pensions, or by assuring us that religious worship displeases the government. In a word . . . they do everything possible to destroy it [the Catholic religion]; this is no exaggeration." Not surprisingly, the minister of the police seems to have sent no reply.[23]

During the course of the Revolution, then, the clergy of the Yonne

[21]AN AFIII 280, Situation du département de l'Yonne, ventôse an VII (February–March 1799), par Housset, le commissaire près les tribunaux civils et criminaux de l'Yonne; Pierre, *Déportation ecclésiastique;* Henri Auclerc, *La déportation ecclésiastique dans le département de l'Yonne sous le Directoire (1797–1800)* (Auxerre, 1958), pp. 13–24; AD Yonne L74–76, Délibérations et arrêtés de l'administration centrale du département, Section du bien public, 21 fructidor an V–11 nivôse an VIII (7 September 1797–1 January 1800).

[22]AN C358, dossier 370, Lettre de Stanislaus Copin au Conseil de Cinq-Cents, 6 février 1799.

[23]AN F7 7585, Lettre de Malary, ministre du culte à Argenteuil, au ministre de la police, 4 germinal an VII (23 March 1799).

not only faced a series of moral dilemmas and confusing or ambiguous situations, they also found themselves subject to forces and laws beyond their control. Despite the best efforts of the leading enclave of jurors in Auxerre and the more successful nonjuror vicar-generals, the clergy had lost spiritual and institutional authority and structure. Paradoxically, the breakdown of the clerical hierarchy gave the laity greater freedom and initiative in defining and creating the sacred. The revolutionary situation forced Catholic villagers not only to fight politically for the legal right to worship in public but also to choose which elements of religious belief and practice were most crucial. Believers faced a period of spiritual questioning as they reconstructed rituals under adverse conditions.

Most strikingly, as villagers struggled to fill the revolutionary void in worship, they seemed willing to accept an ambiguous amalgam of the most traditional and the innovative in their newly defined religiosity. Villagers frequently revived prerevolutionary forms of devotion, such as saints' cults, which the Catholic Reformation had attempted to suppress. Lay Catholics also expanded their role as leaders and creators of forms of religious devotion by assuming the ritual functions of priests and leading their fellow parishioners in worship. Though they were deeply committed to age-old traditions, Catholic villagers used the fluid context of Revolution to transform old forms of worship. They created new rituals to incorporate and express changing attitudes toward the Revolution and toward the sacred. The choices they made in the 1790s affected the long-term practice of Christianity in the region.

Lay Cults

In 1797 Commissaire Housset wrote: "The commune of Châtel-Censoir has no priest; the people who live there still cling to their religion; from among their midst they have chosen three superstitious men who hardly know how to read and write [and] commissioned them on Sundays and holy days to carry out the sham imitation of the religious worship that they miss." In this same era, Rathier, the radical dechristianizing national agent of Auxerre, and Viart, the refractory vicar-general representing the émigré bishop, both complained of the "aping of priests' functions" by lay villagers in the countryside. The revolutionary officials and the bishop's envoy held diametrically opposed religious and political views and objected to the "abuse" for very different reasons, but they all pinpointed a pervasive and unorthodox religious practice in the Yonne.[24] Without clerical leadership lay Catholics in the late 1790s maintained the external necessities of their cult, above all the public rituals—the mass, vespers, festivals, and processions—they had attended in the Old Regime. These groups of lay worshipers went beyond simply gathering to sing hymns, recite the rosary, read religious texts, or pray litanies in common. Under the leadership of "lay ministers" the congregation reenacted the official rites of the church, with as much publicity and official ceremony as possible.

Frequently, the lay minister performed a "white mass." In other words, he performed the entire ceremony of the mass, making all the gestures and singing all the prayers normally sung only by a priest. Many accounts of lay worship routinely called the services masses, and the *comité révolutionnaire* of Auxerre reported that lay ministers "distributed blessed bread," although they rarely went so far as to consecrate the bread and wine.[25] The lay minister of Champs in 1795 performed the consecration and distributed communion, but in most cases the celebrant would either omit the consecration, substitute another ritual gesture, or leave time for private veneration of the host. The lay minister of Vaux elevated a cross rather than the host and chalice. This same minister, clothed in a surplice, did not hesitate to marry Catholic couples and to bury the dead according to the rites of the church.[26]

---

[24]AN F7 7237, Enquête sur l'exercice des cultes, ventôse an v (February–March 1797); AD Yonne V9, Lettre de Viart au préfet, 23 pluviôse an xi (12 February 1803), L782, Lettre de l'agent national d'Auxerre à la municipalité de Vincelottes, 26 nivôse an iii (15 January 1795).

[25]AD Yonne L1118, PV du comité révolutionnaire d'Auxerre au Comité de salut public, 1 nivôse an iii (21 December 1794). "Blessed bread" (*pain bénit*) often referred to bread donated by parishioners, which had been blessed but not consecrated. Although such bread had no sacramental qualities, many believed blessed bread had the power to provide general well-being or good fortune; some thought it could heal sick livestock or induce hens to lay more eggs, for example. Luria, *Territories of Grace*, chap. 3.

[26]AD Yonne L1118, PV du comité révolutionnaire d'Auxerre au comité de salut public, testimony of Guibert, marchand de vin, 4 nivôse an iii (24 December 1794), 1J231, Duplessis, "Mémoire," p. 89. Lay ministers in other areas of France were also hesitant to offer communion. See Hufton, "Reconstruction of a Church," p. 49; and Frank Tallett, "Religion and Revolution: The Rural Clergy and Parishioners of Doubs, 1780–1797" (Ph.D. diss., University of Reading, 1981), pp. 388–92. In contrast, the schoolteacher in Jouanne in Seine-et-Marne consecrated the bread and wine. Fernand

In addition to saying mass and administering the sacraments, lay ministers took over other Old Regime functions of priests. They read laws, announced the upcoming saints' festivals, took up collections for the *fabrique* or for their own services, and performed various rituals other than the mass. Lay ministers regularly led ceremonies of benediction, veneration of the Eucharist, matins and vespers, or even outdoor processions. For example, the commissaire of Villeneuve-la-Guyard complained in 1795 that the rural schoolteachers in his canton "leave their schools at any hour to sing at funerals and other ceremonies." One notable, Jacob Moreau-Dufourneau, reported that the lay ministers of Saint-Florentin said mass, led vespers, including "the *capitale* and the *confession* (Compline)," managed parish finances, and provided for "wax, candles, brooms, etc., as well as the wages of the employees of the church: cantors, sacristan, beadle, church guardian, bell ringer, children of the choir, who carried out their services as usual."[27]

Lay cults were widespread and persistent in the Yonne. Though most prevalent in the Auxerrois and Senonais, lay-led worship took place throughout the department. The national and departmental archives contain at least a hundred reports of lay-led masses in violation of the law during the period just between Thermidor and the Concordat in the Yonne. Many more instances no doubt went unreported and the existing sources referred more often than not to a habitual practice rather than an isolated incident. While it is impossible to know exactly how well attended and frequent lay-led ceremonies were, the commissaires' reports, court records, memoirs, and local *procès verbaux* reveal that in many villages lay cults became a

---

Bridoux, *Histoire religieuse du département de Seine-et-Marne pendant la Révolution*, 2 vols. (Melun, 1953), 2:220.

[27] AN F7 7348, Certificat de l'agent de Vincelles, 7 frimaire an VI (27 November 1797), F7 7483, PV écrit par l'agent de la commune d'Ouanne, 25 messidor an VI (13 July 1798). The schoolteacher of Ouanne was accused not only of singing mass and breaking into the local church but also of going from hamlet to hamlet with a cart to collect *gerbes* for his services. AD Yonne L1080, PV du canton de Toucy, 10 messidor an IV (28 June 1796). The commissaire of Toucy complained that lay ministers in Eglény and Beauvoir led outdoor processions and violated other laws of police des cultes. Outdoor processions led by lay ministers became more common in the nineteenth century when outdoor practice was legal, although the bishop and vicar-generals did not approve of lay-led processions. AN F19 4814⁻⁵, Lettre du commissaire de Villeneuve-la-Guyard, 15 nivôse an III (4 January 1795); "Mémoires de Jacob Moreau-Dufourneau," cited originally by Camille Hermelin, as quoted in Henri Forestier, "Nicolas Chamon, fileur de laine et ministre de culte à Butteaux (an VII)," *Echo d'Auxerre* 40 (1962): 13.

regular form of practice, followed by the majority of Catholics in the area. Resistance or disapproval came from government officials and followers of revolutionary cults but not from fellow Catholics. Rival services were rare or nonexistent. Furthermore, many parishes continued the practice into the early 1800s.[28]

The first public lay worship generally occurred when villagers initially reclaimed their parish churches. Religious activists consistently struggled more avidly to regain their local churches than to recover any other single aspect of their religion. The largest percentage of petitions (27 percent) and of riots (40 percent) had access to the church as their goal.[29] The dechristianizer viewed the church building as the locus of "fanaticism and superstition" and the physical embodiment of the wealth and power of the clergy and the Catholic Church, but to the believer, the church building represented, contained, and even perpetuated many of the key goals of the religious activists. Quite clearly, earthly as well as spiritual motives stirred parishioners to cling to their parish church, for while it was holy, the church building was also a valuable material possession and the prime emblem of communal pride. When the Catholics of Butteaux reclaimed their church, they pointed out matter-of-factly that "their fathers had built it" and that it therefore belonged to them.[30]

Yet the church building also embodied two central religious tenets of the religious activists. First, they believed that collective religious ritual was the most certain way to fulfill one's duty to God and earn

[28]The sources for this discussion of lay cults include AD Yonne, particularly the police des cultes and court records as well as departmental and local administrative records and memoirs; AN, esp. F7 (police) series and the F19 (cults) series; and incidents described by Henri Forestier in his articles on lay cults in the Yonne: "Le culte laïcal," *AB* 24 (1952): 105–10; "Le culte laïcal. Messes blanches à Auxerre," *AB* 24 (1952): 175–77; "Le culte laïcal à Chablis," *BSSY* 97 (1957–58): 338; "Le culte laïcal dans l'Yonne (1795–1828)," in *L'abbé Lebeuf et le jansénisme: 23e congrès de l'Association bourguignonne des Sociétés savantes, Auxerre, 20–22 mai 1960* (Auxerre, 1962), pp. 237–44; "Le 'culte laïcal' et la crise des effectifs"; and "Nicolas Chamon."

[29]Housset remarks on the high percentage of communes that had made legal declarations of church use by 1797 (91 percent of those communes that reported had made declarations to use their churches). AN F7 7237, Enquête sur l'exercice des cultes, ventôse an v (February–March 1797). Information regarding the various religious riots and petitions from the Yonne comes from diverse sources, including AD Yonne, the police des cultes and court records, departmental, district, and municipal deliberations; AN, esp. F7 (police) and F19 (cults) series, BN, newspapers; and various archives communales within the Yonne.

[30]AD Yonne L706, Déclaration de l'assemblée communale de Butteaux, 24 brumaire an IV (15 November 1795).

his good will, as well as to encourage morality and devotion among the people. Second, they believed that sacred power, which could be tapped for its moral and emotional, as well as pragmatic uses, rested in local places, statues, and objects. Public ritual, localized sacred power, the interwoven texture of the sacred and profane, individual or communal prestige and identity, patterns of sociability and festivity, divine aid, strengthening of faith, moral order, salvation—all these were bound up with the idea of the church building.

When the inhabitants of Villeneuve-sur-Yonne petitioned on behalf of their church building, for example, they noted God's "presence on the altar" and proclaimed that their church was the sacred location of rituals where "the ignorant learns, the weak grows stronger, the just feels his most cherished joys multiply. . . . There, finally, grace triumphs and forms the bonds of charity." Likewise, the petitioners of Val-de-Merci, fearing the closing of their church in 1793, lamented dramatically that they would be "deprived of the aid of religion. . . . Already fear and sadness invade every heart, work languishes undone, everyone becomes discouraged." Petitioners and witnesses reapeatedly defended their lay cults and illegal seizure of churches by declaring that "the law of God commanded it," that they wanted only "to follow the ancient customs," "to address their wishes to God," and "to sing the praises of God and thank him for his daily gifts to us." In some cases these popular defenses of religious activism were tinged by fear that the loss of church and ritual had incurred God's wrath and weakened the instrumental power of the sacred to protect people and animals. In the spring of 1794 when nut-sized hailstones pelted the fields, for example, some Catholics were convinced that the storm was evidence of God's anger over dechristianization.[31] In the view of many believers, the return to the church

---

[31]Bibliothèque municipale d'Auxerre, "Invitation de quelques habitants de la commune de Villeneuve-sur-Yonne à leurs concitoyens, sur les réparations à faire à leur église" (printed), an IX (1800–1); AD Yonne L717, Pétition des citoyens de Val-de-Merci à l'administration départementale de l'Yonne, 13 frimaire an II (3 December 1793), L1118, PV de l'interrogation de quelques citoyens de Vaux, comité révolutionnaire d'Auxerre, 18 nivôse an III (7 January 1795); Pétition des citoyens de Volgré au conseil municipal de Volgré, 10 brumaire an III (31 October 1794), as quoted by A. M. Moreau, "Volgré pendant la Révolution et l'Empire," *Annuaire de l'Yonne* 62 (1898): 34; Déclarations des citoyens de Fleury, 26 prairial an III (14 June 1795), as quoted in A. M. Moreau, "Fleury sous la féodalité et pendant la Révolution," *Annuaire de l'Yonne* 56 (1890): 93; AD Yonne L206, Pétition des citoyens de Valichères à l'administration cantonale de Tonnerre, 29 frimaire an VII (19 December 1798); AN F7 7191, Lettre du

and to the public practice of Catholicism was urgent for myriad reasons by the fall of 1794.

At the early stages of the revival in 1794 and 1795, Catholic festival days, particularly Christmas, Easter, and the feast days of local patron saints, became rallying points, moments of extraheated fervor which spurred religious activists to demand church keys or to storm the doors of the village church. But merely to occupy the church building physically was not enough: villagers immediately took real repossession of the church through public rituals, very often led by lay ministers. Some Catholics thought that their church buildings had been desacralized or profaned when they were used for secular functions, such as storehouses for weapons or grain, stables for the *armées révolutionnaires*, or temples for revolutionary festivals. As the Theophilanthropists who shared the cathedral of Sens commented in 1800, "[The Catholics] seem to believe the choir [of the church] is profaned, poisoned by us."[32] Particularly in 1795 and again in 1800, Catholics frequently felt the need to scrub clean and rebless altars, statues, cemeteries, bells, baptismal fonts, as well as the building itself.[33] By purifying the church building, Catholics reactivated the localized sacred, focused their spiritual commitment, and made a public promise that they intended to uphold the newly reestablished sanctity of their religion and their way of life, unsullied and unchallenged. The clear-cut rite of purification seemed to resolve the ambiguity of the position of Catholicism vis-à-vis the revolutionary cults or, in some cases, of the

citoyen Trocher au ministre de la police, n.d., an v (1797–98); AD Yonne 1J231, Duplessis, "Mémoire," p. 72, L782, Rapport de Rathier, agent national du district d'Auxerre, 9 floréal an II (28 April 1794), 7 brumaire an III (28 October 1794); F. J. Fortin, *Souvenirs*, 2 vols. (Auxerre, 1865–67), 2:20–22.

[32] AD Yonne V151, Pétition des théophilanthropes de Sens au ministre de la police et au préfet, 29 thermidor an VIII (17 August 1800); BN, *Observateur de l'Yonne*, 5 nivôse an VI (25 December 1797), 25 pluviôse an v (13 February 1797). The town of Auxerre provides an illustrative range of church uses during the Revolution. Saint-Pierre became a saltpeter factory. Notre-Dame-de-la-D'hors served as an arsenal and a grain storehouse and was later torn down. The Popular Society met in the Ursulines' chapel, which was also used as a garrison. The former cathedral Saint-Etienne became the Temple of Reason. The chapel of the Visitandines became a military hospital. Gendarmes lodged in the Benedictines' former church, and the Cordeliers' chapel became a market. Some of the parish churches were sold and then torn down. AD Yonne 1J231, Duplessis, "Mémoire," p. 30.

[33] BN, *Observateur de l'Yonne* 5 nivôse an VI (25 December 1797), 15 germinal an VI (4 April 1798); AN F19 481⁴⁻⁵, Lettre anonyme [of a citizen of Avallon] au citoyen ministre de la police, 25 ventôse an IV (15 March 1796).

Roman Church vis-à-vis the "profaned" Constitutional one. Finally, for the believer, the purification ritual absolved remorse over letting religious practice be suppressed, and it renewed the personal contract with God for the future.[34]

Ideally, this purification ceremony would be performed by a priest and follow a series of prescribed stages as authorized by the bishop.[35] But in most cases no priest was available to perform an official purification or even to say mass. The laity, therefore, spontaneously turned to the words, music, objects, and gestures of their tradition. A peasant who led his fellow villagers in breaking into the local church on Christmas, reblessed the building with holy water, and then led everyone present in singing the words of the mass found himself endowed with a new spiritual authority and responsibility as well. The commissaire of Mailly-le-Chateau commented that the "idea of the birth of the Messiah gave [the villagers] the audacity" to break into the parish church and attend mass performed by lay ministers. The first ritual paved the way for more regular religious practice. Geneviève Courlet, daughter of a roofer in Courson, confessed to attending lay masses every Sunday and feast day since the villagers had broken into the church on Christmas Eve 1794.[36]

Lay cults were not official and were not authorized by either church

[34]Mary Douglas, *Purity and Danger: An Anthropology of Concepts of Pollution and Taboo* (London, 1966), pp. 2–3, 51–54; Roy Rappaport, *Ecology, Meaning, and Ritual* (Richmond, Calif., 1979), p. 186.

[35]Porée, "Mémoires du chanoine Frappier," p. 139. Frappier gives an account of the refusal by Viart, the vicar-general of the émigré bishop, to let unabsolved Constitutional clergymen participate in the public blessing of holy water and baptismal ceremonies in the cathedral of Saint-Etienne in Auxerre in 1795. The letter writer from Avallon also mentions similar behavior by nonjuring clergy in general in other areas of the Yonne. Bishops in other regions proposed purification rites also. M. Pecheur, "Etude bibliographique sur l'abbé Houillier," *Bulletin de la Société archéologique, historique, et scientifique de Soissons* 11 (1880): 114. The vicar-general of Gravier delegated the canon of the cathedral of Soissons to bless the cathedral and to reconcile about eighty priests who had retracted the oaths they had taken. Registres paroissaux de Soisy-sous-Etoiles, as quoted in E. Colas, "Histoire d'un village: Soisy-sous-Etoiles," *Bulletin de la société historique et archéologique de Corbeil, d'Estampes, et du Hurepoix* 6 (1900): 102. Abbé Dorget at Soisy recorded that he "reconciled and blessed with the ceremonies prescribed by the ritual of Paris, the church of Soisy, the altar, tabernacle, ciborium, linen, ornaments, and solemnly celebrated High Mass." See also Ledré, *Le culte caché*, pp. 220–30; Archives de l'évêché de Tournai, "Règles provisoires," as cited in Jules Plumet, *L'évêché de Tournai pendant la Révolution française* (Louvain, 1963), pp. 90–91.

[36]AD Yonne L714, Lettre du commissaire de Mailly-le-Chateau au commissaire du département de l'Yonne, 7 nivôse an VII (27 December 1798), L1118, PV du comité révolutionnaire d'Auxerre, 28 nivôse au 3 pluviôse an III (17–22 January 1795).

or state. Lay ministers were not priests in any officially recognized sense; they had not received Holy Orders from the bishop, nor had they been given any training in theology. To create their own spiritual authority and to ensure the symbolic validity of these unorthodox celebrations, lay ministers followed the established prayers, gestures, and rituals of the clergy as closely as possible. Traditional sacred symbols and the rituals themselves became the means of forging the validity of lay assemblies and the sacredness of the participants' beliefs.

In Saint-Cyr-les-Colons when two weavers and a cultivator led their fellow believers they leafed through church books to find the appropriate prayers, then rang the church bell to announce the offices, sang the *"Asperges me, Domine* and the *Ostende nobis"* as a prelude to their mass, which "began with the *introytte* sung by Edme Delinotte, former marshal, [and] Jean Petit, son of Jacques, . . . and ended with *Paterre et Fillius* [sic], pronounced as a blessing by Edme Barbette, who performed all the habitual gestures of a priest." A roof thatcher and his fellow celebrants in Préhy "sang mass, vespers, evening prayer, and the rosary, finally everything, and even more than the former pastors sang." The lay minister of Ouanne broke into the parish church to steal the antiphonary, the liturgical hymnbook, just before the church inventory.[37] The singing of the psalms, the words of the mass, the intonation of the Te Deum, the benediction, the liturgy of vespers and matins sung in Latin or French—these formed the verbal core of the liturgies performed by the lay ministers. Lay ministers tenaciously guarded sacred books and strove to reproduce the exact rites of the official church because they needed the power inherent in the sacred *word.* The words and gestures were a code or a formula set down by the law of tradition and sanctified by years of use and popular belief, by the authority of the church, and by the Scriptures. To control the sacred word was powerful and essential.

Likewise, lay ministers drew upon the sacredness of bells, holy objects, and saints' statues. Christophe Berthier of Précy-le-Sec had his pupils dig up the statues he had buried during the Terror; "thereafter," commented the local agent, "he performed the functions of a

---

[37]AD Yonne L782, PVs de la municipalité de Saint-Cyr-les-Colons, 18 frimaire an III (8 December 1794), 2 nivôse an III (22 December 1794), as quoted in Forestier, "Le culte laïcal," p. 108; AD Yonne L715, PV de la municipalité de Préhy, 11 ventôse an III (1 March 1795); AN F7 7483, PV de la municipalité d'Ouanne, 25 thermidor an VI (12 August 1798).

minister of the Catholic cult." His fellow villagers believed that the schoolteacher who had protected the saints from the perils of the Terror in turn would receive added sacred power and protection from the saints themselves. For he had maintained and cultivated the villagers' sacred friendship with these powerful patrons. During the Terror in Auxerre a vigneron who led fellow Catholics of the faubourg Saint-Martin-et-Saint-Julien in clandestine prayer carefully set up an altar with a crucifix and candles in his home; he wore a "sort of chasuble sewn by his wife." J.-A. Lemain, another vigneron, who officiated in his home despite the availability of clergy in Auxerre a few years later, had transformed his table into an altar adorned with "a cloth, several pots of flowers, a crucifix above and several paintings and images on the table, a vase containing water and a palm branch, two lighted candlesticks on a stand, and an open missal."[38] The vigneron apparently realized that he had to make his ritual seem even more sacred or authentic than that of an ordained priest to create an aura of holiness.

Ideally, the lay ministers would perform their ceremonies in the parish church not only because of the holiness of the building itself but also because of the sacred power of public, communal ritual. If the church doors were securely locked, they would lead worship on the front steps of the building or in the cemetery. The parishioners of Seignelay carried out the "sham of Catholic ceremonies on Sundays and holy days in the parish cemetery" after government authorities closed their church and deported their priest. Whenever they could, lay worshipers used church bells to give added publicity and ritual appeal to their ceremonies. In Molesme in the spring of 1799 Nicolas Bouillé regularly rang the church bell to announce Pierre Guillot's lay services. In the neighboring town of Taingy the shepherd Jean Ducrot announced with a church bell his Te Deum of thanksgiving for the restoration of Catholicism in the fall of 1794 and also his Easter mass four years later.[39]

[38]AD Yonne L715, PV du commissaire de Joux-la-Ville et l'agent national de Précy-le-Sec, 24 frimaire an VIII (15 December 1799); Abbé Boussard, *Le docteur Paradis et sa famille* (Auxerre, 1903), p. 346. Boussard writes that this vigneron was not the only one to perform sacerdotal functions in Auxerre in the absence of the clergy. PV du juge de paix du canton d'Auxerre, 6 messidor an VII (24 June 1799), as quoted in Forestier, "Le culte laïcal à Auxerre," p. 176.

[39]AD Yonne L714, Lettre de l'agent national d'Irancy à l'administration départementale de l'Yonne, 11 brumaire an VII (1 November 1798). The parishioners of Irancy sang offices on the front steps of the church when the government officials closed the

Some lay ministers wore vestments to add to their aura of religious authority. As he impatiently awaited the hour for the Catholic ceremony in the local temple, Charles Rousseau, the schoolteacher and lay minister of Thury, wearing a clerical cassock, surplice, and biretta, paraded up and down, gesticulating to distract attention from the *décadi* ceremonies of law reading and civil marriages. Early in the year VII (1798–1799) the republican newspaper at Sens, the *Observateur*, implied that the lay ministers made a burlesque of their own religion. These "disguised" or "dressed up" priests were travesties, hardly legitimate leaders of an established religion.[40] The Catholics who attended the lay masses apparently did not share this interpretation. For many lay ministers who had worn the surplice of a cantor in the Old Regime, to don the cassock of a priest was not merely in keeping with the solemnity and responsibility of their increased role, it was absolutely necessary. The vestments, like the words of sacred offices, the pealing of the church bell, and the presence of the patron saint, endowed the ministers with added authority and transformed the ceremonies from unofficial, makeshift gatherings into powerful, sacred actions. Only then could the lay-led rituals become dramatizations that focused and defined the participants' emotions and assumptions.

In addition, lay ministers and worshipers were keenly aware that the political context and ideology of the Revolution lent further legitimacy to their innovations. The Revolution had validated popular activism and had inculcated the notion that the people had the right to freedom of expression. Lay ministers peppered their religious ceremonies with political declarations of religious liberty and popular sovereignty. A landowner from Dinon gave a sermon announcing that religious practice was and should be free. Nicolas Allard of Courson read "a decree authorizing the freedom of religious worship." The cantors of Pont-sur-Yonne reminded the people that their will was sovereign and argued that the officials' attempts to force Catholics to worship on *décadis* instead of Sundays were based on illegal decrees, not real laws. The lay minister of Précy claimed he did

---

building. AN F1cIII Yonne 9 and AD Yonne L75, Arrêté du département de l'Yonne, 8 frimaire an VII (28 November 1798); AD Yonne L717, PV du district de Saint-Fargeau, 24 brumaire an III (14 November 1794), PV du canton de Druyes, 25 germinal an VII (14 April 1799).

[40]AN F7 7508, PV du canton de Thury, 10 brumaire an VII (31 October 1798); BN, *Observateur de l'Yonne* 25 nivôse an VII (14 January 1799).

not need to make a church declaration because "liberty of practice" had been promised by the government to all.[41] The sacred power of ritual fused with revolutionary ideology to give added force and aura to the lay ministers' claims.

Perhaps the most noteworthy evidence of parishioners' belief in the legitimacy of lay cults was their continuation into the nineteenth century. After the Concordat most villages welcomed back curés and the official reestablishment of orthodox Catholicism. Yet lay cults persisted in some parishes in the Yonne through the 1820s, despite the repeated attempts of prefects and bishops to suppress them. The prefect of the Yonne and the bishop of Troyes issued edicts against lay-led worship in 1803 to no avail. In 1814 the subprefect of the Sens area noted that in many communes, "despite the prohibitions made so many times, laymen, and especially schoolteachers, do not hesitate to usurp the functions of the priesthood. . . . This scandal must end." As late as 1828, the bishop of Sens reminded an offending parish of his 1824 ordonnance against lay cults.[42]

Although lay cults endured largely because of the dearth of priests after the Concordat, some parishioners clung to these rituals because they viewed them as a valid or at least adequate form of regular worship and preferred their lay minister to the official priest. For example, in 1803 the villagers of Servins insisted on attending the offices of their schoolteacher and second cantor despite the legitimate service at Pailly, their official post-Concordat parish. The lay ministers of Jussy and Charentenay in 1810 "sang the mass with such exactness that the villagers would be angry to go to a commune where a priest said the mass." These ministers even consecrated the bread

[41]AD Yonne L717, PV du canton de Druyes, 25 germinal an VII (14 April 1799), L207, PV de la municipalité de Courson, 22 nivôse an III (11 January 1795); AN F1cIII Yonne 7, Lettre du commissaire de Pont-sur-Yonne au ministre de la police, 26 prairial an VI (14 June 1798); AD Yonne L715, PV du commissaire de Joux-la-Ville et l'agent et l'adjoint de Précy-le-Sec, 24 frimaire an VIII (15 December 1799).

[42]The department of the Yonne became part of the diocese of Troyes from the Concordat until 1814, when Sens became the seat of the diocese of the department of the Yonne. AC Auxerre Dépôt 3 P5, Décret de l'évêque de Troyes, 15 germinal an XI/5 avril 1803; AD Yonne V9, Ordonnance de l'évêque du diocèse de Troyes, 1 août 1803, Lettre de l'évêque de Troyes au préfet de l'Yonne, 26 mai 1803, Circulaire du préfet de l'Yonne Rougier-Labergerie aux maires du département, 12 prairial an XI (1 June 1803), as quoted in Henri Drouot, "Le culte laïcal: Sa persistance après la Révolution," AB 22 (1950): 204; Rapport du sous-préfet de Sens, 23 novembre 1814, as quoted in Forestier, "Le 'culte laïcal' et la crise des effectifs," 36:4–5; Forestier, "Le culte laïcal dans l'Yonne," p. 237.

and led processions in full panoply to neighboring towns.[43] Through their very persistence as well as their expansion of ritual, lay cults proclaimed and created their own legitimacy in the eyes of parishioners.

Who were these lay ministers? The professions of lay ministers ranged widely, from cultivator to weaver to national agent, but schoolteachers were the most frequent leaders of lay worship ceremonies and were the most likely to continue leading parish worship over a sustained period of time. The sources that list professions of lay ministers mention schoolteachers one-quarter of the time.[44] Old Regime schoolteachers had often acted as sacerdotal aids to the priest. Not only did they teach catechism; they also had specific duties to help local parish priests. For example, according to his Old Regime contract in Bussy-le-Châtel (Marne) the schoolteacher was to "help the curé to carry the sacrament to the sick, ring the Angelus in the morning, at noon, and in the evening, and carry the holy water every Sunday." Later his contracts expanded his responsibilities to include sacerdotal duties formerly reserved for the priest. In 1794 the town added provisions that he sing offices every Sunday and holy day, and it set exact fees for burials, marriages, baptisms, and low and high masses performed by the teacher. In 1795 the town added a clause providing that if a priest returned to the parish, the schoolteacher would revert to his duties as the priest's assistant.[45]

Although schoolteachers stepped in most easily to replace the priest, lay ministers came from a wide variety of professions, span-

[43]AN F19 2381, Tableau de l'ordination des prêtres dans le diocèse de Troyes (Yonne and Aube), an x (1801–2) à 1810; AD Yonne V13, Rapport de sous-préfet de Sens au préfet de l'Yonne, 30 octobre 1807; Lettre du maire de Saint-Martin-sur-Oreuse au préfet de l'Yonne, 28 mars 1816; Authorisation de préfet de l'Yonne au maire de Saint-Moré, 9 october 1818; Forestier, "Le culte laïcal dans l'Yonne," esp. p. 241. In this same article Forestier mentions various examples of lay cults in the Yonne through the 1820s. AD Yonne V11, Lettre du curé Lebrun au préfet de l'Yonne, 31 août 1810.

[44]This discussion is based on seventy specific references to lay cults that give information on the occupation or identity of lay ministers in the 1790s. See note 28 for sources on lay cults.

[45]Reception de maître d'école, Jean-Claude Gauthier à Bussy-le-Châtel, 1747," as reprinted in Abbé Puiseux, "La condition des maîtres d'écoles aux XVIIe et XVIIIe siècles," Mémoires de la Société d'agriculture, commerce, sciences, et arts du département de la Marne (1881–82): 156, 158–60. Apparently the townspeople worried that the lay minister's usurpation of the priest's functions might present problems later on.

ning the whole gamut of village trades and agriculture. Artisans, vignerons, even a few cabaret owners—lay ministers represented the middling social groups of the average village in the Yonne in the eighteenth century. The very poorest members of society did not lead lay masses. Likewise, although government officials occasionally led their fellow villagers in prayer, very few lay ministers had professional or high status: two notables, a doctor, and one former seigneur were the exceptions. Usually lay ministers were literate, active community members. Often they had reputations for piety or had been engaged in parish organizations and ceremonies before the Revolution. Former cantors, *marguilliers,* or confraternity members had familiarity with traditional rituals and could more easily establish spiritual authority. The commissaire of Coulanges-la-Vineuse complained to the minister of the interior in the year VII (1799) that townspeople chose former "beadles, bell ringers, and priest's valets" to perform the functions of priests on the feast days of the Old Regime. Confraternity members, such as the river boatmen of Auxerre in the confraternity of Saint Nicolas, celebrated their saints' festivals and distributed blessed bread.[46]

Women were in the forefront of the revival: they often led religious riots, dominated the attendance at lay assemblies, and did not hesitate to perform in public the private rituals of the Old Regime, such as saying the rosary or singing hymns. Women sometimes mounted to the altar to lead each other in worship, but they apparently never sang white masses on a regular basis. More often than not, women drafted a male lay minister to celebrate the established rituals of the church, particularly the mass. Barbe Dorotte, wife of a roofer in Vaux, led her fellow townswomen to pressure the mayor into surrendering the church keys in January 1795. Her son sang mass for the group of women present. Later two older vignerons joined him as lay ministers.[47] The forms of religious activism carried out by men and women were partly set by their Old Regime religious and social roles. Men could more easily create the kind of claim to spiritual authority neces-

---

[46]AN F1cIII Yonne 10, Lettre du commissaire de Coulanges-la-Vineuse au ministre de l'intérieur, 30 brumaire an VII (20 November 1798); AD Yonne L712, PV de l'administration du département de l'Yonne, 1 fructidor an VI (18 August 1798); Boussard, *Docteur Paradis,* pp. 345–46; AD Yonne G2385, Registre des comptes de la confrérie de Saint Nicolas en l'église Saint-Loup-d'Auxerre, 1645–1799.

[47]AD Yonne L207, Lettre de l'agent national de Préhy à l'agent national d'Auxerre, 25 ventôse an III (15 March 1795), L714, PV du comité révolutionnaire d'Auxerre, 28 nivôse–3 pluviôse an III (17–22 January 1795), L1118, PV du comité révolutionnaire d'Auxerre, 18, 19 nivôse an III (7, 8 January 1795).

sary to lead fellow villagers in a more formal, full-blown ritual. As the comité révolutionnaire of Auxerre reported, "The old schoolteachers take the place of priests, and the women play a large role in these riotous assemblies."[48]

Lay cults, then, were popular and successful in the Yonne and elsewhere in France in the late 1790s. A combination of factors encouraged their development. The scarcity and reluctance of priests played a part, as did particular political or personal situations within parishes. Perhaps most significant was a shift in popular attitudes as many believers, influenced by events of the Revolution and the Old Regime, felt encouraged to seize autonomous initiative in ritual as well as in politics and welcomed a more egalitarian and less clerical form of religious expression.

Although lay-led worship took place throughout the late 1790s and into the nineteenth century, lay ministers were most active at those times when the clergy were least able to lead public worship, especially in 1794–1795 and again during the second dechristianization campaign, 1797–1799.[49] During the eras of severest repression of public practice, lay ministers were less vulnerable than priests. In many instances, laity complained that their former clergymen were cowards or, at the very least, too reluctant to lead the revival. Lay villagers frequently urged timid or hesitant priests to take action. In fact, instances in which parishioners coerced pastors to celebrate rituals against the law became common enough throughout France in 1795 for one deputy in the National Convention on 11 prairial an III (30 May 1795) to propose that all "priests who broke the law only because they were forced to by the people, and who have been arrested only for this action, be set free."[50] Priests had good reason to be wary, particularly during the post-fructidorean period when the depart-

[48]AD Yonne L1118, Compte analytique par le comité révolutionnaire d'Auxerre pour le comité de sécurité générale, 1 nivôse an III (21 December 1794).

[49]Forestier, "Le 'culte laïcal' et la crise des effectifs," shows that the insufficiency of clergy persisted after the Concordat and encouraged the continuation of the lay cults.

[50]"Journal d'un Auxerrois," p. 255. The Auxerrois journal keeper suggested that the priests of Auxerre were sometimes stingy with their time and prayers on the false pretext that the authorities would be annoyed. Forestier, "Le culte laïcal à Auxerre," p. 177; AN C341, PV de la Convention nationale, séance de 11 prairial an III (30 May 1795). Marie-Paule Biron notes the pervasive pattern of lay people coercing and cajoling timid priests to say mass. See "La résistance des laïcs à travers les messes clandestines pendant la Révolution française," Bulletin de la Société française d'histoire des idées et d'histoire religieuse 1 (1984): 20, 26.

mental administration left few practicing priests free from arrest and none free from fear.

Lay ministers, on the other hand, could more easily escape the full weight of the law. Neither local nor national government authorities ever implemented a consistent policy requiring lay ministers to make the various legal declarations imposed upon the clergy. Many lay ministers simply made these *soumissions,* and the departmental commissaire listed as refractories regularly practicing lay ministers who did not.[51] On the other hand, when the departmental administration attempted to prosecute Rousseau, the schoolteacher-minister of Thury, for not taking the oath of hatred of royalty required by the 19 fructidor an v (5 September 1797) law, the Ministry of the Police overruled the attempt since Rousseau was not a priest. The commissaire of the Yonne acknowledged that if Rousseau had been a priest he would have been deported, but he was a "married citizen and father of a family" and therefore implicitly much less dangerous.[52] Even if the central government authorities had agreed that all those who led worship services must take an oath of loyalty, the law would have been difficult to enforce because in some towns several lay ministers took turns leading the ceremonies.

Priests were bound more tightly by laws and the laws were more zealously enforced against them in part because many government officials viewed them as living symbols of religious fanaticism and as instigators of political rebellion. Lay religious activists could plead that they were ignorant, socially useful, or repentant far more easily than could priests. The women of Courson, for example, petitioned successfully for the release of the lay ministers, their "children and husbands," claiming that they had been "led astray" by the evil example of neigh-

[51]AN F19 481⁴⁻⁵, Lettre du commissaire de Châtel-Censoir au ministre de l'intérieur, 22 nivôse an VIII (12 January 1800), Lettre du ministre de l'intérieur à l'administration départementale de l'Yonne, pluviôse an VIII (January–February 1800); AN F7 7237, Enquête sur l'exercice des cultes, par Housset, ventôse an v (February–March 1797). Housset also recorded the illegal practice of lay ministers in the Yonne in 1799: AN AF III 280, Situation du département de l'Yonne, germinal an VII (March–April 1799). Olwen Hufton gives other examples of confusion regarding whether an oath was required or not. The local authorities in the Ardennes in 1796 were told that these oaths were required only of priests, while in the Franche-Comté all those who led assemblies were required to take an oath. Hufton, "Reconstruction of a Church," pp. 49–50; Tallett, "Religion and Revolution," p. 391.

[52]AN F7 7508, Arrêté du département de l'Yonne, 15 nivôse an VII (4 January 1799) (overruled by minister of police), and Lettre du commissaire de l'Yonne au ministre de la police, 18 pluviôse an VII (6 February 1799).

boring communes and by "better-educated men who interpreted the law wrongly." One of the cantors was only fifteen years old.[53]

Even the very language of accusation betrays the authorities' automatic differentiation between lay ministers and priests. For example, at Cravant in 1799 "men had interfered and begun to play the role of ministers and performed their functions, without making any declaration or oath." The department closed the building because the church might become "a dangerous meeting place, . . . because one could go there furtively at any hour of day or night, under the pretext of religious worship, and foment rebellion in secrecy." In contrast, when the priest Joseph Gantes was arrested, he was accused not only of being a political rebel who spread antirepublican ideas and supported insurrection but also of "sowing division among families, . . . troubling consciences, . . . and carrying worry and despair into the hearts of all."[54] Authorities saw lay assemblies as potentially dangerous because as *groups* they might grow unruly and lead to subversion or full-scale revolt, but *individual* lay ministers were rarely seen as powerful or dangerous. Priests, on the other hand, as preachers with divine authority, were virtual sorcerers. In the eyes of republican authorities they were magicians of rebellion who used all the mysterious incantations and hocus-pocus of their religion to lead the people astray in every way.[55]

Just as they felt less threatened by the political and spiritual authority of lay ministers, republican leaders also assumed that Catholicism would die without the leadership of priests. Republican officials had confidence in their own ability to reeducate the masses, if only they could shake the people free from the grasp of the clergy. The satirical republican newspaper at Sens, the *Observateur,* was even willing to accept the lay ministers as an interim stage in the abolition of fanaticism. The paper reported a rumor in 1796 that a new law would

[53]AD Yonne L207, PV de la commune de Courson, 4 pluviôse an III (23 January 1795).

[54]AD Yonne L76, Arrêté du département de l'Yonne, 26 pluviôse an VII (14 February 1799); AN F7 7424, Lettre du commissaire d'Epineuil au ministre de la police, 4 floréal an VI (23 April 1798).

[55]Pierre, *Déportation ecclésiastique.* Pierre reprinted the official *arrêtés de déportation* issued by the Directory between 1797 and 1799. The arrêtés repeatedly used certain formulas of accusation which reveal the authorities' assumptions that priests universally possessed magical control over the superstitious and naïve minds of the people. In the authorities' view, the priests would use these means solely to undermine the Republic and the Revolution through fanatical subversion and political rebellion.

require priests to stop practicing and relocate in larger towns but
would allow schoolteachers to continue singing masses and even ringing bells in the countryside. "If such a law has just appeared, fanaticism is destroyed and the Republic is saved: because it is not the sound
of bells which can ruin the Republic, it is the terrible priests."[56] Amid
the anticlericalism of the Directory, lay ministers, not priests, could
carry on the ancient practices of Catholicism when the revolutionary
government cracked down on public worship.

Politics mingled with religion to motivate Catholics to support their
lay ministers. Many villagers set out purposely to defy or taunt public
authorities. The municipal agent of Saint-Cyr-les-Colons complained
of this "esprit de contrariété" and reported to the national agent of
the district that one of his fellow citizens had said, "They want us to
attend the *décadi;* but to enrage them, we must always ring the fêtes
and Sundays and sing the ceremonies without giving a damn about
them." Government authorities may have often exaggerated the political, rather than religious, motivation behind lay assemblies; yet some
Catholics complemented their attendance at lay-led Catholic ceremonies with ritual defiance of *décadi* services. Françoise Garnier
showed her disdain for revolutionary cults by boldly parading up and
down nursing her child during the festival of 10 August while waiting
for the lay mass.[57]

In some cases lay ministers used their new spiritual authority to
increase their own prominence within the community. One lay minister, Jollivet of Ouanne, took it as a personal insult when the municipality locked the church. He "ran the streets, crying 'the f___ scoundrel of an agent has taken the church keys to prevent ME from saying
the mass, we must break down the doors, we must not observe the
décadi.'" This schoolteacher, who had gone from house to house to
take up a collection for his services, seemed as anxious to preserve his
personal acquisition of prestige and power as to maintain the holiness
of his religion. Some of the schoolteachers who became lay ministers

---

[56]BN, *Observateur de l'Yonne,* 15 germinal an IV (4 April 1796).

[57]Les minutes de la justice de paix de Saint-Bris, frimaire–nivôse an III (November
1794–January 1795), as quoted in Forestier, "Le culte laïcal," 106; AD Yonne L712,
Lettre du commissaire près Coulanges-la-Vineuse au commissaire près l'Yonne, 2 brumaire an VII (23 October 1798); AN F1cIII Yonne 10, Lettre du commissaire près
Coulanges-la-Vineuse au ministre de la police, 30 brumaire an VIII (21 November
1799); AN F7 7483, PV de la municipalité d'Ouanne, 25 thermidor an VI (12 August
1798).

quite possibly had been rivals of the parish priest in the Old Regime;
some may have even studied unsuccessfully for the priesthood and
welcomed the opportunity to increase their religious authority.[58]

Other lay ministers perhaps hoped to augment their political influence. The *Observateur* mocked the agent of Egriselles-le-Bocage for
picking up the former curé's clerical habits solely to increase his self-
importance in the eyes of his fellow citizens, whom he deceived by
bawling "a long *Dominus vobiscum* which they didn't understand."
Likewise, the commissaire of the Yonne accused the citizen Chevreau
of making himself lay minister just to "win influence over the people
to get himself elected agent next germinal" (that is, at the April elections.)[59] As Catholics struggled against Theophilanthropists or *décadi*-
followers, the politics of personal and communal power repeatedly
came into play, for to control the altar was also to have political influence. Former Jacobins strove to become leaders of the Theophilanthropists, just as some Catholic villagers drew political and personal
authority from roles as lay ministers.

Lay cults could also sustain the pride of a parish or community that
had struggled to survive the various parish suppressions of the revolutionary era. The parishioners of Saint-Pierre of Chablis preferred
to carry on their lay cults after the Concordat rather than attend the
official services at Saint-Martin. They had continually come into conflict with the municipality in their fifteen-year-long struggle to maintain their church and parish. Finally, late in the Revolution, the parishioners had actually *bought* their church to prevent its destruction.[60]
They continued to celebrate lay mass there in the nineteenth century.
Loyalty to the parish community won out over conformity to clerical
mandates.

On the other hand, lay cults could also grow out of parochial conflicts. Both during and after the Revolution parishioners might turn
to a lay minister because they had a feud with the local curé. In 1797
when the curé of Vincelles refused to baptize one parishioner's child
for political and personal reasons, the parents called on a lay minister

[58]AN F7 7483, PVs de la municipalité d'Ouanne, 25 messidor an VI (13 July 1798)
and 25 thermidor an VI (12 August 1798).

[59] BN, *Observateur de l'Yonne*, 15 nivôse an VII (4 January 1799); AN F7 3699², Lettre
du commissaire de l'Yonne au ministre de la police, 27 ventôse an VII (17 March 1799).

[60]AC Chablis, Dépôt 296, 1P1, and AD Yonne L975, 696, Délibérations de l'administration municipale du canton de Chablis, 30 brumaire an IV–30 germinal an VIII (21
November 1795–20 April 1800); Forestier, "Le culte laïcal à Chablis," p. 338.

from a neighboring town. Likewise, fifteen years later, the parishioners of La-Chapelle-Vaupelteigne had grown so accustomed to the lay worship led by their schoolteacher that they refused to attend mass said by the priest Dom Alvarez, sent from nearby Rouvray. Apparently, they disliked Alvarez, who had trouble getting even his own parishioners to attend his services and contribute toward his salary.[61] No doubt other villagers were relieved to practice their cult without paying a pastor regularly. A schoolteacher-minister performed two jobs for one salary.[62]

Specific circumstances—such as feuds within parishes, the personal goals of certain lay ministers, or above all the scarcity of priests and the relative immunity of laymen before the law—were important elements encouraging the development of lay cults. Yet in order to understand why lay cults were so pervasive and persistent, another extremely significant factor must be examined: the widespread shift in attitudes toward social and religious hierarchy in general and toward the clergy in particular.

Certain aspects of revolutionary ideology left their impact in the realm of religious practice. In the first place, the same egalitarian notions that made the Revolution catch fire and spread so quickly through France found their reflection in popular religious attitudes. The lay cults acted out in ritual form a widespread willingness to accept a more egalitarian framework for worship as well as for social and religious organization. Old Regime clerical hierarchy clearly had little role in a lay-led worship ceremony in which not even a priest participated. Just as they had welcomed early reforms that abolished seigneurial privilege and feudal dues, attempted to equalize taxation, and overhauled local political structures, so too most of the citizens of the Yonne approved of the suppression of clerical privileges and the confiscation of church lands, other than parish churches. In fact, the cahiers of the Third Estate in the Yonne had suggested exactly these reforms.[63] Resentment of the wealth of the church would lead some

[61]AN F7 7348, Certificat de l'agent de Vincelles, 7 frimaire an VI (27 November 1797); AD Yonne V11, Lettre de Viart au préfet, 14 janvier 1812; Forestier, "Le culte laïcal dans l'Yonne," p. 241. Forestier quotes a letter written to Viart by the mayor of Rouvray about the difficulties between Alvarez and the citizens of Rouvray in 1816.
[62]Hufton, "Reconstruction of a Church," p. 50; AN AFIII 280, Situation du département de l'Yonne, germinal an VII (March–April 1799).
[63] Courtaut, "Etudes sur l'esprit public," pp. 312–15; Demay, "Cahiers des paroisses," 38:66, 72–76, 116–17.

inhabitants of the Yonne to the violent and strident anticlericalism of the dechristianizers; for others who were less willing to surrender their religious perspective, these egalitarian notions led them to accept forms of practice without the clergy.

In the late 1790s groups and individuals that formerly had little political clout within the parish were able to define themselves as new leaders through political activism and religious initiative. Admittedly, schoolteachers or *fabriciens* were often members of prerevolutionary village elites, but lay ministers of widely varying backgrounds forged new spiritual and communal authority through their new religious roles. Among the lay worshipers, prerevolutionary standards of privilege and wealth no longer determined one's place in the religious assembly or in the community at large. In the lay cults authority and status rested with villagers who dared to occupy the church and lead their fellow parishioners in worship, not with those who had the money and prestige to rent pews closest to the altar.

Moreover, these rituals grew out of the independent and autonomous action of rioting combined with the revolutionary valorization of popular sovereignty and popular voice. The Revolution's emphasis on popular political activism seemed to offer justification for a corollary increase in lay religious activism and lay innovation in ritual. As the lay leaders of the revival in Pont-sur-Yonne claimed, "The people are sovereign and should follow only their own wishes." In many cases when lay ministers made declarations to use the parish church, they commented that they were to practice "on the invitation of their fellow citizens." When three landowners of Coulanges-la-Vineuse asked to take the oath of hatred of royalty, they sent a petition signed by twenty fellow inhabitants, including the canton president, adjunct, and juge de paix. They called for the continued right to lay-led worship and concluded, "Vive la République! Vive la Constitution de l'an III!"[64] The ideology of Revolution had vindicated popular, autonomous activism, and lay religious activists extended this ideology of activism into greater lay initiative in the realm of ritual.

Parishioners were strikingly aware of the link between the Revolution's guarantees of liberty and equality and their own desire to estab-

[64]AN F1cIII Yonne 7, Lettre du commissaire de Pont-sur-Yonne au ministre de la police, 26 prairial an VI (14 June 1798); AD Yonne L692, PV de Quarré, 19 floréal an IV (8 May 1796), L712, Pétition des habitants de Coulanges-la-Vineuse au canton de Coulanges-la-Vineuse, 4 vendémiaire an VII (25 September 1798).

lish unorthodox, public lay cults. In demanding the right to hold lay assemblies, villagers noted that the Revolution had promised them religious liberty and freedom of public practice. For example, in 1794 when the local agent of Beine read the National Convention's decree of "liberty of cults," the villagers spontaneously proclaimed their thanks to the legislators for "delivering them from slavery and destroying tyranny." They announced jubilantly that they "intended to assemble in the temple of Reason only to invoke the Supreme Being and sing hymns and canticles, not to compromise the cause of liberty; they swore to live both as good republicans and Catholics without ministers. . . . As for priests, source of their unhappiness, they didn't want them any more and . . . would turn them in to denouncers."[65] Likewise, in that same winter the worshipers in Mailly-le-Vineux ardently proclaimed the "liberty of cults" decreed by the National Convention, claimed that the "temple of the Supreme Being belonged to them," and promised to pray for the armies of the Republic. The national agent argued that his fellow citizens were in fact good republicans, except for their religious fanaticism.[66]

Gradual religious changes in the Old Regime helped to pave the way for this less clerical and less hierarchical form of religiosity. People turned to the lay cults in part because they incorporated in ritual form an increasingly common attitude: a growing detachment from the clergy even among those who still wanted to practice their religion. Many villagers petitioned for the release of their deported or imprisoned curés, and municipalities often supplied certificates of civism to help their deported priests regain freedom. The parishioners of Appoigny who rioted at the arrest of their curé in 1796 were not at all unusual.[67] Priests were still considered vital leaders of the religion, and most lay ministers practiced only until a legitimate priest resurfaced. But although they came to the defense of the local curé with petitions, personal aid, and even riots, the villagers of the Yonne frequently clung to church buildings and bells, saints' festivals and outdoor processions, crosses and statues with equal or even greater fervor. Housset complained of the pervasive "fanatic" defense of

65AD Yonne L208, PV de Beine, 18 frimaire an III (8 December 1794).

66AD Yonne L207, Lettre de l'agent national de Mailly-le-Vineux au comité révolutionnaire d'Auxerre, 4 pluviôse an III (23 January 1795).

67AD Yonne L710, PVs des gendarmes nationaux d'Auxerre, 5, 7 ventôse an IV (24, 26 February 1796).

Old Regime religious festivals and churches, and commented, "The people cling singularly to this cult whose ministers they scorn."[68]

Rathier, the national agent of the district of Auxerre, repeatedly despaired over the popular attachment to "ancient habits," although "not a word, not a sigh was given for their priests." Rathier also noticed that when communes drew up "declarations that they meant to live and die in the Catholic religion, some even said without a priest." The parishioners of Courson, for example, added to their petition for church use, "We ask for the office all without priests. Vive la République!" Likewise, four years later when their church had been closed in the wave of religious repression following the fructidorean coup d'état, the citizens of Irancy would ask to practice their religion in the local church "without a priest."[69] Furthermore, as we have seen, in some towns lay cults continued to rival the legitimate priests and persisted into the nineteenth century.

The events of the Revolution helped to undermine the authority of the clergy. Early in the Revolution they lost their role as local representatives of the central government: they no longer announced laws or recorded and sanctified births, marriages, and deaths. The issue of clerical oaths caused a deeper crisis of conscience. The divisions created among the clergy hindered their ability to lead a unified and dignified revival. One anonymous journal writer complained that infighting among the parish priests of Auxerre caused some of them to boycott the procession and celebration at the cathedral in 1797 to commemorate the recent reestablishment of Catholicism and the anniversary of Auxerre's delivery from the Huguenots in 1568. The clergy had missed "a most beautiful occasion . . . to manifest the spirit of union and peace which pastors should offer as an example to their flock."[70] In short, the uproar over the Civil Constitution, the emigra-

[68]AN AFiii 280, Situation du département de l'Yonne, germinal an vii (March–April 1799).

[69]AD Yonne L782, Correspondance de Rathier, agent national du district d'Auxerre, 8 vendémiaire, 18 pluviôse an iii (29 September 1794, 6 February 1795), as quoted in Forestier, "Campagnes de l'Auxerrois," p. 195, 199; AD Yonne L712, Pétition des habitants de Courson à la municipalité de Courson, 11 brumaire an iii (1 November 1794), L714, Pétition des citoyens de la commune d'Irancy à l'administration du département de l'Yonne, n.d. [c. vendémiaire an vii (September–October 1798)].

[70]"Journal d'un Auxerrois," pp. 261–62; AN AFiii 280, Situation du département de l'Yonne, germinal an vii (March–April 1799).

tion of many of their leaders, the abdication and imprisonment of many priests, and the disputes about successive oaths inevitably weakened the prestige and authority of the clergy.

Long before the specific crises of the Revolution, some of the religious reforms of the eighteenth century had brought about a shift in religious perspective. As noted, when the parish curé attempted to become a better-educated and morally upstanding leader of his flock, he also gradually became more distant. Rural believers could not always follow their educated and reformed pastors into the "enlightened" world of the eighteenth century. Furthermore, tensions, or at least lack of familiarity, between villagers and curé may have increased in the many parishes where the local curé was an "outsider," perhaps from Lorraine or Picardy.

Lay cults were particularly extensive and vigorous in the formerly Jansenist Auxerrois area. Between 1794 and 1799, 46 percent of the reported violations by lay ministers in the Yonne took place in the district of Auxerre, occurring in thirty-one of the eighty-six communes in the district. The district of Sens, where the influence of Jansenism was present but weaker, accounted for another 16 percent of the reported instances of lay cults.[71] Jansenism no doubt helped pave the way for popular acceptance of practice without priests and without the Eucharist. Jansenist clergymen had stressed that sacraments were not easy tickets to God's grace: confession and the corollary sacrament of Penance were not to be undertaken lightly. Communion should be taken only when the recipient was morally and theologically ready. Although the Jansenists had intended to purify and *elevate* the sacraments and their grace-giving power, their practice had the opposite effect. The theological fine points of a purified sacrament might well be lost on the uneducated villager, for whom the moral stringency demanded by the priest could result quite simply in a gradual detachment from the sacraments. The laity in such a region might well be willing to accept a lay mass without the central sacrament of the Eucharist. Over the long run the villager who turned less frequently to the sacraments would also turn less often to the priest.

Jansenist clergy had also encouraged the laity to take the initiative both at home and at church, to become more active in prayers and rites. In fact, in 1732 Languet de Gergy, the anti-Jansenist bishop of

[71]Lay cults were fairly evenly scattered throughout the remaining districts.

Sens, reported with alarm that Jansenist priests in the Puisaye and
Auxerrois were urging the laity to recite the words of the mass along
with the priest: "I have learned in this country [the Puisaye] about a
custom introduced in the *Jansenist* parishes of saying . . . dry masses.
The priest, instead of going to the altar, ascends the pulpit without a
chasuble. There, he reads or recites aloud the whole mass *in French*,
except the words of the Consecration. They say this mass every week-
day. . . . *The people are told to follow the priest, pronouncing under their
breath the same words as he.* Thus they are taught to celebrate the
mass."[72] The bishop complained that on Sundays and holy days one
priest in the pulpit translated into French the words of the mass being
sung in Latin by a priest on the altar. Indeed, Caylus, the Jansenist
bishop of Auxerre, issued ordonnances urging his parish clergy to
read at the very least the epistle and the gospel in French. His 1751
"Lenten Pastoral Letter" supported lay participation; the laity should
follow along in their missals. "Why not teach the simple faithful the
right to offer the adorable sacrifice with the priest? What can they
fear in uniting with the priest and practicing in this way?" The words
of the mass, claimed Caylus, were not secret, mysterious, or shameful
but should be shared by all. In 1756 Bishop Condorcet, Caylus's anti-
Jansenist successor, forbade priests to say the canon aloud in a voice
intelligible to the laity.[73] Jansenist encouragement of lay participation
in the mass helped remove the taboo on sacred rites formerly reserved for the priest alone. The lay cults would take participation one
radical step farther, for it was one thing to follow the priest's words
and quite another to pronounce them in his absence.

[72]Collection Languet: Languet, archevêque de Sens, à Cardinal Fleury, ministre
d'état, n.d., vol. 34, no. 8, as quoted in Chanoine Grossier, "Correspondance entre le
cardinal Fleury, ministre d'état, et Monseigneur Languet, archevêque de Sens, sur le
jansénisme en Puisaye," in *L'abbé Lebeuf et le jansénisme*, p. 262. I am grateful to Jean-
Pierre Rocher for pointing this passage out to me.
[73]Caylus, "Mandement pour le carême," 1751, as quoted in Henri Brémond, "Une
guerre de religion," *Revue de Paris* 38 (1931): 258; AD Yonne 1J183: 49, Ordonnance
de Caylus, as cited by Dinet, "Jansénisme et déchristianisation," p. 15; Ordioni, *Résistance gallicane et janséniste*, p. 137. On Jansenist attitudes to liturgy, see also Préclin,
Jansénistes du XVIIIe siècle, pp. 179–97. The rituals proposed by Jubé, the curé
d'Asnières, and the missal of Troyes both encouraged lay participation in mass and
found imitators and supporters in the Auxerrois and Senonais. Bishop Caylus's own
Rituel d'Auxerre apparently also encouraged lay participation. Jean Viguerie, "La devotion populaire dans la France des 17e et 18e siècles," in *Histoire de la Messe: Actes de la
troisième rencontre d'histoire religieuse de Fontevraud* (Angers, 1980), pp. 17–18. Viguerie
reports that the anti-Jansenist bishop Languet de Gergy of Sens ordered le curé of
LaFerté not to say the canon in an audible voice.

Finally, Jansenists had also urged the laity to pray as a family and to read devotional works at home. Languet of Sens worried about the secret printing and distribution of various Jansenist devotional books, "sold to the peasants at low cost." The six Jansenist primary schools in Auxerre run by the Tabourin Brothers sent home a manual to parents urging them to go over catechism lessons and texts from the Old and New Testaments with their children. The manual suggested that the parents could contribute toward their own salvation as well by devotional reading and by giving their children a Christian education. Restif de la Bretonne, who grew up in Sacy in this atmosphere of Jansenist rigorism and spiritual education, depicts his youthful reading of devotional literature. In the autobiographical work *L'enfance de Monsieur Nicolas,* for example, he reports that he "found at the beginning of his psalm book, the *Ordinary of the Mass,* in both Latin and French." Using this book, the youthful Restif then imitated the curé's performance of the mass. Though his imitation of the ritual was only child's play, Restif's tale nonetheless provides clues to the education and setting that made a more devout lay mass possible several decades later.[74]

The Jansenists, like the Protestant reformers before them, meant to offer their parishioners a purer Christianity, stripped of unnecessary externals and absorbed through reading and prayer at home. Yet ultimately, the Jansenists, like the Catholic reformers, seem to have had a mixed impact on lay religious attitudes. Some Catholics of the Yonne incorporated the moral stringency and austere practices of the Jansenist clergy into their own belief structures. In a broader sense, the Jansenists succeeded in training the laity to take greater initiative in prayer and worship. But for the most part, they failed to suppress the deep popular attachment to localized forms of devotion. In their refusal to maintain their formal sacerdotal roles, some priests may have unwittingly driven their parishioners back toward those very "superstitions" that the Catholic Reformation and Jansenism alike, despite their differences, both sought to purify or abolish.[75] The priest's aura as spiritual voice of the people grew fainter as they

[74]Collection Languet: lettre de Languet à Fleury, 26 août 1732, vol. 34, no. 7, as quoted in Grossier, "Correspondance entre le Cardinal Fleury et Languet," p. 260; "Avis aux pères et aux mères qui veulent se sauver par l'éducation chrétienne qu'ils donnent à leurs enfants," as quoted in Gazier, *Ecoles de charité,* p. 25; Restif de la Bretonne, *L'enfance de Monsieur Nicolas,* pp. 88–93.

[75]Quéniart, *Hommes, l'église,* p. 275; Hoffman, *Church and Community,* pp. 160–61; Dinet, "Jansénisme et déchristianisation."

learned to speak more boldly for themselves. Paradoxically, over
the long run, encouraging the laity to imitate priests while lessening
the clerical role in other ways would perhaps ultimately contribute to
the gradual secularization and anticlericalism of the Yonne.

In fact, some of the clergy of the Yonne in the late 1790s were
painfully aware of this danger. Vicar-General Viart was particularly
outraged by the lay cults, especially when they rivaled official worship
services and when they persisted beyond the Concordat. Just before
the Revolution, Bishop Cicé of Auxerre had appointed Viart as his
vicar-general to reward him for his loyal service in leading the anti-
Jansenist faction of cathedral canons at Saint-Etienne of Auxerre.
Already in 1795 Viart was concerned about the "mimicry of priests"
by laity in the countryside. While Vicar-General Verdier in the diocese of Autun to the south even encouraged lay worship services in
churches without priests, Viart reacted explosively against any form
of "laïcisme," fearing that it "will grow deep roots and will prevent us
from reaching our goal of reestablishing religious morality among the
people." The lay cults, Viart complained, "join scandal with ridicule."[76] He worried that parishioners who had been attached to Jansenist priests in the Old Regime would use the lay worship services to
avoid having recourse to anti-Jansenist priests. In the midst of the
Revolution and into the 1800s Viart persisted in fighting the ecclesiastical civil wars of the Old Regime.

When lay cults continued after the Concordat, Viart and the newly
appointed bishop of the diocese both wrote to the prefect, urging him
to put an end to the "apery of ecclesiastical functions" by the laity in
many parishes in the Yonne.[77] Bishop de la Tour-du-Pin went so far
as to issue an ordonnance on 1 August 1803 threatening excom-
munication and expressly forbidding "laymen to wear surplices in any
church in the absence of the pastor . . . to sing or recite the prayers of
the mass, in the midst of the assembly of people, or to perform any
ecclesiastical function." Likewise, the prefect sent a circular to all may-
ors instructing them to close churches if the laity insisted on celebrat-

---

[76]Abbé René Fourrey, *Dans la cathédrale Saint-Etienne d'Auxerre* (Auxerre, 1934), p.
111–17; J. Richard, "Le culte laïcal," *AB* 34 (1962): 206; AD Yonne V9, Lettre de Viart
au préfet de l'Yonne, 23 pluviôse an XI (12 February 1803).

[77]AD Yonne V9, Lettre de M. Viart au préfet du département de l'Yonne, 23 pluviôse an XI (12 February 1803), Lettre de l'évêque de Troyes au préfet de l'Yonne, 6
prairial an XI (26 May 1803). The department of the Yonne became part of the diocese
of Troyes from the Concordat until 1814, when Sens became the seat of the diocese of
the Yonne.

ing these unauthorized offices. Yet the practice lingered. Well aware of the laws against lay ministry, the schoolteacher of Voutenay wrote to the subprefect of Avallon in 1816 to assure him that he led prayers only at the urging of his fellow villagers and that he never usurped "the functions of a priest." Highly suspicious of the many instances of lay-led devotions, such as this one in Voutenay, successive prefects and bishops of the Yonne repeatedly issued warnings and decrees against lay leadership of ritual throughout the Empire and Restoration, even as late as 1828.[78]

Perhaps Viart was right to worry about the "danger" of lay cults that extended into the nineteenth century and continued even as the clergy returned or as new clergy were recruited in the 1820s.[79] Much research remains to be done in order to map the geography of lay cults in France as a whole and, above all, to analyze the various types of lay-led practice during the Revolution. But I suggest that in the Yonne, as in surrounding regions where clerical density had been low in the Old Regime and where the Catholic Reformation had the least success in bridging gaps between clergy and people, lay-led masses often betrayed a growing willingness to do without the clergy, which in turn paved the way for secularization and detachment from regular practice in modern times. It seems clear that lay masses were especially prevalent in areas later known for weak devotion, particularly in the departments surrounding Paris, including the Loiret, Seine-et-Oise, Seine-et-Marne, Marne, Aube, and Aisne. In some cases participants expressed a preference for lay-led services over those of the priests. The dechristianizer Crassous in Seine-et-Oise complained, for example, that the "parishioners, [who] to hear them speak are 'disgusted' with priests, nonetheless themselves perform ceremonies and sing offices."[80]

[78]AD Yonne V9, Ordonnance de l'évêque du diocèse de Troyes, 1 août 1803; Circulaire du préfet de l'Yonne Rougier-Labergerie aux maires du département, 12 prairial an XI (1 June 1803), as quoted in Drouot, "Le culte laïcal," p. 204; AD Yonne V13, Lettre de l'instituteur de Voutenay au sous-préfet d'Avallon, 17 mars 1816, V13, Rapport de sous-préfet de Sens au préfet de l'Yonne, 30 octobre 1807, Lettre du maire de Saint-Martin-sur-Oreuse au préfet de l'Yonne, 28 mars 1816, Authorisation de préfet de l'Yonne au maire de Saint-Moré, 9 october 1818; Forestier, "Le culte laïcal dans l'Yonne," p. 241; AD Yonne V11, Lettre du curé Lebrun au préfet de l'Yonne, 31 August 1810.

[79]AD Yonne V11, Lettre de Viart au préfet, 14 January 1812; AD Yonne V11 includes other reports of lay cults in the 1810s. AD Yonne V13, Lettre du maire de Saint-Martin-sur-Oreuse au préfet de l'Yonne, 28 March 1816, marginal note by Viart: "danger à souffrir qu'un laïc fasse des lectures au peuple dans l'église."

[80]Biron, "Résistance des laïcs," pp. 30–37; Bridoux, Histoire religieuse du Seine-et-

Unquestionably, white masses also occurred in regions that were more "pious" in modern times, including the Franche-Comté, Lyonnais, Normandy, and at least on occasion in the Aveyron. Yet many participants voiced less independence from the clergy than the more audacious and persistent lay ministers of the Yonne. For example, in the commune of Morlhon near Villefranche in Aveyron, as the villagers were attending their white mass, "someone came to announce that a mass [by a priest] was about to be said in the hamlet of Périer; everyone hastily left to go hear the mass at that place." Moreover, in the Lyonnais, the lay leadership of worship was largely controlled by the network of missionary nonjurors. The refractory Abbé Jacques Linsolas instructed priests to appoint lay *chefs des paroisses* to preside over Sunday assemblies and even "recite . . . the prayers and ordinary of the mass." These more clerically disciplined lay masses were to remain private and small in scale, in contrast to the Yonne's highly public and well-attended lay masses outside of clerical control.[81]

Obviously, the form, persistence, and independence of lay worship varied widely. Marie-Paule Biron has remarked on the different levels of defiance toward the clergy expressed in lay cults in various regions.[82] Nor did lay cults always have the same implications for nine-

---

Marne, pp. 220–21; M. Bouchel, "Essai historique sur Presles-et-Boves," *Bulletin de la Société archéologique, historique, et scientifique de Soissons* 3.3 (1893): 88; Emile Bouchez, *Le clergé du pays rémois pendant la Révolution et la suppression de l'archevêché de Reims (1789–1821)* (Reims, 1913), p. 548; Alfred Charron, "Boësses (Loiret): Notes d'histoire locale," *Annales de la Société historique et archéologique du Gâtinais* 33 (1916–17): 290; Georges Clause, "Un journal républicain à l'époque directoire à Chalons-sur-Marne: *Le Journal de la Marne*, 1796–1800," *Mémoires de la Société d'agriculture, commerce, sciences, et arts du département de la Marne* (1975): 311; Hufton, "Reconstruction of a Church," pp. 48–50; René Pillorget and Suzanne Pillorget, "Les messes clandestines en France entre 1793 et 1802," in *Histoire de la Messe*, pp. 155–67, esp. 162–63; Plongeron, *Conscience religieuse*, p. 128; Tackett and Langlois, "Ecclesiastical Structures," pp. 358, 360–64; Tackett, "The West in France," pp. 742–43; Isambert and Terrenoire, *Atlas de la pratique religieuse*.

[81]"Notes historiques sur la paroisse de Morlhon, district de Villefranche (Aveyron) par un curé qui a recueilli les souvenirs des survivants en 1847," quoted by Biron, "Résistance des laïcs," p. 33; L. Duval, "La messe de Monsieur des Rotours," *Bulletin de la Société historique et archéologique de l'Orne* 28 (1909): 198–99; Hufton, "Reconstruction of a Church," pp. 48–50; Ledré, *Culte caché*, pp. 88–92, 228–30; Patry, *Le régime de la liberté des cultes*, pp. 131–32; Pillorget, "Messes clandestines," pp. 162–63; Tallett, "Religion and Revolution," pp. 388–96; Viguerie, *Christianisme et Révolution*, pp. 246–49. Marquis de Roux also mentions two incidents that may have included lay masses in *Histoire religieuse de la Révolution à Poitiers et dans la Vienne* (Lyon, 1952), pp. 261, 309 n. 44.

[82]Biron, "Résistance des laïcs," esp. pp. 32–35, notes that the lay cults in the Yonne seemed to express more anticlericalism than lay-led ceremonies in other regions.

teenth-century practice. At least in the Paris Basin, however, where clerical shortages were acute in the early 1800s and where religious practice had declined drastically by modern times, lay cults may have indeed been worthy of concern among existing clerical leaders. These unorthodox religious habits allowed the laity to develop an increasing independence from both the clerical hierarchy and the Eucharist. In the late 1790s, even in the Lyonnais, some clergymen began to worry that lay participants in white masses were growing too detached from priests. One of the vicar-generals complained to Bishop Yves-Alex-andre de Marbeuf of Lyon that "these laymen, anxious to persuade, to charm by their talents, seem to forget about the need for the minis-try. . . . The people grow accustomed to doing without the mitre. They are lulled to sleep, fooled by appearances. They no longer have the same ardor for the sacraments in the regions where they have these sorts of assemblies."[83]

Lay Catholics who found the opportunity to express latent anti-clericalism, egalitarianism, or at least lay independence in white masses during the Revolution might more easily drift away from nineteenth-century Catholicism, which relied so heavily on the hierarchical lead-ership of Rome and was profoundly conservative socially and politi-cally. Catholics in these areas were still religious, but they often seemed to hold fast to remnants of traditional popular devotion more than to their priests. Initially, the post-Concordat church also found it difficult to absorb this popular belief in the localized sacred. Although the nineteenth-century clergy would eventually shift back toward encour-aging a more localized and thaumaturgical religiosity, immediately after the Revolution bishops continued their effort to purge Catholi-cism of "superstition" and of potentially immoral practices. In the early 1800s they issued ordonances restricting saints' festivals and unruly outdoor processions.[84] Some villagers would decide that religion with-out these popular practices was no religion at all.

The development of lay cults thus provides an insight into gradual secularization in large areas of France. Lay cults did not "cause" de-christianization; rather, at least in the Yonne and probably in other

---

[83]Lettre du vicaire-général Ruivet à Monseigneur Marbeuf, n.d. [c. 1798], quoted in Ledré, *Culte caché*, p. 229.

[84]AC Auxerre, Dépôt 3, P5, Ordonnance de Monsieur l'évêque de Troyes and Indult pour la réduction des fêtes, both ratified by préfet on 5 messidor an x (24 June 1802). These ordonances reduced the number of holy days and increased restrictions on outdoor processions.

parts of north-central France, they expressed a curious mixture of religious fervor and detachment from the clergy. This attitude—Viart's dangerous "laïcisme"—made it easier to drift gradually away from regular practice. Nonetheless, the dechristianization of the nineteenth century should not be projected back too quickly onto the participants in lay cults during the Revolution. The lay cults illustrate above all the vigor and resiliency of the villagers' religious beliefs and bear witness to the adaptability of religious forms.

The Revolution created a pressure-cooker situation, a cauldron of political and cultural turmoil in which the lay-led rituals became a field of cultural transformation, a field for playing out the tensions among tradition, revolution, and religious belief. The lay people who broke into churches to conduct white masses and brought buried saints' statues out of hiding to sanctify and preside over their prayers certainly felt a deep-rooted attachment to the "religion of their fathers." They defended the age-old, localized sacred and enacted public, collective rituals that would link the believer to God and produce powerful emotional and moral responses in the participants. Yet they went beyond merely returning to old practices or making up for the scarcity of clergy: they adapted and created new rituals to respond to the Revolution's challenge to traditional religious assumptions, social structure, and community identity. Catholic villagers took advantage of the revolutionary context to express changes in their religious attitudes which had begun in prerevolutionary days. In short, believers created the lay cults to express their fervent need for the sacred, to overcome the material difficulties and the ambiguities of Revolution, and to establish the reality of their changing religious world view.

CHAPTER FOUR

Redefining Revolutionary Liberty:
The Rhetoric and Politics
of Religious Revival

When the radical leaders of the French Revolution set out to challenge and overthrow the traditional cultural framework that supported church, king, and status quo, they unleashed a vast debate on culture and politics. Sweeping and fundamental questions, such as the right to individual freedom, the role of the popular will, the meaning of the sacred, and the relationship of state to society, were suddenly thrown open for discussion. Not only did they instigate a far-reaching controversy over basic issues, the revolutionaries also fashioned a discourse of dynamic and powerful concepts. Such central principles as liberty, popular sovereignty, general will, equality, and freedom of opinion were peculiarly powerful, yet elusive goals. Even the revolutionary leaders themselves could not agree on the exact meaning and nature of these notions.[1] Part of the very strength of these concepts, like that of the Revolution itself, lay in their ambiguity. But this same ambiguous power left the discourse open for redefinition and varied uses. Moreover, the revolutionaries created or expanded many political mechanisms through which to voice popular demands: the petition, the electoral system, the communal assembly, and the section all provided means for exerting influence on revolutionary politics.

As Catholic activists in the Yonne waged a political battle to win the right to public religious practice, they often made use of revolutionary political structures and revolutionary language, for the Revolu-

[1]Hunt, *Politics, Culture, and Class*, chap. 3.

[122]

tion influenced their perceptions of their rights, their expectations of state response to popular protest, and their methods of political expression. I want to challenge the prevalent assumption that Catholics virtually inevitably adopted counterrevolutionary attitudes. On the contrary, many Catholics in peaceful regions of France, such as the Yonne, not only consistently supported the Revolution but turned its promises, ideology, and political techniques to their own advantage. They actively participated in revolutionary politics and, above all, reinterpreted the meaning of revolutionary ideology to accord with their traditional religious assumptions and their current demand for public worship.

Two tenets of revolutionary ideology—liberty and popular sovereignty—were the primary ideological underpinnings of the Catholics' campaign to worship in public. For example, when the national deputies first began to define "liberty" as part of their new political ideology, they conceived of it essentially as a political and secular right, a guarantee against arbitrary government and the inequities of privilege. They sought to establish freedom from the unjust legal system of the monarchy, freedom of conscience and expression, and freedom to consent to taxes and to demand an accounting from the government. *Liberté*, however, represented by bonnets of liberty and liberty trees and repeated in the revolutionary slogan "Liberté, Egalité, Fraternité," soon took on a symbolic life of its own. Rural villagers' interpretations of the meaning of liberty did not always coincide with those of their revolutionary leaders. To a villager liberty might indeed mean freedom from seigneurial dues or protection from arbitrary arrest, as the revolutionary leaders in Paris expected, but it might also mean the freedom to dance on Sundays and saints' days or the right to lead a funeral procession through the village streets: "Where then is liberty if we cannot dance whenever we want to? If we are not free, then we must cut down the liberty tree."[2] For many Catholics during the Directory, liberty came to mean the freedom of religious worship.

Certain new political techniques and structures, created or extended by revolutionary leaders, allowed the religious activists to voice and promote their claim for religious liberty. Catholics took

---

[2]This was the complaint of many villagers of the Yonne according to the commissaire. See AN F1cIII Yonne 5, Compte analytique de la situation du département de l'Yonne, par commissaire Collet, thermidor an VI (July–August 1798).

advantage of the expanded process of petitioning to impress their religious demands on authority figures. Communal assemblies, sectional politics, and the election of local and national officials gave lay believers increased opportunities to influence policy. In short, although they were not always successful, Catholic activists did not hesitate to make use of revolutionary political structures and to refashion revolutionary discourse to demand the return to Catholic practice.

Petitioning

Petitioning had existed long before the Revolution. Under the Old Regime village assemblies had petitioned seigneurs, intendants, judges in the various courts, or even the king or his ministers. On occasion, village assemblies appealed to an authority figure's personal sense of justice. For example, shortly before the Revolution the villagers of Civry wrote to their seigneur, requesting that he lighten their seigneurial dues and pointing out that he had no legal right to collect a *tierce générale*.[3] More frequently, Old Regime petitions took the form of legal *requêtes*, as village assemblies went to court to defend communal rights. If villagers wanted, for example, to bring a lawsuit against the local seigneur before a royal bailliage court, the notables, representing the village as a whole, would first petition the intendant in hopes of gaining his support and then send a requête to the court itself.[4] During the course of the lawsuit villagers sent petitions aimed at influencing the outcome. The inhabitants of Isle-sous-Montréal appealed to the comte de Maurepas regarding their seven-year-old

[3]AN 80 AP 64, Pétition des habitants de Civry à M. Berthier, seigneur et intendant, n.d. [c. 1770s or 1780s]. As the control of intendants increased, villagers petitioned them more frequently about local affairs. For example, Noyers requested permission to collect money for road repair: AD Yonne Dépôt 5 (AC Noyers), CC[1], Pétition du maire et échevins de Noyers à M. Amelot, intendant, n.d. [c. August 1773]. I am grateful to the Abbé Guillaume de Bertier de Sauvigny for allowing me to use the private archives of his family. Mary Ann Quinn has given me useful information about Old Regime petitioning and several archival illustrations. See also "Doléances sur l'injustice de la taille, 17 novembre 1731" (from the inhabitants of Aprey to the Elus des états de la province de Bourgogne), in Pierre Saint-Jacob, *Documents relatifs à la communauté villageoise en Bourgogne* (Paris, 1962), pp. 74–75.

[4]Hilton Root, *Peasants and King in Burgundy: Agrarian Foundations of French Absolutism* (Berkeley, Calif., 1987), chaps. 2, 5. Root argues that intendants in the eighteenth century increasingly supported village assemblies in their legal struggles against local seigneurs.

lawsuit against the seigneur, who had appropriated communal wood-lands. Forty years earlier, their fathers had petitioned the king for the right to intervene in a case before the royal court regarding the juris-diction and use of the Forêt d'Hervaux.[5]

Yet although petitioning was fairly common in the Old Regime, its use was limited by the legal and bureaucratic structures of the royal administration and the seigneurial system. Although individuals or groups other than the village assembly occasionally drew up petitions, the power to petition lay primarily in the hands of the notables or syndics of each village, who used petitioning to bring cases to court or to make a special request from a seigneur, intendant, or bishop.[6] Seigneurs often questioned petitions from other groups, sometimes claiming that they were clandestine and illicit.[7] Essentially, petitioning village assemblies relied on the complex and uncertain workings of the Old Regime justice system or on the willingness of authority fig-ures to grant their demands.

The Revolution transformed the process of petitioning. The free-dom to petition was one of the first rights guaranteed by the National Assembly. According to the law of 28 December 1789 "active citizens" were guaranteed the "right to meet peacefully without arms in assem-blies of private citizens to draw up addresses and petitions, either for the legislative body (or for the king) with the condition that municipal officers be notified of the time and place of these assemblies, and that not more than ten citizens be appointed to carry and present these addresses and petitions."[8] A wider range of people now had the legal right to petition, and petitions during the Revolution tended to have

[5]AN 80 AP 9 (F2B 10), Plainte des habitants de l'Isle à M. le comte de Maurepas, janvier 1780; AD Yonne 1J561, Requête des habitants de l'Isle au roi et son conseil, [c. 14 June 1742]. See also J. H. Shennan, *The Parlement of Paris* (Ithaca, N.Y., 1968), p. 58; Roland Mousnier, *Les instititutions de la France sous la monarchie absolue*, 2 vols. (Paris, 1980), 2:388–89.

[6]See, for example, AD Yonne 32 B 180, Plainte de Jean Barnabé, tisseur à Origny, contre François et Jean Barbier, père et fils, laboureurs à Origny; Jean-Pierre Gutton, *La sociabilité villageoise dans l'ancienne France* (Paris, 1979), pp. 265–68. On individual appeals to the king for private justice, see Arlette Farge and Michel Foucault, *Le désordre des familles: Lettres de cachet des Archives de la Bastille* (Paris, 1982), pp. 345–54.

[7]See, e.g., AD Yonne 1J561, Délibération des habitants de l'Isle-sous-Montréal et dépendances, 28 mai 1768, E576, PV de l'assemblée des habitants de la terre de l'Isle, 22 mai 1741.

[8]Lettres-patentes du roi, sur un décret de l'Assemblée nationale pour la constitution des municipalités, 28 décembre 1789, article 62, *Lois et actes du gouvernement, août 1789 au septembre 1790* (Paris, 1834).

more signatures than those during the Old Regime as more emphasis was placed on popular political participation. The revolutionary guarantee of freedom of opinion, the ideology of popular sovereignty, the ambiguity of the law on petitioning, and above all the restructuring of local and national government—all encouraged more widespread use of petitions.[9] Throughout the Revolution various groups, such as Popular Societies, town assemblies, and Parisian sections, showered local, departmental, and national governments with demands and addresses. Petitioners begged the national legislature to lower their grain requisitions; they denounced local suspects or appealed for enforcement of antiseigneurial laws. Now that popular politics had suddenly been given greater credibility, any request, complaint, or commendation could become the subject of a petition. For example, a group of cultivators in Saint-Martin-des-Champs in the Yonne petitioned the National Convention on 28 August 1793, requesting a more complete abolition of seigneurial dues in their village and noting that the titles of feudal rights had not been burned. They also observed that there were too few curés in the countryside while the former monks and vicars of the bishop remained idle.[10]

The religious revivalists of the Yonne eagerly took advantage of this loosely defined and widespread system born of the Revolution. Especially when the Thermidorean period brought high hopes for the return to public Catholic practice in the winter and spring of 1795, France as a whole witnessed an explosion of religious petitions to municipal and departmental authorities, to the national legislatures, and later to the Directors as well. In the Yonne, Catholics most frequently demanded the use of their parish church: almost 40 percent of religious petitions between Thermidor and the Concordat had this goal. Requests for the right to keep sacred objects or to ring church bells made up about 25 percent of petitions. Villagers asked for the release of their priests in almost one-fifth of their appeals; these pleas were especially prevalent during the second anticlerical campaign between 1797 and 1799. They also made a wide variety of

[9]Questioned about the imprecision of the law on petitioning, the legislative committee responded that the law had been enacted quickly "in a time of Revolution" and, despite its lack of clarity, had been effectively put into action throughout France. AN DIII 305, Lettre de Guéniot au citoyen président, 30 avril 1793, Réponse du comité législatif à Guéniot, n.d. [c. summer 1793].

[10]"Pétition des cultivateurs de Saint-Martin-des-Champs à la Convention (1793)," from AN DIII 307, reprinted by M. R. Mothu, BSSY 90 (1936): 175–77.

other religious requests, ranging from general appeals for freedom of worship to more specific claims for the parish rectory, the maintenance of the Catholic calendar, or the repair of their church.[11]

Lay religious activists were keenly aware that numbers gave strength; they used popular assemblies or door-to-door soliciting to gain as many signatures as possible. In some cases, local leaders of the religious movement, often the village schoolteacher or the *fabriciens*, drew up formal petitions to read at a village assembly or to circulate to their fellow citizens. One Sunday in October 1790 after mass the *fabriciens* of Saint-Pierre of Auxerre read aloud a petition arguing against the suppression of their parish; the parishioners voted unanimously that the petition "absolutely contained their will" and charged the *fabriciens* to present their request to the department and "even to gather signatures if necessary from the inhabitants who were absent." In other instances, the composition and signing of petitions was more spontaneous. A particularly heated incident, an illegal gathering, or an inspiring devotional ceremony could easily spur petition signing. In Brienon on the evening of 26 brumaire an VIII (17 November 1799) a crowd anxiously awaited the arrival of the post with more news of the coup d'état of Napoleon. When the post arrived, the citizens thronged before the church doors until Pierre Denis, a local merchant and sergeant major of the national guard, got the church keys and let the crowd enter. In the church different newspapers were read aloud and citizens Denis and Gaillais read a petition in favor of religious worship and collected signatures.[12]

[11]My discussion is based on 102 religious petitions sent by parishioners in the Yonne between Thermidor and the Concordat. I include any written request by groups of citizens in favor of some aspect of Catholic practice. My calculations do not include petitions sent by priests, lay individuals, or municipal councils, nor do I include declarations of church use made according to the laws of 11 prairial an III (30 May 1795) and 7 vendémiaire an IV (29 September 1795). Although most petitions had one main request, a few made multiple central demands and are classified under more than one category of "goals." Sources: AD Yonne, police des cultes and court records, departmental, district, and municipal deliberations; AN, esp. the F7 (police) and F19 (cults) series; AC Auxerre, Saint-Florentin, and Chablis, among others, esp. the D (municipal deliberations) and P (cults) series; BN, newspapers.

[12]AD Yonne G2396, Registre de la fabrique de Saint-Pierre, 24 October 1790, L220, PV par l'administration de la commune de Brienon, 26 brumaire an VIII (17 November 1799). See also AD Yonne L716, Lettre de Leclerc-Racinnes aux citoyens administrateurs de Saint-Florentin, 7 fructidor an VI (24 August 1798), Pétition des habitants catholiques de Saint-Florentin aux citoyens administrateurs de la commune de Saint-Florentin, 12 fructidor an VI (29 August 1798), L710, PV du conseil général de la commune d'Auxerre, 9 germinal an III (29 March 1795); AN F7 4439¹, Lettre des

Leading religious activists sometimes circulated petitions by carrying them door-to-door throughout the community. For example, a friend or relative of a deported priest might gather signatures on a petition asserting the priest's innocence and requesting his release. In 1798 when Audin returned from fighting in Italy to discover that his brother, the curé of Saint-Bris, had been deported a couple of months earlier, he circulated a certificate in his brother's defense. According to local government officials, his activism stirred up so much religious sentiment that the parishioners forced the locks of the local church yet again.[13] During the Revolution, as in the Old Regime, authorities viewed this door-to-door solicitation with suspicion and warned against "secret agitators."[14]

Composers of religious petitions had several obstacles to overcome in gathering signatures. When the Catholics of Aillant petitioned to the minister of police on behalf of their deported curé, they noted that they had collected only fifty-four signatures. Despite widespread support for the curé, they claimed that they could not amass more signatures because some parishioners could not sign their names, others were afraid to make a public statement, and still others were overcome by the "*esprit de parti*" of certain fellow citizens.[15] In fact, illiteracy and factional town politics did hinder many Catholics from signing petitions. Illiterate villagers sometimes added x's to the lists of names or had fellow villagers sign "in their name." Nevertheless, in the poorest and least literate areas of the department, not only were there fewer signatures but petitioning itself was curtailed. Petitioning was rarest in the least-educated regions of the Yonne, the Puisaye and the Morvan.[16] Furthermore, to sign a petition was to make a public

---

députés du département de l'Yonne au citoyen Mailhe, représentant en mission, 20 germinal an III (9 April 1795), PV de la commune d'Auxerre, 11, 13 floréal an III (30 April, 2 May 1795); Gaston David, "Tableaux de l'histoire d'Auxerre," *Echo d'Auxerre* 88 (1969): 27–28.

[13]AD Yonne L75, Arrêté du département de l'Yonne, 14 thermidor an VI (1 August 1798).

[14]AN F7 7340, Lettre du commissaire de l'Yonne au ministre de la police, 25 prairial an VI (13 June 1798); AN 80 AP 15, Lettre de Wion, régisseur, à M. Berthier, intendant, 1 November 1779. Wion accused Labbé, a village notable, of persuading fellow villagers to sign away the right to cut the communal woods by reading them a false version of the petition. The villagers subjected him to a charivari.

[15]AN F7 7412B, Pétitions des citoyens d'Aillant au ministre de la police, 11 prairial an VI (30 May 1798), and prairial an VI (May–June 1798).

[16]The Puisaye, for example, with a male literacy rate of only 19 percent, sent far fewer petitions than the more literate (40 percent male literacy) and high-petitioning Auxerrois. See Netter, "Alphabétisation," pp. 33–34, 39, 47–48. AD Yonne L706,

religious and political statement. Some Catholic villagers were no doubt hesitant to take this step in small face-to-face communities that were already bitterly factionalized. Doubts about the legality of Catholicism made others, particularly priests, wary of signing petitions. On the other hand, in communities where Catholicism received virtually unanimous support, some villagers may have felt pressure to conform and sign, particularly if a petition was circulated by a powerful *laboureur* or notable.[17]

Petition signers were predominantly male, were at least partially literate, and in theory had to be heads of household in order for their signatures to be legal. Petitioning was not dominated by a village elite, nor was the desire for a return to public Catholic practice confined to poorer members of society. The signers made up a wide social spectrum and seem most often to have represented the social composition of the town or village as a whole, with a slightly higher representation of the just above average taxpayer. For example, in wine-producing areas where vignerons dominated the village population, their signatures also dominated the pages of petitions. In the tiny grape-growing village of Bernouil, 46 of the 205 inhabitants signed the declaration to use the village church. Among the signers were fifteen cultivateurs, including the agent and adjunct; seventeen vignerons; one day laborer; eleven artisans of varied crafts, including four weavers; and two widows who were wool workers. The occupations of the petitioners reflected the social makeup of a small, wine-producing village. Since the average household contained four to five members, the forty-six signers must have included by far the majority of the heads of household in this particular pro-Catholic village.[18]

---

comprising "déclarations des communes pour l'exercice du culte, conformément à la loi du 7 vendémiaire an IV (29 September 1795)," includes many examples of literate citizens signing on behalf of all those present. See, for example, the declarations made by the Catholics of Sennevoy, Chémilly, Yrouerre, Poilly-sur-Serein, Bernouil, Percey, Jouancy, etc. In the commune of Sainte-Vertu 25 citizens, including 1 woman, signed in the name of 82 women and 93 men listed who supported the declaration. In Viviers 42 signed on behalf of 236 women and 256 men who appeared before the *adjoint* to request use of the church. If a curé lived in the town, he often signed the declaration and also made a separate promise to submit to the laws of the Republic.

[17]Although subtle pressure to sign may have existed, no opponents of the revival specifically reported coercion. They did, however, complain of being ridiculed for failing to celebrate Sunday and Catholic festival days. AD Yonne L209, PV du canton de Saint-Georges, 3 floréal an IV (22 April 1796).

[18]AD Yonne L719, Registre de la commune de Bernouil, 5 nivôse an IV (26 December 1795); AN F20*20, Dénombrement et population du département de l'Yonne, an III (1794–95).

In larger towns, with more diverse populations, petitioners likewise came from more diverse backgrounds. For example, in the larger town of Toucy, with about nineteen hundred inhabitants, those who made the church declaration in the fall of 1795 included several *propriétaires,* a schoolteacher, a doctor, an *homme de loi,* and a merchant-druggist, as well as various artisans. Likewise, when the parishioners of Saint-Julien of Avallon petitioned in 1792 to protect their church and its bells, the names of artisans and shopkeepers dominated the list of signatures, in a pattern found in other towns as well.[19]

In those few villages where it was possible to find petition signers in existing tax rolls and so to evaluate their relative wealth within the community, petitioners tended to pay slightly more taxes and earn slightly higher revenues than the average citizen. Since signing a petition presumed some level of literacy and of politicization, it is not surprising that the average petition signer was a bit better off than his or her fellow villagers. Widows tended to be among the poorest signers. But by and large, the very poor did not sign as often for the obvious reasons that they tended to be illiterate and to be marginalized within village politics. Conversely, at the other end of the spectrum, the very rich also were underrepresented; some were absentee landlords with less investment in village affairs. In short, petitions, as well as the less explicitly political declarations of church use, seem to have represented a broad middling portion of village opinion.[20]

[19]AD Yonne L692, PV de la commune de Toucy, 25 brumaire an IV (16 November 1795); AN F20*20, Population de l'Yonne, an III; AD Yonne L711, Pétitions des inhabitants d'Avallon au conseil général d'Avallon, 7 juin, 12, 24 septembre 1791, 6 février 1792, PV du conseil général de la commune d'Avallon, 7 février 1792. The town council of Avallon analyzed the social background of the petition signers in order to invalidate many of them for not being "active citizens." For another example of the importance of artisans in petitioning, see AD Yonne L716, Pétition des catholiques de Saint-Julien-du-Sault à l'administration départementale de l'Yonne, 23 nivôse an VIII (13 January 1800).

[20]Unfortunately, few villages offered the necessary combination of a religious petition with signatures and individual tax rolls for the revolutionary period. In each case, only some of the signatures were identifiable. Moreover, in calculating village averages, I omitted the several wealthiest individuals whose high taxes single-handedly skewed the village averages and made them artificially high. AC Chablis 4E68 1G9, Tableau des déclarations des contribuables à la contribution personelle, mobilaire, et somptuaire de l'an v (pour Chablis et les communes du canton), 4E68 1P1, Pétition des citoyens de Chablis à l'administration du district d'Auxerre, n.d. [c. ventôse an III (February–March 1795], 4E68 1P8, Déclaration par les citoyens de la commune de Courgis, 20 germinal an IV (9 April 1796), Déclaration des citoyens de Préhy, 7 germinal an IV (27 March 1796), Déclaration des citoyens et citoyennes de la commune de Milly, n.d. [c. March 1796]; AC Ligny-le-Châtel 4E228 G3, Contribution foncière de l'an 1790; AD

Irancy provides a final illustration of petition signing. In this fairly large village of 1,122 people in the hilly, grape-growing region south of Auxerre, Catholics petitioned in 1793 to keep their parish and curé, in 1795 to reclaim their church, and in 1798 to worship freely in their church "without a priest." A case study of the occupations, revenues, and taxation levels of these petition signers in this unusually well documented village reveals that they spanned the gamut of income and professions from those who were too poor even to pay direct taxes to wealthy propriétaires or *distillateurs* whose revenues exceeded three hundred livres a year. Not surprisingly in a village that is still known primarily for its wine, by far the majority of the petitioners were vignerons or distillateurs (63 percent). Artisans made up the next substantial group of petition signers (22 percent). A striking number of men who served as municipal officers or notables at some point during the Revolution (21) signed the petitions. On the average, petitioners had a modest level of fortune, typical for the town: they had a reported annual revenue of 182 livres in the year v (1796–1797), notably above the village average of 159 livres. (Given the low level of these figures, much revenue must have gone unreported.) In the year III (1794–1795) petition signers paid an average of 29 livres of direct tax, distinctly higher than the 19 livres paid by the average villager.[21] In Irancy, Catholic petitioners came from varied backgrounds and represented a wide spectrum of wealth and occupations. Two noteworthy groups, the radical politicians of the

Yonne L207, Pétition des habitants de Ligny-le-Châtel à l'administration départementale de l'Yonne, janvier 1792; Maurice Minoret, *La contribution personnelle et mobilière pendant la Révolution* (Paris, 1900), intro., and pp. 540–49.

[21]AD Yonne L714, Pétition des citoyens d'Irancy à l'administration départementale de l'Yonne, 7 frimaire an II (27 November 1793), Pétition des citoyens de la commune d'Irancy à l'administration départementale de l'Yonne, n.d. [c. vendémiaire an VII (September–October 1799)]; AC Irancy, Dépôt 506 1D3, Registre des délibérations municipales, 15 germinal an IV (4 April 1796), 1G1, Montant de la contribution foncière de 1793, personnelle et somptuaire de l'an III, Dépôt 506 1G2, Contribution personnelle de l'an v (1796–97). The petitions were signed by 48, 53, and 55 people respectively, but the overlap of some signatures reduced the number of separate signatures to 111. Of these 111 petitioners, 54 could be identified in one or both of the taxation rolls. It was not possible to identify the remaining petitioners definitively, primarily because many shared one of several common last names; those petitioners who gave neither first name nor initial or who had the same entire name as another villager were frequently impossible to identify with certainty. Some of the other signatures were indecipherable, or the name did not seem to appear in the tax rolls. As noted, I omitted the taxpayers whose exceptionally high taxes skewed village averages.

year II and several of the wealthiest members of the village, made no move to support Catholicism. But the revival succeeded in Irancy notwithstanding, because many citizens, including powerful village officials and leading vignerons, consistently offered their backing. In Irancy, as in other areas of the Yonne, the success of the revival depended on the activism and initiative of lay Catholics from different groups within the community.[22]

Finally, religious petitions came from towns and villages of all sizes. Catholics in all but one of the ten towns in the Yonne with over two thousand inhabitants submitted written requests, but petitions were also strikingly widespread in tiny communes throughout this rural department. Rural petitioning was not only extremely pervasive, but the petitions were also original. Apparently, no model petitions comparable to the models of cahiers de doléances in 1789 seem to have been circulated. Furthermore, although one petition claimed to speak for "the citizens of the department of the Yonne," virtually all religious petitions were local, presenting the demands of Catholics from one particular commune or canton.[23] And despite the suspicions of the authorities, priests had very little role in the composition of petitions in the Yonne. Nor did clergymen sign lay-written petitions, since the shifting laws made priests vulnerable before the law and understandably wary of putting their names on the line. Priests did petition on their own behalf for freedom from imprisonment or deportation, for back pay of their pensions, or for the right to remain in their

---

[22]Powerful local figures who supported the revival included members of the important Rojot, Melon, and Cordier families, also Edme Cantin, a wealthy propriétaire, Timothé Daviot, a vigneron and barrel maker who repeatedly served as town adjunct, and Grégoire Guillaume and Germain Melon, representing other well-off wine producers and government officials. AD Yonne L75, Arrêté de l'Yonne, 17 prairial an VI (5 June 1798), L76, Arrêtés de l'Yonne, 14, 25 thermidor an VII (1, 12 August 1799). Important figures who opposed Catholicism included Jean Cottin-Roux, the wealthiest local négociant and propriétaire, who served as a municipal officer (1791–92), national agent (1797–99), and as mayor for several years after 1800; Michel Sonnet-Morel, also an extremely wealthy propriétaire, early municipal officer, district archivist, and supporter of Theophilanthropy; Jean-Baptiste Roux, mayor from 1792 to 1794; most of the men who held office late in the Terror; and finally, Michel Radu, a stranger to Irancy and a man of small income, who became mayor of Irancy from 1789 to 1792. See Suzanne Desan, "The Revival of Religion during the French Revolution (1795–1799)" (Ph.D. diss., University of California, Berkeley, 1985), pp. 196–207, for a more detailed discussion of the petitioners of Irancy.

[23]AN F7 7585 and AN C568, dos. 370, Pétition des citoyens du département de l'Yonne aux citoyens législateurs, 14 ventôse an VII (4 March 1799). In other areas of France, neighboring villages sometimes composed model petitions. Tallett, "Religion and Revolution," p. 267.

villages.[24] But by and large, petitions for public religious practice were the indigenous and spontaneous product of local Catholic villagers. The revolutionaries had in some ways been notably successful in their attempt to politicize the people of the countryside; yet, paradoxically, Catholic peasants and townspeople would turn this political education to their own ends against the visions of the radical revolutionaries.

The formats of petitions varied. Sometimes petitioners worked to give their petitions a formal and official appearance. Marie-Catherine Huguenin submitted a printed eleven-page "Mémoire," complete with ninety signatures, to defend her relative, the deported curé of Beine. Few petitions were as elaborate as this. Most were one or two pages long, handwritten by a literate lay member of the parish, such as a *fabricien* or teacher. To endow their petitions with authority, religious activists did not hesitate to remind the authorities of their legal right to petition and hold assemblies to determine the general will. They frequently used formulaic, legal phrases to legitimize their requests. For example, in 1793 when the citizens of Irancy wrote to the departmental administration to protest the suppression of their parish, they used the formula "by virtue of the right to petition guaranteed to us by the constitutional act, at this moment we claim in favor of our commune. . . ."[25]

The success or failure of petitions depended in part on the attitudes of local authorities. Many municipal officers were sympathetic to the revival and willingly granted petitions. (These same officials might turn a blind eye to violations of the laws, actively participate in illegal religious festivals, or make official religious requests on behalf of the

[24]BN, *Observateur de l'Yonne,* 5 nivôse an VI (25 December 1797). The dossiers AD Yonne L694–99 contain numerous requests of individual priests in the Yonne concerning imprisonment, pensions, legal status, oaths, etc. See also AN C568, dos. 370, Pétition des ministres pensionnés par l'état, des différentes communes du département de l'Yonne au Conseil des Cinq-Cents, 10 pluviôse an VII (29 January 1799). Viart did send a form letter to local curés, suggesting that they compose and circulate petitions requesting the return of the exiled bishop Cicé in 1800, but this incident of clerical intervention seems to have been an exception rather than the norm. AC Auxerre, Dépôt 3, P5, Lettre de Viart, 15 avril 1800 (he uses the old-style dating); AD Yonne L717, Lettre du commissaire de Thury au préfet de l'Yonne, 5 floréal an VIII (25 April 1800).

[25]AN F7 7353, dos. 9558, "Mémoire que présente Marie-Catherine Huguenin au directoire exécutif, pour la justification de son parent, Jean-Louis Jacquin, ministre du culte catholique à Beine, commune du département de l'Yonne, condamné à la déportation, en vertu d'un arrêté du 6 nivôse an VI"; AD Yonne L714, Pétition des citoyens de la commune d'Irancy à l'administration départementale de l'Yonne, 7 frimaire an II (27 November 1793).

municipality.)[26] On the other hand, many republican authorities refused religious demands outright. Government officials often sought
to discredit the validity of petitions, to make the gathering of signatures difficult, or to warn citizens not to be "duped" into signing
petitions.

To bring the validity of a petition into question, an official could
argue that it had an illegal format, suggest that the signatures did not
all come from heads of households, or speculate that coercion was
involved in collecting signatures. The departmental administration of
the Yonne advised the municipal administrators of Neuvy-Sautour
that they need not accept a petition claiming the rectory for the curé
Edme-Nicolas Fouinat since the collective petition violated article 364
of the Constitution of the year III, which stipulated: "All citizens are
free to address petitions to public authorities, but they should be
individual; no association can present collective petitions, except the
constituted authorities, and only for objects pertaining to their duties." Likewise, when the parishioners of Maligny sought daily access
to their church, the commissaire of the canton claimed the appeal was
invalid because young women and children had signed it.[27] Opponents of the revival and local authorities continually warned that petition circulators could easily deceive the peasantry about the contents

[26]For instances in which municipal officers supported the revival, see the *liasses* AD
Yonne L694–99, which contain the police dossiers of individual priests and frequently
include statements of support by municipal governments. On lenient authorities, see
AD Yonne L717, Lettre du commissaire de Sergines au commissaire de l'Yonne, 27
fructidor an VI (13 September 1798), L72, Arrêté de l'Yonne, 16 brumaire an V (6
November 1796). For many examples of the dismissal of local government officials for
being Catholic sympathizers, see AD Yonne L74–77, Registres des délibérations et
arrêtés de l'administration centrale du département de l'Yonne (Section du bien public:
Police civile et militaire), 21 fructidor an V–11 nivôse an VIII (7 September 1797–1
January 1800). On the problem of lenient judges, see AN F[19] 1017, Lettre du commissaire près les tribunaux du département de l'Yonne au ministre de la justice, 11
floréal an IV (30 April 1796); AN F7 7487, Lettre du commissaire Jean-Baptiste Hérard
au ministre de la police, 17 frimaire an VIII (8 December 1799).

[27]AD Yonne L717, Réponse de l'administration départementale de l'Yonne aux
administrateurs de Neuvy-Sautour, 2e jour complémentaire an IV (18 September
1796); Jacques Godechot, ed., *Les constitutions de la France depuis 1789* (Paris, 1970), p.
140. The wording of article 364 is ambiguous, for collective petitions not presented by
"associations" were accepted as legal. AD Yonne L714, Lettre du commissaire du
canton de Ligny aux citoyens administrateurs du département de l'Yonne, 13, 14
vendémiaire an VIII (5, 6 October 1799). When the inhabitants of Flogny retracted their
signatures from a petition that they thought favored religious liberty and supported the
local officials, they too noted that women and children had been allowed to sign the
discredited petition. AD Yonne L713, Lettre des habitants du canton de Flogny au
commissaire de l'Yonne, 5 pluviôse an VIII (25 January 1800).

of the petition or even extort signatures. The Republican newspaper of Sens, *Observateur du département de l'Yonne,* repeatedly accused the *"honnêtes gens* of Sens" and the "messieurs of the town or their valets" of circulating dangerous pro-Catholic petitions in the countryside and extorting signatures from the unsuspecting peasantry. According to the municipal administrators of Saint-Georges, Edme Riotte worked at night, using threats and persuasion to pressure "weak and blind men" to sign a petition "in favor of a deported priest." His petition apparently demanded a return to the Constitution of 1791, but he presented it to the peasantry as a petition in defense of Catholicism. In a very few cases villagers did claim they had been deceived and retracted their signatures; nevertheless, government accusations of duplicity far exceeded the real threat.[28]

All these attempts by the opponents of the revival to discredit or invalidate petitions bear witness to their power. In the context of a revolution based on a promise of popular sovereignty, which had guaranteed the right to assemble, petition, and voice the general will, petitioning had more authority than it had under the Old Regime. The national government had brought about a whole series of local institutional changes designed to give more political voice to "the people"; the administrative structures of government on the level of the commune, canton, district (until 1795), and department provided an institutional framework for voicing popular demands. Although petitions did not always succeed, petitioning had become a forceful tool that administrative officers could not ignore or take lightly.

The Revolutionary Rhetoric of Religious Activists

The religious activists who petitioned for free use of their churches or for the return of sacred objects did not always intend to make counterrevolutionary demands. On the contrary, they believed that the Revolution itself guaranteed the right to religious freedom. They made their requests within the context, language, and assumptions of

[28]BN, *Observateur de l'Yonne* esp. 15, 25 messidor, 5 thermidor an v (3, 13, 23 July 1797); AD Yonne L1288, PV de l'administration de Saint-Georges, 25 brumaire an VII (15 November 1798), PV du département de l'Yonne, 17 frimaire an VII (7 December 1798); AN F7 7283, Lettre de Joseph et Edme Gauchot, laboureurs, et Nicolas Charles et Gesle Truffot, vignerons, au ministre de la police, 1er jour complémentaire an v (17 September 1797), Lettre du ministre de la police à l'administration du département de l'Yonne, 18 vendémiaire an VI (9 October 1797); AD Yonne L713, Lettre des habitants du canton de Flogny au commissaire de l'Yonne, 5 pluviôse an VIII (25 January 1800).

the revolutionary discourse on religion, culture, and politics. The petitioners took the revolutionary promises of liberty and popular sovereignty and applied them together with the revolutionary political techniques to defend an aspect of their daily lives which seemed threatened—the realm of religious practice and belief. In all regions within the department, protesters reinterpreted revolutionary concepts to suit their religious convictions and their own conception of freedom. They voiced these assumptions regarding the guarantees of the Revolution most clearly in written petitions, but it is important to note that the same concepts also found expression in their speeches in village assemblies, in shouts at riots, in testimony at trials, and in threatening placards tacked to liberty trees, parish churches, and town walls. The notion that the Revolution itself was the basis of popular sovereignty, religious liberty, and freedom of belief and expression was more than a rhetorical tactic to appeal to authorities: it was a deep-rooted conviction among people newly educated in the heat of Revolution.

On the most general level, religious activists invoked liberty as a basic right. After five years of Revolution, villagers no longer conceived of liberty in the Old Regime sense of privilege; rather, it had become for them a natural right, an inherent characteristic and inalienable possession of humankind. Catholic activists repeatedly proclaimed that the Revolution guaranteed them religious liberty as a basic human right. As one anonymous letter writer warned the president of the Council of Five Hundred, the antireligious actions of the government were "contradictory and did not conform to the wishes of the public who have elected you and whose opinion and liberty you must respect. . . . You want to impose tyranny over our thoughts, as well as our actions, and [we are] men whom you like to call free." In fact, Catholic villagers frequently became deliberately defiant and stubborn in their claims for liberty of conscience; they seem on occasion to have acted illegally just to prove that they had the right to defy the government. In 1796 in a brawl with the guardsmen who tried to disband an illegal festival in the town of Saint-Georges one villager made this taunting claim in defense of liberty as a general principle: "People are free to gather every day and amuse themselves; the fair only existed to prove that the citizens were free; there is no law that could change Saint-Pierre."[29]

[29]AN C568, Lettre anonyme au président du Conseil des Cinq-Cents, n.p., n.d. [c. fructidor an VI (August–September 1798)]; AD Yonne L230, PV de la commune de Saint-Georges, 11 messidor an VI (29 June 1798).

For the most part, protesters were more specific in their use of the word *liberty*. Most frequently, they referred explicitly to the promise of *liberté des cultes*, "so often and so strongly pronounced by the National Convention" as the villagers of Courgis were quick to point out.[30] The Declaration of the Rights of Man and the successive constitutions, as well as various explicit laws, had in fact repeatedly guaranteed this freedom of religious practice. Catholic petitioners, rioters, letter writers, priests, municipal officers, and court witnesses alike referred again and again to this guarantee in a wide variety of contexts as they demanded freedom of public worship. In 1799 the citizens of Noyers, like many other Catholics of the Yonne, cited the *liberté des cultes* to assert their right to use the local church. The inhabitants of Fontenailles based their claim for the return of sacred objects on the "Constitution, which allows the freedom of religion."[31] A speaker at a village general assembly in Ligny in 1793 gave a classic formulation of the argument:

> We have obtained liberty. The principle is incontestable, it is constitutional: this liberty includes the practice of whatever religion we judge appropriate to adopt. The freedom of worship cannot be forbidden—Article VII of the Declaration of the Rights of Man. The commune of Ligny has therefore the right to continue the practice of the Catholic religion if [the inhabitants] think it is good and to follow the religion in which they have been brought up and which their fathers have taught them.[32]

This villager's plea for the continued practice of Catholicism combined the revolutionary principle of constitutional liberty with the traditional reference to the "religion of our fathers" in a typical fashion. Priests as well as lay villagers appealed in the name of the constitutional guarantee of freedom of religious practice, especially in the spring of 1798 when the departmental administration decreed that priests must perform Catholic services only on *décadis*. Countless priests, who vowed to stop practicing rather than abandon Sundays

---

[30]AD Yonne L712, Pétition de l'assemblée des citoyens de la commune de Courgis à l'administration départementale, n.d. [c. early frimaire an III (November–December 1794)].

[31]AD Yonne L715, Pétition des habitants de la commune de Noyers au canton de Noyers, 4 prairial an VII (23 May 1799), L707, Pétition des habitants de la commune de Fontenailles au district de Saint-Fargeau, 19 frimaire an II (9 December 1793).

[32]Speech given by villager at general assembly, Ligny, 11 December 1793, as quoted in Michel Valot, "Maître Louis Bouteille, curé de Ligny," *BSSY* 107 (1975): 108.

and traditional festival days, claimed that the Constitution guaranteed freedom of religious practice every day of the week, including Sunday.[33]

Although Catholic activists made claims based on the promise of freedom of religious practice throughout the revolutionary era, at certain moments this type of claim became particularly prevalent or opportune. Catholic protesters were keenly aware of the political tone of different eras of the Directory, and they shifted their rhetoric accordingly. The law of 3 ventôse an III (21 February 1795) promised religious liberty and allowed small groups to worship together, although the law did not grant the use of churches and continued to prohibit public practice and public Catholic symbols; on 11 prairial an III (30 May 1795) the Convention went a step farther, allowing parishioners to reclaim unsold parish churches. Inspired by these new promises, religious activists referred triumphantly and optimistically to the laws increasing religious liberty. When the primary assembly of Bléneau rejected the Constitution of the Year III in the summer of 1795, it also proposed that the National Convention grant "definitively the use of churches and rectories" and guarantee that "religious practice be free and public as in the past." In a triumphant mood that same summer citizen Islème from Asquins-sous-Vézelay wrote to the legislators that the 11 prairial law was "an inexhaustible source of joy for all good citizens. 'Vive la Convention! A bas les Jacobins, les terroristes!' These are the cries repeated by the people who swear their attachment to the great principles of liberty."[34]

In the aftermath of the fall of Robespierre, petitioners used the language of the Thermidorean reaction. They associated the repressive religious policy of the year II (1793–1794) entirely with the politics of Robespierre and the Terror. In December 1794 when the municipality of Mont-Saint-Sulpice appealed for the return of its

[33]AD Yonne L715, Lettre de Gourousseau, curé de Quenne, à l'administration cantonale de Saint-Bris, 16 ventôse an VI (6 March 1798), L212, Réponses des curés de Joigny à l'administration communale, ventôse an VI (February–March 1798), 1J418(10), PV de Ligny, 19 ventôse an VI (9 March 1798); BSPR, Déclaration faite à l'administration municipale d'Auxerre par Paiard, 12 ventôse an VI (2 March 1798); AD Yonne L717, Lettre des ministres catholiques de Sens à l'administration municipale, 11 ventôse an VI (1 March 1798). The ministers of Sens asserted their loyalty and donated their prayers for both religion and Republic.

[34]AD Yonne L208, PV de l'assemblée primaire de Bléneau, 20 fructidor an III (6 September 1795); AN DIII 304, Lettre du citoyen Islème à la Convention nationale, 17 prairial an III (5 June 1795).

church bells, the petitioners spoke of the bell-removing brigands with a peculiar mixture of religious and Thermidorean rhetoric. "We still *pardon* them for this act of *tyranny* and of *despotism*, [emphasis added]" proclaimed the petitioners with the self-righteous assurance of Thermidoreans. The religious activists were quick to warn against a return to the Terror, particularly during the attempt by the Directory to enforce observance of the republican calendar and fêtes décadaires following the coup d'état of 18 fructidor an v (4 September 1797). The religious agitators of Charny who violated the republican festival laws cried out deliberately against the Terror. The gendarmes who went to prevent the celebration of a religious festival in Vézelay in the year vi (1797–1798) were met with defiance: "Where are your orders? Those are only departmental decrees. We don't give a damn. This won't last long. If we had a flute, we would dance despite you. *We are no longer under the reign of Robespierre* [emphasis added]."[35]

Lay Catholic protesters were very conscious of specific laws that guaranteed their religious rights. Sometimes the petitioners made precise references to laws that had just been passed. A petition addressed to the legislature and the minister of police by "the citizens of different communes of the department of the Yonne" in 1799 formally quoted the most important legislation on religious liberty, including the laws of 3 ventôse an iii (21 February 1795) and of 7 vendémiaire an iv (29 September 1795), as well as article 354 of the Constitution of the year iii. (Article 354 stipulated, "No one can be prohibited from practicing, in accordance with the law, the religion that he has chosen.") The petitioners appealed to the legislators to crack down on those who threatened and troubled the freedom of worship and concluded their plea with the observation that no other right of the Constitution was dearer to the people and more sacred for the state than the right to religious freedom. Likewise, the inhabitants of Coulanges-la-Vineuse cited several laws and concluded their petition, "Vive la République, vive la Constitution de l'an iii!" when they objected to the closing of their church. Not all petitions quoted sections of the laws at such length, but they cited them with great frequency.[36]

[35]AD Yonne L712, Lettre de la municipalité de la commune de Mont-Saint-Sulpice à l'administration départementale de l'Yonne, 14 frimaire an iii (4 December 1794), L217, PV de Charny, envoyé à l'administration départementale de l'Yonne, 25 brumaire an vii (15 November 1798); AN F7 7488, PV des gendarmes à Vézelay, 11 thermidor an vi (29 July 1798).

[36]AN F7 7585, and AN C568, Pétition des citoyens du département de l'Yonne aux

Even when they did not have knowledge about an exact law, protesters insisted that they had legal backing. When the women of
Toucy marched to the town council on 22 March 1795 to demand the
keys of the church, "built by their ancestors," three leading women
"insisted that there was a decree which they didn't have, but which
authorized their actions." In a similar fashion, the villagers of Charny
who celebrated an illegal festival accompanied their threats, gestures,
and assaults with the claim that the requirement to observe the republican calendar "was not a law." "They objected continually against
the attacks on the Constitution and the free practice of religion,"
reported the municipal officers.[37] In short, while the composers of
petitions more frequently cited specific laws, the leaders of spontaneous religious uprisings were not as precise in their information.
In the heat of the moment, they called on their general certainty that
the Constitution, the Declaration of the Rights of Man, and some
unspecified laws supported their claim to religious liberty.

In a sense the exact content and wording of the laws had become
less important than their existence as symbols of the villagers' rights.
The villager at Ligny who objected to the reading of the decree closing churches by waving an almanac that contained the text of the
Constitution, asserting vociferously that this document guaranteed
freedom of religious practice, may never have read the Constitution,
but reference to its written word had become a source of authority.
The commissaire of the Yonne noted in the winter of 1800 that the
law of 7 nivôse an VIII (28 December 1799) "seemed to have put into
the hands of malevolent people a weapon for striking and destroying
republican institutions."[38] Interestingly enough, municipal officers

citoyens législateurs, 14 ventôse an VII (4 March 1799); AD Yonne L712, Pétition des
habitants de Coulanges-la-Vineuse à l'administration municipale du canton de Cou-
langes-la-Vineuse, 4 vendémiaire an VII (25 September 1798). See also AD Yonne L710,
Pétition des paroissiens de Saint-Etienne à l'administration du département de l'Yonne,
n.d. [c. nivôse an VIII (winter 1799–1800)], L716, Pétition des catholiques de Saint-
Julien-du-Sault au département de l'Yonne, 23 nivôse an VIII (13 January 1800), L68,
Arrêté du département de l'Yonne (regarding petition from Blenne), 13 messidor an
III (1 July 1795); and Pétition des citoyens du faubourg Saint-Martin d'Avallon à l'ad-
ministration municipale d'Avallon, 29 messidor an III (17 July 1795), as quoted in
Giraud, "La ville d'Avallon," p. 475. See also the church-use declarations in AD Yonne
L706. See Godechot, *Constitutions de la France*, p. 139.

[37] AN F7 4439[1], PV du conseil général de Toucy, 4 germinal an III (24 March 1795);
AD Yonne L217, PV de la municipalité de Charny, envoyé à l'administration départementale de l'Yonne, 25 brumaire an VII (15 November 1798).

[38] AD Yonne L714, PV de la municipalité de Ligny, 6 nivôse an III (26 December

also tried to use laws or decrees as concrete symbols. They routinely read decrees to rioters, as if the very words of the law, as manifestations of their authority, would convey a power beyond their actual verbal content.

Villagers in some cases misinterpreted laws, either deliberately or inadvertently, in such a way as to give more legitimacy to the religious revival. The law of 7 vendémiaire an IV (29 September 1795) required parishioners and priests to make a formal declaration *if* they intended to use their parish church, but when they made their church declarations to local municipalities, several groups of Catholics went so far as to suggest that the law *required* them to choose a church. The inhabitants of Gland commented that "they assembled to obey the law that *obliged* them to select a place to practice the Catholic religion [emphasis added]," while the Catholics of Butteaux spoke of the law that "*ordered* them to choose a locale for worship [emphasis added]."[39]

Rumors about laws on religious practice or about speeches given at the national legislature were not always well founded, but they clearly influenced the actions of the villagers. News of Grégoire's speech in favor of freedom of worship in December 1794 fueled the early stages of revival. As early as 2 March 1795 the national agent of Préhy complained of the adverse effect of the law of 3 ventôse an III (21 February 1795), "not yet promulgated, but already known." Rumors about the address given by the deputy Camille Jordan calling for a return to bell ringing set bells ringing throughout France in the summer of 1797. In early September 1797 the cantonal administration of Epineuil, for example, decreed that local agents should seize bell tower keys and bell cords because "many people took the motion made in the Council of Five Hundred on bell ringing as a pretext for violating the law."[40]

In any event, authorities noted that religious activists acted as if the guarantee of *liberté des cultes* was more fundamental than any other

---

1794); AN F19 481⁴⁻⁵, Lettre du commissaire de l'Yonne au ministre de l'intérieur, 9 pluviôse an VIII (29 January 1800). The law of 7 nivôse an VIII allowed parishioners to reclaim unsold churches once again and simplified the declaration of loyalty required of the clergy.

[39] AD Yonne L706, PV de la commune de Gland, 16 fructidor an IV (2 September 1796), PV de la commune de Butteaux, 24 brumaire an IV (15 November 1795).

[40] AD Yonne L714, Bulletins de la police, 5 nivôse an VII (25 December 1798), 19 ventôse an VII (9 March 1799), L715, Lettre de l'agent national de Préhy au district d'Auxerre, 12 ventôse an III (2 March 1795); AN F7 7283, PV du canton d'Epineuil, 22 fructidor an V (8 September 1797).

national law. The représentant en mission Mailhe complained in the spring of 1795 that fanatics and royalists misinterpreted the "humane and philsophical decree on the freedom of religious practice [as a] pretext for persecuting good citizens in the name of heavenly vengeance." The municipality of Flogny complained that no law, no letter from the minister of police, no departmental decree—in short, no legal authority—could diminish the villagers' insistence on performing "their ancient religious ceremonies with great pomp" on Sundays and holy days; the inhabitants would only respond "that they were free to practice these ceremonies, that no one had the right to force them to change these days." When the department decreed that all church goods be inventoried and returned to the municipality in August 1798, the inhabitants of Flogny immediately took most of the religious objects from the temple, apparently assuming that the promise of *liberté des cultes* gave them the right to do so.[41]

Just as Catholic villagers relied heavily on their own interpretation of the liberty promised to them by the Revolution, so too they used the ideology of *popular sovereignty* to lend greater authority and certainty to their cause. Under the Old Regime village assemblies had made demands of seigneurs and intendants and had taken these higher authorities to court on occasion. The villagers' expectations for success, however, had been entirely in the hands of the justices of various courts. After 1789 the people were able to act on their own in a new way. The Revolution altered popular conceptions of political roles, for it brought both the ideological guarantee of popular sovereignty and the formation of new political structures that, in theory at least, were meant to convey the general will and to ensure representation of the masses.

Catholic activists made use of the ideological argument of popular sovereignty in their struggle for the right to practice religion publicly. A woman from Joigny tacked a placard to the stump of a newly cut liberty tree in the summer of 1799:

Wake up people of France. No government is as despotic as ours. They tell us, 'You are free and sovereign,' while we are enchained to the point

[41] AN F7 4439[1], Lettre de Mailhe, représentant en mission, à Maure, représentant du peuple, 7 floréal an III (26 April 1795); AD Yonne L1407, PV de la municipalité de Flogny, 17 fructidor an VI (3 September 1798).

where we are not allowed to sing or to play on Sundays, not even allowed
to kneel down to offer homage to the Supreme Being. . . .

    After this, *are we sovereign?* Isn't this playing with the people?
[emphasis added]

In this remarkable document "Suzanne sans peur" went on to criticize
the factionalism of the government and the schisms in popular assemblies as well as the national war policy.[42]

    The protesters' interpretation of popular sovereignty was local and
communal, rather than national, in basis. Villagers had no desire to
sacrifice their communal support for Catholicism to an abstract and
Rousseauian general will of the "nation" as a whole, interpreted by
authorities in Paris. In any event, Catholics of the Yonne remained
convinced that the majority of French people shared their religious
feelings. Sometimes petitioners pointed out that antireligious policy
went against the wishes of the population in general, but for the most
part villagers gave a concrete and local interpretation to political representation and the general will. Since they were aware that the will of
the majority carried weight, Catholic villagers consistently strove to
prove that their desire for public Catholic practice represented the
dominant, if not the universal or unanimous will of the village. The
citizens of Noyers based their petition for church use on the constitutional guarantee of "freedom of religious practice" and insisted that
Catholicism was "the religion of the *major part, if not the totality of the
citizens of Noyers.* Since your intention, citizen administrators, is not to
deprive your people of their *rights,* [you will please grant us the use of
the church]. . . . In doing this you will show more and more that you
are worthy of fulfilling the honorable office *to which the people have
called you* [emphasis added]."[43] This petition combines the political
language of the Old Regime and the new. For while the Catholics of
Noyers used the legal formula of prerevolutionary village assemblies,
"the major part," they deliberately extended their claim beyond the
ambiguous and quite often elite group referred to in the Old Regime
phrase.[44] Aware of revolutionary changes in the nature of politics,

[42]AN F7 3699[2] and AD Yonne L217, Affiche trouvée à Villethierry au pied de
l'arbre de la liberté, signée Suzanne sans peur, 16 messidor an VII (4 July 1799).
  [43]AD Yonne L715, Pétition des habitants de la commune de Noyers à l'administration cantonale de Noyers, prairial an VII (23 May 1799).
  [44]On the ambiguous use of the term "la majeure et saine partie" and on the trend
toward elite representation within the village assembly, see Gutton, *Sociabilité villageoise,*
esp. pp. 76–80, 269–70.

they claimed support from virtually *all* "citizens" and did their best to
marshal the arguments of *liberté des cultes*, the rights of the majority,
and popular sovereignty. Above all, they specifically reminded the
cantonal officers that they were responsible for listening to the demands of the people who had elected them to office.

Petitioners used different tones as they reminded government authorities of their duties to their constituents. The Catholics of Sens
simply expressed their confidence that "their magistrates loved and
cherished this liberty [of religious practice] as they did and that they
would eagerly seize any circumstance to prove it." The parishioners of
Saint-Etienne were more direct; they pointed out that returning the
cathedral to Catholic practice would illustrate the wisdom of the administrators in "procuring happiness and peace in all that could accord with the glory of the Nation." The *marguillers* of Saint-Lazare in
Avallon reminded the municipality that if they met resistance in their
commune, "they should hasten to do everything necessary to discover
the general will [*volonté générale*]"; the Catholics of Lavau urged the
cantonal authorities to "uphold the interest of their *administrés*" by
presenting their request for bell ringing to the department.[45]

The petitions of Catholic villagers had power in part because local
officials too were aware of the power of popular demands and of the
validity of claims based on popular sovereignty. The national agent of
Courgis wrote to the revolutionary committee of the district of Auxerre that it would be oppressing his villagers to deprive them of their
religion; not only were they supported by the Declaration of the
Rights of Man, but "it would be breaking the law of the Sovereignty of
the People" to oppose their peaceful assemblies. Convinced that they
could be both Catholic and republican, he commented, "As for the
public opinion of our fellow citizens, firmly attached to the principles
of the Constitution, they love and intend to conserve their religion." A
private citizen from the town of Saint-Florentin wrote to the National
Convention in the winter of 1795 warning the representatives that
they must hurry to institute revolutionary festivals to reeducate the

[45]AD Yonne L717, Pétition des habitants de Sens à l'administration communale et au
commissaire de Sens, 27 frimaire an VIII (18 December 1799), L710, Pétition des
paroissiens de Saint-Etienne [d'Auxerre] à l'administration départementale, n.d., [c.
nivôse an VIII (December–January 1800)], L711, Mémoire pour la paroisse de Saint-
Lazare d'Avallon au sujet des cloches contre le conseil général de la commune présenté
aux citoyens administrateurs du département de l'Yonne, n.d., [c. July 1792]; AN F7
7174, Pétition des citoyens de Lavau à l'administration cantonale de Lavau, 11 vendémiaire an v (2 October 1796).

people, for Catholicism was quickly taking root again as Catholics argued that the Rights of Man and Citizen gave them the right to practice their religion.[46]

Town authorities were also afraid of the physical power of the majority. The municipal officers of Pont-sur-Yonne, for example, pointed out to the departmental authorities that they had better grant the Catholic petitioners use of the local church, lest violence result. Already laws regulating religious worship were being broken.[47] Town officials were painfully aware that if petitioning failed, villagers might very well turn to more violent means to regain the use of their churches and the right to worship in public. Government figures found themselves in a delicate and sometimes dangerous position, suspended between popular demands to restore Catholicism and pressures from higher authorities to institute the new revolutionary cults and culture. In the midst of a Revolution whose origins and legitimacy were built on popular political activism, whether peaceful or violent, the voice of the people had power.

The writers of petitions and the participants in religious riots had varied attitudes toward the Revolution. Although the Yonne was not a counterrevolutionary region of France, undoubtedly some of the Catholics who demanded free religious practice had counterrevolutionary leanings. Particularly during the crackdown on public worship following the fructidorean coup d'état, some protesters' invocations of their religious rights and liberties seemed to grow more threatening and resonated with disillusionment. Some religious activists protested in a bitter tone that if the promises of revolutionary liberty had been broken, then the current law too should be broken. At the very least, Catholic villagers could use illegal symbolic actions to express their disenchantment with revolutionary promises. The disappointed counterrevolutionaries who stripped the bark off the liberty trees at Junay left an inscription claiming, "We are destroying the liberty trees because they bear no fruit." Likewise, another poster, left on the freshly planted liberty tree at Vermenton in December 1797, warned, "You

[46]AD Yonne L712, Lettre de l'agent national de Courgis au comité révolutionnaire du district d'Auxerre, 5 pluviôse an III (24 January 1795); AN DIII 306, Lettre du citoyen Germain Regnard (barbouilleur à Saint-Florentin) aux citoyens représentants, 1 pluviôse an III (20 January 1795).

[47]AD Yonne L715, Lettre de l'administration cantonale de Pont-sur-Yonne à l'administration centrale du département de l'Yonne, 15 prairial an VII (3 June 1799).

who were supposed to make the peace of the nation, you will die."[48] Furthermore, even those Catholics who were willing to accept many of the ideological and political changes brought by the Revolution nonetheless rebelled against the revolutionary cults and calendar created as cosmological rivals of Catholicism.

Yet although Catholic villagers of the Yonne could not accept many of the rituals and symbols of the revolutionary cults, they did not reject the Revolution out of hand.[49] What is most striking and widespread in the Yonne is the pervasive conviction of religious activists that they could be loyal to both Catholicism and the Revolution. Frequently, petitioners and letter writers sought to disabuse government officials of the conviction that Catholicism equaled counterrevolution and fanaticism. In July 1796 one anonymous letter writer, as he appealed to the "citizen president" to give satisfaction to the people by allowing the return of the mass, assured him that he was "among those citizens most loyal to the Republic and most attached to the Roman Catholic, apostolic religion, which according to his opinion could go together very well." Petitioners routinely included assurances that religion would support the moral fabric of the nation and that religion and the Republic were compatible. The petitioners of Courson in the fall of 1794 demanded the right to practice Catholicism "as real republicans, all having sworn to be loyal to the laws of the Republic," and they concluded their petition with the postscript, "We demand [the celebration of] offices, all without priests. Vive la République!" As the petitioners of Chablis claimed in 1795, "We wish to be Catholics and republicans and we can be both one and the other."[50]

Obviously, Catholics' assertions of loyalty to both religion and Republic must be taken with a grain of salt, for to a certain extent, petitioners no doubt felt compelled to reassure authority figures who were wary of counterrevolution. Yet, whereas some petition writers

---

[48]AD Yonne L218, Lettre du commissaire de Vézinnes au commissaire de l'Yonne, 21 thermidor an VII (8 August 1799); BN, *Observateur de l'Yonne*, 5 nivôse an VI (25 December 1797).

[49]On the favorable attitude toward the Revolution among the Catholics of the Yonne, see also Rocher, "Aspects de l'histoire religieuse," pp. 5–6, 28.

[50]AN F7 7182, Lettre anonyme au citoyen président, 7 thermidor an IV (25 July 1796); AD Yonne L712, Pétition des habitants de Courson à la municipalité de Courson, 11 brumaire an III (1 November 1794); AC Chablis, Dépôt 296 1P1, Pétition des citoyens de Chablis à l'administration du district d'Auxerre, n.d. [c. ventôse an III (February–March 1795)].

no doubt recognized the strategic values of such statements, many factors help dispel the notion that revolutionary rhetoric and assertions of loyalty were primarily tactical ploys. In the first place, Catholic villagers did not use this language solely in carefully planned petitions, they also shouted out the same sentiments spontaneously at riots, declared them on anonymous posters, and expressed them in response to questioning, often in quite simple terms. Furthermore, these proclamations were not only extremely widespread, they also went beyond simple promises of obedience and tranquility to more explicit and enthusiastic declarations of revolutionary conviction. Sometimes they included expressions of anticlericalism which the revolutionaries would share. The existence and persistence of lay cults even when priests were available belies the possibility that this anticlericalism was also feigned.

Moreover, in many instances Catholics expressed in *actions* as well as *words* their loyalty to the Revolution. The Catholics of the town of Beine provided a striking example of fidelity to both religion and Republic in their reactions to the reading of the decree of *liberté des cultes:*

> The agent was interrupted by all the citizens of the assembly, more than 350, with shouts of Vive la Convention! Vive la loi! Vive la République! exclamations repeated so often that it was impossible to bring them to order. . . . They cried that the National Convention . . . had delivered them from slavery and destroyed tyranny, that they . . . intended to assemble in the Temple of Reason only to invoke the Supreme Being and sing hymns and canticles, not to compromise the cause of liberty; they swore to live both as good republicans and Catholics without ministers. . . . As for priests, source of their unhappiness, they didn't want them any more and . . . would turn them in to denouncers.

The villagers made further promises to remain loyal to the Convention and the law, to live as good republicans, even to "pour out their blood for the country and the unity of the Republic." Likewise, in that same winter of 1795 the worshipers of Champs broke into the church and "required [the municipal officers] to represent their cause as one generally held by all." These Catholic citizens of Champs assured the authorities that they had "assembled to pray to God, the Supreme Being, for the conservation of all the goods of the Republic, the preservation of the National Convention, and the protection of the armies," but they also proclaimed that they would sooner "shed blood" than compromise their loyalty to Catholicism.[51] Republicanism and Catholicism seemed perfectly compatible to them, and to many other citizens of the Yonne.

Finally, it is clear that Catholics in other regions of France used different types of appeals for religious freedom. I discuss these differences in detail later in this chapter. Here, it is sufficient to note that like those in the Yonne, petitioners in counterrevolutionary regions of the west also referred to revolutionary laws and promises, but counterrevolutionary Catholics did not claim compatibility between Republic and religion, and their petitions possessed a very different tone. They referred to revolutionary guarantees primarily during short periods when the political opportunities for reconciliation seemed greatest and were quick to abandon this language at inopportune moments (after the fructidorean coup, for example). Comparison with the widespread, diverse, and persistent use of revolutionary rhetoric by Catholic activists in the Yonne should help to clarify regional differences in the political beliefs and expectations of Catholics. First, however, let us turn to the religious activists' reliance on revolutionary political institutions to complement their struggle for religious freedom.

The Possibilities of Democratic Politics

As they assimilated revolutionary rhetoric, the Catholics of the Yonne also learned to use new democratic political techniques to accomplish their religious goals. French villagers had long used village assemblies to influence authority figures or instigate court actions.[52] The revolutionaries had gradually built upon these existing local political structures and created a climate that encouraged and expanded the potential of grass-roots participation and national influence. Despite their limitations, the vote and the popular assembly offered institutional means of at least attempting to put into effect the ideology of popular sovereignty and the popular demand for religious freedom. Believers used assemblies to draw up and circulate petitions,

[51]AD Yonne L208, PV de Beine, 18 frimaire an III (8 December 1794), L712, Extrait du PV de la municipalité de Champs, 14 pluviôse an III (2 February 1795).
[52]Gutton, *Sociabilité villageoise*, chaps. 3–5; Quinn, "Pratiques et théories de la coutume"; Root, *Peasants and King*, chap. 5.

to pressure local authorities, to implement specific religious goals directly, and to elect pro-Catholic local officials and electors.

In the early stages of dechristianization, Catholics in many villages passed local resolutions or decrees in a fruitless attempt to halt or slow dechristianization. In 1793 the community of Baon approved a unanimous resolution on behalf of the citizens and town council demanding to keep their priest and to continue to worship on Sunday; they reminded the National Convention that the recent decree of *liberté des cultes* and earlier laws protected free Catholic practice. Late in that same fall of 1793 the town assembly of Merry-sur-Yonne formally protested the suppression of their parish, and the assembled citizens of Nitry reclaimed "the church, ornaments, sacred vases, and a priest at the expense of the Nation or of the commune, and in this last case, a *priest of their own choice* [emphasis added]."[53]

After the Terror religious activists renewed this use of village assemblies to support specific religious requests and policies. Various communes in the year III (1794–1795) voted to reopen their churches, pay for repairs, reclaim the village rectory or cemetery, or invite a priest or lay minister to lead them in worship. Late in 1794 the town council of Volgré granted the request passed by the general assembly, to allow parishioners "free entry to the temple to say their prayers and to practice their accustomed religion there." Catholics in the tiny village of Guerchy attempted, ultimately without success, to protect their parish priest in 1795 by suspending the sale of his rectory, while the assembly of Héry declared (illegally) that it had "chosen" the rectory to lodge the parish priest. The citizens of LeVault selected a schoolteacher and decreed that he must "teach catechism and sing mass and vespers every Sunday and holy day." When the villagers of Courlon assembled in 1797 to pass a formal appeal for the return of their church bell, they declared their loyalty to religion and Republic and assured the authorities that bell ringing had many pragmatic, secular uses.[54] Obviously many of these actions by village assemblies

---

[53]AN DIII 305, Extrait du registre de la municipalité de Baon, 9e jour du 2e mois de l'an II (30 October 1793); AD Yonne L714, Pétition des officiers municipaux et des habitants de Merry-sur-Yonne à l'administration de l'Yonne, 7 frimaire an II (27 December 1793); Pétition de la commune de Nitry, n.d. [c. frimaire an II (November– December 1793)], as quoted in J. Cuillier, "Nitry pendant la Révolution (1790–1795)," *BSSY* 79 (1925): 311. See also Délibérations municipales de Fleury, 24 mars 1793, as quoted in A. M. Moreau, "Fleury pendant la Révolution," *Annuaire de l'Yonne* 54 (1890): 11–103, esp. 87–88.

[54]Délibérations du conseil général de la commune de Volgré, 8, 10 brumaire an III

were overruled or curtailed because they went against departmental decrees or national laws, but assembled citizens nonetheless persisted in their attempts and repeatedly asserted the legality of their meetings and demands. Just as petitioners emphasized their wide popular backing, village assemblies stressed the "unanimity" or "general will" of their proposals and cited the support of the "totality" or at least the "majority" of local citizens.[55]

Moreover, although the Yonne certainly did not witness any massive, violent backlash against the Jacobins comparable to the White Terror of the southeast, in the year III (1794–1795) religious activists sometimes used assemblies to denounce or disempower vocal opponents of Catholicism. The assembly of Pourrain denounced the local agent, two municipal officers, and the juge de paix, who had made "irreligious remarks against the *liberté des cultes*," thus going against the "general will." A large group of Catholics in Diges, calling themselves "new patriots," assembled in April 1795 and offically voted to force the resignation of two municipal officers, the local agent, two tax assessors, and the municipal secretary because they had supported dechristianization.[56]

(29, 31 October 1794), as reprinted in A. M. Moreau, "Volgré pendant la Révolution et l'Empire," *Annuaire de l'Yonne* 62 (1898): 34; AD Yonne L829, Arrêté du district de Joigny, 16 fructidor an III (2 September 1795) (this district decree overruled the commune of Guerchy's attempt to suspend national law), 1J418 (10), PV de la commune d'Héry, 30 brumaire an IV (21 November 1795), L217, Lettre du commissaire de LeVault à l'administration départementale de l'Yonne, 4 brumaire an VII (25 October 1798), L712, Pétition des citoyens de Courlon à l'administration départementale de l'Yonne, 5 frimaire an VI (25 November 1797).

55AD Yonne L67 and AN F1cIII Yonne 6, Arrêté du département de l'Yonne, 27 ventôse an III (17 March 1795) (regarding Vermenton church opening), L1407, PV de la commune de Fontenailles, 30 germinal an III (19 April 1795), L691, Rapport du commissaire de Coulanges-sur-Yonne, 21 floréal an IV (10 May 1796); Bonneau, *Clergé de l'Yonne*, p. 40; AD Yonne L712, PV de la municipalité de Champs, 14 pluviôse an III (2 February 1795), Délibération des citoyens de Courgis, 14 frimaire an II (4 December 1793), L706, Pétition des citoyens composants les faubourgs Saint-Pierre de Chablis à l'administration du canton de Chablis, 14 nivôse an VIII (4 January 1800). See also various declarations of church use in the year IV in AD Yonne L706.

56AN F7 4439¹, Lettre des habitants de Pourrain à Mailhe, représentant en mission, 25 floréal an III (14 May 1795), PV de la commune de Pourrain, same date; AD Yonne L208, PV des gendarmes du district d'Auxerre, 30 germinal an III (19 April 1795), Lettre de huit citoyens de Diges au district d'Auxerre, 23 floréal an III (12 May 1795), L763, PV du district d'Auxerre, 2 floréal an III (21 April 1795), Arrêté du district d'Auxerre, 24 floréal an III (13 May 1795); AN F7 4439¹, Dénonciation à Mailhe (représentant en mission) par la municipalité de Diges, contre divers terroristes de la commune, 8 floréal an III (27 April 1795).

Likewise, religious activists took advantage of yearly elections to select local authorities and national electors who would support the religious revival. It is extremely difficult to interpret voting patterns and electoral results during the Revolution, particularly at the national level. The lack of a party system with clear alignments, the low number of voters by the late 1790s, and the two-tiered system of legislative election via primary assemblies and then electors makes it especially hard to link local views with the policies of elected national representatives. National election results were annulled several times and scissions in primary assemblies continually created doubt about the validity of vote counts. Finally, the commissaires, who provided the most information on the impact of religion on electoral politics, displayed a particular bias in their reporting: they assumed that any pro-Catholic candidates were necessarily "royalists" and "counter-revolutionaries" who "seduced the people by promising them the return of priests and the splendor of the altar."[57]

Despite the difficulties of interpretation, however, it is clear that Catholic voters in the Yonne selected candidates who promised to facilitate public worship. Although one deputy of the Yonne, Charles Tarbé, was a right-wing supporter of the legislative attempt in 1797 to overthrow the Republic by legal means, Catholic voters did not necessarily share this goal.[58] Rather, above all on the local level, villagers repeatedly elected agents, adjuncts, and electors, including some priests, simply because they favored the return to Catholicism.[59] Gov-

---

[57]Hunt, *Politics and Culture*, p. 127; Jean-René Surrateau, "Heurs et malheurs de la 'sociologie électorale' pour l'époque de la Révolution française," *Annales: Economies, sociétés, civilisations* 28 (1968): 556–80; Melvin Edelstein, "Vers une 'sociologie électorale' de la Révolution française: Citadins et campagnards," *Révue d'histoire moderne et contemporaine* 22 (1975): 508–27; AN F1ciii Yonne 7, Compte analytique par Collet, commissaire de l'Yonne, pluviôse–ventôse an vii (February–March 1799). See also AD Yonne L212, Addresse de l'administration cantonale de Courson à ses citoyens, 22 pluviôse an vi (10 February 1798), PV de l'administration cantonale de Flogny, 11 ventôse an vi (1 March 1798); AN F7 7321, Lettre de Coudren aux directeurs, 15 vendémiaire an vi (6 October 1797).

[58]On the use of religious issues by right-wing legislators, see W. R. Fryer, *Republic or Restoration in France* (Manchester, Eng., 1965), esp. chap. 8; Albert Meynier, *Les coups d'état du Directoire*, 2 vols. (Paris, 1927), 1:38–44; Georges Lefebvre, *The Thermidoreans and the Directory*, trans. Robert Baldick (New York, 1964; orig. 1937), pp. 304–6; Harvey Mitchell, *The Underground War against Revolutionary France* (Oxford, 1965). The Yonne deputy Edme-Charles-François Leclerc was also purged by the fructidoreans, although his attachment to the Club de Clichy was not so clear as was Tarbé's. Adolphe Robert, *Dictionnaire des parlementaires français*, 5 vols. (Paris, 1891), 4:28, 5:367.

[59]AN F7 7508, Lettre de l'administration municipale de Vénizy à l'administration

ernment officials often accused victorious candidates of using religious propaganda and ceremony to gain the electoral support of
Catholic voters. For example, in 1797 the departmental deputy Alex-
andre Villetard denounced the newly elected agent of Saint-Sauveur
for his ostentatious religiosity: "To gain supporters he gratified the
people by praising their errors." In 1797 Villetard also inveighed
against Fatou, a lawyer in the village of Mont-Saint-Sulpice, for successfully campaigning to become an elector by having himself "baptized with greatest possible ceremony" on the eve of the primary
assemblies. In 1799 the citizen Taillandier of Villeneuve-sur-Vanne
reportedly "bought the popular confidence by means of a Christ and
a pair of silver candlesticks that he gave to the church."[60]

During the purges following the left-wing coup d'état in fructidor
an v (September 1797), very many of the suspended local officials
were accused of "protecting fanaticism" by hiding subversive priests,
preventing the sale of rectories, saying mass themselves as lay ministers, ignoring national festivals, or treating them with "derisive
coldness."[61] Fructidorean authorities exaggerated the "counterrevolutionary" nature of local officials' religiosity and used these declarations of suspension more to pronounce a new policy than to
make accurate accusations of specific individuals. Nonetheless, in this

---

départementale de l'Yonne, 29 vendémiaire an VII (20 October 1798); AN F7 7425,
Lettre de l'administration centrale de l'Yonne au ministre de la police, 9 floréal an VI
(28 April 1798); AN F1bII Yonne 1, Lettre du commissaire de l'Yonne au ministre de
l'intérieur, 6 floréal an v (25 April 1797); AD Yonne L715, Lettre du commissaire
de Neuvy aux commissaires de l'administration départementale et des tribunaux de
l'Yonne, 13 pluviôse an v (1 February 1797). For a description of priests chosen as
electors in spring 1797, see BN, *Journal politique et littéraire*, 15, 25 germinal an v (4, 14
April 1797). For sample denunciations of priests as officials, see AN F7 7283, Lettre des
habitants d'Epineuil au ministre de la police, 17 brumaire an VI (7 November 1797);
AN F19 1017, Lettre du chef du bureau des émigrés au département de l'Yonne aux
directeurs exécutifs, 30 nivôse an v (19 January 1797); AD Yonne L696, Lettre de
l'administration cantonale de Saint-Sauveur à l'administration centrale de l'Yonne, 29
thermidor an VI (16 August 1798); AN F7 7143, PV du tribunal correctionnel d'Auxerre, 14 germinal an IV (3 April 1796); AD Yonne L75, Arrêté du département de
l'Yonne, 12 thermidor an VI (30 July 1798).

[60]AN F7 7312, Dénonciation par Villetard au ministre de la police, 20 vendémiaire
an VI (11 October 1797); AN F7 3699², Lettre du commissaire près l'administration
centrale de l'Yonne au ministre de la police, 27 ventôse an VII (17 March 1799); AN F7
6612, Lettre du commissaire du canton de Villeneuve-sur-Vanne au ministre [de la
police?], 8 messidor an VII (26 June 1799).

[61]AD Yonne L74, Délibérations et arrêtés de l'administration centrale de l'Yonne, 21
fructidor an v–11 germinal an VI (7 September 1797–31 March 1798). This register is
full of denunciations forcing the resignations of local officials.

moment of cultural and political instability, the religious beliefs and behavior of local candidates no doubt influenced the political choices of villagers. Catholics throughout the Yonne willingly applied electoral politics to promote the revival. In short, religious activists combined their petitioning and their references to revolutionary ideology with a complementary use of participatory politics.

A brief but close look at the religious movement in Auxerre in 1794–1795 reveals this fusion of revolutionary rhetoric with democratic politics. Without turning against the Revolution, Catholic activists simply sought to appropriate revolutionary politics and turn them toward their own ends. Auxerre had been in some ways a model Jacobin town in 1793–1794. Fervent local revolutionaries dominated the Popular Society and controlled the municipal and district administrations. As we have seen, these local revolutionaries joined with the représentant en mission and National Agent Rathier to conduct a lively dechristianization campaign in Auxerre and nearby villages. Although the cathedral of Saint-Etienne served briefly in January 1794 as both the Temple of Reason and a Catholic church, by early February it, too, was closed as the other churches of Auxerre had been a few months earlier. The public practice of Catholicism was nonexistent, though several vignerons had taken on the role of priests and led their fellow parishioners in clandestine white masses on makeshift altars in their homes. Many citizens actively participated in revolutionary festivals, such as the ritual building of a mountain in April and the celebration of the festival of the Supreme Being on 20 prairial an II (8 June 1794).[62]

Yet despite the apparent success of dechristianization during the year II, immediately after the fall of Robespierre Catholic activists in Auxerre began to agitate for a return to public, collective ritual, especially in the winter and spring of 1795. On Palm Sunday, 9 germinal an III (29 March 1795), a large crowd of townspeople persuaded the local bell ringer to hand over the coveted key to the cathedral of Saint-Etienne. Ignoring the exhortations of local officials who arrived on the scene, the rioters declared defiantly that "religious

[62]David, "Tableaux de l'histoire d'Auxerre," Echo d'Auxerre 85 & 87 (1968): 42–45, 39–40; Forestier, "Campagnes de l'auxerrois"; Jean-Pierre Rocher, "La Révolution," in Histoire d'Auxerre, pp. 271–300, esp. 284–92; AD Yonne 1J231, Duplessis, "Mémoire," 37J5, "Mémorial d'un Auxerrois," 2:245–65; Cobb, Armées révolutionnaires 2:661–64, 690; AN AFII 146, Arrêté de Guillemardet, représentant en mission dans l'Yonne, 4 nivôse an III (24 December 1794).

liberty had been decreed," referring to the recent law of 3 ventôse an
III (21 February 1795) (which promised limited religious rights,
though it explicitly denied the use of churches). While the helpless
local authorities left to consider what action to take, the ever-growing
crowd of parishioners began to pray together. One group of "women,
children, old people, and even inhabitants from the surrounding
countryside" tore down the scaffolding and platform built for the
celebration of the fêtes décadaires. They carefully set aside the altar
of the Nation and protected the revolutionary flag from harm, but
some children built a bonfire in the square to burn painted images of
Brutus, Mutius Scaevola, and the goddess of Liberty, whom they reportedly mistook for the "goddesse décadaire." In the midst of this
action several priests arrived on the scene. (A week later Vicar-General Viart would lead some local clergy in blessing and purifying the
cathedral and then performing a triumphant Easter mass.)

Meanwhile, the Catholic activists sent a delegation of fifty people to
the municipality to petition for use of the cathedral. Several citizens in
the crowd carried the tricolor flag, loudly proclaiming their loyalty to
the Republic and "swearing that they would rather lose their lives
than let the flag suffer the tiniest tear or stain because of the demolition [of the *décadi* platform]." At the town hall, the Catholics "protested their fidelity to the laws, to the peace and tranquility of the
commune, which they believed depended on the free practice of religion in their church." The demonstrators concluded by crying "Glory to God! Respect to the Convention and the constituted authorities!
Vive la République!"[63]

The municipal council remained paralyzed with indecision. Wary
of exacerbating popular discontent at a moment of severe grain shortage, they hesitated to oust the several hundred occupants of Saint-
Etienne by force. Furthermore, the four sections pressured the municipal council to allow the Catholics to use the cathedral. Ten days
earlier the sections had already chosen twelve members to report on
the repairs needed for the parish churches of Auxerre and had decided to send deputies to the town council to request the reopening of
Saint-Etienne. When the Catholics of Auxerre took matters into their
own hands, the sections supported the spontaneous popular movement by peppering the town council with formal petitions advocating

[63]AD Yonne L710, PV du conseil municipal d'Auxerre, 9 germinal an III (29 March
1795); AN F7 4439[1], Lettre des députés de l'Yonne à Mailhe, représentant en mission,
20 germinal an III (9 April 1795); AD Yonne 1J231, Duplessis, "Mémoire," pp. 77–79.

joint use of the cathedral for Catholic and civic purposes. Like the demonstrators, the section members were anxious to assert their loyalty to the Republic and to prove that religious and revolutionary ideology were compatible. Seeking to protect the initiators of the cathedral takeover from any accusations of counterrevolution, the sections sent deputies to the municipality to apologize for the "innocent" destruction of the image of Liberty by *children* and to request its ceremonial replacement with a new statue of the same goddess. On 20 floréal an III (9 May 1795) a festival was held to dedicate the new statue of Liberty, with full backing and attendance by the section members.[64]

In fact, the sections played a critical role in the Catholic revival from its beginnings in the fall of 1794 through the summer of 1795, for numerous leading Catholic activists, including some demonstrators, recognized their possible influence as section members. In the Old Regime many of them had been active confraternity members and *fabriciens* in their parishes, and some of them had held political office early in the Revolution.[65] Religious and political leadership was intertwined in the new regime as in the old, although other former parish leaders became radical leaders and promoters of dechristianization in the year II (1793–1794). During the Thermidorean reaction, the moderates who dominated the sections became increasingly powerful, particularly as the Jacobin Popular Society and revolutionary committee first lost influence and then ceased to exist. Three interconnected themes dominated the debates and requests of the sections in the spring of 1795: they repeatedly pressured the town council to alleviate the grain shortage, to undermine the power of the

[64]AD Yonne 37J5, "Mémorial d'un Auxerrois," 2:332–33, 349–54; AN F7 4439¹, PV du conseil municipal d'Auxerre, 11, 13 floréal an III (30 April, 2 May 1795).

[65]On Auxerrois political leadership, see David, "Tableaux de l'histoire d'Auxerre"; Charles Demay, "Procès verbaux de l'administration municipale de la ville d'Auxerre pendant la Révolution," BSSY 45–47 (1891–93); AC Auxerre Dépôt 3, K5 (Elections politiques 1798–an XII). On confraternities, *fabriques*, and parish assemblies, see AD Yonne G2372–99, comprising many registers of confraternity memberships and activities as well as parish and *fabrique* assembly records for the various parishes of Auxerre. Also Demay, "Confréries de métiers." AC Auxerre Dépôt 3 P5 contains many of the petitions sent by Catholics of the various Auxerrois parishes, e.g., Pétition des mariniers d'Auxerre à l'administration municipale d'Auxerre, n.d., granted by PV de l'administration municipale d'Auxerre, 27 messidor an III (15 July 1795), Pétition des citoyens de Saint-Eusèbe au conseil général d'Auxerre, n.d. [c. June 1795], Pétitions des paroissiens de Saint-Pierre au conseil général d'Auxerre, 1 ventôse an IV (20 February 1796), 7 messidor an V (25 June 1797), 16 nivôse an VIII (6 January 1800).

Jacobins, and to facilitate the open practice of Catholicism. In their rhetoric the Thermidorean section leaders linked these three motifs as they sought to build new political and cultural power at the expense of the Jacobins. The new sections applauded the decision of the représentant en mission Guillemardet to disband the Popular Society and later aided his successor Mailhe in reviewing and denouncing Jacobin members to be disarmed. Some of these accusations singled out former leaders of the dechristianization campaign for specific crimes against Catholicism.[66]

The Thermidorean sections also sought to seize control of the creation of revolutionary meaning; they conducted a cultural campaign against the leaders of the year II (1793–1974) by accusing them of distorting true revolutionary culture. Early in ventôse an III (February 1795) the sections successfully lobbied for the annihilation of any "hateful reminders of the Terror." They voted to destroy the mountain built by the Jacobins and demanded that the words "liberté ou la mort" be replaced with the more moderate slogan "liberté, égalité" on the sections' letterhead and on all public and private buildings.[67]

Moreover, the sections aided the Catholic revival more directly by lobbying for greater freedom of worship. As early as brumaire an III (October–November 1794) the sections of Unité, Liberté, Egalité, and Fraternité began once again to petition the municipality to allow church bells to be rung three times a day as they had been under the Old Regime. When the National Convention passed the 3 ventôse an III (21 February 1795) law allowing greater freedom of religious practice, all four sections urged the municipal council of Auxerre to send the Convention this wholehearted commendation of the new law:

> The people demanded the freedom of worship [*libre exercice des cultes*], their enemies had destroyed this liberty; they intended to extend their

[66]AD Yonne 37J5, "Mémorial d'un Auxerrois," 2:318–63; Demay, "PV de l'administration municipale de la ville d'Auxerre"; AD Yonne 1J231, Duplessis, "Mémoire"; AC Auxerre Dépôt 3 I2, PV de l'administration municipale d'Auxerre, 1 ventôse an III (19 February 1795); AD Yonne L1118, PV du comité révolutionnaire d'Auxerre, 28 ventôse an III (18 March 1795). The revolutionary committee dissolved itself at the end of ventôse an III (mid-March 1795); the Popular Society was disbanded by Guillemardet on 26 pluviôse an III (14 February 1795); Mailhe disarmed certain Jacobins in floréal an III (April–May 1795).

[67]AC Auxerre Dépôt 3 P5, Pétitions de quatre sections à l'administration municipale d'Auxerre, 10 ventôse an III (28 February 1795), Dépôt 3 I2, PVs des sections, 20, 30 ventôse an III (10, 20 March 1795). The mountain was in fact "solemnly destroyed" later that spring.

tyrannical empire even over consciences; to raise one's soul toward the creator of one's being had become a crime. The virtuous citizen is assured the enjoyment of his rights; each one of us is allowed to address homage to the eternal in his own way. This is a victory won over those agents of disorder who wanted to deprive man of the most powerful restraint and the sweetest of consolations.

In language both revolutionary and religious, the sections reminded the deputies of popular "rights" and "freedoms" as well as of the emotional sway of religion over the people. Soon afterwards the sections would support the reopening of several parish churches and suggest a return to the Catholic calendar, allegedly for commercial reasons.[68]

Although each of the four sections frequently sent deputies to the other three in order to present united addresses to the municipal council, each section could also act to represent its own neighborhood. In fact, section lines had been drawn along Old Regime parish boundaries, and Catholic section members used this political mechanism to convey the requests of their fellow parishioners to the municipality. The section of Unité, which coincided geographically with the former parish of Saint-Pierre, repeatedly sent petitions to the municipal and departmental administrations requesting the use of the parish church and the return of sacred objects. Saint-Pierre had been leased to a saltpeter manufacturer and the parishioners faced a two-year struggle to regain access. Likewise, the section of Egalité petitioned to recover Notre-Dame-de-la-D'Hors, since it was no longer being used for fodder storage.[69]

Throughout the Thermidorean reaction of the year III (1794–1795), then, Catholic activists, who held the majority in all four of Auxerre's sections assimilated the malleable discourse of revolution and used the framework of sectional politics to support the wide-

[68]AC Auxerre Dépôt 3 P5, PVs des sections de Fraternité, Unité, Liberté, et Egalité au conseil général d'Auxerre, 20 brumaire an III (10 November 1794), Dépôt 3 I2, Addresse de quatre sections à la Convention nationale, ventôse an III (February–March 1795); AD Yonne 37J5, "Mémorial d'un Auxerrois," pp. 332–33, 344, 357–63.

[69]Auxerre Dépôt 3, K5, PV de la section de l'Egalité, 20 germinal an III (9 April 1795), Dépôt 3, P5, PV de la section de l'Unité, 20 prairial an III (8 June 1795); Demay, "PVs de l'administration municipale de la ville d'Auxerre," 47:209: Pétitions de la section de l'Unité à l'administration d'Auxerre, 25 messidor, 10 thermidor an III (13, 28 July 1795); AD Yonne L733, PV de l'administration centrale de l'Yonne, 17 thermidor an III (4 August 1795).

spread popular reaction against the dechristianization policies of the Terror and to demand a return to public Catholic practice. Although they opposed the radical politics and revolutionary cults of the Jacobins, the revivalists did not view their actions as counterrevolutionary and had no desire to overthrow the Revolution. Political moderates, rather than counterrevolutionaries or royalists, Catholic section leaders in Auxerre remained loyal to religion and Republic and tapped the legitimacy granted to popular politics. Although the Catholics of Auxerre were particularly well educated and well versed in the political possibilities of the Revolution, they nonetheless indicate what was occurring on a smaller scale throughout the department of the Yonne. Catholics often sought to work peacefully within the Republic. They used revolutionary ideology and participatory politics to support their demand for freedom of religious practice.

The Regional Character of Religion and Politics

This amalgamation of religious and revolutionary discourse and the corresponding use of democratic political structures was most possible in prorevolutionary parts of France where a majority of the local clergy had accepted the Civil Constitution of the Clergy. In those regions of France where the Civil Constitution had kindled early opposition to the Revolution and where hopes for a union of Catholicism and Republic had died long before dechristianization, such a combination of revolutionary and religious discourse was less likely. In the "troubled" departments of the west, for example, Catholics petitioned for freedom of religious practice and tried to elect pro-Catholic candidates. But whereas they sometimes referred to the laws guaranteeing specific religious rights and to the constitutional promise of freedom of worship, religious activists in the *chouan* regions of the west, not surprisingly, were unlikely to assert in words and action that they could be both Catholic and republican. *Chouan* Catholics generally shared the view of the radical revolutionary leadership that republicanism and Catholicism were fundamentally opposed to each other; *chouans* tended to see patriots as outsiders and enemies, or even as "devils" or "black-hearted" individuals who were damned.[70]

On the other hand, Catholic petitioners who supported Constitu-

[70]Sutherland, *The Chouans*, pp. 255–56, 279.

tional clergymen or who lived in "bleu" (prorevolutionary) villages in sharply divided departments, such as the Sarthe, Côtes-du-Nord, and Ille-et-Vilaine, were intently anxious to voice their patriotism and republicanism, as well as their opposition to the counterrevolutionary behavior of their neighbors.[71] Catholics of the west who had remained loyal to the Republic seemed to view *liberté des cultes* as a particular right, earned by their loyalty. In 1796, for example, the Catholic republicans of one village in the Ille-et-Vilaine claimed that when their town was "surrounded by misguided communes, the butt of all the furor of the *chouans*, the commune of Gahard found patriotism . . . to be an invincible wall against its enemies and those of the country." Noting that they had perhaps done more than any other commune for the Republic, these villagers went on to request freedom of religious practice in exchange for all their "sacrifices."[72]

In the west the guerrilla warfare against the Revolution, the massive lay and clerical resistance to the Civil Constitution, and the heavily clerical nature of Old Regime Catholicism had all left their mark on the religious requests and political style of the religious activists.[73] In many cases, when petitioners from the west demanded freedom of practice, whether they were *chouan* or not, their petitions took on an almost threatening tone, claiming that Catholics had "fought" to gain religious freedom and predicting that if this freedom were not granted, war would return. In 1795 the petitioners of Corlay in the Côtes-du-Nord, for example, belligerently claimed newly won "liberty" for themselves and asserted, "The people armed themselves in order to have religion. . . . Since they only demand what has been given to them by their fathers, you cannot refuse their request."[74] Catholics of the west generally seemed certain that freedom of public

---

[71]AD Sarthe L380, Pétition des habitants de Montailler au département de Sarthe, 16 floréal an IV (5 May 1796); AD Ille-et-Vilaine L445, Pétition des habitants de Guipry et Loudéac à l'administration départementale d'Ille-et-Vilaine, 22 pluviôse an VII (10 February 1799), Pétition de Saint-Ganton à l'administration départementale d'Ille-et-Vilaine, 26 floréal an VII (15 May 1799); AN F7 7265, Pétition des partisans de l'église constitutionelle à Lannion [Côtes-du-Nord] au ministre de la police, 10 juin 1797 (they used the old-style dating).

[72]AN F19 1018, Pétition des habitants de la commune de Gahard [Ille-et-Vilaine] au Conseil des Cinq-Cents, 7 messidor an IV (25 June 1796).

[73]See Tackett, *Religion, Revolution,* esp. chap. 10, on the correspondence between refusal of the oath in 1791 and a high density of clergy in the Old Regime, particularly in western France.

[74]AD Côtes-du-Nord, LM5 87, Pétition des citoyens de Corlay à l'administration du district de Loudéac, 8 floréal an III (27 April 1795).

worship and, above all, the return of their nonjuring priests were the necessary conditions for public tranquility and conformity to the republican government.

Not only did the religious activists of the west harp more frequently on the themes of warfare and public tranquility than did their fellow Catholics of the Yonne, they also placed a much heavier emphasis on the necessary role of the clergy. The petitioners of Rennes summed up the essence of the western revival when they referred to the "obvious truth that the freedom of priests is inseparable from the freedom of religion, and that this is inseparable from public tranquility, especially in the countryside."[75] This attitude was reflected also in the actions of the departmental and local officials in the west. In many cases, they apparently moved more gingerly than the authorities in the Yonne and were especially hesitant to take action against returning refractory priests. During the second dechristianization campaign, for example, the administrators of the Yonne deported priests far more zealously than did those of the western departments.[76] As one government official of the Calvados commented in 1796, "We promised them liberty and equality, and after that we tyrannized them and denied them religious freedom, which would bring peace to all if we would only grant it to them."[77]

Even in the counterrevolutionary west, there were moments during the Revolution when it seemed as if the legal structures of republican government might offer a peaceful solution and religious liberty, particularly in the springs of 1795 and 1797. Especially in the spring of 1797, when the newly elected moderate and right-wing national deputies staged an attempt to turn around the Revolution from within the councils, there was a corresponding campaign in the provinces to use the very structures of Revolution against the political culture of

---

[75]AD Ille-et-Vilaine L1006, Pétition des citoyens de Rennes et des communes environnantes au Conseil des Cinq-Cents, 11 brumaire an v (1 November 1796).

[76]Pierre, *Déportation ecclésiastique,* pp. xviii–xx. Pierre notes that local administrations had more control over deportation in the west and in Brittany than in the Yonne and other areas. The departments of the west lay between the Yonne and the distinctly laxer departments of the Midi in numbers of priests deported in this second dechristianization period. AN F19 418, Lettre de l'administration départementale et du commissaire des Côtes-du-Nord au ministre de l'intérieur, 13 nivôse an III (2 January 1795); Patry, *Le régime de la liberté des cultes,* pp. 123–24; Pommeret, *L'esprit public,* pp. 357, 415–19; Reinhard, *Département de la Sarthe,* pp. 124–25, 568.

[77]AN F7 7192, Lettre de Laneuve au président du conseil, 11 fructidor an IV (28 August 1796), as quoted in Patry, *Le régime de la liberté des cultes,* pp. 122–23.

the Revolution and to restore Catholicism. In western towns, such as Rennes and Saint-Brieuc, petitions with ample references to revolutionary laws and constitutional promises of religious freedom were circulated and gained hundreds of signatures. In contrast to the practice in the Yonne, model petitions were sent out to the countryside; some villagers copied these urban-based petitions word for word. The petition campaign was linked to the right-wing leadership of the *honnêtes gens;* priests were sometimes instrumental in circulating these petitions and in composing rural ones as well. Petition warfare broke out between factions within towns and villages as anticlerical, left-wing republicans accused right-wing Catholic activists of gathering false signatures in their attempt to "overthrow the constitution by the constitution" and to conceal their attack on the Republic "beneath the mask of the religion of humanity and of patriotism."[78]

However, once the fructidorean coup d'état put an end to the hopes for a peaceful reconciliation between the government and Catholicism until the coming of Napoleon, Catholics of the west seem to have lost hope in the idea that religion could exist under the Republic. The flurry of petitioning died down amid the general certitude that the republican promises of religious liberty and popular sovereignty were indeed empty. The years VI and VII (1797–1799) brought a return of both *chouan* guerrilla warfare and the Vendéan civil war. Although the west had witnessed cases of republican Catholicism during the revolution, this combination became less and less possible in a region where the "golden legend" of the heroes of the Vendée who had "died for the faith" became etched on the collective memory. The Vendéan and *chouan* resistance left a deeply rooted ideological legacy:

[78]Pommeret, *Esprit publique,* pp. 397–99; Reinhard, *Le département de la Sarthe,* p. 272; Patry, *Le régime de la liberté des cultes,* pp. 137–39; AN F7 7255, Pétition des habitants de Moncoutour [Côtes-du-Nord] aux représentants du peuple, 10 floréal an v (29 April 1797), F7 7263, Lettre du commissaire de Paimpol [Côtes-du-Nord] au ministre de la police, 1 messidor an v (19 June 1797), Lettre du commissaire des Côtes-du-Nord, 24 prairial an v (12 June 1797), Pétition des catholiques romains de Saint-Brieuc aux deux conseils (printed), n.d. [c. prairial an v (May–June 1797)]; AD Ille-et-Vilaine L1006, Pétition des citoyens de Rennes et des communes environnantes au Conseil des Cinq-Cents, 11 brumaire an v (1 November 1796); AN F7 7262, Pétition des habitants [républicains] de Lamballe au Directoire, 24 messidor an v (12 July 1797), Lettre de mareschal au ministre de la police, 2 thermidor an v (20 July 1797). Model petitions also circulated in the spring of 1795; AD Côtes-du-Nord LM5 86, Pétition des catholiques romains de Saint-Brieuc au district, reçue le 22 germinal an III (11 April 1795), LM5 87, Pétition des catholiques de Pleury à l'administration du district de Loudéac, 29 floréal an III (18 May 1795).

throughout the modern period Catholicism in the west would remain
in some sense the prisoner of counterrevolutionary ideology. It became impossible to conceive of religion that was not opposed to any
and all forms of republicanism.[79]

In noncounterrevolutionary regions such as the Yonne, on the
other hand, confidence in the power of popular demands without
recourse to counterrevolution was more pervasive and persistent.
Well before the hopeful spring of 1797 and even under the severe
weight of the postfructidorean dechristianization campaign of 1797–
1799, Catholics in tiny villages and large towns alike in the Yonne
continued to bombard the authorities with requests for religious liberty, still couched in the revolutionary language of popular sovereignty,
the general will, and the promises of freedom. Many Catholics in
other prorevolutionary regions of France shared this optimism. They
might invoke Jean-Jacques Rousseau, the "general interest," and the
"will of the majority of French people," as did some villagers in
Nièvre, or they might assert, along with the self-proclaimed "Catholics" and "patriots" of De-Griège in the Saône-et-Loire, that the return to Catholicism was "the well-known will of all the communes of
the department and of the neighboring departments, in one word,
the will of the people." Their declarations might contain more bravado, as did the petition from nine hundred "Catholics and republicans" in the Nord, who demanded the use of their church in
1795: "We declare to you. . . . We will celebrate our divine mysteries
in our church on the first of germinal if our priest does not flee, and if
he does flee, we will find another one. Remember that *insurrection is a
duty* for the people when their *rights* are violated" (my emphasis).[80]

---

[79]Chaline, Lagree, and Chassagne, *L'église de France: L'Ouest*, pp. 13, 41, 50–52, 59–
60, 86; Reinhard, *Le département de la Sarthe*, pp. 627–30. Lagrée gives examples of
republican Catholicism in the West, but also discusses its limitations.

[80]AN F19 1018, Pétition des habitants de Saint-Leger de Fougeret [Nièvre] au Conseil des Cinq-Cents, 23 fructidor an IV (9 September 1796), Pétition de Mèves au
Conseil des Cinq-Cents, n.d. [c. messidor–thermidor an IV (summer 1796)], F19 467–
68, Pétition de la commune de Griège [Saône-et-Loire] aux citoyens législateurs, n.d. [c.
9 nivôse an IV (30 December 1795)]; AD Nord L8075, folio 183 and L8917, dos. 2,
Pétition de 900 catholiques et républicains à l'administration du district de Bousbecque,
26 ventôse an III (16 March 1795), as quoted in Joseph Peter and Charles Poulet,
Histoire religieuse du département du Nord pendant la Révolution (1789–1802), 2 vols. (Lille,
1930), 2:31. Multiple examples of petitions with revolutionary language from Catholics
in northern and central France can be found in AN F19 398–481 and in various
regional histories of Catholicism during the Revolution. A closer examination of those
departments that were not counterrevolutionary and yet favored Catholicism would no
doubt reveal many more instances of this combination of republican and religious
discourse.

Obviously, regional attitudes toward the Revolution varied, but to view the alliance of counterrevolution and Catholicism as invariable throughout France is to take at face value the rhetoric and viewpoint of revolutionary officials. In much of France, Catholic villagers sought to reconcile loyalty to their religion with loyalty to the Revolution. They shared the view of the citizen Serret, who protested when the district of Saint-Fargeau characterized Catholicism as "fanaticism" and equated it with "royalism." On the contrary, he claimed, "the freedom of religious practice is the only way to bring all the individual spirits of the Republic to unity."[81]

Paradoxically, the Revolution opened up surprising and unexpected possibilities for the laity in prerevolutionary regions of France to find within the Revolution itself political techniques and ideology to aid their reestablishment of Catholicism. In effect, the Catholic villagers of the Yonne assimilated those aspects of revolutionary political techniques and language which they could incorporate within their traditions and beliefs. As they infused their petitions and placards with revolutionary rhetoric and used the political institutions of the Revolution to voice their claims, the religious activists continued to draw as well on traditional forms of protest and to combine religious activism with their political strategies. This fusion of the religious and the political and of the traditional and the revolutionary increased the power of the Catholic revival.

Examination of the language of the religious revival also illustrates the need to reevaluate how the Revolution was received on the local level. The revolutionary discourse was a live entity; the politicians and journalists in Paris and in large provincial cities were not the only ones who struggled to create and control it. Catholic villagers constantly integrated revolutionary innovations into their old traditional patterns of life and assumptions. In doing so, French villagers transformed and reinterpreted the Revolution in an active and dynamic way. They redefined the goals of the Revolution to accord with their religious beliefs and their own conception of freedom. Perhaps the citizen Laire spoke with some truth when he commented about the citizens of the Yonne, "The French heart may well be republican, but the customs are still monarchical."[82]

The revolutionaries tried to do something radically different: to

[81]AN F19 481(4–5), Lettre du citoyen Serret de Saint-Fargeau au Comité de salut public, 15 messidor an III (3 July 1795).

[82]BSPR, Carton Yonne, Lettre de Laire à Grégoire, 21 nivôse an III (10 January 1795).

separate the religious from the political or at least to draw a clear-cut dichotomy between Catholicism and the Revolution. But it was not so simple to divide traditional religious culture from the new secular political culture of the Revolution in the minds and attitudes of the people. Popular attitudes toward the Revolution were not always what politicians in Paris might expect. Would revolutionary deputies understand the thinking of the villagers in the Périgord who had insisted early in the Revolution that their curé put a revolutionary tricolor cockade on the host and that he leave the doors of the tabernacle open "so that the good God might be free?"[83] God, too, according to these villagers should benefit from revolutionary liberty. Religion and revolution might mix in unusual ways. To create a secular, political culture, entirely independent of religion, was not as easy as the radical revolutionaries hoped.

[83]Lettre de Vergniaud, 16 janvier 1790, in Vergniaud, *Manuscrits, lettres, et papiers: Pièces pour la plupart inédites*, ed. C. Vatel (Paris, 1873), as quoted in Ozouf, *Fête révolutionnaire*, p. 151.

CHAPTER FIVE

Rioting in God's Name:
Activism, Gender, and Community

In January 1795 a group of Catholics in the tiny village of Pallaye marched to the municipality to demand the parish church keys. When the municipal officers refused, the parishioners, with women in the lead, forced opened a window of a side chapel, rang the church bell to call others to worship, and began to celebrate a lay-led mass to commemorate the festival of Saint Vincent, the patron saint of vignerons. When the mayor of Pallaye arrived on the scene to break up the assembly, Nicolas Balet shouted, "A commune is stronger than a municipality." One woman opted for a less theoretical approach. She cried out to the other women, "Let's band together, take up our sticks. Let's kill him [the mayor], don't let him escape from the church." Meanwhile Jacques Miné urged his fellow worshipers, "Let's keep singing. Do not answer to anything." The lay ministers Jacques Miné and Germain Challaux continued to sing the offertory of their "white mass," while some angry parishioners forced the mayor to exit. The mayor fled his pursuers in despair, certain that the lay ministers were singing the Per Omnia to mock him as he left.[1]

During the late 1790s many Catholic villagers, like those in Pallaye, broke into churches, rang church bells with noisy bravado, danced on saints' feast days in defiance of republican institutions, and hanged local government officials in effigy. Religious rioters mixed the sacred and the violent in powerful ways. This incident in Pallaye provides a

---

[1]AD Yonne L716, PV de la municipalité de Pallaye, 3 pluviôse an III (22 January 1795).

[165]

glimpse of the complex synthesis of ritual, violence, and power struggle that characterized illegal religious activism during the French Revolution. In this typical riot, the Catholics of Pallaye combined political
arguments, unabashed threats of violence, and sheer force of ritual to
achieve their goal of collective public worship. By enacting the ritual,
the vignerons asserted their religious faith, demonstrated their professional pride and identity, focused their hopes for next year's harvest, and reestablished the sacred, ancient bond of friendship and
protection with their patron saint. Yet the illegal seizing of the church
also endowed certain members of the community with new status and
authority at the expense of the retreating mayor. In this case, two
groups, the women who led the riot and the lay ministers who led the
worship, asserted their own positions as arbiters of cultural expression and as collective decision makers in the village.

   In recent years, historians of collective action have paid attention
not only to the social background of the rioters but also to the ritualized and dramatic patterns of crowd behavior. They have studied
the meaning, motivation, and ritualized elements of violent activism
and asked how protesters expressed communal views.[2] This fruitful
approach has enabled historians to examine the role of the community in defining the notions of legitimacy and justice that influence
popular violence. Historians have used this form of inquiry to illustrate the autonomy and "moral economy" of various activists, from
strikers to grain rioters, and to link crowd behavior patterns to their
broader cultural context and significance. At times, however, this
influential method has led historians to exaggerate communal consensus and play down the power of riot to express internal conflicts,
to bring about cultural transformation, and to realign prestige,
power, or roles within the community.[3]

   [2]E. P. Thompson, "The Moral Economy of the English Crowd in the Eighteenth
Century," *Past and Present* 50 (1971): 76–136; Natalie Zemon Davis, "The Rites of
Violence," in her *Society and Culture in Early Modern France*, pp. 152–87. These two
articles have influenced much work on collective activism.
   [3]For critiques and commentary on this approach, see Suzanne Desan, "Crowds,
Community, and Ritual in the Work of E. P. Thompson and Natalie Davis," in *The New
Cultural History*, ed. Lynn Hunt (Berkeley, Calif., 1989), pp. 47–71; Janine Estèbe and
Natalie Zemon Davis, "Debate: The Rites of Violence: Religious Riot in Sixteenth-
Century France," *Past and Present* 67 (1975): 127–35; Clifford Geertz, "Blurred Gen-
res: The Refiguration of Social Thought," in *Local Knowledge*, pp. 19–35, esp. 26–30;
M. Greengrass, "The Anatomy of a Religious Riot at Toulouse," *Journal of Ecclesiastical
History* 34 (1983): 367–91, esp. 389–91; Robert Holton, "The Crowd in History: Some
Problems of Theory and Method," *Social History* 3.2 (1978): 219–33; Michael Taussig,
"History as Sorcery," *Representations* 7 (1984): 87–109, esp. 106, 109 n. 20.

In my analysis of religious riots, I too ask how the protesters legitimized their violence. Yet I wish to emphasize two points of departure
from much of this recent literature on communal violence. First, the
forging of a language of religious protest was no simple appropriation of available symbols and rituals. Rather, it was an experimental,
tenuous, and often violent process, which drew on an amalgam of the
tradition and the new and which in turn transformed the political and
religious cultures it touched. Rioters created spiritual and political
authority by fusing traditional popular culture with new revolutionary techniques. In particular, male and female activists drew at times
on the power of religious ritual, on the traditional violence and mocking customs of the Old Regime, and on revolutionary politics, especially its validation of popular sovereignty and collective action. Yet
in this contested process of symbolic appropriation, they transformed
traditional religious rituals, ascribed new and controversial meanings
to revolutionary ideology, and faced the constant opposition of those
who interpreted and used some of the same symbols and language
differently.

Second, in the highly politicized context of revolution, the rioters'
efforts to invest their actions with authority did not always reflect
communal solidarity. Illegal religious violence had a nuanced range
of effects on the community. Collective action could effectively unify
the parish against outside forces, but it could also spark and fuel local
power struggles, which often pitted Catholic moderates against radical dechristianizers. Moreover, in many cases, religious violence had a
social and cultural rather than purely political impact on the community. Whether the community stood solidly behind Catholicism or
found itself torn by factionalism, activism often reallocated roles and
prestige. For example, lay leaders, especially lay ministers, augmented their spiritual authority and created new forms of religious
expression through rioting. Above all, women created power and
identity and carved out a sphere of cultural influence as the dominant
leaders of goal-oriented religious riots in either divided or united
communities. Their activism would affect female spirituality and
women's position in the community over the longer term, ultimately
contributing to the feminization of religion in the nineteenth century.

Religiosity, Riot, and Ritual

Catholic collective activism and violence took several distinctive,
forms. Sometimes groups of villagers, most often with women in the

Table 8. Religious riots by goal and time period

Goals	July 1794–Sept. 1795	Sept. 1795–Sept. 1797	Sept. 1797–Nov. 1799	Total	Percentage
Church use	23	0	15	38	28
Rectory	4	22	3	29	22
Illegal festivals/ anticalendar	0	4	23	27	20
Statues, crosses, bells/ringing	4	2	6	12	9
Defense of curé	0	5	7	12	9
Attacks on republican symbols	4	1	7	12	9
Attacks on republicans	4	5	1	10	7
Miscellaneous	0	0	3	3	2
Totals (by goals)[a]	39	39	65	143	
Total incidents[b]	34	37	63	134	

Sources: AD Yonne, the police des cultes and court records, departmental, district, and municipal deliberations; AN esp. the F7 (police) and F19 (cults) series; BN newspapers; archives communales within the Yonne.

[a] In most cases riots had one main goal. However, those that obviously had more than one central goal are classified under more than one category of "Goals."

[b] Religious riots include religious gatherings of large groups of people who took action that was violent or highly threatening, not acts of religious violence by isolated individuals.

lead, took direct and coercive action to reclaim or defend the sacred spaces, leaders, objects, and rituals of their faith. They might assemble en masse to demand church keys, defend a priest from arrest, or prevent the demolition of an outdoor cross. As illustrated in Table 8, between Thermidor and Napoleon's takeover, the largest percentage of religious riots in the Yonne arose over church use, especially as villagers tried to reopen churches in 1794–1795 and to combat their renewed closings in 1797–1799. Conflicts over the rectory motivated nearly a quarter of Catholic riots, primarily between 1795 and 1797 when the national government attempted to promote republican schoolteachers and house them in rectories. Finally, 9 percent of religious riots involved the defense of the priest himself; another 9 percent centered on the protection or reclamation of sacred objects, such as crosses or bells. Women were virtually always in the forefront of these goal-oriented religious riots.

Less explicitly religious violence could spring up on the occasion of Catholic celebrations, especially saints' festivals. Although women participated in this form of collective action, they were less likely to initiate it. Whether villagers were dancing, selling vegetables, or forming a religious procession, republican authorities viewed the observation of the traditional, rather than the revolutionary, calendar as political provocation and sometimes came into conflict with participants. Illegal festivals and calendar disputes prompted a fifth of the religious confrontations in the Yonne. As Table 8 shows, by far the majority of these conflicts occurred in the period between September 1797 and December 1799 when the national government sought to enforce the republican calendar during its second dechristianization campaign. Finally, religious violence arose when Catholics attacked or mocked the symbols or supporters of revolutionary cults. Villagers might clandestinely cut down a liberty tree under cover of night or publicly perform a charivari to humiliate a married priest or a particularly authoritarian official. Attacks on republican symbols occurred slightly more often than attacks on republican individuals, and most took place immediately after the passage of Napoleon's first laws allowing Catholics to reclaim certain churches. Apparently, triumphant Catholics felt they could finally take revenge on rival revolutionary cults.

Participants in religious riots came from varied backgrounds within towns and villages and seem to have represented a cross section of the Third Estate in Old Regime rural society. Allegiance to Catholicism did not divide along class lines, and religious violence in the Yonne did not express the demands of poorer citizens against local elites.[4] The prominence of women was the most noteworthy social pattern within the rioting crowd. Illegal religious activism was also geographically widespread in the Yonne. In the districts of Auxerre, Saint-Fargeau, and Saint-Florentin, about one-third of the communes witnessed at least one religious riot during the later 1790s. Even the

---

[4]Most reports provide strikingly little information on the background of rioters, but those sources that mention occupation list a wide variety of professions, from day laborer to notable or propriétaire. Vignerons, cultivateurs, and various kinds of artisans were also frequent participants. AN F1cIII Yonne 9, PV de l'agent et commissaire d'Héry, 8 fructidor an VII (25 August 1799); AD Yonne L715, Lettre de l'agent national de Préhy à l'administration du district d'Auxerre, 12 ventôse an III (2 March 1795), L1281, Interrogatoire du juge de paix du canton de Toucy, 3 thermidor an IV (21 July 1796), L76, Arrêté du département de l'Yonne, 9 germinal an VII (29 March 1799), L1286, PV du commissaire de Treigny, 20 thermidor an VI (7 August 1798).

quieter regions—the Senonais, Avallonais, and Tonnerrois—all experienced collective religious activism in at least one-tenth of their towns and villages (see Chapter 2, Table 3 and Map 4).

Catholic activists aimed above all to promote the public, collective expression of their faith. A variety of factors motivated villagers to demand the right to practice in public, but most had a strong desire to reaffirm the age-old validity of their religious beliefs. Public, collective worship would loudly reinforce their religious convictions, attract other believers, and create solidarity in opposition to rival revolutionary cults. With a conviction akin to the moral economy of grain rioters who appropriated grain wagons and fixed prices, the Catholic rioters of the Yonne used their religious words and actions to create their own authority and to justify their appropriation of sacred symbols, spaces, and times.[5] When the parishioners of Saint-Martin of Chablis rioted to prevent an inventory of their church goods, the *procureur* of the commune commented, "The majority of the people regard the excesses of the furious rioters not as a crime, but as an *act of religious devotion,* and far from blaming them, they heap praise upon them and see as their enemies only those who desire a return to order" (my emphasis). In the aftermath of these illegal religious gatherings, the arrested rioters generally played down the dangerous political potential of their actions and emphasized their feeling that they had a religious right and duty to fulfill. Virtually none of them ever expressed regrets or apologies. Marie Duru testified in 1795 that she had rung the church bell "to call people to mass. It was out of habit." When the national agent of Mailly-le-Chateau asked Catholics why they had assembled in the Temple of the Supreme Being in December 1794, they cried out, "To pray to God," and then chased the official from their former church.[6] Like many Catholics in the Yonne, they believed that religious faith and communal custom legitimized their violence.

[5]Thompson, "Moral Economy." On communal attitudes and price fixing, see also R. B. Rose, "Eighteenth-Century Price Riots and Public Policy in England," *International Review of Social History* 6 (1961): 277–92; William A. Reddy, "The Textile Trade and the Language of the Rioting Crowd at Rouen, 1752–1871," *Past and Present* 74 (1977): 62–89; Louise A. Tilly, "The Food Riot as a Form of Political Conflict in France," *Journal of Interdisciplinary History* 2.1 (1971): 23–58.

[6]AD Yonne L712, Lettre de Charon, procureur de Chablis au ministre de la police, 10 janvier 1792, L1118, PV du comité révolutionnaire d'Auxerre, 28 nivôse an III (17 January 1795), L1407, Lettre de l'agent national de Mailly-le-Chateau au comité révolutionnaire d'Auxerre, 11 frimaire an III (1 December 1794).

At the heart of religious violence in the Yonne lay the defense of ritual: whether they reclaimed the church as its arena, the bell as its voice, the curé as its intermediary, or the *fête patronale* as its enactment, religious activists were proclaiming that ritual would continue to create a context for expressing their emotions, patterning their relationships, and marking out the rhythms of their everyday life from season to season. Ritual gave the riot both goal and form; it provided the context, occasion, location, and means for religious riot. Yet the relationship between ritual and violence took on different forms. An exploration of the riot-ritual connection not only illustrates a powerful technique used by rioters; it also helps to clarify the complex intertwining of the spiritual and the political within community power struggles.

In some cases, the relationship between violence and ritual was straightforward: activists often performed a ritual as the goal and culmination of a religious riot, especially after entering a church illegally. Although this ceremony expressed religious beliefs, it could also be politically defiant. After the Catholics of Treigny had attacked the home of the local commissaire, according to the administrators of the Yonne, they infuriated him even further by celebrating "a solemn mass to insult the republican institutions by triumphantly and insolently performing one of the premier ceremonies consecrated to superstition."[7]

Activists also used riot to extend their religious power. For although rioters often sought to restore traditional practices, riot could also become a fulcrum for the transformation of religious expression, especially by promoting lay cults. Villagers, charged with the excitement of riot and inspired by the revolutionary situation, extended the autonomous action of rioting to independent lay expression within ritual as well. Religious activists often crowned their rebellion with lay-led ceremonies. In late November 1794 when the villagers of Isle-sur-Serein broke into their village church and then pressured the reluctant mayor into surrendering the church keys, they celebrated their victory by ringing the church bells, singing a Te Deum led by the local schoolteacher, and lighting a triumphant "bonfire of joy" in front of the village church.[8] Lay riots prepared the way for popular acceptance of lay-led ceremonies.

[7]AN F7 7487, Lettre de l'administration départementale de l'Yonne au ministre de la police, 15 fructidor an VI (1 September 1798).

[8]AN DIII 305, Rapport des membres du tribunal du district d'Avallon au comité de

Ritual could also act as a powerful technique to guarantee the success of an illegal *rassemblement*. The repeated and ritualized patterns of religious ceremony endowed the riot with both purpose and authority while enabling the uprising to achieve its goal. In the village of Saint-Bris, for example, the four to five hundred Catholics who gathered illegally to sing offices in front of their parish church one Sunday in 1794 refused to stop singing when the municipal officers came to disperse them.[9] Instead, the crowd used the hymns as a shield of legitimacy as well as an expression of their collective faith. Religious ritual within riot had power because it *seemed* to speak for the community as a whole; ritual proclaimed the unity, legitimacy, and traditional authority of a particular cultural system. Indeed, in a community unified behind the revival of Catholicism, the symbolic act of the mass legitimized the rioters' violence, and the ringing of the church bell—irrepressible, noisy, and defiant—voiced communal consensus for a shared world view.

But revolutionary politics had factionalized many villages and all the large towns of the Yonne. Divisions might follow family feuds, deep-rooted Old Regime quarrels, or more recent ideological conflicts. In small villages, rioters might face the opposition of only a few neighbors and local authority figures. In these various situations, Catholics often had only a tenuous hold over cultural perceptions and legitimacy; at least they faced challenges and rivals. Thus religious activists used ritual to dramatize power and unity that they in fact lacked. In Irancy in 1798 an audacious band of Catholics performed a threatening procession in part to intimidate a handful of local dechristianizers and officials. Ostentatiously carrying arms as well as the host and other sacred symbols, the Catholics, who "benefited from their great number," paraded through the streets of their village.

---

législation, 9 frimaire an III (29 November 1794); AN F7 4575, Arrêté du comité de sécurité générale, 28 frimaire an III (18 December 1794); AC Isle-sur-Serein, Dépôt 404, Délibérations du conseil municipal d'Isle-sur-Serein, 3, 6 frimaire, 7, 8 nivôse an III (23, 26 November, 27, 28 December 1794). For other examples of the use of the *feu de joie* and other rituals of triumph, see AC Auxerre, P5 Dépôt 3, Lettres de l'administration départementale de l'Yonne à la municipalité d'Auxerre, 6 messidor an VI (24 June 1798), 28 thermidor an VI (15 August 1798). The departmental administrators complained first about the gunshots and bonfire to commemorate the festival of Saint John in Auxerre and then about ostentatious music and a procession on the feast of the Assumption.
    [9]AN DIII 305, Rapport par Bouranet, accusateur public du département de l'Yonne, au comité législatif, 8 prairial an II (27 May 1794).

Religious and political motives mingled as they strove to project the image of moral authority and unanimity even as they were forging them in reality. In fact, afterward the curé Bichot enjoyed a temporary upsurge in popularity and sacerdotal action until the government authorities noticed this and had him deported. Ritual acted as both tool and triumph, means and end of the religious riot.[10]

Ritual could be associated with collective activism in another way. Riots or conflicts often arose out of a ritual context and mushroomed beyond their ritual origins. On a few occasions, Catholics interrupted or sabotaged a Theophilanthropist or revolutionary festival.[11] Far more frequently, illegal Catholic celebrations, particularly outdoor festivals and processions, ignited confrontations. The conflicts arising out of this ritual context were not necessarily religious. Beyond their religious significance, saints' days in particular possessed social, economic, and—during the Revolution—political aspects: they were social gatherings and market days, comprising moments of business exchange, merry-making, dancing, gossip, courtship, and relaxation after the harvest or sowing. In addition, by honoring a particular patron saint, villagers cultivated their sacred friendship, promoted the communal identity of the village, and clarified the hierarchical relationship of inhabitants to the structure of the community.[12] Catholics resented the new calendar, which disrupted patterns of sociability, work, and seasonal commemoration and sought to inculcate a whole new set of values emphasizing hard work, austere morality, patriotism, and most of all, a more secular and "rational" mindset. In short, since the celebration of Catholic holidays invariably combined

[10]AD Yonne L992, PVs de l'administration cantonale de Cravant, 10 messidor an VI (28 June 1798), 5e jour complémentaire an VI (21 September 1798).
[11]AN F1CIII Yonne 8, Lettre du commissaire de l'Yonne au ministre de l'intérieur, 4 ventôse an VII (22 February 1799); AD Yonne L734, Lettre des citoyens de Malay-le-Petit au commissaire près le tribunal de Sens, 19 nivôse an VII (8 January 1799), Information faite par le juge de paix de la police judiciaire de Véron, 27 nivôse–3 pluviôse an VII (16–22 January 1799), Lettre de l'agent municipal de Malay au ministre de la justice, 27 pluviôse an VII (15 February 1799). See also Henri Forestier, "Catholiques et théophilanthropes dans l'Yonne à la veille du Concordat," Echo de Saint-Pierre d'Auxerre 35 (1961): 3–5.
[12]Charles Phythian-Adams, "Ceremony and the Citizen: The Communal Year at Coventry, 1450–1550," in P. Clark and P. Slack, eds., Crisis and Order in English Towns, 1500–1700 (London, 1972): 57–85; David Underdown, Revel, Riot, and Rebellion: Popular Politics and Culture in England, 1603–1660 (Oxford, 1985). For illustrations of the diverse markets on traditional saints' days, see Arrêté du canton de Sens, 28 floréal an VI (17 May 1798), as reprinted in BN, Observateur de l'Yonne, 15 thermidor an VI (2 August 1798).

sacred and profane activities, it is often hard to untangle religious motivations from the desire for recreation, commerce, or political opposition.

In some cases, the conjuncture of a religious festival with another reason for discontent could impel an illegal gathering in a patently political and violent direction. In 1796 a requisitioner from Auxerre narrowly escaped the furor of the crowd when he tried to requisition horses on First Communion day in the commune of Saint-Privé; the commissaire of Bléneau complained the next Sunday that the Catholics of Saint-Privé had attacked him and threatened to "kill him and eat his liver" for not going to mass.[13] In the eyes of the villagers, the political (and unpopular) act of requisitioning was bound up with the cultural dispute over religion.

Nonetheless, many Catholics ardently defended the traditional calendar for liturgical and devotional reasons. In many instances, the religious origin of conflict is clear. The commissaire of the Yonne and other officials regularly called in gendarmes to suppress pilgrimages and outdoor religious processions led by priests, lay ministers, or groups of women. At the festival of Sainte Béate in Avrolles, for example, fifty gendarmes were called in to squelch dancing as well as illegal religious ceremonies. The curé Mathieu Picard faced deportation for ringing the church bell and saying mass.[14]

In fact, Catholic villagers during the Revolution frequently took advantage of the lack of clerical supervision to participate in festivals that the Catholic reformers, and the Jansenists even more so, had tried to suppress, or at least control, especially if the celebrations included long-distance outdoor processions or raucous festivities. As the curé of Tronchoy commented in his own defense to the cantonal administrators of Epineuil, "Haven't I been forced to concede to the wishes of the inhabitants and *celebrate festivals suppressed many years ago, but to which they are still attached?*" (my emphasis). The commissaire of Saint-Fargeau, sounding like a reforming bishop, complained in

[13]AN F19 1017, Rapport de l'agent de Saint-Privé au commissaire du canton de Bléneau, 3 prairial an IV (22 May 1796), Lettre du commissaire de Bléneau au ministre de la police, 8 prairial an IV (27 May 1796).

[14]AD Yonne L217, Lettre du commissaire de l'Yonne au ministre de la police, messidor an VII (June–July 1799), L1322, PV du tribunal de la police de Tonnerre, 1 brumaire an VII (22 October 1798), L217, Lettre des patriotes de Sainpuits à l'administration départementale de l'Yonne, 15 prairial an VII (3 June 1799); Henri Auclerc, *Les curés d'Avrolles pendant la Révolution française* (Auxerre, 1949), pp. 14–17.

1796 about the "drunk" parishioners of Lavau, who had stirred up a troublesome *rassemblement* on their saint's day: "After an orgy, which Saint Eloi has commanded since the old days, [they] flocked to the church and rang the bell freely at noon."[15]

Saints' festivals constituted at least 45 percent and probably closer to 65 percent of the illegal festivals in the late 1790s.[16] Catholic activists held festivals in honor of the Virgin Mary, Saint Jean-Baptiste, and local village patrons, such as Saint Germain of Irancy or Saint Louis of Héry. The saintly protectors of professions and confraternities—such as Saint Fiacre, patron of gardeners, or Saint Vincent, guardian of wine producers throughout Burgundy—also benefited from the tried and true allegiance of Catholic activists. Villagers' devotion and loyalty to their saints withstood not only the passage of time but also the repeated suppression attempts by Catholic reformers and revolutionary dechristianizers alike.

In fact, the defense of saints' festivals during the Revolution provides clues to the choices, successes, and failures of the Catholic Reformation. Illegal festivals in the Yonne during the Directory honored at least twelve of the twenty saints who could claim the most images, chapels, and confraternities to their names in the diocese of Auxerre in the seventeenth century. Statues of all but one of these saints had been singled out for disapproval in the late seventeenth century by Catholic reform bishops who found them too "indecent," "malformed," "grotesque," or "degraded by the presence of animals." None of these saints, however, had suffered the particularly harsh repression allotted to those whose life stories or representations seemed most inappropriate or offensive. In the diocese of Auxerre, for example, reforming bishops had mixed results in encouraging devotion to Christ and Mary at the expense of saints in general, but Caylus and the Colberts had been markedly successful in doing away

---

[15]AN F7 7424, Lettre du curé de Tronchoy, Jean-François-Joseph Gantès, à l'administration cantonale d'Epineuil, 20 ventôse an VI (10 March 1798); AD Yonne L210, Lettre du commissaire de Saint-Fargeau au celui de l'Yonne, 20 frimaire an v (10 December 1796).

[16]Of the 109 reported illegal Catholic festivals, 45 percent were saints' days, 20 percent were other specific Catholic holy days, 18 percent were other unclear holy days, 10 percent were funerals of well-known individuals, and 7 percent were carnivals in large towns. Undoubtedly, many illegal festivals, especially in the Avallonais, went unreported. Sources on festival statistics include AD Yonne, the police des cultes and court records, departmental, district, and municipal deliberations; AN, esp. the F7 (police) and F19 (cults) series; BN, newspapers; and various archives communales.

with the images and cults of certain targeted saints, such as Sebastien, Martin, and Georges.[17]

Although it is hard to gauge the devotional content and meaning of villagers' attachment to saints' festivals, the persistent celebration during the postfructidorean era of feast days that both the clerical hierarchy and the central government had successively tried to suppress suggests a tenacious and deep devotion. The saints' humanity, their sensitivity and vulnerability, allied them more closely to believers and made them uniquely appealing intercessors and friends.[18] The parishioners of Ligny articulated this special bond when they pleaded in 1792 for the relics of Saint Edme from the disbanded Abbey of Pontigny. "Ligny has been the theater where Saint Edme has . . . performed the most astounding miracles; he even seems to have a special favor for this parish; in gratitude for this apostolic tenderness, this parish has consecrated itself to him with the most absolute devotion; they are afraid they will not be able to carry on if their petition is rejected, refusal will spread consternation in the hearts of all. But what joy, what gladness if their request is granted!"[19]

Many Catholics felt that during the dechristianization campaigns of 1793–1794 and 1797–1799 the saints had been polluted or held in bondage; their bones had been scattered, their statues smashed or clothed in the alien guise of "goddesses of reason." At various times during the later 1790s, as Catholics peeled the masks off their old saints, gathered them together, dug them out of hiding, and restored them to positions of honor, the villagers welcomed them back and celebrated the renewal of their link between heaven and earth. The rediscovery of the saint expressed the confidence of the revival. On their saints' special days, Catholic villagers could only ask, "Why not dance?"

---

[17]Roudil, "Vie religieuse," p. 66 and tableau III. See also Roudil, "Vie religieuse et mentalité collective dans le diocèse d'Auxerre de 1672 à 1712," unpublished paper, pp. 9–18 and tableau I. Of the twenty most popular saints reported by Roudil, Jean-Baptiste, Vincent, Pierre, Nicolas, Laurent, Lazare, Eloi, Fiacre, Roch, Louis, Jacques, and Catherine (as well as the Virgin Mary and some less popular saints) were mentioned in the reports of revolutionary government commissaires as the patrons of illegal *rassemblements*. The Colberts and Caylus had suppressed certain statues of all of these saints, except Saint Lazare.

[18]For a discussion of the nature of the bond between believers and saints, see Peter Brown, *The Cult of the Saints* (Chicago, 1981), pp. 56–68, 92–94; Luria, *Territories of Grace*, chaps. 5, 6.

[19]AD Yonne L707, Pétition des habitants de Ligny-le-Châtel à l'administration départementale de l'Yonne, 9 janvier 1792.

In sum, as villagers celebrated saints' festivals, they reforged an ancient alliance with their sacred friends and took advantage of the revolutionary flux to reassert customs attacked by Catholic reformers and revolutionary authorities alike. Opponents of the revival, such as the editor of the republican newspaper of Sens, *Observateur de l'Yonne*, were well aware that Catholics returned to rituals the church had long ago condemned. Bemoaning the "follies" of the carnival, Benoist-Lamothe asked, "How is it possible to reconcile this attachment of some people to pagan institutions with their apparent zeal for a religion that has always outlawed them?"[20] His question could well have been asked for very different reasons by the Catholic Reformation Bishop Nicolas Colbert over a century earlier.

These festivals included both secular and religious rituals that authorities found particularly threatening. Large festivals have always had the potential of leading to revolt. The combined presence of crowds, strangers, wine, fairs, armed parades, inattentive magistrates, and youths in a rowdy mood could be potentially explosive or disorderly in any age.[21] Although festivals became launching points for revolts, particularly in harsh periods such as the early seventeenth century, in many instances Old Regime festivals acted as an escape valve for village tensions because they contained and condoned violence within a semistructured framework.[22] During the late 1790s, however, outdoor Catholic festivals were illegal and, hence, were protest by definition. Republican officials viewed outdoor processions, illegal gatherings in officially closed churches, and the festive observance of Catholic holy days as demonstrations of political subversion. In 1798, for example, the departmental administrators denounced participants in Catholic festivals for spreading "the spirit of rebellion."[23] The politicization of religious, commercial, and festive days amplified the possibility for confrontation. Whether villagers were solemn, playful, or provocative, trouble could easily occur.

The celebration of holy days sometimes broke beyond ritual into violence even when Catholics defied the authorities in a seemingly

[20]BN, *Observateur de l'Yonne*, 15 pluviôse an VIII (4 February 1800).

[21]Yves-Marie Bercé, *Fête et révolte: Des mentalités populaires du XVIe au XVIIIe siècle* (Paris, 1976), chap. 1.

[22]Ibid., chap. 2, esp. pp. 72–74. See also Emmanuel LeRoy Ladurie, *Carnival in Romans*, trans. Mary Feeney (New York, 1979).

[23]AC Auxerre, Dépôt 3 P5, Lettre de l'administration centrale du département de l'Yonne à ses concitoyens, 15 frimaire an [VI?] (5 December [1797?]).

playful way. Villagers repeatedly used dancing and music to proclaim their religious and political independence. The violin player and villagers of La-Chapelle who played music and danced all through the night on the eve of Saint Nicolas presented a challenge to authorities.[24] Local officials would appear weak if they allowed the dancers to revel in the festive manifestation of their liberty, but the alternative was to display their authoritarianism and use force to suppress the popular desire for the festival.[25] Revolutionary authorities who envisioned a form of politics without factionalism or hidden conspiracy particularly disliked carnival masquerades; they seemed particularly subversive, for they revived "the old customs and ancient prejudices" and, even worse, made a mockery of the revolutionary ideal of transparency and open politics. Some communes, such as Sens and Tonnerre, outlawed the wearing of masks to prevent this furtive and cunning form of festivity.[26]

In short, the relationship among religiosity, ritual, and riot was both powerful and complex. A lay mass as the climax of a church break-in, psalm singing as a tool for drowning out officials' warnings and threats, an outdoor procession as a potentially dangerous moment of heightened collective sensibility—religious ritual could act as end, means, or context of religious riot. Yet this religious violence took place in an unusual structural context. In the eyes of the authorities all outdoor religious gatherings *by definition* broke the law and expressed political defiance. This illegal and oppositional status increased the likelihood that festivals or processions would explode beyond ritual into violence or confrontation. Conversely, the frequent lack of clerical supervision, the confused and often divided nature of secular authority, and the pervasive fluidity of cultural definitions made it all the more likely for riot to enable or even encourage lay independence in ritual. Paradoxically, the religious boldness of the laity, bolstered by the autonomous act of rioting, fostered both the

[24]AD Yonne L1323, PV du tribunal de la police correctionelle de Tonnerre, 11 pluviôse an VII (30 January 1799).

[25]John Berger, "The Nature of Mass Demonstrations," *New Society* 295 (1968): 754–55.

[26]AD Yonne L1356, Information faite sur le carnival de Tonnerre, directeur du jury de l'arrondissement de Tonnerre, 12 germinal an v (1 April 1797), L216, Arrêté de la municipalité de Tonnerre, 1 pluviôse an VI (20 January 1798), L210, Arrêté de la municipalité de Sens, 19 nivôse an v (8 January 1797); BN, *Journal politique et littéraire*, 25 nivôse an v (14 January 1797). On transparency and revolutionary politics, see Hunt, *Politics, Culture, and Class*, pp. 44–46.

inherently conservative resurgence of saints' festivals and the more innovative development of lay cults.

The Power of Traditional and Revolutionary Culture

The link between religious ritual and riot came most strongly to the fore when activists fought for direct control of public and sacred space or time, such as the church building or festival day. But religious activism often took other forms, for the campaign for public worship was part of a much broader power struggle within the community. Old Regime popular culture also offered nonreligious models for voicing and legitimizing popular demands. Activists, as often men as women in this case, tapped the power of violent prerevolutionary customs and burlesques, especially to exert pressure on opponents of Catholicism or to attack the symbols of rival revolutionary cults.

In rural and urban communities of the Old Regime, members of the community, especially young men, had long used various forms of ritualized hostility against individuals or groups who opposed the majority or broke social norms in some way.[27] Ranging from the public ridicule of a charivari to the clandestine threat of a blood-streaked doorpost, these traditional violent or mocking acts spoke a powerful symbolic language and proclaimed the public and communal authority of certain cultural presuppositions. Within the tight boundaries of rural village communities, ritualized humiliation seemed to speak with a frightening and unanimous authority that virtually always made its mark on the victim.

Yet, although these forms of activism created the impression of communal judgment by the whole village, they often allowed participants to remain anonymous or disguised. Thus, ritualized hostility

[27]Davis, "The Reasons of Misrule," in her *Society and Culture*, pp. 97–123. Davis suggests that although ritualized forms of hostility, such as charivaris, usually acted to support the social norms and structures of the community, in certain circumstances they might lead to rebellion (p. 119). See also, Robert Darnton, *The Great Cat Massacre and Other Episodes in French Cultural History* (New York, 1984), esp. chap. 2. Revolutionary activists also drew on the repertoire of Old Regime popular forms of mockery. Dechristianizers, in particular, used burlesque to satirize the clergy and the "superstitious" practices of Catholicism. On this point, for example, Bercé, *Fête et révolte*, pp. 89–90; Bianchi, *Révolution culturelle*, pp. 218–26; Ozouf, *Fête révolutionnaire*, pp. 108–14.

was particularly effective against authority figures who might be too powerful to attack directly.[28] When they attempted to oppose or limit the practice of Catholicism, government officials, purchasers of *biens nationaux*, and republican schoolteachers all had the official power of the law on their side, but they were intensely vulnerable to the unofficial shaming and violence of angry villagers. Confronted in 1797 with mockeries designed "to harass the purchasers [of *biens nationaux*]," the authorities in Lasson were stymied: "It would be difficult to find the source [of the harassments]; they are so *public and common.* [emphasis added]" No one ever caught the people who fired warning shots at the home of the commissaire of Cérisiers when he returned from Sens with collections of Theophilanthropist hymns and verses to convert his commune.[29] The authors of a satirizing or threatening action certainly did not have to be known to be effective.

Ritualized acts of hostility could take either clandestine or blatantly public and noisy forms. Sometimes villagers acted under the cloak of night to give symbolic warnings to fellow villagers. On the night following the arrest of two local priests in 1796, the Catholics of La-Ferté-Loupière put streaks of blood on the doors of the Jacobin opponents of the revival, while the villagers of Junay, Ancy-le-Franc, and elsewhere cut the fruit trees and vines of the local agents who sought to enforce the republican calendar.[30] Villagers used nocturnal attacks on liberty trees to express various kinds of dissatisfaction with republican institutions, including disapproval of the republican calendar and anti-Catholic laws.[31]

[28]E. P. Thompson, "Rough music: Le charivari anglais," *Annales: Economies, sociétés, civilisations* 27 (1972): 290. See also James Scott, *Weapons of the Weak: Everyday Forms of Peasant Resistance* (New Haven, Conn., 1985), chap. 7.

[29]AD Yonne L715, PV de l'agent municipal de Lasson, 17 fructidor an v (3 September 1797); BN, *Observateur de l'Yonne*, 15 nivôse an VII (4 January 1799).

[30]AN F19 1017, Lettre du commissaire de La-Ferté-Loupière au citoyen Jean Précy, représentant du peuple, 20 floréal an IV (9 May 1796); AN F7 7189, Lettre des deux citoyens de Junay au ministre de la police, n.d. [c. vendémiaire an v (September–October 1796)]; AD Yonne L75, Arrêté du département de l'Yonne, 22 vendémiaire VII (13 October 1798); AN F1CIII Yonne 7, Comtes analytiques du commissaire de l'Yonne, pluviôse–ventôse an VII (January–March 1799), thermidor an VI (July–August 1798); AN F7 3699², Lettre de l'administration départementale de l'Yonne au ministre de la police, 11 brumaire an v (1 November 1796).

[31]It is difficult to pinpoint the exact motivation behind mutilating or chopping down liberty trees, and often it is impossible to gauge the religious element within the attacker's discontent. Particularly in the aftermath of the fructidorean coup d'état in 1797, local officials became greatly concerned about the frequency of attacks on liberty trees. See esp. AN F1CIII Yonne 7, Rapport par le commissaire de l'Yonne, thermidor an VI (July–August 1798); AD Yonne L218, Lettre du ministre de la police au commissaire de l'Yonne, 19 germinal an VII (8 April 1799).

Although these villagers chose to act in secrecy to guard their anonymity, they in fact intended the results of their nighttime actions to
become painfully public the next morning. Their secretive attacks
often graphically conveyed a specific symbolic message. For example,
the Catholics of Egriselles-le-Bocage disliked the local commissaire's
attempts to enforce the republican calendar, so they gave him a taste
of his own medicine. To prevent him from working on Sunday, they
disassembled his plow and hung each individual part from a nearby
elm tree without losing or stealing a single piece. The next morning
the commissaire stubbornly reassembled the plow, worked until sun-
set that Sunday, and declared that the villagers' attempt to "frighten"
him had failed.[32]

Frequently, the derision of opponents of the revival was public,
theatrical, and noisy from start to finish. When the former curé of
Sergines married in 1799, a group of "women, children, and even
men" conducted a charivari outside his house the evening of his wedding day; they shouted insults and threats, threw rocks through his
windows, and tore down the merchant clothier signboard from above
his door. Their actions vividly illustrated their disapproval of the
obvious breach—his marriage—and also attacked the symbol of his
new, nonreligious profession as a cloth merchant.[33]

In their public assaults on individuals or their property, Catholic
villagers plainly claimed to be speaking for the community as a whole,
whether or not this was the case. Particularly if the conflict involved
the church building or rectory, Catholic villagers, especially women,
often shouted out their claims of communal prerogative in the midst
of the riot. When the women of Sacy rioted in 1797 to prevent the
acquéreur Edme Champeaux from moving into his newly purchased
rectory, they announced boldly to the local agent that "the building
belonged to them rather than to Champeaux," and insisted, "It is our
business and our property." The women supported their claims of
ownership with direct action both symbolic and practical: two times in
succession they removed all the doors and windows of the rectory and

---

[32]AD Yonne L217, Bulletin de la police de l'Yonne, 29 floréal an VII (18 May 1799).
[33]AD Yonne L717, Lettre du commissaire de Sergines au commissaire de l'Yonne, 27
fructidor an VI (13 September 1798), PV de l'administration départementale de
l'Yonne, 29 fructidor an VI (15 September 1798), L213, Lettre du ministre de la police à
l'administration départementale de l'Yonne, 15 fructidor an VI (1 September 1798);
BN, *Observateur de l'Yonne*, 15 vendémiaire an VII (6 October 1798). This charivari
resembled those taking place at weddings in the Auxerrois in the Old Regime, especially when a villager married an outsider. Roudil, "Vie religieuse," pp. 86–88.

hid them. The implication was clear: only the Catholics of the village would control the entering and exiting of the rectory.[34]

Catholics' conception of community seems to have incorporated both the devotional community of believers who worshiped together and the parish community of inhabitants who owned the church, rectory, and cemetery—all "built by our ancestors." The parishioners of Avallon who broke into their churches illegally in the spring of 1795 "saw these buildings as their property, which they had the right to use as they wished." The citizens who were accused of stealing and burying their church bell at Puits-de-Bon "didn't think they had done anything wrong; they thought of themselves as the owners of the chapel." Just as ritual sought to illustrate and recreate the communion of belief, direct action in riot expressed the community of ownership or control.[35]

Finally, in many cases large groups would act in concert to shield the anonymity of those who had broken the law on behalf of the "community of believers." Various commissaires searched in vain for those who broke into the parish churches of Saint-Cydroine and Bussy-en-Othe under the shadow of night in the winter of 1798–1799. Despite the small size of these villages, in each case the parishioners who assembled illegally early the following morning to sing offices claimed to have no idea who had taken action to reestablish public practice for the parish as a whole.[36]

Sometimes when Catholics proclaimed with words, actions, or rituals that they spoke for the community, they in fact faced local opposition. In 1791–1792 and again in a few places in 1795, rifts had occurred within the Catholic community between supporters of Constitutional clergy and those who remained loyal to nonjurors. During the Directory, however, the Constitutional Church had become so weak that such intra-Catholic disputes were less frequent. Rather, Catholics most often opposed Theophilanthropists or supporters of

[34]AN F7 7233, Lettre du commissaire de Vermenton au Villetard, député du peuple de l'Yonne, 31 pluviôse an v [sic] [c. 19 February 1797]; AD Yonne L716, PVs de la commune de Sacy, 23, 25, 26, 27 pluviôse an v (11, 13, 14, 15 February 1797).

[35]AN F7 4439[1], Lettre du Comité de sécurité générale à Mailhe, représentant en mission, 26 germinal an III (15 April 1795); M. Maillot, "Noyers pendant la Révolution," BSSY 50 (1896): 5–44; AD Yonne L715, PV de la recherche de la cloche au hameau de Puits-de-Bon, 5 fructidor an VI (22 August 1798).

[36]AD Yonne L716, Lettre du commissaire de Saint-Cydroine au celui de l'Yonne, 4 pluviôse an VII (23 January 1799), L218, Lettre du ministre de la police au commissaire de l'Yonne, 20 nivôse an VII (9 January 1799).

the revolutionary cults. The highly theatrical yet flexible nature of Old Regime burlesque provided a rich repertoire of actions with which to play out political and religious rivalries. For example, emboldened by the election of pro-Catholic officials and by a new law promising the reopening of local churches, a group of Catholic youths in Flogny in early 1800 rang the church bells, entered the *temple décadaire,* and made a huge bonfire of the Theophilanthropists' garlands and inscriptions. The celebrators reportedly also hanged three local officials in effigy from a makeshift gallows and burned a dog adorned with a tricolor ribbon to represent the former commissaire. In retaliation several days later a rival group of agitators, apparently Theophilanthropists this time, held a mock trial of the statues of saints from the local church/temple and condemned them to death. To carry out the "execution," these youths paraded the lighter wooden statues through the streets of the village to be dumped into a canal on the outskirts of Flogny. This inversion of the solemn religious processions in which the statues were carried in triumph to a place of honor in the church denuded the saints of supernatural power and left them lying in a ditch.

This incident illustrates the continual battle to appropriate and distort rival symbol systems on one's own behalf. Furthermore, the period of agitation in Flogny coincided with the political turmoil following Napoleon's takeover. The Catholic and Theophilanthropist factions alike used the ritualized tools of popular culture of the Old Regime—the bonfire, the effigy, the mock trial, and execution by drowning—not only to attack the symbols and underlying cultural systems of their rivals but also to align themselves with local political factions. The burlesque inversions were illegal but potent political and cultural statements made in the context of village power struggles.[37]

As this incident at Flogny suggests, Catholics sometimes removed

[37]AD Yonne L713, PV de l'administration cantonale de Flogny, 16 nivôse an VIII (6 January 1800), Lettre du commissaire de Flogny au commissaire de l'Yonne, 23 nivôse an VIII (13 January 1800); AN F1cIII Yonne 10, Lettre du juge de paix du canton de Flogny au ministre de l'intérieur, 28 nivôse an VIII (18 January 1800); AN F19 481⁴⁻⁵, Rapport du commissaire de Flogny au ministre de l'intérieur, 8 pluviôse an VIII (28 January 1800), Lettres du juge de paix du canton de Flogny au ministre de l'intérieur, 6, 11 pluviôse an VIII (26, 31 January 1800), PV de l'administration centrale de l'Yonne, 21 nivôse an VIII (11 January 1800). On similar youth behavior in the Old Regime, see Henri Forestier, "Les 'droits des garçons' dans la communauté villageoise aux XVIIe et XVIIIe siècles," *AB* 13 (1941): 109–14; Roudil, "Vie religieuse," pp. 86–88.

and destroyed revolutionary symbols as part of their triumphant re-
conquest of churches, particularly in the spring of 1795 and in the
winter of 1799–1800, when Catholics anticipated a loosening of laws
regarding the public practice of Catholicism. To validate their claims,
villagers formally paraded, mutilated, and burned rival symbols. In
April 1795 the Catholics of Toucy forced open the church door, rang
the civic bell, removed the image of Liberty, flaunted it in the streets
and mutilated it; they finally abandoned it in a barn with the tablets of
the Rights of Man and the Constitution, also taken from the church.
Sometimes religious activists used the stolen symbols to express their
political opinions in a dramatic way. To remind elected officials of
their desire for religious freedom, Catholic activists in Joux-la-Ville
moved the statue of Liberty unharmed from the parish church to the
town hall early in 1800. They also tore a canvas painted with an image
of Liberty from chin to knee and from thigh to arm. This graphic
laceration of Liberty's image, reportedly carried out by women and
children, voiced popular protest and disillusionment with a revolution that had not delivered on its promise of freedom.[38]

In effect, religious activists used traditional customs to assert their
opinions and demands in the revolutionary context. Yet religious
activists often fused more traditional methods with revolutionary
techniques or ideology. For Catholics were keenly aware that the Revolution had recast the nature of collective action by transforming the
means, arguments, and framework of popular protest. Revolution
lent the rioters a new validity, new arenas of activism, and new arguments to support popular demand. As I have shown, Catholic villagers had varied attitudes toward the Revolution. Many Catholics,
though they opposed the revolutionary calendar and cults and sometimes attacked revolutionary symbols, believed that the Revolution in
fact guaranteed them the right to religious freedom and to popular
sovereignty. Even during riots, they used these arguments to justify
their popular activism. Religious activists became engaged in a war
with authority figures and republican rivals over the correct meaning
of revolutionary promises. "Where then is liberty if we cannot dance
whenever we wish?" demanded many villagers, confronting gen-

[38]AN F1cIII Yonne 6, Analyse des délibérations de l'administration générale du
département de l'Yonne, pour germinal an III (March–April 1795), 7 germinal an III
(27 March 1795); AN F7 3699², PV par le commissaire de Joux-la-Ville, 29 nivôse an
VIII (19 January 1800).

darmes sent to suppress festivals in 1797.[39] Furthermore, protesters recognized that the revolutionary ideology of popular sovereignty and the proven success of crowd action throughout the 1790s endowed popular protest with particular authority and reinforced its Old Regime validity in the popular mind. Finally, the reformulation of popular politics offered rioters further opportunities for making their wishes known: municipal meetings and primary assemblies became prey to bands of activists, who recognized that numbers meant political authority and not just strength through force.

In fact, Catholics sometimes marched to municipal or cantonal meetings to pressure local elected government officials to heed the popular will. For example, shortly after the germinal an VI (April 1798) elections in Thorigny, a group of citizens who were "irritated at having been defeated in the nomination of republican electors" invaded a governmental meeting of the administrators who had been named during the postfructidorean purges and tried to reinstate the pro-Catholic administrators who had been forced to resign. The rioters refused to leave the administrative session and "claimed to have the right to trouble them in their functions . . . on the pretext that this locale belonged to all the administered inhabitants." In 1795 citizen Degonde led his fellow Catholics of Rogny "to the office of the municipality and beat the drum to call the council to a meeting." When the assembled municipal officers refused to turn over the church keys, Degonde abandoned legal forms of pressure and simply seized the keys by force.[40]

The revolutionary language of rioters illustrated many Catholics' certainty that revolutionary ideology and law not only guaranteed freedom of worship but also reinforced their traditional right to take collective action. Rioters did not necessarily view this rioting as counterrevolutionary. For example, in the spring of 1795 protesters in Mailly-le-Vineux invoked the law of *liberté des cultes* and claimed that to prevent them from entering the Temple of the Supreme Being "was to go against the opinion of the Convention; it was to abolish their freedom to give to God what he deserved, to pay him homage

[39]AN F1cIII Yonne 5, Compte analytique de la situation du département de l'Yonne, par le commissaire, thermidor an VI (July–August 1798).

[40]AN F7 7422, Dénonciation par les administrateurs du département de l'Yonne contre le ministre du culte de Thorigny Perrier au ministre de la police, 23 germinal an VI (12 April 1798), PV du canton de Thorigny, 12 germinal an VI (1 April 1798); Délibérations municipales de Rogny, n.d., [c. spring 1795], as quoted by M. Gauthier, "Rogny et Saint-Eusoge depuis les origines à nos jours," BSSY 50 (1986): 379.

and glory in his temple. They were not even afraid to claim that the Temple of the Supreme Being belonged to them and to attribute the successes of the armies of the Republic to their own prayers." The national agent reported that if he reminded his villagers of the benefits of the Revolution and the conservation of their rights, "they responded, 'All the more reason to return to us the Temple of the Supreme Being.' This is their language." The Catholics in Champs who broke into their church early in 1795 professed loyalty to religion and Republic and observed calmly to the municipal officers that their "assembly was peaceful, that no tumult occurred, nothing against the Revolution and its laws." (They apparently exaggerated their peacefulness.) Likewise, the women of Vaux excused their violent demands for the parish church keys with the comment, "Since everyone had the freedom of opinion, we desired our religion and thought we were authorized to demand it."[41]

Other Catholic activists were more indignant and daring in their repudiation of local authority. In Chichée in the fall of 1794 when some villagers were caught forcing the door to the church bell tower, one of them cried out to the national agent, "Confounded villain! Damned rogue! Show me your orders that you have the right to prevent us from entering the bell tower." He threatened to call together the whole village to revolt against the officers. Just as protesters used religious ritual and communal customs to forge symbolic unity, they reminded authorities that they had the "right" to speak for the community and the ability to call up large numbers to support their demands.[42]

Villagers often gained their understanding of revolutionary ideology or specific laws through secondhand reports or rumors. In the summer of 1797 rumors of Camille Jordan's speech in favor of bell ringing provoked widespread violations as villagers assumed his motion would soon become law. Likewise, authorities in Druyes and Thorigny in the winter of 1798–1799 reported rumors that the *décadis* would soon be suppressed, that the priests would soon return, that many of them had been released from imprisonment at

[41]AD Yonne L207, Lettre de l'agent national de Mailly-le-Vineux au comité révolutionnaire d'Auxerre, 4 pluviôse an III (23 January 1795), L712, PV de la municipalité de Champs, 14 pluviôse an III (2 February 1795), L1118, PV du comité révolutionnaire d'Auxerre, 18 nivôse an III (7 January 1795).
[42]AD Yonne L712, PV de la municipalité de Chichée, 7 brumaire an III (28 October 1794).

Rochefort already, and that Napoleon (not yet even in the country) wanted to reestablish the mass and Catholic worship.[43] Since most rural citizens had a less than perfect grasp of national politics and republican ideology, it became easier for them to reformulate revolutionary notions to complement the traditional moral and religious economy, which validated both riot and public worship.

The revolutionary context and the villagers' declarations of popular support heightened the awareness of republican authorities that they were in a delicate situation. They feared the power of popular activism; even the most radical officials recommended care in handling volatile Catholic peasants and went out of their way to avoid touching off greater popular violence. In 1794 the représentant en mission Maure warned the national agent and municipality of Mont-Armance (Saint-Florentin) that they might have been more prudent in their actions against the "uneducated and misguided" Catholics of Champlost, who poured out of a psalm-singing ceremony to insult and attack supporters of dechristianization. Maure commented, "Your responsibility is terrible if [closing the church] results in disturbances."[44]

At the same time, however, republican officials contested the villagers' attempts to redefine revolutionary ideology on their own terms. When the parishioners of Toucy broke into the church and stole the goddess of Liberty, the deputies of the Yonne urged local authorities to take action; they turned popular claims to "religious liberty" on their head and noted that the rioters had "strangely abused the law on the freedom of religion. The people have been duped." Because officials were aware that certain revolutionary arguments seemed to support the popular desire for religious liberty, it became imperative for authorities in turn to repossess revolutionary ideology and secure its support for dechristianization. They repeatedly proclaimed that Catholicism was not the people's choice but, rather, a subversion of the general will. The municipality of Charny worried that rioters on the illegal market/festival day had added power because "the majority of the inhabitants of this canton contrib-

[43]AN F7 7283, PV du canton d'Epineuil, 22 fructidor an v (8 September 1797); AD Yonne L217, Bulletins de la police, 5 nivôse an vii (25 December 1798), 19 ventôse an vii (9 March 1799), PV de l'administration cantonale de Thorigny, 30 vendémiaire an vii (21 October 1798).

[44]AN AFii 163, dos. 1337, Lettres du représentant Maure à l'agent national de Mont-Armance et à l'administration municipale de Mont-Armance, 5, 6 floréal an ii (24, 25 April 1794).

uted to this revolt with their presence, their warnings, gestures, threats, or assaults," as well as their claims of legal support from the Constitution. To counter this threat of popular choice in action, the municipality pronounced that the priests who supported the celebration of illegal Catholic festivals opposed their "private will to the general will."[45]

Likewise, when the commissaire of Pont-sur-Yonne called for the maintenance of the republican calendar in 1800, he admitted that people had the "right to work and rest as they wished, but we must not confuse this natural liberty of individuals with the political liberty of the city, for which the laws should set the limits and regulate the practices." Revolutionary authorities argued that republican education would eventually overcome the misguided ignorance of the peasantry and refashion them to recognize the true general will. "It will no doubt be sufficient to show the good people the traps held out to them through malevolence," declared the Committee of General Safety optimistically. The district administrators of Mont-Armance, who observed the growing "fanatic" agitations in the aftermath of the fall of Robespierre, wondered, "We don't know which individuals fool the people, but certainly they are fooled [trompé]."[46] In the meantime, activists frequently used their limited republican education for ends quite different from those of the authorities.

Religious Violence and Community Dynamics

As Catholic villagers combined violence with religious ritual, traditional mocking customs, and revolutionary arguments to demand public Catholic practice, their violent collective activism had a number of different possible effects on the village community. Religious vio-

[45]AN F7 4439[1], Lettre de Villetard et Maure, députés du peuple, à Mailhe, représentant en mission, 21 germinal an III (10 April 1795); AD Yonne L217, Arrêté du canton de Charny, 5 thermidor an VI (23 July 1798), PV de Charny, envoyé à l'administration centrale de l'Yonne, 2 brumaire an VII (23 October 1798).
[46]AN F1cIII Yonne 10, Lettre du commissaire de Pont-sur-Yonne au ministre de l'intérieur, 8 pluviôse an VIII (28 January 1800); AN F7 7129, Lettre du ministre de la police au commissaire de Pont-sur-Yonne, 17 pluviôse an IV (6 February 1796); AD Yonne L208, Lettre du Comité de sécurité générale à l'administration municipale de Joigny, 5 frimaire an III (25 November 1794), L707, Lettre de l'administration du district de Mont-Armance au citoyen Etienne Finot, représentant du peuple, 2 sansculotides an II (18 September 1794).

lence could effectively unite or divide the community and could re-
distribute political power. Rioting also affected the informal allocation of power and roles in both divided and united communities.

Religious activism was not necessarily divisive. In communities
where almost everyone supported Catholicism, villagers used riot or
ritualized hostility to take a united stand against a few local officials,
dechristianizers, or Theophilanthropists, or against a detachment of
gendarmes from the cantonal or district administration. The gendarmes who came from Auxerre to arrest the curé of Appoigny faced
the threats and blows of several hundred armed citizens, including
the mayor and several municipal officers; evidently, the commune
was united behind its curé against outside forces. Likewise, in 1799
when gendarmes from Pont-sur-Yonne went to the village of Plessis-
du-Mée to enforce calendar laws prohibiting work on the *décadi,* they
faced the apparently united opposition of "the whole commune." The
gendarmes later claimed that "the whole populace," including all the
men, women, and children, stopped work and gathered to chase them
away with "words and a shower of stones and sticks, which fell on us
like hail." While gendarmes who had failed to enforce a law might
exaggerate the strength and unity of their opposition, their perceptions were often not far wrong. In many villages a large majority of
the heads of household signed the declaration to reclaim the village
church. Even if a few villagers opposed their Catholic neighbors, the
sheer number of Catholics joined in an illegal *rassemblement* could
intimidate a few local opponents into silence and guarantee the dominance of public Catholicism and Catholic leaders.[47]

In many instances, especially in communities where Catholics had a
strong majority, villagers could succeed in illegally seizing the parish
church or evicting a schoolteacher from the rectory because of the
leniency of the local officials. Authorities in the Avallonais and Tonnerrois were especially recalcitrant, yet throughout the department,
commissaires bemoaned the lack of indictments by local juges de paix.
In 1797 Commissaire Housset concluded his report on the police des
cultes with the observation, "The indulgence of the tribunals embold-
ens the guilty ones." Frequently, it became difficult to prove violations
because of the scarcity, wilyness, and recalcitrance of witnesses. All

[47]AD Yonne L710, PVs de la gendarmerie nationale d'Auxerre, 5, 7 ventôse an IV
(24, 26 February 1796), PV du tribunal criminel de l'Yonne, 26 ventôse an IV (16 March
1796), L218, PV des gendarmes à Pont-sur-Yonne, 20 prairial an VII (8 June 1799).

too often villagers claimed ignorance of the identity of lawbreakers, and sympathetic judges failed to push the searches any further. In the case of a particularly recalcitrant pro-Catholic community, departmental administrators might send in troops, but many violations went unrepressed and the unified community succeeded in resisting national policy.[48]

While some pro-Catholic authorities shut their eyes entirely to religious violations, others clearly thought they could absolve themselves of all responsibility by going through the motions of "attempting" to enforce the law and then drawing up a procès verbal without really enforcing laws against Catholic worship. In the typical scenario of an illegal church entry or an illegal Catholic festival, the local agent would arrive on the scene, wearing his tricolor scarf, the symbol of his office and authority. Then he would read a decree and attempt to persuade people to disband, perhaps by threatening to write up a procès verbal. The villagers' typical response was to continue performing their rituals; if necessary, they would threaten and insult the official. If he still refused to leave, the crowd, especially the women and children, would drive him away physically with kicks and sticks and stones. The government official generally escaped unharmed and drew up a report recounting his legal and peaceful efforts as well as his narrow escape from the furor of the crowd.

Some officials sincerely tried to enforce laws, even when faced with violent crowds, but the set actions to be performed by the local agent—the reading of a decree, the hurried departure, the drawing up of a procès verbal—could also allow the agents to manifest their authority, detach themselves from the illegal activism of fellow villagers, and voice formal disapproval of Catholic agitation without actually enforcing the law. Despite their assertions of crowd violence, very few officials were seriously injured. Their clothes might be torn, their ears might smart from insults, but they survived with little harm

---

[48]AN F7 7237, Rapport sur l'exercice des cultes par Housset, ventôse an v (February–March 1797). On the evasion of justice and the leniency of officials, see also Housset's reports in late 1796 in F7 7162; AN FIcIII Yonne 7, Compte décadaire du commissaire de l'Yonne au ministre de l'intérieur, 3 nivôse an vI (23 December 1797); Forestier, "Catholiques et théophilanthropes," pp. 3–5. For example, in order to "preserve peace and unity within families," the judge at Vénizy decided to release the Catholics who had destroyed the Theophilanthropists' decorations and pews. For multiple examples of witnesses' evasion of questioning, see AD Yonne L1118, PV du comité révolutionnaire du district d'Auxerre, an III (1794–95); BN, Observateur de l'Yonne, 25 ventôse an v (15 March 1797).

to write up the reports that effectively absolved them from responsibility.[49]

In fact, some municipal officials seem to have seen the drawing up of an official report as a means of fulfilling the duties of their office without provoking their fellow villagers to further anger and activism. The agent of Héry surrendered the church keys to insistent parishioners with the warning that he would in any event write a report (he did). Several months later, he and the commissaire wrote to the departmental administration that rather than take "other extremely strict measures, which could bring about angry results," they thought it was better simply to send a procès verbal with a description of their failed attempt to break up the illegal gathering on the festival day of Saint Louis. Early in March 1795 the national agent and secretary of Préhy duly recounted an illegal ceremony, led by a local roofer/lay minister and attended by a "large number of *citoyens* and *citoyennes*, as well as by the notables and assessors of the commune." The national agent informed the district that he had been unable to take any action and was sending a report "so as not to compromise my personal responsibility." In these and other cases, the officials were anxious to demonstrate that though their attempts to restore order were of no avail, at least their intentions were good. This type of ritualized "non-enforcement" of the laws was most likely to occur in communes where most or all the citizens supported the return to Catholicism.[50]

While some pro-Catholic communes viewed dechristianizing laws and ceremonies as an outside imposition, in other instances powerful local figures supported the republican cults and calendar. Often, re-

[49]Andrée Corvol discovered a similar pattern of only seeming to enforce the law among gendarmes in the Old Regime. "L'homme et l'arbre sous l'ancien régime" (Thèse d'état, Université de Paris IV, 1983), pp. 497–518.

[50]AD Yonne L714, PV par l'agent d'Héry, 23 floréal an VII (12 May 1799), Lettre de la municipalité d'Héry à l'administration centrale de l'Yonne, 16 fructidor an VII (2 September 1799), PV par le commissaire et l'agent d'Héry, 8 fructidor an VII (25 August 1799); AD Yonne L715, Lettre de l'agent national de Préhy à l'administration du district d'Auxerre, 12 ventôse an III (2 March 1795), PV par l'agent national et le sécretaire de Préhy, 11 ventôse an III (1 March 1795). On festivals, see AD Yonne L75, Arrêté du département de l'Yonne, 11 prairial an VI (30 May 1798); AN F1cIII Yonne 7, Compte décadaire du commissaire de l'Yonne, 24 prairial an VI (12 June 1798). On the attempt to remove church bells, see AD Yonne L712, PV des gendarmes et officiers municipaux et commissaire de Chassy, 24 frimaire an II (14 December 1793). On church entry, see AD Yonne L716, PV de la municipalité de Pallaye, 3 pluviôse an III (22 January 1795), L1286, PV de la municipalité de Treigny, 20 thermidor an VI (7 August 1798). On defense of church goods, see AD Yonne L712, PV de l'administration communale de Chablis, 2 octobre 1793.

ligious violence expressed and augmented local political conflicts between radical republicans and more moderate Catholics who might or
might not support the Republic. Time and again, confrontation over
Catholic practice had a political fallout within the community. To give
but a few examples among many, after the commissaire of Aillant
attempted to suppress an illegal festival of Saint Jean in the hamlet of
Mornay in 1799, his Catholic anti-Jacobin political opponents sought
to oust him from office by accusing him of murdering one of the
participants in the festivities.[51] In an equally complex scenario of local
in-fighting, the commissaire of the canton of Charny claimed that the
organizers of a recent riot in defense of traditional festival and market days were trying to get rid of the president of the municipality,
whom they accused of purging pro-Catholic local agents in the aftermath of the fructidorean coup d'état. In Diges in 1795 a group of
Catholics violently took over the church and prevented the sale of the
rectory. The fearful mayor confessed that he had allowed these violations of national law because "it was the will of the commune and
[he] had been forced by the commune." Having cowed the Jacobin
national agent as well, the Catholics, proclaiming themselves "new
patriots," soon formed a popular assembly to expel the municipal
government and elect a new one. District authorities at Auxerre finally sent in the national guard to calm the tumult and suppress the
"fanatics'" new government.[52]

Certain conditions fostered greater factionalization. First, the large
towns of the Yonne invariably experienced more intense political battles than did most smaller villages. Tonnerre, Auxerre, and Sens in

[51]Although the sources do not reveal the results of this accusation, it probably failed
since the commissaire of the Yonne came to the support of his accused colleague at
Aillant. AD Yonne L220, Lettre du commissaire d'Aillant au ministre de la police, n.d.
[c. messidor an VII (June–July 1799)], Lettre du commissaire d'Aillant à celui de
l'Yonne, 22 messidor an VII (10 July 1799), PV des gendarmes l'Aillant, 6 messidor an
VII (24 June 1799).

[52]AD Yonne L218, Lettre du commissaire de Charny à l'administration départementale de l'Yonne, 8 nivôse an VII (28 December 1798), Lettre du président de l'administration cantonale de Charny à l'administration départementale de l'Yonne, 4 nivôse
an VII (24 December 1798), L207, Lettre de l'agent national de Diges au comité révolutionnaire d'Auxerre, 10 pluviôse an III (29 January 1795), L208, PV des gendarmes du
district d'Auxerre, 30 germinal an III (19 April 1795), Lettre de huit citoyens de Diges
au district d'Auxerre, 23 floréal an III (12 May 1795), L763, PV du district d'Auxerre, 2
floréal an III (21 April 1795), Arrêté du district d'Auxerre, 24 floréal an III (13 May
1795); AN F7 4439[1], Dénonciation à Mailhe [représentant en mission] par la municipalité de Diges contre divers terroristes de la commune, 8 floréal an III (27 April 1795),
L68, Arrêté du département de l'Yonne, 24 floréal an III (13 May 1795).

particular witnessed heated political contests that incorporated religious issues. Second, towns and villages with a strong Theophilanthropist following faced sharp political and religious divisions more often than other villages. Thus, religious riots in the Senonais and Auxerrois were often more divisive than those in the Avallonais, Tonnerrois, or Puisaye. In Malay-le-Petit, for example, Theophilanthropists and Catholics came into violent confrontation when the municipal agent and the parish priest decided to do a church inventory during the Theophilanthropist service early in 1799. The ensuing dispute and investigation factionalized the small village, with the Catholics ultimately holding the majority position. At the April elections the Theophilanthropist adjunct lost his position, and the priest and municipal agent carried the election.[53] In Saint-Florentin, too, there was a prolonged political and religious battle between Theophilanthropists and Catholics. At one point the Theophilanthropists actually bolted down the pews in the shared church so that the Catholics could not move them to face their altar.[54]

Third, these disputes tended to be more hotly contested throughout the department when religious violence coincided with an electoral period or a particular crackdown in the laws regarding religious worship. Religious practice became especially politicized in 1797 and 1798 during the postfructidorean purges when many members of cantonal and communal administrations were forced to resign because of their support for public Catholic worship. The pro-Catholic crimes of government officials varied from taking up collections for priests to hindering the celebration of the fêtes décadaires to conducting outdoor processions as lay ministers for their fellow villagers. The agent and the adjunct of Bléneau, for example, were suspended for leading a detachment of national guardsmen and villagers to take

[53]AD Yonne L734, Lettre des citoyens de Malay-le-Petit au commissaire près le tribunal de Sens, 19 nivôse an VII (8 January 1799), Information faite par le juge de paix de la police judiciaire de Véron, 27 nivôse–3 pluviôse an VII (16–22 January 1799), Lettre de l'agent municipal de Malay au ministre de la justice, 27 pluviôse an VII (15 February 1799), Lettre du citoyen Larcher à l'administration cantonale de Véron, 9 floréal an VII (28 April 1799), Registre des élections, Malay-le-Petit et Véron, 10 germinal an VII (30 March 1799). See also Forestier, "Catholiques et théophilanthropes," pp. 3–5.
[54]AD Yonne V151, esp. Lettre de neuf citoyens de Saint-Florentin au préfet, 16 pluviôse an IX (5 February 1801). AD Yonne L734 and the *Observateur de l'Yonne* (BN) provide further illustrations of struggles between Theophilanthropists and Catholics, mainly in the Senonais and Auxerrois regions.

over the parish church and force the priest to sing mass. The municipal agent of Lucy-sur-Yonne had apparently supported local "at-
troupés" who rioted to prevent the sale of the rectory. In Thorigny
the whole cantonal administration was suspended for "preaching the
dispossession of owners of *biens nationaux* and the imminent return to
traditional customs." The department had to send in gendarmes to
subdue local defenders of the purged pro-Catholic administration.[55]
At highly controversial turning points or electoral transitions, political
and religious animosity was especially likely to divide the community
and to enable local Catholic politicians to use illegal religious activism,
consciously or unconsciously, to increase their local authority and
popularity.

Most difficult to assess is the impact of clerical participation in
collective activism. In fact, religious riot was primarily a lay phenomenon in the Yonne; few riots had priests as leaders or even as
participants. A few key points stand out with regard to clerical participation. First, because of the assumptions and biases of governmental figures reporting on clerical activism, it is hard to judge the nature,
let alone the effect, of clerical religious activism. Government officials
tended to play up clerical subversion and to exaggerate the "tyrannical," almost magical ability of priests to influence their parishioners,
especially women. The municipal officials of Maligny made a typical
accusation when they charged the priest Jean Desvoitines with having
"influenced the weak minds of several women so that they would in
turn lead their husbands astray." During the crackdown on priests
between 1797 and 1799, denunciation after denunciation reported
that clergymen won political authority as spiritual leaders. But even
though republican authorities viewed priests as violent and dangerous figures, what is striking is that for the most part they were *not*
accused of direct participation in violence. Rather, they were denounced for less direct "crimes," such as preaching counterrevolution, leading processions, collecting the tithe, or influencing the outcome of the germinal an v (April 1797) elections. Claude-Gabriel
Beranger, the curé of Saint-Valérien, for example, faced judgment

[55]For many examples of local officials denounced and suspended for supporting the
Catholic revival, see esp. AD Yonne L74, Délibérations et arrêtés de l'administration
centrale du département, [section du bien public], 21 fructidor an v–11 germinal an vi
(7 September 1797–31 March 1798), L74, Arrêtés du département de l'Yonne, 22
vendémiaire an vi (13 October 1797), 17 pluviôse an vi (5 February 1798), L75, Arrêté
du département de l'Yonne, 18 vendémiaire an vii (9 October 1798).

for stirring up hatred toward the married former priest, now the schoolteacher, by telling "lies and perfidious tales under the false pretext of religion."[56]

Since authorities no doubt wanted to emphasize clerical violence, their failure to discover much of it reinforces the impression that the clergy did not participate in riots very often in the Yonne. When they did, they seem to have been behind the scenes more often than in the forefront of the crowd. Curé Jean Breton apparently egged on the women of Montillot who assembled to defend outdoor crosses from destruction; he encouraged the villagers to pray, dance, and confront authorities on the feast day of Saint Laurent in 1797. The commissaire claimed that Breton earned "the highest reputation of holiness" for his efforts, as the villagers' expressions of loyalty seemed to demonstrate. Breton nonetheless was deported, despite his repeated assertions that he was about to marry.[57]

The example of Breton suggests not only that priests tended to leave the violent aspects of the religious struggle to the laity, especially women, but also that they had more to lose than to gain from participating in violence. Because of their dangerous position before the law, priests were less likely than lay men and women to garner communal advantages from leading riots. Priests who came out of hiding and flouted the law in the name of religion sometimes enjoyed great communal and spiritual respect and even were elected to office. If they broke the law too flagrantly, however, they quickly faced arrest and deportation for their bravery, especially between 1797 and 1799. Jean-Joachim Chabrol, the curé of Treigny, for example, had been elected municipal agent in 1797 and escaped the fructidorean purges, only to be denounced and deported for stirring up a protest against the calendar laws in 1798. Likewise, Charles Delassue led his parishioners in breaking the laws prohibiting outdoor worship, was chosen as municipal agent, continued to lead illegal processions and funer-

[56]AD Yonne L236, PV de la municipalité de Maligny, 20 ventôse an VI (10 March 1798). Pierre, *Déportation ecclésiastique*, and AD Yonne L690–700 provide multiple examples of denunciations of the priests in the Yonne. AD Yonne L74, Arrêté du département de l'Yonne, 12 ventôse an VI (2 March 1798), L694, PV du canton de Chéroy, 27 frimaire an VI (17 December 1797).

[57]AN F7 7488, Lettre du commissaire de Châtel-Censoir à l'administration de l'Yonne, 14 fructidor an VI (31 August 1798), PV des gendarmes de Vézelay, 1 brumaire an VII (22 October 1798), Rapport par le ministre de la police pour les directeurs, ventôse an VII (February–March 1799), Pétition de Breton aux directeurs, 7 pluviôse an VII (26 January 1799).

als, and found himself suspended from office and briefly jailed in 1796.[58]

Conversely, lay individuals were especially likely to gain prestige or popularity from their role in religious violence if they complemented their illegal acts of defiance with spiritual leadership. As noted, lay ministers who led church break-ins and white masses augmented their prestige among Catholics. Some anti-Catholic authorities accused them of using their spiritual authority to support their political ambitions. The commissaire of Saint-Bris complained bitterly about the local agent's "aspirations for a certain popularity," gained by helping the Catholics illegally reopen their church: "Imagine this *good man* in the midst of a group of *dévots* saying, 'Let me handle this; the commissaire closed your church; me, I can open it for you. . . .' They heap him with blessings, crying 'Vive l'agent! May the commissaire die!'" In other instances, lay ministers who were already serving as elected local officials took advantage of their governmental status to validate breaking the law in the name of religion. For example, the district administrators of Tonnerre reported an illegal seizure of a chapel in Tonnerre in the fall of 1794: "Two citizens, one of whom is a member of the General Council of the Commune, were dressed up as pontiffs and sang the mass and vespers." The angry district administrators suggested tearing the chapel down.[59]

[58]For examples of priests elected to office, see AN F7 7283, Lettre de 27 habitants d'Epineuil au ministre de la police, 17 brumaire an VI (7 November 1797). AD Yonne L74 and L75 give examples of curés who held municipal office suspended in the postfructidorean purges in the year VI in Champignelles, Villegardin, Saint-Denis, Châtel-Gérard, Saint-Sauveur, and Sainte-Colombe, for example. For earlier examples, see AN F19 481[4–5], Lettre du commissaire de Thorigny au ministre de l'intérieur, 12 pluviôse an IV (1 February 1796), F19 1017, Lettre du commissaire de Ligny-sur-Serein au ministre de la police, 15 pluviôse an V (3 February 1797); Vathaire de Guerchy, "Notice sur Treigny et la vie des nos ancêtres," *BSSY* 89 (1935): 36–40; AD Yonne 1J418 (10), PV du canton de Chablis, 10 frimaire an IV (1 December 1795), L73, Délibérations de l'administration départementale de l'Yonne, 23 pluviôse an V (11 February 1797); AN F7 7143, PV du tribunal correctionnel d'Auxerre, 14 germinal an IV (3 April 1796), Arrêté du département de l'Yonne, 23 floréal an V (12 May 1797).

[59]AD Yonne L716, Lettre du commissaire de Saint-Bris à celui de l'Yonne, 16 germinal an VI (5 April 1798); AN F1cIII Yonne 5, Analyse de la correspondance du district de Tonnerre, n.d. [c. brumaire an III (October–November 1794)]. See also AN F7 3699[2], Bulletin de la police, Yonne, 25 ventôse–1er germinal an VII (15–21 March 1799). For further examples of local authorities denounced for their role in worship, see AD Yonne L217, Lettre des patriotes de Sainpuits à l'administration de l'Yonne, 15 prairial an VII (3 June 1799), L218, Délibérations de l'administration cantonale de Pont-sur-Yonne, 29 thermidor an VII (16 August 1799). AD Yonne L70, L71, Délibérations et arrêtés de l'administration centrale de l'Yonne, 17 brumaire an IV–14 thermidor an

Officials and villagers alike recognized that alliance with the religious movement won support for local leaders, even when the ramifications were not explicitly political. In Sormery in 1796 the agent gained strong local backing for allowing Catholic citizens to harass the republican schoolteacher, who was trying to celebrate a revolutionary festival in the temple with his students. In this town, where the curé openly performed processions in full clerical garb and took up collections for the church with the agent at his side, local patriots called for armed support and feared assassination. "The Republic is not strong enough to support us here," commented citizen Massy.[60]

In short, in the highly politicized atmosphere of the late 1790s, many individuals found that illegal religious activism had an impact on village politics and public opinion. To argue that religious violence was embroiled in local power struggles is not to discount the religious motivation of Catholic rioters. Rather, I wish simply to emphasize that the struggle to construct meaning—in this case to control definitions of the sacred and to legitimize violence in God's name—also contributed to realigning power and social roles within the community. Often, the reallocation of prestige or roles was informal and did not explicitly affect political alignments or offices. In some cases, those without much formal power could use violence to gain a certain cultural prerogative and voice. Just as male lay ministers gained spiritual authority, so too women, in particular as leaders of the most goal-oriented religious riots, carved out a cultural niche within the community.

Female Activism and the Feminization of Religion

Both men and women participated in the movement to resurrect Catholicism in the late 1790s. But traditional prerevolutionary roles combined with the social and legal structures of France in the 1790s to bring about a gender-based dichotomy in uses of religious violence and in the *means* of the religious revival as a whole. Catholic men, as

---

iv (8 November 1795–1 August 1796), offer many prefructidorean examples of municipal agents suspended or reprimanded for participating in (or leading) illegal outdoor worship or for aiding priests.

[60]AN F19 1017, Extrait d'une lettre du commissaire de Neuvy Edme-Jean-André LeClerc au représentant Villetard, 24 ventôse an iv (14 March 1796), Lettre du citoyen Massy au commissaire [de Neuvy?], 20 ventôse an iv (10 March 1796).

legal citizens, could use the petition, the vote, and the village assembly to put legal pressure on local and national authorities. Women, however, more often voiced their demands through direct and illegal actions, for the legal, political, and social structures tightly limited the official voice of women and channeled them toward illegal forms of activism. In the winter of 1794, for example, 106 men of Courson, professing to be both "Catholics and republicans," petitioned for the use of the local church to conduct Catholic ceremonies "without a priest." The request failed, but soon afterward a group of villagers, led by women who boosted their children through the windows, broke into the village church. In 1797 when the men of La-Ferté-Loupière thronged into the meeting of the municipal council to demand the freedom of two priests who had just been arrested, most of the women stayed outside: they shouted insults and hurled garbage through the windows onto the municipal officers inside.[61]

When men initiated religious violence, their motivation often seemed to reflect political rivalries and commercial interests as well as religious belief.[62] Thus men were most likely to engage in ritualized hostility against specific individuals or to instigate riots to protect their right to dance, drink, or sell goods on a traditional Catholic festival day. Women, on the other hand, were constantly in the forefront of religious riots that had a specific religious goal, such as reclaiming the parish church, defending the rectory, preventing the arrest of a priest, or protecting bells and crosses from confiscation or destruction. And according to most testimony of the time, Catholic women seemed even more intent than their husbands on returning to public Catholic practice. As early as 1792 the mayor of Ravières expressed his "fear of a popular uprising" if he persisted in collecting sacred objects, "especially by the women, who still regret the loss of their crosses, their candlesticks." When the curé of Fontaines bemoaned

[61]AD Yonne L1118, PVs du comité révolutionnaire d'Auxerre, 28, 29 nivôse an III (17, 18 January 1795), L712, Pétition des habitants de Courson à la municipalité, 11 brumaire an III (1 November 1794), L209, Lettre de l'administration cantonale de La-Ferté-Loupière à l'administration départementale de l'Yonne, 20 floréal an IV (9 May 1796), PV du canton de La-Ferté-Loupière, 20 floréal an IV (9 May 1796).

[62]Timothy Tackett, "Women and Men in Counterrevolution: The Sommières Riot of 1791," *Journal of Modern History* 59 (1987): 680–704, esp. 701–3. Tackett makes a similar discovery in his analysis of a riot against the oath in 1791; he finds that men combined religious motivations with political considerations and clan rivalries more frequently than did the more devotionally minded women rioters.

the laws curtailing Catholic practice in 1796, he commented, "It is the women who are always the first to disobey."[63]

Why, then, did women act as the prime movers of religious riots during the Directory? In the first place, French women had a strong tradition of taking collective action to defend the interests of family and community. Just as women frequently led grain riots under both the Old Regime and the new, so too they led riots to demand the spiritual bread.[64] As guardians of the family, Catholic women felt responsible for the spiritual as well as the physical sustenance of their families. The concept of religion as nourishment was an accepted image in eighteenth-century France. In 1793 the petitioners of Val-de-Merci, for example, commented that they had been "nourished and penetrated by the maxims of Religion." In fact, the metaphor of religion as sustenance lay at the heart of Catholicism. Through the central sacrament of the Eucharist, God nourished the believer and offered the ultimate form of sustenance: salvation. In famine times of the 1790s, the theological link between bread and salvation took on added poignancy in the demands of rioters who sought both grain and religion. At Bayeux in Normandy, angry women claimed, "When God was there, we had bread." Likewise, at a market day in Charny in 1798 on an illegal Catholic saint's day, they cried out, "They want to abolish our religion and make us die of hunger."[65]

Authorities, too, were aware of this inflammatory link between subsistence and religion. In 1795 the deputy Villetard warned Mailhe, the représentant en mission, to be careful in acting against widespread church break-ins, occurring "at a moment when people are short of provisions." "If grain prices were reasonable," commented the commissaire of the Yonne in 1798, "Sunday would no longer be celebrated." Likewise, in 1796 the municipal officials of Chablis noted

[63]AD Yonne L708, Lettre du maire de Ravières au "citoyen," 22 octobre 1792; AN F7 7353, Lettre du curé de Fontaines au C. Deboissards, 2 floréal an IV (21 April 1796).
[64]Hufton, "Women in Revolution," pp. 104–8. For an example of women's roles as leaders of grain riots in the Yonne, see Georges Moreau, *Tonnerre pendant la Révolution* (Tonnerre, 1890), p. 256. On 8 vendémiaire an IV (30 September 1795) outside Tonnerre a group of women took over a grain convoy to distribute it; their action seems to have followed E. P. Thompson's model of the "moral economy" of grain riots.
[65]AD Yonne L711, Pétition des habitants de Val-de-Merci à l'administration départementale de l'Yonne, 13 frimaire an II (3 December 1793); Hufton, "Women in Revolution," p. 105; AN F1cIII Yonne 7, Compte décadaire par le commissaire de l'Yonne, 24 prairial an VI (12 June 1798).

that the spread of religious assemblies and "fanaticism" grew more threatening because the inflation of *"assignats* and the scarcity of grain make the women and worker[s] growl against the Revolution. Tranquility reigns here, but it would require very little to trouble it." Wary of the link between grain shortages and religious riots, authorities urged prudence in dealing with religious violence.[66]

Women rioters drew motivation and legitimacy for their actions above all from their religious faith. Continually, the actions of women rioters betrayed their conviction that they had the right and duty to provide religious worship. Through their use of religious symbols and language, women both illustrated and reinforced their belief that God, the Virgin Mary, and the saints sanctioned and even demanded riots to regain the right to worship in public. When the women of Avallon occupied the bell tower of Saint-Julien for several days to prevent its destruction, they held up a crucifix in the midst of their *rassemblement* and proclaimed threateningly, "Here, see our master who chases you!" In a riot in Chablis to prevent an inventory of church goods, Marie Anne Baillot, "carrying a huge stick," furiously threatened one town notable: "Stop there, damned scoundrel! You are all confounded thieves of *churches*" (emphasis added). In some cases the women voiced in words or actions their special link with the spiritual female leadership of their faith. They felt in particular that they had the right to defend the Virgin Mary. For example, they insulted the republican schoolteacher of Saints, calling him a Jacobin and a thief, especially because he had "stolen the candles and the contributions of the Virgin."[67] Religious ritual and belief provided female activists with both motive and a sense of moral conviction.

Women more often than men used violence to defend the integrity of a religious ceremony. In the spring of 1794 in the hamlet of Courcelle a republican passerby stepped into the village church and taunted a group of Catholics singing psalms, "You sing now, but you won't be singing for long." Although "almost the whole community of male and female citizens" was present, it was the women who poured out of

---

[66]AN F7 4439¹, Lettre de Villetard et Maure à Mailhe, 21 germinal an III (10 April 1795); AN F1cIII Yonne 7, Compte analytique du commissaire de l'Yonne au ministre de l'intérieur, fructidor an VI (August–September 1798); AD Yonne 1J418 (10), PV de Chablis, 29 nivôse an IV (19 January 1796).

[67]AD Yonne L711, PV de l'administration du district d'Avallon, 7 novembre 1791, L712, PV de la commune de Chablis, 2 October 1793; AN DIII 307, Dossier 33, PV du juge de paix de Saints, 30 thermidor an III (17 August 1795).

the chapel to "attack him and pursue him with a shower of stones." Women apparently viewed it as their particular prerogative to protect the communion of believers from outside insults. Likewise, it was the women of Epineuil who "formed a sort of barrier and refused to let [the municipal officers] enter the choir" of the church to prepare for the fête décadaire early in 1800.[68]

Indeed, women seemed to view themselves as preordained protectors of both the spiritual and physical community. Just as the women of Dye banded together in 1797 to resist the takeover of the communal ovens by their new owner, so too, when authorities attempted to inventory and perhaps requisition some church furniture and sacred objects in Sens in 1798, far more women than men arrived at the church to defend this communal property. Village women often shared with the schoolteacher the duties of tending the altar, washing linens, and caring for the church building; like him, they may have felt a special responsibility to protect this sacred space and its contents. Furthermore, as noted earlier, women were more likely than men to proclaim communal ownership in riots to defend rectory, church, or cemetery. As the *citoyennes* Tessier, Languier, and Vauquet commented to their mayor in 1795 when they demanded the church keys, "the temple belongs to us; [it was] built by the contributions of our ancestors." Likewise, in 1795 the women of Saints took to heart the complaints of their disgruntled, dispossessed curé that the schoolteacher had no right to enjoy the fruits of the rectory garden; after mass on the festival day of Saint Prix the women stole "the onions, cabbage, lettuce, peas, and leeks" from the garden while daring the new republican schoolteacher to oppose them.[69] They asserted their power to represent the community and to control its possessions as well as its culture.

Women's assertion of their public role as leaders of religious riots also grew out of informal social networks within the village. Women not only would find support and friendship in the collective practice

[68]AN AFII 163, dos. 1337, Extrait du registre de Mont-Armance, 3 floréal an II (22 April 1794), Lettre de l'agent national de Mont-Armance à Maure, représentant du peuple, n.d. [c. late April 1794]; AD Yonne L236, Lettre du commissaire d'Epineuil au commissaire de l'Yonne, 1 pluviôse an VIII (21 January 1800).

[69]AN F7 7237, no. 7048, Lettre du commissaire de l'Yonne, au ministre de la police, 25 ventôse an V (15 March 1797), Lettre de Villetard au ministre de la police, 30 ventôse an V (20 March 1797); BN, *Observateur de l'Yonne*, 15 thermidor an VI (2 August 1798); AN F7 4439¹, PV du conseil général de Toucy, 4 germinal an III (24 March 1795); AN DIII 307, dos. 33, PV du juge de paix de Saints, 30 thermidor an III (17 August 1795).

of their regained cult but would also inspire one another to action.[70] Women in many villages of the Yonne seem to have followed the same patterns as they gathered to reclaim their religion through collective action. A core group of a few dedicated women sparked others into a mass demonstration. For example, in late December 1794 in the town of Vaux the rumor passed from one woman to the next that neighboring communes were openly practicing Catholicism. On the morning of 13 nivôse an III (2 January 1795) several women decided to demand the church keys from the mayor; they went door-to-door to find other women at home sewing or doing housework who would join them in their march. As Marguerite Pierre reported, the two most vocal leaders, Barbe Dorotte and Renée LaValle, stopped by to ask, "Do you want to be with us? Do you want the keys to the church?" Marguerite responded that she would do as the other women did. Although the judge tried again and again to find evidence of an outside source inciting the women to take action, the women of Vaux repeatedly testified that "we incited each other to make the demand." As Héleine Dujon commented, she "would have been quite angry to have missed it."[71]

Although reclaiming church keys was generally a communal venture by many of the village women, religious conviction and the desire to participate was by no means always universal. Tensions and rivalries among village women played themselves out over the issue of

[70]Many historians have written about the capacity of religious devotion to offer communal networks of female sociability. See, for example, Nancy Cott, *The Bonds of Womanhood: "Woman's Sphere" in New England, 1780–1835* (New Haven, Conn., 1977), pp. 138–45; Laura Thatcher Ulrich, "Daughters of Liberty: Religious Women in Revolutionary New England," in *Women in the Age of the American Revolution,* ed. Ronald Hoffman and Peter J. Albert (Charlottesville, Va., 1989), pp. 211–43. On women's organization for rioting, see Michelle Perrot, "La femme populaire rebelle," in *L'histoire sans qualités,* ed. Christiane Dufrancatel, Arlette Farge, and Christine Faure (Paris, 1979), pp. 123–56.

[71]AD Yonne L1118, PVs du comité révolutionnaire d'Auxerre, 18, 19 nivôse an III (7, 8 January 1795); Arrêté de Guillemardet, représentant du peuple, 21 nivôse an III (10 January 1795). For other examples of similar actions and attitudes by women, see AD Yonne L1118, PVs du comité révolutionnaire d'Auxerre, 28, 29 nivôse an III (17, 18 January 1795) on the women of Courson, L1281, PV de la municipalité de Moulins, 30 prairial an IV (18 June 1796); AN F7 7233, Lettre du commissaire de Vermenton au Villetard, député du peuple de l'Yonne, 31 pluviôse an V [*sic*] (19 February 1797); AD Yonne L716, PVs de la commune de Sacy, 23, 25, 26, 27 pluviôse an V (11, 13, 14, 15 February 1797). See also Roger Dupuy, "Les femmes dans la contre-Révolution dans l'ouest," *Bulletin d'histoire économique et sociale de la Révolution française,* 1979 (Paris, 1980): 61–70, esp. 69. Dupuy suggests that religious practice played a larger role in the daily lives of women than of men.

religious activism. Just as male political and religious violence took the form of ritualized hostility against specific rivals, women rioters sometimes singled out reluctant or opposed women as special objects of persuasion or humiliation. The women who led a rectory riot at Moulins in the spring of 1796 locked one widow in her house because they thought she was responsible for giving incriminating information to the local commissaire. A year earlier the Catholic women of Diges echoed the anti-Jacobin political activism of their husbands by blocking the church door to prevent the wives or daughters of leading Jacobins from entering; they even ejected the wife of one recently ousted municipal officer with threats and kicks.[72] Religion did not always reinforce female solidarity and express shared interests; sometimes it could provoke bitter controversy or could force conformity.

Another reason women were so active in religious riots was that they were held less culpable for their actions before the law since they were believed to be more hysterical by nature and more easily duped than men. The language of the rioting crowds and of reporting officials, revolutionary authorities, and Catholic villagers reveals this pervasive conception of women either as weak, malleable souls or as uncontrollable furies. Government officials were especially wary of the influence of wily priests on the impressionable hearts of women. For example, Jacques Boileau, a deputy for the Yonne, warned the members of Avallon's Popular Society about priests who "worked on feeble souls and especially on the consciences of women, because they know how much this sex has both the arms and the means to proselytize for them." Boileau argued that women were pliable and vulnerable creatures who should be controlled and directed by good republican husbands rather than by priests. Although republican authorities often portrayed priests as cunning, they also insinuated that irrational priests shared the superstitious and credulous character of women, making it particularly easy for priests to enflame their suggestible female counterparts. According to one government official, when the curé of Malay-le-Grand became enraged at the presence of the Theophilanthropist minister during vespers, the priest easily in-

<hr />

[72]AD Yonne L1281, Détails postérieurs au PV du canton de Toucy du 30 prairial an IV (18 June 1796), L208, Lettre des citoyens de Diges à l'administration du district d'Auxerre, 23 floréal an III (12 May 1795). The Catholic moderates of Diges had called a town assembly to vote the forced resignation of the leading Jacobins from municipal offices. See also AN F7 7353, Lettre du commissaire près Vermenton au commissaire près les tribunaux de l'Yonne, 5 frimaire an VI (25 November 1797).

cited kindred spirits in the crowd to echo his anger, especially the excitable women, who joined in the "atrocious insults vomited by the holy pastor."[73]

Because of the assumption that they were hysterical by nature and therefore less responsible for their violence, women enjoyed greater leeway than men in collective action. Both during and after riots male and female religious activists turned this perception of female hysteria and irresponsibility to their own advantage. When the municipal officers of Chablis tried to remove sacred objects from the church of Saint-Pierre in 1793, groups of men and women gathered to prevent the confiscation of church goods. One vigneron cried out, *"Let the women do as they wish. They are in a state to kill them [the government officials]"* (emphasis added). In the spring of 1795 Catholic women of Toucy, accused of breaking the church doors, claimed in their defense, "We are only women; they don't do anything to women [*on faisait rien aux femmes*]." Likewise, at a rectory riot at Sacy, women cried out to the commissaire that "they could do no harm to women [*on ne pouvait faire aucun mal aux femmes*]." (In this case some of the women nonetheless were taken to trial at the civil tribunal of the department, and the commune of Sacy was fined 313 livres.) The women who attacked the new owner of the rectory in Chassy in 1796 declared that "they didn't care, that there would be no more proof against them than against those who had cut down the liberty tree." In Charbuy early in 1795 the two teenage girls who were caught prying a lock off a church door admitted that a male neighbor had explained how to remove the lock and had told them, "You are just young girls; no one will say anything." When this case came before the revolutionary committee of Auxerre, the youth and lack of judgment of the girls protected them from enforcement of the law; Thomas Michel, the thirty-six-year-old day laborer, who admitted having shown the girls how to remove the lock, was also freed since he had not actually touched the lock himself.[74]

[73]Discours par Jacques Boileau à la Société populaire d'Avallon, 1792, in M. Léger, ed., *Lettres des représentants du peuple dans l'Yonne*. (Excerpts reprinted from *Annuaire de l'Yonne*, 1892–98). N.p., n.d., pp. 80–81; AD Yonne L212, Lettre de Magny, instituteur de Malay-le-Grand, à l'administration du département de l'Yonne, n.d. [c. early frimaire an VI (December 1797)].

[74]AD Yonne L712, PV de la commune de Chablis, 2 October 1793; AN F7 4439¹, PV du conseil général de Toucy, 4 germinal an III (24 March 1795); AD Yonne L716, PV de la commune de Sacy, 27 pluviôse an V (15 February 1797), Lettre de l'administration cantonale de Vermenton à l'administration départementale de l'Yonne, 17 messidor an VI (5 June 1798); L72, Arrêté du département de l'Yonne, 21 thermidor an IV (8

When women rioters were arrested, husbands who petitioned for the release of their wives downplayed the threatening and serious aspects of collective religious action by women. The petitioners in Avallon successfully argued that when the townswomen took over and occupied the bell tower for several days, "it was just a few hysterical cries and the agitations of women out of control." The municipal officers of Pallaye appealed for clemency for *la femme* Chévillard, who had called for the murder of those opposed to the celebration of the mass of Saint Vincent. Her defenders admitted that she had committed "an imprudence in speaking in that way." Nevertheless, "her intention was not to put her threats into effect." In any case, noted the municipal authorities, "her husband had strongly reprimanded her . . . and she had immediately repented." The leniency toward women before the law was so great that some men dressed as women to avoid arrest. When the Convention decreed a form of temporary house arrest of all women in Paris after the grain riots of 1 prairial an III (20 May 1795), they denounced men who "misled or incited" women as well as those "troublemakers [who] dress like women in hopes of enjoying impunity."[75]

Although most female religious activists were not especially well educated, they shared their husbands' awareness that certain revolutionary laws and tenets supported the freedom of religion and the right to popular self-determination. These revolutionary concepts and context reinforced what women perceived as their traditional right to riot to protect certain community values. As Marie Anne Rémy testified in 1795, she had participated in a *rassemblement* to regain the church "to follow the ancient custom, and anyway, one heard that we had religious liberty [*on disait que tous les cultes étaient libres*]." When Marianne Michaut, a seamstress in Chichée, pressured the national agent to let her ring bells and hold public worship in 1794, she reminded him of the power of his constituents' opinion: "You will be esteemed by everyone if you let me do these things and if you put the statues back in place."[76] Many Catholic women were

August 1796), L1118, PV du comité révolutionnaire d'Auxerre, 27 nivôse, 3, 4 pluviôse an III (16, 22, 23 January 1795).

[75] AD Yonne L711, Pétition des habitants d'Avallon à l'administration départementale de l'Yonne, n.d. [c. November 1791], L716, Lettre de la municipalité de Pallaye à l'agent national du district d'Auxerre, 14 pluviôse an III (2 February 1795); AN C341, Arrêté de la Convention nationale, 4 prairial an III (23 May 1795).

[76] AD Yonne L1118, PV du comité révolutionnaire d'Auxerre, 18 nivôse an III (7 January 1795), L712, Lettre de l'agent national de Chichée au comité révolutionnaire d'Auxerre, 7 brumaire an III (28 October 1794).

conscious of the betrayal of revolutionary promises; at the very least, they knew that the Revolution increased the potency of popular activism.

In short, various factors contributed to women's leadership of religious riots: women's traditional role as leaders of grain riots and defenders of community, the networks of female sociability within the village, women's lack of official political voice combined with their impunity before the law, and their moral certainty that both revolutionary ideology and Catholic tradition validated their actions. What inspired female religious activists most of all was the tremendous strength of their religious devotion and belief. When asked why they had broken into churches, defended priests from arrest, or stolen church bells and statues, by far the majority of women witnesses echoed the straightforward sentiments of the villagers of Champs, who claimed in 1795 that they had assembled quite simply "to pray to God. . . . We would sooner pour out our blood than renounce the Catholic religion which we have always professed." As an old woman commented to a soldier in Auxerre when she refused to attend the festival of the Supreme Being, "It is not your god I adore. He is too young; it is the old one."[77]

Women were apparently more strongly attached than men to the public practice of Catholicism. As Commissaire Housset said, "Everywhere, it's the women who prove to be most ardently attached to Catholicism."[78] Why did women seem to feel the need for public devotion more than men did? A partial answer to this question may lie in women's position as traditional guardians of the nourishment and unity of the family.[79] Within the subsistence economy of early modern Europe, both men and women lived from day to day with death hovering over their shoulders. Women, as bearers of children, providers of sustenance, and nurturers of the family were made aware, even more than men, of the fragility of human life. At the core of women's consciousness lay the struggle not only to bear life but to preserve it as well.[80] In women's world view traditional religious be-

[77]AD Yonne L712, PV de la commune de Champs, 14 pluviôse an III (2 February 1795); Abbé F. J. Fortin, *Souvenirs*, 2 vols. (Auxerre, 1865–67), 1:18.

[78]AN F7 7237, Rapport sur l'exercice des cultes par Housset, ventôse an v (February–March 1797).

[79]See esp. Hufton, "Women in Revolution," and "Reconstruction of a Church," pp. 23–25.

[80]Temma Kaplan, "Female Consciousness and Collective Action: The Case of Barcelona, 1910–1918," *Signs: Journal of Women in Culture and Society* 7 (1982):545–66, esp. 545–47.

liefs and practices had become inextricably connected with the affir-
mation of life. The sacred provided a context for living: the church
bell rang out the hours of work and prayer, of birth and death; the
festival of Saint Anne established a bond of protection and devotion
for the young pregnant woman and focused her hopes for a healthy
birth; the funeral procession closed life with dignity, consoled the
bereaved family, and enabled all to anticipate salvation. Particularly in
a time of hardship, when war, famine, and the uncertainties of revolution seemed to threaten the family with incoherence and confusion,
women may have clung to Catholicism because it did more than provide a framework for living: it endowed the critical moments of life
with a transcendental significance, celebrated the unity of family and
community, and reinforced an overall cosmological order and whole-
ness.

The link between religious and subsistence riots suggests the correlation in women's minds between physical and spiritual sustenance.
Furthermore, many Catholic women expressed in words and action
their certainty that religious ritual acted as a force for morality and a
source of emotional support. Citoyenne Boylau, who proclaimed her-
self both Catholic and republican, fused Christian and *sans-culotte*
visions of women's duties to claim that women must bring their children up in the Catholic religion, which ensured morality and trained
sons to become good citizens and "defenders of the country." One
anonymous woman noted in a letter in 1798 that only God, not the
government, had the right to command people's feelings; she commented that "[religion] alone can give us the courage to withstand the
calamities of such a long revolution. . . . This religion has been en-
graved on the hearts of the French and cannot be erased."[81]

Women's powerful consciousness of their role as preservers of life
was an essential motivation for persistent attachment to Catholicism.
It does not, however, tell us the whole story. It is critical to take into
account women's position in the early modern social structure, for
their lack of formal political voice influenced their sense of spiritual
commitment both by encouraging them to seek otherworldly rewards
and by directing them toward less political forms of public, communal
influence here on this earth.

Village women in Old Regime or revolutionary France could not

[81]AN DIII 304, Protestation de la citoyenne Boylau à la Convention nationale, 22
avril 1793; AN F7 7303, Lettre d'une femme anonyme aux citoyens directeurs, 17
septembre 1797 (she used the old-style dating).

expect to become powerful public, political figures within the community. They could not hold office, vote in village assemblies, or even legally sign petitions as recognized citizens (except for widows as heads of households). Although the Revolution initially seemed to open up the doors to political participation, the opportunities granted to women in any *official* capacity were slight and were rapidly curtailed from 1793. In the early years of the Revolution women were prime movers of revolutionary movements; they were particularly active in the *journées* that intertwined issues of subsistence and politics, such as the October Days of 1789 and the ill-fated uprisings of germinal and prairial an III (May and June 1795). In addition to agitating for revolutionary political and economic reforms, the more radical feminists of the Revolution appealed for greater equality between the sexes and even demanded representative and political roles for women. Male leaders of the Revolution, however, did not conceive of politics as an arena for women. Women's clubs were closed in October 1793, and by 1795 women had been excluded from the Jacobin clubs and from the galleries of the Convention. They had virtually no direct involvement in the military or political affairs of the Revolution. In short, although the revolutionary years contributed to women's long-term political education, the Revolution did not effectively increase their political rights in the 1790s. Few women in the Yonne and other provinces anticipated a radical increase in their own political participation, but they did recognize that the Revolution, which promised a greater political voice to their husbands, offered them no corollary increase in public power.[82]

To women deprived of public political power, in the Old Regime as in the new, the public practice of Catholicism might have special appeal for two paradoxically interconnected reasons. First, Christianity legitimated and even acclaimed the potential spiritual value of those without earthly power. Second, it simultaneously provided women with an earthly arena for collective activism, initiative, and voice in the community at large.

[82]Jane Abray, "Feminism in the French Revolution," *American Historical Review* 80 (1975): 43–62; Dominique Godineau, *Citoyennes tricoteuses: Les femmes du peuple à Paris pendant la Révolution française* (Aix-en-Provence, 1988), pp. 169–77 and 319–51; Joan B. Landes, *Women and the Public Sphere in the Age of the French Revolution* (Ithaca, N.Y., 1988), esp. chap. 4; Darlene Gay Levy, Harriet Branson Applewhite, and Mary Durham Johnson, *Women in Revolutionary Paris, 1789–1795* (Chicago, 1979), pp. 3–12, 309–12; Leonora Cohen Rosenfield, "The Rights of Women in the French Revolution," *Studies in Eighteenth-Century Culture* 17 (1978): 117–38.

Religious devotion offered a realm where worldly power and office were not the only or the ideal goals. In other words, some women were perhaps more attached to religion than men were because in the spiritual realm, at the deepest level of significance, worldly power did not have ultimate importance.[83] One's position within institutionalized or informal power structures mattered less than the depth of one's devotion and the strength of one's faith. In their defense of religious worship, women guarded the *public* expression of their *private* attachment to an internal world where those without power could find ultimate reassurance. Women's creation of both personal and collective forms of piety became an expression of their autonomy and self-worth within the patriarchal structures of the village community.[84]

But paradoxically, Catholicism also had a particular power to attract women because it became a domain within the village community in which women could have a public voice and take independent action, particularly during the Revolution. For despite the efforts of the dechristianizers and the promoters of revolutionary cults, the context of revolution made the late 1790s in many ways an extremely creative and fertile period for lay Catholic activism by both men and women. The lack of clear clerical leadership and the breakdown of the institutional and hierarchical structures of the church made it both possible and necessary for the laity to take the lead in religious activism during the Revolution. Although women clearly supported the clandestine practice of Catholicism by hiding refractory priests, cultivating prayer in the home, and teaching catechism to their children, above all they strove to return religion to the *public realm,* to the visible position of authority and publicity which it had held in the Old Regime.[85]

[83]Caroline Walker Bynum, "Women's Stories, Women's Symbols: A Critique of Victor Turner's Theory of Liminality," in *Anthropology and the Study of Religion,* ed. F. Reynolds and R. Moore (Chicago, 1984), pp. 105–25, and "Women Mystics and Eucharistic Devotion in the Thirteenth Century," *Women's Studies* 11 (1984): 179–214, esp. 194.

[84]Eugene Genovese makes a similar point regarding the role of slave religion within the paternalistic system of the Old South in *Roll, Jordan, Roll: The World the Slaves Made* (New York, 1972), pp. 162–68, 181–83, 280–84. See also Judith Herrin, "Women and the Faith in Icons in Early Christianity," in *Culture, Ideology, and Politics: Essays for Eric Hobsbawm,* ed. Raphael Samuel and Gareth Stedman-Jones (London, 1982), pp. 56–83, esp. 67–69.

[85]On the role of women in the Yonne in maintaining clandestine religion in the home during the Revolution, see the accounts of Pierre Paradis about his mother's role

As Catholic women expanded their liturgical roles in the absence of the clergy, they built upon the existing models and patterns of female piety which had grown out of both the Catholic Reformation and popular cultural resistance to the reforms. During the Old Regime women and girls had certainly been encouraged to be pious and to make devotional and charitable contributions. The imagery and history of Catholicism provided women with models of active females, including many saints and, of course, the Virgin Mary. While Catholic women in the early sixteenth century had a decidedly smaller role than their husbands in organized and formal religious expression, the Catholic Reformation partially redressed this balance by encouraging the institutionalization of a more public and well defined place for women through the creation of new women's religious orders and lay confraternities. Lay women could take a more active and creative part in religious ritual, charity, and education as members of new confraternities and charitable organizations, such as the confraternities of the Rosary, the Sacred Heart, or Saint Catherine.[86] Participation in confraternities would also encourage female spirituality. In the Yonne the small village of Arthonnay, for example, had two all-female confraternities until they were suppressed in 1792: Sainte Vierge (Rosary) for young girls and Sainte Anne for married women; each confraternity sponsored elaborate processions, songs, and special rituals. While women's confraternities were generally under the supervision of the parish priest, his control was by no means guaranteed. In Avallon the women in the female Confraternity of Charity,

---

in Boussard, *Docteur Paradis,* pp. 28–34. Also, on women as protectors and hiders of nonjuring priests, see Fortin, *Souvenirs* 1:11. The literature on religion during the French Revolution abounds with examples of women as supporters of clandestine Catholicism. See, for example, Langlois and Tackett, "A l'épreuve de la Révolution," p. 273; Daniel-Rops, *L'église des Révolutions,* p. 93.

[86]On the importance of female imagery in the Catholic tradition and on the restricted role of women in organized religiosity before the Catholic Reformation, see Davis, "City Women and Religious Change," in her *Society and Culture,* pp. 65–96, esp. 74–76, 88–89, 94. On the development of this new spirituality of the Catholic Reformation as regards women's roles and position, see, for example, Robert Sauzet, "Présence rénovée du catholicisme (1520–1670)," in *Histoire des catholiques en France,* ed. Lebrun, pp. 75–145; Hoffman, *Church and Community,* pp. 126–28, 144–46; Elizabeth Starr Cohen, "The Socialization of Young Women in Early Modern France" (Ph.D. diss., University of Toronto, 1978), esp. chap. 6. The Catholic Reformation spawned (and controlled) new active orders, such as the Ursulines, the Daughters of Charity, and the Visitandines, which gave religious women a larger role in teaching, caring for the sick, and aiding the poor. At times, lay women participated in activities organized by these orders.

established in 1655, came into conflict with local clergymen in 1770 when they tried to exercise tighter control over the women's choice of beneficiaries for their charity.[87]

In fact, toward the end of the Old Regime, women in many parts of France already seem to have remained more faithful than men to Catholic practice. Recent studies of confraternity membership and of pious language in bequests indicate that men drifted away from devotional religiosity more quickly than women did in the eighteenth century.[88] Yet, although women rioters of the 1790s built upon their Old Regime religious tendency, the Revolution crystallized this spirituality by challenging it so forcefully, by inadvertently encouraging women to take a more public religious role, and by infusing religious actions with political importance.

Once they had regained their churches, women actively encouraged their sons and husbands to take over the traditional liturgical role of the clergy by performing white masses. But women too, although they apparently did not say white masses, rushed to fill the void left by priests by leading religious worship on their own. Women have often had an increased role in the public expression of religiosity at critical moments of religious transition or oppression.[89] During the Revolution women rang bells for the Angelus, met to pray and sing psalms, led religious processions, and insisted on the celebration of saints' festivals. For example, the women of Préhy broke into their church in the winter of 1795, rang the church bell, and began to sing offices. In Courson early in 1795 women mounted to the lectern to sing vespers. The Catholic women of Châtel-Censoir, who repeatedly

[87]S. La Loire, "Notes historiques sur Arthonnay," *BSSY* 64 (1910): 59–64; Ernest Blin, "La charité à Avallon," *BSSY* 59 (1905): 85–94.

[88]Pierre Chaunu, *La mort à Paris aux XVIe, XVIIe, et XVIIIe siècles* (Paris, 1978), pp. 434–36; Hoffman, *Church and Community*, pp. 126–27, 144–45; Kathryn Norberg, *Rich and Poor in Grenoble, 1600–1814* (Berkeley, Calif., 1985), pp. 250–52, 337–38; Quéniart, *Hommes, l'église*, p. 296; Tackett, *Religion, Revolution*, p. 248; Vovelle, *Piété baroque*, pp. 133–40, 298–300.

[89]For example, in the early years of the Catholic Reformation, Catholic women created activist, noncloistered women's religious orders; at the outset of the Quaker and Anabaptist movements, women as well as men preached or prophesied. In all these cases, as the religious movements became institutionalized, the public role of women became more limited. See, for example, Ruth P. Liebowitz, "Virgins in the Service of Christ: The Dispute over an Active Apostolate for Women during the Counter-Reformation," in *Women of the Spirit: Female Leadership in the Jewish and Christian Traditions*, ed. Rosemary Ruether and Eleanor McLaughlin, pp. 131–52, and see their introduction, pp. 21–22; Margaret Fell Fox, *Women's Speaking Justified* (1665); Phyllis Mack, "Women as Prophets during the English Civil War," *Feminist Studies* 8 (1982).

broke into their church in 1794 and 1795, also did not hesitate to dethrone the goddess of Reason, draft a young boy to ring the church bell, and lead worship on their own. Likewise, women in Auxerre broke into their cathedral for the second time in 1798 to conduct religious rituals for themselves. That same fall the wife of the suspended municipal agent in Vézelay led an illegal outdoor procession of young men and women singing litanies. When questioned, she responded, "Religion must be respected," and continued unperturbed with the procession.[90]

Above all, the peculiarly politicized context of revolution created a situation in which public religious activism took on added significance and communal influence. Those without power could forge authority by fusing powerful symbolism with political activism. In the midst of the revolutionary campaign to enlighten French people with the secular and rational ideals of the Revolution, to bury one's husband with a public Catholic funeral or to dance on the festival of the Virgin was to make a statement at once political and religious. In the politically and symbolically charged atmosphere of the Revolution, the slightest symbolic action could take on subversive significance and force authority figures to listen to those who had no legal voice within the official power structures. When women broke into bell towers, chopped down liberty trees, or replanted crosses by the roadside, revolutionary officials had no choice but to heed this doubly powerful assertion of spiritual and temporal power. The march to the mayor's house to demand church keys was a political act and a threat of social disorder, but for the women as they sang psalms and prayed litanies, it also became a procession without priests, a profoundly religious expression of their own autonomy, of communal solidarity, and above all of their right to affirm the coherence of their world view and to consecrate the life of the family as they saw fit and as they had done for centuries.

The religious activism of women during the Revolution profoundly

[90]Among the numerous examples of women initiating various services without a priest, see, for example, AD Yonne L207, Lettre de l'agent national de Préhy à l'agent national d'Auxerre, 25 ventôse an III (15 March 1795), PV de la municipalité de Courson, 22 nivôse an III (11 January 1795), L1118, PV du comité révolutionnaire d'Auxerre, 28 nivôse an III (17 January 1795); E. Pallier, "Recherches historiques sur l'histoire de Châtel-Censoir," pp. 103, 147; AC Auxerre P5 Dépôt 3, PV par l'officier de la poste d'Auxerre, 11 fructidor an VI (28 August 1798); AD Yonne L714, PV du comité révolutionnaire d'Auxerre, 28 nivôse–3 pluviôse an III (17–22 January 1795), L75, Arrêté de l'Yonne, 15 vendémiaire an VII (6 October 1798).

affected community dynamics and gender roles. Women had long had a traditional role as guardians of family and community values, but their willingness to use violence to defend Catholicism during the Revolution contributed over the longer term to their appropriation of public religious expression as women's prerogative and women's duty within the family and community. Their activism made a critical and lasting impression precisely because the Revolution was a moment of such all-encompassing cultural change. Not only were social and political structures in flux, but the new revolutionary culture challenged the fundamental underpinnings of traditional Catholic culture. Whereas this dechristianizing assault grew out of the Enlightenment and the gradual secularization of the eighteenth century, as well as the particular politics of the year II, the Revolution brought matters to a head: it engendered a moment of cultural crisis which heightened the importance of the popular response.[91] The revolutionary situation put faith to the test; in so often clinging more passionately than men to religious culture, women increasingly carved out lay religiosity as their own arena of informal control. In short, women's role in religious violence helped to lay the groundwork for the gradual feminization of religious practice in the nineteenth century. This development had ambiguous ramifications for women, particularly as the structures of authority and clerical control were developed once again in the years following the Concordat.

A parallel can be drawn between the Revolution's impact on secularization generally and its tendency to promote the feminization of religion. The revolutionary era was not single-handedly responsible for secularization. Rather, it intensified and hastened an existing trend away from regular religious practice, which various nineteenth-century factors would in turn encourage. Likewise, the Revolution's promotion of the feminization of religion built on an Old Regime tendency toward a gender dichotomy in religious devotion. In turn, over the longer term, many factors enhanced female commitment and male rejection, including the transformation of the domestic

[91]Many works discuss the gradual secularization of eighteenth-century society. See esp. Vovelle, *Piété baroque*. On the decline of religious literature in the late eighteenth century, see François Furet, "La librairie du royaume de France au XVIIIe siècle," in *Livre et société dans la France du XVIIIe siècle*, vol. 1, ed. François Furet et al. 2 vols. (Paris, 1965–70), 1:3–32, esp. 20–22, 28; Jean-Louis Marie Flandrin, "La circulation du livre dans la société du XVIIIe siècle: Un sondage à travers quelques sources," *Livre et société* 2:39–72, esp. 67–68.

economy, the increasing division of labor according to gender, and
the development of lay forms of education and leisure for boys and
men.[92]

But in part men and women sought different things from the
church in the nineteenth century because they had profoundly different revolutionary experiences. For men, even in counterrevolutionary regions of France, the Revolution opened up unprecedented ave-
nues for political participation and left behind the expectation that
politics, like work and leisure outside the home, offered a viable
means of defining one's identity, of taking meaningful collective action, and of forming alternative symbolic systems to make sense of the
world. For women, on the other hand, the continuing exclusion of
women from the political structures during the Revolution reinforced
women's subordinate social position and continued to channel wom-
en's political participation toward unofficial or illegal means. It also
encouraged women to turn to religion to find identity, friendship,
consolation, and meaning that men might seek elsewhere. Politics and
religion were not two diametrically opposed and mutually exclusive
arenas of activism for men and women in the 1800s. In fact, the two
realms would interact in complex and interesting ways in the nineteenth century. But in many parts of France men and women alike
came increasingly to view regular religious practice as a female responsibility and female domain. The roots of this phenomenon lay
not only in women's position in the family and in the domestic economy but also in the particular character of women's experience of the
Revolution.

[92]There are many explanations for the sexual division in religious practice which
became so prevalent in nineteenth- and twentieth-century France. Girls were generally
educated at religious institutions, while boys had the possibility of attending lay, state-
run schools. Women often found a nexus of sociability in activities connected to the
local church, while male leisure time became laicized and politicized. For many men,
the café replaced the church as the focal point of the town. Some historians have
argued that the association of the church with the temperance movement was more
repellent to men than to women. For discussions of the sexual divisions in religious
practice, see Philippe Boutry and Michel Cinquin, *Deux pèlerinages au XIXe siècle: Ars et
Paray-le-Monial* (Paris, 1980), chaps. 1, 2; Dupuy, "Les femmes dans la contre-Révolution," 61–70; Claude Langlois, "Permanence, renouveau, et affrontements, 1830–
1880," in *Histoire des catholiques*, ed., Lebrun, pp. 291–368, esp. 323–25; Hufton, "Reconstruction of a Church," esp. pp. 23–25. Other European countries, most notably
Spain and Italy, witnessed a similar division of religious practice by gender. See Christian, *Person and God in a Spanish Valley*.

At the heart of the cultural clash between Catholic villagers and the revolutionaries lay two fundamentally different conceptions of the role of the sacred in everyday life. "The people no longer want *mysteries;* they want *truth;* they want bread, freedom, and peace" (emphasis added), wrote the republican editor of the *Observateur de l'Yonne* optimistically in 1796. The minister of the interior urged local officials in 1799 to "make people see that republican institutions are *purely political and moral*" (emphasis added).[93] But the Catholics of the Yonne clearly were not ready for a form of truth without mystery, or for a way of life that was "purely political and moral." Instead, they used every means at hand to defend a way of life in which the sacred and the profane were continually intertwined. Festival days that combined dancing, sale of farm produce, and processions in honor of saints; bells that rang to invoke God's blessing and to mark out the hours of the day; churches that housed the sacred and provided a place for communal gatherings and village assemblies—Catholics repeatedly chose to defend the elements of village life whose meaning and function were both sacred and profane.

Indeed, the Catholic villagers' very means of activism manifested this same intermingling of the sacred and the profane as their violence combined the popular culture of the Old Regime, revolutionary political activism, and the timeless force of religious ritual to proclaim their right to practice Catholicism. Yet, as religious activists effectively fused violence, ritual, politics, and old and new customs to make their claim, their struggle left its mark on religious practice, as well as on revolutionary politics and community life. The context of riot and revolution both forced and enabled lay activists to seize the initiative in religious ritual and to lead each other in unorthodox forms of worship, such as lay masses, female-led ceremonies, or resurrected saints' cults. Moreover, since the Catholic revival was a political and cultural contest deeply entangled within local power struggles, religious violence could either unite the bulk of the community against a few dechristianizers or outsiders or, alternatively, provide fuel for tensions between moderate Catholics and radical republicans. Certain lay individuals gained prestige or in some cases political power from

---

[93]BN, *Observateur de l'Yonne*, 15 pluviôse an IV (4 February 1796); AN F1cIII Yonne 8, Lettre du ministre de l'intérieur aux administrateurs de Montréal, 26 floréal an VI (15 May 1798).

their role in religious violence. Finally, in a variety of local political situations, the prominent leadership role of women in riots contributed to the gradual redefinition of public lay religiosity as a particularly female sphere and responsibility. In sum, religious violence during the Revolution indeed sought to preserve age-old ways and beliefs, but it was not simply a conservative attempt to defend traditional practices by traditional means. Instead, rioting had a dynamic impact on the ritualistic creation of religious meaning as well as on the distribution of power and roles within the community.

CHAPTER SIX

Conclusion

On 5 June 1803 the parish curé Dinet of Chablis, attired in full ecclesiastical alb and chasuble, solemnly entered his former parish church to perform the ritual of repossession prescribed by the new bishop of the diocese. After kissing the "master altar with respect," he opened the tabernacle to incense the Blessed Sacrament, sat briefly in the confessional, kissed the baptismal fonts, rang the church bell once, and finally returned to the "choir where he read aloud in a clear voice to [the parishioners] the act of his canonical installation." To complete the ritual, the curé Dinet solemnly sang the mass and the Te Deum. "These ceremonies bore testimony to the repossession of the church," certified the act signed by priest, parishioners, and municipal officers alike. In the aftermath of the revolutionary struggles, this traditional ritual of *prise de possession* served to demarcate the curé's sacerdotal functions once again and to reappropriate and purify the newly regained church building.[1]

After the promulgation of the Concordat in 1802, priests throughout the Yonne performed elaborate rituals such as this one to mark the official reestablishment of Catholicism. The Concordat, proclaimed with heavy ceremony from Paris to the Pyrenées, cemented the official reinstatement of Catholicism as the "religion of the majority of the French people" and consolidated a new accord between church and state. The attempt to replace Catholicism with a new revolutionary culture had officially come to an end. The church had

[1]AN F19 5705, Acte de prise de possession de l'église, Chablis, 5 juin 1803.

[217]

retained its position as a fundamental national institution and a forceful arbiter of culture, and the radical revolutionaries had fallen short of their ambitious goal: the total transformation and "regeneration" of the French people. Yet although the years of revolutionary strife and uncertainty were over, the post-Concordat church would never regain the political power, immense wealth, or cultural hegemony of the Gallican Church of the Old Regime. For the Revolution had made a profound mark on lay religious attitudes as well as on the position and role of the Catholic Church as an institution. Furthermore, the events of the Revolution had transformed the essentials of the relationship between religion and politics.

Catholicism Emerging from the Revolution

In the aftermath of the Revolution, Catholicism not only had to overcome vast material losses of property and personnel but also had to face the deeper cultural challenge of the rival secular culture promoted by the Revolution. The post-Concordat church had to reconcile itself to directing its appeal to certain sectors of the population, rather than expecting the widespread support it had enjoyed in earlier centuries. Catholicism became predominantly rural, particularly as the century progressed and the church found it hard to respond to the growing challenges of industrialism and science.[2] Second, regional differences in levels of devotion became more pronounced after the Revolution. The west, Massif Central, parts of the Pyrenées, and northeastern and far northern France became known for their piety, while the population of many other regions slipped gradually toward indifference or at least toward lower levels of practice. Third, in most areas of France during the nineteenth and twentieth centuries, women were more dedicated to religious practice than men were.[3] Moreover, the intense politicization of religion, the clergy's dependent position as salaried civil servants, and the growth of anticlericalism all increased the tendency toward conflict between church and state and

[2]Jean Godel, *La réconstruction concordataire dans le diocèse de Grenoble après la Révolution (1802–1809)* (Grenoble, 1968), esp. pp. 364–65; Langlois, "Permanence, renouveau, et affrontements," pp. 320, 351–55.

[3]Langlois, pp. 323–25; Roger Mehl, *Catholicisme français dans la société actuelle* (Paris, 1977), chap. 1; Boulard, *Matériaux pour l'histoire religieuse,* esp. pp. 88–91, 552–53; Isambert and Terrenoire, *Atlas de la pratique religieuse.*

encouraged Ultramontane attitudes among the clergy. Finally, although some French people combined Catholic beliefs and practices with left-wing politics, for the most part, Catholicism became increasingly allied with the right.[4]

The Revolution did not single-handedly bring about all these transformations, but it marked a watershed, a fundamental divide in religious practice and belief. More than that, the Revolution was a crucial catalyst of religious change. As many historians have emphasized, the cultural construction of an alternative secular world view and the political alignment of the church with the right reduced the appeal of Catholicism for large parts of the population. But a complementary examination of *religious responses* during the 1790s provides further insights into the process of religious transformation extending into the nineteenth century. By looking within the religious movement itself, we can see the interwoven strands of past influences, present choices, and future implications.

The revolutionary decade was a unique and pivotal period for lay expression and for the metamorphosis of French Catholicism. Despite, or perhaps because of, its hard-hitting attack on Christianity, the Revolution created an opening, a moment of crucial and influential choices for the laity. Although the critiques of the *philosophes* throughout the eighteenth century had already set religion on the defensive, the revolutionary era marked the first time that Christianity was challenged to its very core. The revival of the 1790s in some ways set patterns of possible response, resistance, and accommodation, for although nineteenth-century Catholics would not have to struggle against the legal constraints that had curtailed and enclosed Catholic practice during the Revolution, they would continually face the challenge of expressing and cultivating their religiosity in an increasingly secular age and in an atmosphere in which religious devotion had become a political issue.

The religious adaptations made by the laity during the Revolution included both experimental and customary choices. Indeed, the re-

[4]Adrien Dansette, *Histoire religieuse de la France contemporaine: L'église catholique dans la mêlée politique et sociale*, 2d ed. (Paris, 1961), esp. books 5–7; Isambert and Terrenoire, *Atlas de la pratique religieuse*, chap. 6; *Histoire des catholiques*, ed. Lebrun, chaps. 5, 6; John McManners, *Church and State in France, 1870–1914* (New York, 1972). On attempts at alliances between Catholicism and the left, see Edward Berenson, *Populist Religion and Left-Wing Politics in France, 1830–1852* (Princeton, N.J., 1983); Paul Cohen, *Piety and Politics: Catholic Revival and the Generation of 1905–1914 in France* (New York, 1987).

ligious revival of the 1790s in the Yonne bore witness to the dogged
defense of old customs and beliefs, but also to a widespread willingness to make changes in ritual expression. When they broke into
churches, recovered statues, bells, crosses, and altars, and turned back
to the celebration of saints' cults, religious activists drew on the symbolic power of traditional religious rituals. Even as they took advantage of the fluid context of Revolution to create new or altered rituals,
such as lay cults or female-led ceremonies, they incorporated attitudes
developed during the Old Regime. Villagers also seized religious initiative and forged new ceremonies to deal with the cultural ambiguities and material difficulties of the revolutionary situation and to
express in ritual form their own changing attitudes toward the Revolution and toward the essential means of reaching the sacred. Moreover, within the very activism of villagers, whether traditional or innovative, lay the seeds of change. The religious movement during the
Revolution contained antecedents of future religious trends, including the feminization of religion and the growing detachment of many
people from the clergy and from formal devotion in general. The
analysis of religiosity during the Revolution, then, must simultaneously encompass the tenacity and influence of the past, the dynamism of the present, and the foreshadowing and formation of the
future.

What form did Catholicism take in the wake of the Revolution? In
the years following the Concordat the institutional weakening of the
church is the easiest legacy of the Revolution to discern. In the early
1800s when priests and people returned to the legal, public practice of
their faith in the Yonne, as in the rest of France, they faced immediate
structural and material obstacles. The church emerged from the Revolution poorer in wealth and numbers. The decade of Revolution had
witnessed the confiscation and sale of church lands, of many rectories,
and of some church buildings. Often, the remaining churches were
badly in need of repair, and sacred objects, statues, bells, and crosses
were missing or damaged. Church coffers contained no funds to salary
priests, aid the poor, or hire schoolteachers. As late as 1820 a royal
ordinance allowed *fabriques* to reappropriate unsold church goods in
order to deal with their great shortage of funds and supplies. As the
post-Concordat curé F. J. Fortin commented about the early nineteenth century, "In effect, the elements of the earthly presence of the
church among us had disappeared. To reconstruct them would be to
do in a few days the work of centuries." In addition, religious orders

had been suppressed and schools shut down. Thousands of children had grown up without Catholic catechism and the regular public practice of their faith.[5]

More crippling still was the scarcity of clergy in the aftermath of the Revolution. Only about a quarter of the prerevolutionary parish priests of the Auxerrois, for example, were reported to be practicing in the year x (1801–1802), although more would return gradually, and former monks and canons filled some parish posts.[6] Some priests were reluctant to take up their former duties because they doubted, with good reason, that they would be given housing and paid at least a subsistence wage. It would take the clergy of the Yonne several decades to recover from the losses of the Revolution. The handful of clergy who were trained and ordained in the early 1800s could not even fill the positions of the older prerevolutionary clergy who died during the First Empire. While the French clergy as a whole had a difficult time recovering from the 1790s, the Yonne was among those departments hardest hit by clerical shortages in the early 1800s. In 1821, in fact, fewer parish priests were practicing in the Yonne than in 1803.[7] This shortage of clergy contributed to the persistence of lay cults into the nineteenth century and, more fundamentally, accustomed many villagers to life without priests—a dangerous prece-

[5]AD Yonne V33, Ordonnance du roi, 28 mars 1820. AD Yonne V15 and V27, on diocesan churches and rectories, contain many reports between 1802–25 on the need for repair or replacement of church buildings and goods. See esp. AD Yonne V27 (and AN F19 643), Rapport sur les besoins du culte dans le département de l'Yonne, 17 juillet 1811. AN F19 5705 contains letters from priests to the newly appointed "ministre des cultes," bemoaning the poverty of the Yonne's parishes and requesting higher salaries, repairs to churches and rectories, funds for the poor, etc. See Fortin, *Souvenirs* 2:73; Godel, *Réconstruction concordataire*, pp. 355–71.

[6]AN F19 866, Tableau des prêtres du département de l'Yonne, envoyé par le préfet au ministre de la police, 15 vendémiaire an x (7 October 1801); AN F19 2381, Tableau des ordinations, 1801, cited by Jean-Pierre Rocher, "Une séquelle des querelles jansénistes au XVIIIe siècle à Saint-Fargeau (1818–19)," *BSSY* 101 (1967): p. 29. See also Rocher, "Aspects de l'histoire religieuse," pp. 38–40, tableau 2.

[7]AN F19 965B, Etat général des communes où sont placées les cures et les succursales de ce département [de l'Yonne] avec les noms des ecclésiastiques, 27 septembre 1804/3 vendémiaire an XIII. AD Yonne V1 also contains several successive "Etats statistiques et nominatifs" of the priests of the Yonne from 1800 to 1810. From 1802 to 1808, for example, only six new priests were ordained in the diocese of Troyes, which included the Yonne and the Aube. Forestier, "Le 'culte laïcal' et la crise des effectifs," 36:3–6, 37:3–6. Tackett and Langlois, "A l'épreuve de la Révolution," esp. map p. 283, illustrates that the Yonne, along with its neighbor departments from the Ardennes in the north stretching on a broad diagonal southwest through the center to the departments of Charente-Inférieure and the Gironde in the southwest, had the highest percentage of vacant parishes in 1814–15.

dent in a clericalized religion such as Catholicism. In short, the institutional impact of the Revolution—the results of its all-out campaign against the wealth, power, and clerical leadership of the Old Regime church—left a tangible mark on religious devotion and on the morale of parishioners and priests.

Faced with a weakened church and a scarcity of clergy in the early nineteenth century, some villagers abandoned public religious devotion entirely. Others combined orthodox rituals with the stubborn defense of unorthodox forms of lay devotion. Following patterns of religious expression created during the French Revolution, religious activists clung to a somewhat paradoxical mixture of the revolutionary and the traditional. Bishops, clergy, and government officials in the early 1800s waged an age-old battle against the illegal celebration of saints' festivals and also struggled to suppress the more innovative lay cults. Parishioners apparently saw no troubling contradictions in this fusion of revolutionary and traditional forms of devotion. For example, the *acquéreur* of the church Saint-Pierre in Chablis complained in 1799 that the former parishioners held "daily *rassemblements.* . . . With the pretext of looking for a saint, . . . some participants took the liberty of digging and creating wreckage" on his newly acquired property. These same parishioners had rioted against the transfer of their sacred objects to a nearby parish in 1793, held illegal outdoor processions and dancing on a festival day in 1798, barricaded their church bell tower to save the bell in 1803 and 1807, and at one point succeeded in buying back their church to prevent its destruction. Yet the parishioners of Saint-Pierre also persistently celebrated lay masses in the late 1790s and early 1800s, despite the availability of a priest at the nearby parish of Saint-Martin.[8]

For believers increasingly independent of the clergy, innovative and timeworn forms of devotion converged to satisfy their fervent desire to reach the divine through the localized sacred and through collective ritual. As activists in the Yonne reconstructed their religion

[8]AD Yonne L696, Délibérations municipales de Chablis, 30 germinal an VII (19 April 1799), L712, PV de la commune de Chablis, 2 octobre 1793, L75, Arrêté du département de l'Yonne, 21 thermidor an VI (8 August 1798); AC Chablis 1 P1, dépôt 296, Lettre du maire de Chablis au préfet de l'Yonne, 27 nivôse an XI (17 January 1803), Arrêté du département de l'Yonne, 23 floréal an XI (13 May 1803), PV du maire de Chablis, 26 nivôse an XII (17 January 1804), Arrêté du préfet de l'Yonne, 30 November 1807, Lettre du maire de Chablis au préfet, 23 December 1807, Lettres des acquéreurs de Saint-Pierre au maire de Chablis, April 1808; Forestier, "Le culte laïcal à Chablis," p. 338.

within the fluid context of the Revolution, they often chose to pursue what Nicole Perin has described as "popular religion of disorder."[9] Largely inadvertently, the laity and clergy alike exacerbated the tendency, already growing in some regions of France, toward distance between priests and people.

Indeed, as they rebuilt the hierarchical structures of the post-Concordat church, the clergy often found it difficult to absorb these manifestations of lay autonomy and unorthodoxy. In fact, authorities were aware of a dangerous link between lay cults and older types of "superstitious" or "irrational" worship. Lamenting the pervasiveness of lay cults, the bishop of Troyes wrote in 1803, "Many schoolteachers and others continue to usurp all the sacerdotal functions, singing or reciting aloud the offices and even the ordinary of the mass in the churches. The results in a short while will be either the *abolition of religion* in the parishes or the *introduction of many superstitions*, and the government is as opposed to impiety as to superstition" (emphasis added).[10]

Lay cults and older "superstitions" seemed to elude clerical control and to signal the growing gap between villagers and educated clergy and notables, who envisaged a more "enlightened" Catholicism.[11] When the bishop of Troyes sought to enforce the reduction of saints' festivals in 1803, he appealed to the prefect of the Yonne to protect priests from the violence and disobedience of unruly parishioners: "It is important that curés are safeguarded from any violence that hinders them from promoting the intentions of the Holy See and the government [to reduce festival days]."[12] Indeed, the prefect reported

[9]Nicole Perin applies the term to the diocese of Reims in the 1770s. "La religion populaire: Mythes et réalités: L'exemple du diocèse de Reims sous l'ancien régime," in *La religion populaire,* pp. 221–28, esp. 225.

[10]AD Yonne V9, Lettre de l'archevêque de Troyes au préfet du département de l'Yonne, 26 mai 1803. Arguably, the unpopularity of the clergy increased because of the attempt to suppress popular festivals in the early 1800s. Forestier suggests that this anticlerical sentiment encouraged the tenacity of lay cults. See his "Notes sur le culte laïcal," *AB* 25 (1953): 210–11.

[11]Yves-Marie Hilaire, "Notes sur la religion populaire au XIXe siècle," *La religion populaire,* pp. 193–98, esp. 195. Hilaire points out that notables and clergy were part of the "Second Enlightenment," which increased their distance from "popular religion," which was "agrarian, festive, and panic-oriented." Berenson, *Populist Religion and Left-Wing Politics,* chap. 2. On the training and character of priests in the Yonne, see Fortin, *Souvenirs,* esp. 2:365ff.

[12]AD Yonne V9, Lettre de 'évêque de Troyes au préfet du département de l'Yonne, 26 mai 1803.

that "curés are forced to cede to the insistence of the citizens" and commemorate "all possible festivals" with pomp, celebration, and flamboyant bell ringing. One priest in Auxerre, for example, gave in to his parishioners' demands for bell ringing, outdoor processions, and ceremonies after dark on the festival of the Nativity of the Virgin.[13] While it is hard to gauge the exact religious motivation of villagers, clearly they sought to defend customs rooted in traditional Catholic culture.

Although the church had repeatedly confronted the challenge of either incorporating or weeding out unorthodox lay practices, it found the task more delicate and difficult in an era when secularism presented a viable alternative to religion as a cultural system. Gérard Cholvy has suggested that lay attachment to "popular religion" in the nineteenth century was perhaps stronger, or harder to assimilate and christianize, "in the 'dechristianized' areas such as the Parisian Basin." Particularly in regions of "Jansenist or simply rigorist" clerical traditions, the reserved attitude of the clergy tended to increase the distance between villagers and their pastors, just as it had in the eighteenth century. Indeed, in areas such as the Yonne and other departments of central France where clergy were especially scarce during the critical postrevolutionary years 1800–1830, this conflict and distance between clerical desires and lay forms of practice may have been especially detrimental.[14] Later, in the mid-nineteenth century, the church was able to cultivate popular allegiance by amalgamating and even embracing certain forms of "popular" religious practice, such as pilgrimages and miracle cults.[15] But for some regions and sectors of

[13]AC Auxerre, Dépôt 3 P5, Lettre du préfet de l'Yonne au maire d'Auxerre, 17 frimaire an XII (9 December 1803), Réponse du maire d'Auxerre au préfet, 18 frimaire an XII (10 December 1803). On the persistence of festivals in the Yonne into the later 1800s, see Charles Moiset, "Les usages, croyances, traditions, supersititons, etc., ayant existé ou existant encore dans les divers pays du département de l'Yonne," *BSSY* 42 (1888): 5–157; Jean-Pierre Rocher, ed., *Les paysans de l'Yonne au XIXe siècle: Du lendemain de la Révolution à la Grande Guerre* (Auxerre, 1978), pp. 33–35.

[14]Gérard Cholvy, "Expressions et évolution du sentiment religieux populaire en France du XIXe siècle, du temps de la restauration catholique (1801–1860)," *Actes du 99e congrès national des Sociétés savantes* (Paris, 1976), 1:301; Louis Pérouas, "Entre le XVIe et le XIXe siècles, de regards différents sur le culte des saints en Limousin," in *La religion populaire*, pp. 85–94; Alain Corbin, *Archaïsme et modernité en Limousin au XIXe siècle, 1845–1880*, 2 vols. (Paris, 1975), pp. 619ff., as cited in Pérouas, p. 85. Pérouas and Corbin analyze the coexistence of detachment from the clergy with fervent attachment to "popular" forms of traditional devotion in the Limousin.

[15]Thomas Kselman, *Miracles and Prophecies in Nineteenth-Century France* (New Brunswick, N.J., 1983); Hilaire, "Notes sur la religion populaire," pp. 196–97.

the population, particularly in the huge central area of France known for "indifference" in the modern era, this flexibility of the institutional church offered too little change too late.[16]

Although some choices of the laity seemed in the long run to facilitate or herald the growth of secularism or anticlericalism, during the French Revolution itself these lay actions bore witness to Catholic villagers' determined and heartfelt defense of their living religion. As the citizen Laire of Sens commented in a letter to Grégoire in 1795, "I think it will be difficult to restrain the countryside back within the narrow boundaries of society except by giving them back their churches and the freedom to practice the religion in which they have been brought up and nourished."[17] In the Thermidorean and Directorial periods, many parts of France experienced an outburst of religiosity which could not be sustained into the nineteenth century. Lay cults did not express "irreligion." Rather, they expressed a dynamic and creative form of religiosity which allowed independence from the clergy to flourish. The post-Concordat church found it difficult to incorporate this ritual detachment from the institutional hierarchy and from orthodox Catholic practice, especially because the shortage of clergy exacerbated the cultural trend toward distance from the clergy.

Likewise, the development of female devotion and male detachment was born of nascent Old Regime tendencies, intensified and furthered by the choices of lay religious activists during the Revolution. Although this development contained secularizing elements, it too grew out of devotion and activism. For the fervent religious response of women in the 1790s accentuated an existing tendency toward the feminization of religion. Many nineteenth-century developments promoted this sexual division of religious practice, among them the laicization of male education and leisure time, the transformations in domestic habits and in gender labor patterns, and the clergy's focus on the family as the launching pad for religious, moral, and social reform movements. Men may have resented more than their wives did the church's condemnation of left-wing politics, its association with the temperance movement, and its disapproval of forms of contraception, for which the male was held morally responsi-

[16]Isambert and Terrenoire, *Atlas de la pratique religieuse;* François Goguel, *La politique en France* (Paris, 1980), esp. map p. 246.

[17]BSPR, Fonds Grégoire, Carton Yonne, Lettre de Laire à Grégoire, 21 nivôse an III (10 January 1795).

ble. Particularly as science seemed to highlight the irrational and passive aspects of religion, men in the late 1800s who wished to associate themselves with the active, rational images of science and politics left religious devotion to their wives. As the century progressed, the association of Catholicism with the domestic (female) sphere only increased, and the sexual dichotomy in religious practice grew more pronounced.[18] This modern allocation of religious responsibility within the family stemmed from inclinations existing in the Old Regime and channeled by nineteenth-century social, economic, and political trends. Yet the activism of women during the Revolution first crystallized this development. As women charged to the fore in defense of churches, bells, and priests, they proclaimed their vibrant attachment to Catholicism and demarcated public religious expression as their own sphere within community and family.

New Political Definitions

A final ramification of the revolutionary era for Catholicism was a basic change in the political position of religious culture and of the church as an institution. Just as the post-Concordat church had to accept a decline in religious practice, so it had to come to terms with a very different political status. In the Old Regime, public Catholic rituals on the national level had endowed the monarchy with legitimate sacred power, and on the local level public participation in Catholic processions, the rental of expensive pews near the altar, and membership in *fabriques* or in respected confraternities bestowed prestige on the wealthiest and most powerful villagers. But once the Revolution had simultaneously undermined the hierarchical structure of Old Regime society and the religious system that helped to unfold it, Catholic culture no longer held sway as the universal bestower and reinforcer of political power.

Although the Concordat had reestablished the Catholic Church as a legitimate institution, the loss of its financial and political indepen-

[18]Boutry and Cinquin, *Deux pèlerinages au XIXe siècle*, chaps. 1 and 2; Dupuy, "Les femmes dans la contre-Révolution," pp. 61–70; Langlois, "Permanence, renouveau, et affrontements," pp. 323–25; Hufton, "Reconstruction of a Church," pp. 23–25; Pat Holden, ed., *Women's Religious Experience: Cross-Cultural Perspectives* (Totowa, N.J., 1983), p. 6; Vieda Skultans, "Mediums, Controls, and Emminent Men," in *Women's Religious Experience*, 15–26, esp. pp. 23–25; Ruether and McLaughlin, eds., *Women of the Spirit*, p. 26.

dence, combined with its status as an *église fonctionarisée*—a church of civil servants—made repeated disputes with the state inevitable. As the wealthy Gallican Church ceded its place to the poorer Ultramontane Church of the nineteenth century, many clergymen would look to Rome rather than to the state for guidance and support. Above all, faced with the perennial decision of whether to accept or reject the principles of 1789, the Catholic leadership followed an indecisive path, wavering between a liberal and, more often, an authoritarian and rigid approach. Most Catholic clergymen and many lay Catholics found it difficult to make accommodations with republican politics and secular culture, and—to oversimplify somewhat—the less accommodating attitude came to dominate Catholic response to left-wing politics. The church chose to cast its lot increasingly with right-wing or monarchical parties. (For example, the decision to support Louis Napoleon in 1851 was crucial in allying religion with "order" and the right, as was the failure of the *ralliement* in the 1890s.)[19] These transformations in the political, cultural, and social position of the church necessarily affected lay religious expression. They contributed to the church's inability to incorporate certain political groups of the population. Many republican men and some women deliberately chose to avoid Catholic services in order to state their opposition to clergy who were not only right-wing but also seemed to be excessively authoritarian and at times even disloyal to France.

This particular position of the church grew out of the revolutionary era and also out of choices made in the nineteenth and twentieth centuries by many French people, whether Catholic or anticlerical, republican or monarchist, laity or clergy. The tendency of republicans both during and after the Revolution to define themselves in opposition to Catholicism, as well as a certain rigidity of many Catholic leaders facing modern political and social challenges—both of these were crucial in defining the modern relationship between religion and politics. Yet I have argued that it is wrong to assume that Catholicism and the left were irreconcilable from the 1790s on. Rather, I have sought to emphasize the striking flexibility of culture and politics during the upheaval and uncertainty of the revolutionary years, for the revolution was a moment of cultural transformation when both religion and politics were in a complex process of reformulation.

[19]Dansette, *Histoire religieuse*, esp. books 5–6, 10: 5; McManners, *Church and State*, esp. chaps. 3, 8, 9.

During the course of the Revolution itself the most radical revolutionaries came increasingly to characterize Catholicism as entirely alien to the goals and ideals of the Revolution. Out of Catholicism they forged a residual category of stereotyped characteristics—a type of theatrical stage onto which they projected all the cultural and political attributes of the Old Regime which they hoped to abolish or transform.[20] In Catholicism, the revolutionaries saw only a dramatization of deception, counterrevolution, and tyrannical power—political, emotional, and moral—played out on a stage of superstition and inequality. Against this schematized representation of Catholicism as counterrevolutionary, the revolutionaries could define their own new culture more easily, showing it in clear-cut opposition. Reason, equality, popular sovereignty, virtue, and transparency stood out in sharp relief against the perceived fanaticism, privilege, authoritarianism, corruption, and mysterious duplicity that seemed to define Catholicism.

The prerevolutionary position as political ally of the monarchy and promoter of religious faith made Catholicism the natural enemy of the revolutionaries in their crusade to create a representative political structure and a secular culture. The revolutionaries assumed that in order to reeducate the people according to their new ideals, they had to obliterate Catholicism, but in their fervor to construct a new world, they underestimated the resiliency and flexibility both of Catholicism and of their own revolutionary discourse. In effect, by irrevocably equating Catholicism with counterrevolution not only did the revolutionaries underrate the tenacity and adaptability of religious culture; they also oversimplified the connections between religion and politics and failed to recognize the ability of Catholic villagers to assimilate the Revolution. Admittedly, Catholics were frequently unable or unwilling to accept the new symbolic system promoted by the revolutionaries. But while they may have found the Supreme Being distant or alien, chafed against the revolutionary calendar, and resented the destruction of their saints' statues and the imprisonment or deportation of their priests, many Catholic villagers did not reject the Revolution in its entirety.

Catholicism fueled counterrevolution in the west and in parts of

[20]Edward W. Said, *Orientalism* (New York, 1978), pp. 69–73. Said argues in a similar fashion that the West projected onto the Orient certain stereotyped traits that helped the West to define and assert its cultural and moral superiority over the Orient as well as to validate its political dominance.

southeastern France, but in much of the country the connections between revolutionary politics and religious affiliation were much subtler. In the Yonne, and in many other regions that were religious yet not counterrevolutionary, the politics of religious resurgence took a different and perhaps unpredictable form. The Revolution provided Catholic villagers with a political ideology and political structures that enabled them to demand freedom of worship. Beyond this, the centrality of Catholic practice and belief in the lives of many French people made religion an inevitable point of debate in local politics; local conflicts over religious issues augmented the political education of some villagers.[21] In some situations, the desire to demand the return to religious practice increased villagers' exposure and openness to revolutionary political institutions and ideology as they strove to use petitions, the structures of electoral politics, and the revolutionary promises of liberty and popular sovereignty to put their demands into effect. Religious activists incorporated revolutionary political discourse into their existing attitudes toward politics. They used some political tactics from prerevolutionary days, now made more powerful as the events and the ideology of the Revolution validated and expanded the power of popular activism.

In short, although the battle lines between the left and the church were indeed being drawn during the Revolution, the Revolution was also an era of cultural and political flux that allowed multiple recastings and varied interpretations of discourse and politics. Cultural change and realignment, perhaps especially in the countryside, was not always as thorough and clear-cut as the revolutionaries hoped. In 1798 the *Observateur de l'Yonne* complained that many women attended Theophilanthropist ceremonies with crosses around their necks, failing to see that this "superstitious" practice was inconsistent with their revolutionary regeneration and a deist turn toward Theophilanthropy. Their syncretism bears witness to the complex and many-layered nature of cultural change and to the cultural fluidity of the Revolution itself. When the religious activists of Auxerre, seeking to regain their cathedral in 1795, used sectional politics, violence, and a march on the municipality with the tricolor flag to petition for their church and to assert their loyalty to Republic and religion, they com-

---

[21]See Peter M. Jones, *Politics and Rural Society: The Southern Massif Central, c. 1750–1880* (Cambridge, Eng., 1985), chap. 6. Jones suggests that religion may have done more than the state to promote political awareness.

bined old and new methods and proclaimed both revolutionary and traditional loyalties.[22]

This analysis calls into question the assumption that Catholics virtually inevitably chose to take right-wing or monarchical political positions during the Revolution and also suggests the possibility for coalitions between the left and Catholicism in the modern era. The attempt of Catholic villagers to assimilate revolutionary ideology into their religious expression and into their political defense of Catholicism may have paved the way for later attempts to join popular Catholicism with radical political views. The Yonne and the surrounding regions, for example, were prime locations for the development of the alliance between popular Christianity and Democratic Socialism between 1848 and 1852, which has been analyzed by Edward Berenson.[23]

The Revolution brought about an intense clash of two conflicting cultures; yet both cultures seemed to many French people to contain appealing elements, and the conflicting cultures were able to influence each other even as they clashed. In fact, the Catholic activists of the Yonne faced the cultural challenge of the Revolution with unexpected adaptability. The religious movement drew strength from the dynamic attempt to forge a new cultural reality out of old and new beliefs and practices. In the religious realm, as they recreated their spirituality, Catholic activists combined the defense, and even resurrection, of old traditions with lay religious innovation and experimentation to incorporate the revolutionary culture and context. Likewise, in the realm of political struggle, activists relied on old forms of protest infused with new life, method, and ideology born of the Revolution. Above all, the religious activists of the Yonne, as in much of the rest of France, succeeded in fusing symbol and action, religion and politics, to bring about cultural change at this critical juncture in modern history.

[22]BN, *Observateur de l'Yonne*, 25 floréal an VI (15 May 1798).
[23]Berenson, *Populist Religion and Left-Wing Politics*.

APPENDIX

National Religious Policy

2 November 1789: Nationalization of church lands.
19 December 1789: Law authorizing sale of nationalized lands.
13 February 1790: Law withdrawing official recognition of monastic vows.
12 July 1790: Law of Civil Constitution of the Clergy.
27 November 1790: Law imposing clerical oath:

> "I swear to look carefully after the welfare of my parishioners, to be faithful to the nation, the law, and the king, and to maintain with all my power the Constitution determined by the National Assembly and accepted by the king."

26 December 1790: King sanctions the oath to Civil Constitution.
4 May 1791: Pope condemns Civil Constitution.
26 August 1792: Law requiring deportation of refractory clergy.
3 September 1792: Law requiring all ecclesiastics to take Liberté-Egalité oath:

> "I swear to be faithful to the nation, and to maintain with all my power Liberty, Equality, and the security of persons and property, and to die, if need be, for the execution of the law."

7 October 1793: Revolutionary calendar adopted.
10 November 1793 (20 brumaire an II): Festival of Reason.
8 December 1793 (18 frimaire an II): Law guaranteeing freedom of worship.
7 May 1794 (18 floréal an II): Law instituting national festivals and cult of the Supreme Being.
8 June 1794 (20 prairial an II): Festival of Supreme Being.
27 July 1794 (9 thermidor an II): Fall of Robespierre.
18 September 1794 (2e sans-culottides an II): Law not to salary ministers of any cult.

12, 17 November 1794 (22, 27 brumaire an III): Laws establishing secular primary education system.

21 December 1794 (1 nivôse an III): Grégoire's speech in favor of freedom of religious practice; debate on the *culte décadaire*.

17 February 1795 (29 pluviôse an III): LaJaunaye truce with the Vendée allowing limited freedom of worship.

21 February 1795 (3 ventôse an III): Law allowing limited freedom of religious worship; no signs, bells, churches, collections, or outdoor processions permitted; no state support for any cult or any ministers.

15 March 1795 (25 ventôse an III): Encyclical sent out to all Constitutional clergy by Grégoire's standing council of Constitutional Bishops to re-establish the Constitutional Church and make a profession of faith in Catholicism and the Republic.

30 May 1795 (11 prairial an III): Law allowing parishioners to reclaim use of churches provided that the curé make a declaration of "submission to the laws of the Republic."

23 September 1795 (1 vendémiaire an IV): Proclamation of the Constitution of the Year III.

29 September 1795 (7 vendémiaire an IV): Law regulating police des cultes; communes and priests may declare use of churches; whether practicing or not, priests must make the declaration: "I recognize the universality of French citizens as sovereign, and I promise submission and obedience to the laws of the Republic." Those priests who intended to practice must also declare where they would lead worship.

25 October 1795 (3 brumaire an IV): Reapplication of 1792 and 1793 law against priests subject to deportation.

9 April 1796 (20 germinal an IV): Law against bell ringing.

25 November 1796 (14 frimaire an V): Weakening of 3 brumaire an IV law; liberation of more priests.

15 January 1797 (26 nivôse an V): First Theophilanthropist ceremony in Paris.

March–April 1797 (germinal an V): Elections bringing many pro-Catholic moderate and right-wing deputies to power.

17 June 1797 (29 prairial an V): Camille Jordan's speech for freedom of religious practice and bell ringing.

15 August 1797 (28 thermidor an V): Opening of National Council of Constitutional Bishops.

24 August 1797 (7 fructidor an V): Repeal of 1792 and 1793 laws against nonjuring and deportable priests.

4 September 1797 (18 fructidor an V): Coup d'état against the right.

5 September 1797 (19 fructidor an V): Law imposing on practicing clergy the oath of "hatred of royalty and anarchy, of attachment and loyalty to the Republic and to the Constitution of the Year III"; and reenacting the 1792 and 1793 laws against nonjuring and emigré clergy; all deportable clergy must leave France within fifteen days.

4 December 1797 (14 frimaire an VI): Law enforcing republican calendar and institutions.

3 April 1798 (14 germinal an VI): Law making republican calendar and festivals obligatory for markets, spectacles, fairs, etc.

5 July 1798 (17 messidor an VI): Law ordering search for hidden nonjurors.

5 August 1798 (18 thermidor an VI): Law enforcing various republican institutions, such as wearing the *cocarde,* using the title citizen, closing public offices and schools on *décadi.*

9 September 1798 (23 fructidor an VI): Law making *culte décadaire* obligatory.

9 November 1799 (18 brumaire an VIII): Coup d'état by Napoleon.

24 December 1799 (3 nivôse an VIII): Napoleon becomes first consul; Law suppressing *fêtes nationales* except 14 July and 22 September.

28 December 1799 (7 nivôse an VIII): Law allowing unsold churches to be used for worship, even on Sundays, and requiring priests to promise loyalty to new constitution.

26 July 1800 (7 thermidor an VIII): Law ending obligatory celebration of *fêtes décadaires.*

8 April 1802 (18 germinal an X): Promulgation of Concordat.

Bibliography

PRIMARY SOURCES

The primary documents listed in this section provided the core of information for this study. They consist mainly of police and court records, letters and reports written by government officials and priests, petitions by Catholics, departmental, district, and municipal deliberations, and some memoirs. General descriptions of the sources are listed here; more detailed citations can be found in the footnotes.

Archives nationales
ADvii 37 & 48. Printed pamphlets and speeches on religious policy.
Série AFii. Correspondence and reports by représentants en mission, among papers of the Committee of Public Safety and the Committee of General Security.
Série AFiii. Papers of the Directory, including reports, correspondence, and notes on the politics and *esprit public* of the departments.
Bii 66. Elections to accept or reject the Constitution of the Year iii (1794–95).
Série C. Papers of the national legislatures. Petitions and letters sent to the legislatures. Minutes of the debates.
Série Diii. Papers of the National Committee of Legislation.
Série F1bii. Reports on administrative personnel.
Série F1ciii. Reports on *esprit public*.
Série F7. Police records on violations of religious laws and on refractory clergymen.
F13 772. "Enquêtes sur les monuments religieux par le Ministre de l'intérieur (an iv/1795–96)."
F18 23. Correspondence and reports on publishers.
Série F19. Papers of the Ministry of the Interior regarding *cultes*.

F20*20. Statistics. Population estimates for the Yonne in the year III (1794–95).

Archives départementales de l'Yonne
F441–442. Notes on the revolutionary period collected by Charles Porée.
Série G. Old Regime ecclesiastical records, including pastoral visits by bishops and registers of confraternities and parish *fabriques*.
Série L. Departmental papers from the revolutionary period.
Série V. Reports and correspondence on *cultes* after 1800.
1 Fi Cassini 1–7. Cassini's eighteenth-century maps of the Yonne.
Série 1J and 37J. Diverse collections, especially 37J5, "Mémorial d'un Auxerrois de ce qui s'est passé à Auxerre, 1793–96"; 1J231, Jacob-Nicolas-Edme Duplessis, "Mémoire historique pour continuer l'histoire de l'église d'Auxerre: L'épiscopat de Monseigneur Champion de Cicé (1761–1805)."

Archives départementales de la Côte-d'Or
C6351. Taille roll of Auxerre (1789).
Série L. Departmental papers from the revolutionary period.

Archives départementales des Côtes-du-Nord, de l'Ille-et-Vilaine, et de la Sarthe
Série L. Departmental papers of the revolutionary period.

Archives communales
Auxerre: Série D. Municipal deliberations and decrees.
    G1-2. Taxation records (revolutionary period).
    Série I. Police records.
    Série K. Election results.
    Série P. Papers concerning *cultes*.
Chablis: Série G. Taxation records.
    Série P. Papers concerning *cultes*.
Irancy: D1-3. Municipal deliberations and decrees.
    G1-2. Taxation records (revolutionary period).
Ligny-le-Châtel: Série G. Taxation records.
Saint-Bris: D2. Municipal deliberations and decrees.
Saint-Florentin: Série D. Municipal deliberations.

Bibliothèque municipale d'Auxerre
The Collections Bastard, Lorin, and Tarbé contain many pamphlets, almanacs, poems, and songs from the revolutionary period.

Bibliothèque nationale: Newspapers
Le journal politique et littéraire du département de l'Yonne, 15 nivôse–15 fructidor an V (4 January–1 September 1797).
L'observateur du département de l'Yonne, 25 nivôse an IV–9 frimaire an IX (15

January 1796–30 November 1800).
Some of the issues of these journals missing from the Bibliothèque nationale are available at the Bibliothèque municipale d'Auxerre.

Bibliothèque de la Société de Port Royal (BSPR)
Fonds Grégoire. Correspondence, especially Carton Yonne. Letters to Grégoire from the Constitutional clergy of the Yonne.

Printed Primary Sources
Demay, Charles, ed. "Cahiers des paroisses du bailliage d'Auxerre pour les Etats-généraux de 1789." *BSSY* 38 (1884): 65–400, and 39 (1885): 5–150.
———. "Procès verbaux de l'administration municipale de la ville d'Auxerre pendant la Révolution." *BSSY* 45–47 (1891–93).
Fortin, F. J. *Souvenirs.* 2 vols. Auxerre, 1865–67.
Garreau, Antoine. *Description du gouvernement de Bourgogne,* 2d ed. Dijon, 1734.
Grégoire, Henri. *Mémoires.* Ed. H. Carnot. 2 vols. Paris, 1840.
"Journal d'un Auxerrois du 19 novembre 1796 au 7 septembre 1797)." *Annuaire de l'Yonne* 30 (1866): 247–91.
Lebeuf, Abbé Jean. *Mémoires concernant l'histoire civile et ecclésiastique d'Auxerre . . . continués jusqu'à nos jours.* Ed. Challe, A. and Max Quantin. 4 vols. Auxerre, 1848–55.
Léger, M., ed. *Lettres des représentants du peuple dans l'Yonne.* (Excerpts reprinted from *Annuaire de l'Yonne,* 1892–98). N.p., n.d.
Lois et actes du gouvernement, août 1789 au septembre 1790. Paris, 1834.
Monceaux, Henri, ed. *Procès verbaux de l'administration départementale de 1790 à 1800.* 7 vols. Auxerre, 1888–1913.
Porée, Charles, ed. *Cahiers de doléances du bailliage de Sens pour les États-généraux de 1789.* Auxerre, 1908.
———. *Sources manuscrites de l'histoire de la Révolution dans l'Yonne.* Auxerre, 1918–27.
———. "Mémoires du chanoine Frappier sur le clergé d'Auxerre pendant la Révolution (de 1789 à l'an IV)." *BSSY* 77 (1923): 101–42.
———. *Cahiers des curés et des communautés ecclésiastiques du bailliage d'Auxerre pour les Etats-généraux de 1789.* Auxerre, 1927.
Relation de la visite générale faite par Monsieur de Condorcet, évêque d'Auxerre, dans son diocèse. N.p., n.d. [c. 1760].
Restif de la Bretonne, Nicolas-Edme. *La vie de mon père.* Paris, 1970, orig. ed., 1778.
———. *L'enfance de Monsieur Nicolas.* Ed. Gilbert Rouger. Paris, 1955, orig. ed., 1794–97.

SECONDARY SOURCES
General Studies
Abray, Jane. "Feminism in the French Revolution." *American Historical Review* 80 (1975): 43–62.

Agulhon, Maurice. *1848, ou L'apprentissage de la République, 1848–1852*. Paris, 1973.

Audard, E. *Actes des martyrs et des confesseurs de la foi pendant la Révolution*. Tours, 1916–20.

Aulard, F. A. *Le christianisme et la Révolution française*. Paris, 1924.

Bauzon, Louis, Paul Muguet, and Louis Chaumont. *Recherches historiques sur la persécution religieuse dans le département de Saône-et-Loire pendant la Révolution*. 4 vols. Chalons-sur-Saône, 1889–1903.

Beidelman, T. O. *Moral Imagination in Kaguru Modes of Thought*. Bloomington, Ind., 1986.

Bercé, Yves-Marie. *Fête et révolte: Des mentalités populaires du XVIe au XVIIIe siècle*. Paris, 1976.

Berenson, Edward. *Populist Religion and Left-Wing Politics in France, 1830–1852*. Princeton, N.J., 1983.

Berthelot du Chesnay, Charles. *Les missions de Saint Eudes*. Paris, 1967.

———. *Les prêtres séculiers en Haute-Bretagne au XVIIIe siècle*. Rennes, 1984.

Bertrand-Geoffroy, Monique. "Le culte révolutionnaire et l'opposition à la France dans le département des Alpes-Maritimes (1793–1800)." *Actes du 99e Congrès national des Sociétés savantes* (Paris, 1976): 1:199–209.

Bianchi, Serge. *La révolution culturelle de l'an II: Elites et peuple (1789–1799)*. Paris, 1982.

Biron, Marie-Paule, "La résistance des laïcs à travers les messes clandestines pendant la Révolution française." *Bulletin de la Société française d'histoire des idées et d'histoire religieuse* 1 (1984): 13–37.

Bois, Paul. *Paysans de l'ouest*, abrev. ed. Paris, 1971.

Bossy, John. "Essai de sociographie de la messe, 1200–1700." *Annales: Economies, sociétés, civilisations* 36 (1981): 44–70.

Bouchard, Gérard. *Le village immobile*. Paris, 1972.

Bouchez, Emile. *Le clergé du pays rémois pendant la Révolution et la suppression de l'archevêché de Reims (1789–1821)*. Reims, 1913.

Boulard, Fernand. *Premiers itinéraires en sociologie religieuse*. 2d ed. Paris, 1954.

———. *Pratique religieuse urbaine et régions culturelles*. Paris, 1968.

———. *Matériaux pour l'histoire religieuse du peuple française, XIXe–XXe siècles*. Paris, 1982.

Boussolade, J. *L'église de Paris du 9 thermidor au Concordat*. Paris, 1950.

———. "Le presbytérianisme dans les Conciles de 1797 et 1801." *AHRF* 121 (1951): 17–37.

Boutry, Philippe, and Michel Cinquin. *Deux pèlerinages au XIXe siècle: Ars et Paray-le-Monial*. Paris, 1980.

Brelot, J. *La vie politique en Côte-d'Or sous le Directoire*. Dijon, 1932.

Bresson, A. *Les prêtres de la Haute-Marne déportés sous la Convention et le Directoire*. Langres, 1913.

Bridoux, Fernand. *Histoire religieuse du département de Seine-et-Marne pendant la Révolution*. 2 vols. Melun, 1953.

Brown, Peter. *The Cult of the Saints*. Chicago, 1981.

Burke, Peter. *Popular Culture in Early Modern Europe.* New York, 1978.

Bussière, G. *Etudes sur la Révolution en Périgord.* 3 vols. Bordeaux, 1897–1903.

Bynum, Caroline Walker. "Women Mystics and Eucharistic Devotion in the Thirteenth Century." *Women's Studies* 11 (1984): 179–214.

_____. "Women's Stories, Women's Symbols: A Critique of Victor Turner's Theory of Liminality." In *Anthropology and the Study of Religion.* Ed. F. Reynolds and R. Moore. Chicago, 1984: pp. 105–25.

Bynum, Caroline Walker, Stevan Harrell, and Paula Richman, eds. *Gender and Religion: On the Complexity of Symbols.* Boston, 1986.

Castex, J., et al. *L'église de France et la Révolution: Histoire régionale. Le Midi.* Vol. 2. Paris, 1984.

Certeau, Michel de. "L'histoire religieuse du XVIIe siècle: Problèmes de méthode." *Recherches de science religieuse* 57 (1969): 231–50.

Certeau, Michel de, Dominique Julia, and Jacques Revel. *La politique de la langue.* Paris, 1975.

Chaline, Nadine-Josette, Michel Lagrée, and Serge Chassagne. *L'église de France et la Révolution: Histoire régionale. L'ouest.* Vol. 1. Paris, 1983.

Charrier, Jules. *Histoire religieuse du département de la Nièvre pendant la Révolution.* 2 vols. Paris, 1926.

Chartier, Jacques. "Texts, Symbols, and Frenchness." *JMH* 58 (1986): 218–34.

Chaunu, Pierre. "Jansénisme et frontière de la catholicité: A propos du jansénisme lorrain," *Revue historique* 227 (1962): 115–38.

_____. *La mort à Paris aux XVIe, XVIIe, et XVIIIe siècles.* Paris, 1978.

Chaussinand-Nogaret, Guy. *La noblesse au XVIIIe siècle.* Paris, 1976.

Cholvy, Gérard. "Expressions et évolution du sentiment religieux populaire en France du XIXe siècle, du temps de la restauration catholique (1801–60)." *Actes du 99e Congrès national des Sociétés savantes* (Paris, 1976): 1:289–320.

_____. "Religion et Révolution: La déchristianisation de l'an II." *AHRF* 233 (1978): 451–64.

Christian, William. *Person and God in a Spanish Valley.* New York, 1972.

_____. *Local Religion in Sixteenth-Century Spain.* Princeton, N.J., 1981.

Cobb, Richard. *Les armées révolutionnaires: Instrument de la Terreur dans les départements.* 2 vols. Paris, 1961–63.

_____. *The Police and the People: French Popular Protest, 1789–1820.* Oxford, 1970.

Cohen, Elizabeth Starr. "The Socialization of Young Women in Early Modern France." Ph.D. diss., University of Toronto, 1978.

Cohen, Paul. *Piety and Politics: Catholic Revival and the Generation of 1905–1914 in France.* New York, 1987.

Compère, Marie-Madéleine, Roger Chartier, and Dominique Julia. *L'éducation en France du XVIe au XVIIIe siècle.* Paris, 1976.

Cott, Nancy. *The Bonds of Womanhood: "Woman's Sphere" in New England, 1780–1835.* New Haven, Conn., 1977.

Croix, Alain. *La Bretagne aux 16e et 17e siècles: La vie, la mort, la foi.* 2 vols. Paris, 1981.

———. *Les Bretons, la mort, et dieu.* Paris, 1984.

Daniel-Rops, Henri. *L'église des révolutions.* Paris, 1960.

Dansette, Adrien. *Histoire religieuse de la France contemporaine: L'Eglise catholique dans la mêlée politique et sociale.* 2d ed. Paris, 1961.

Darnton, Robert. *The Literary Underground of the Old Regime.* Cambridge, Mass., 1982.

———. *The Great Cat Massacre and Other Episodes in French Cultural History.* New York, 1984.

Davis, Natalie Zemon. *Society and Culture in Early Modern France.* Stanford, Calif., 1975.

———. *The Return of Martin Guerre.* Cambridge, Mass., 1983.

Delarc, Odon. *L'église de Paris pendant la Révolution française.* 3 vols. Paris, 1895–98.

Delarue, Paul. *Le clergé et le culte catholique en Bretagne pendant la Révolution.* 6 vols. Rennes, 1903–10.

Delcambre, E. *La vie dans la Haute-Loire sous le Directoire.* Rodez, 1943.

Delumeau, Jean. *Le catholicisme entre Luther et Voltaire.* Paris, 1971.

Desan, Suzanne. "Redefining Revolution Liberty: The Rhetoric of Religious Revival during the French Revolution." *Journal of Modern History* 60 (1988): 1–27.

———. "Crowds, Community, and Ritual in the Work of E. P. Thompson and Natalie Davis." In *The New Cultural History.* Ed. Lynn Hunt. Berkeley, Calif., 1989: pp. 47–71.

———. "The Role of Women in Religious Riots during the French Revolution." *Eighteenth-Century Studies* 22 (1989): 451–68.

Dommanget, Maurice. *La déchristianisation à Beauvais et dans l'Oise (1790–1801).* Paris, 1918–22.

Douglas, Mary. *Purity and Danger: An Anthropology of Concepts of Pollution and Taboo.* London, 1966.

Dubois, Eugène. *Histoire de la Révolution dans le département de l'Ain.* 6 vols. Bourg, 1931–35.

Dupuy, Roger. "Les femmes dans la contre-Révolution dans l'ouest." *Bulletin d'histoire économique et sociale de la Révolution française,* 1979 (Paris, 1980), pp. 61–70.

Duval, Louis. *La réouverture des églises en l'an III dans le district de Bellême.* Bellême, 1907.

———. "La messe de Monsieur des Rotours." *Bulletin de la Société historique et archéologique de l'Orne* 28 (1909): 156–204.

Eich, Jean. *Histoire religieuse du département de la Moselle pendant la Révolution.* Metz, 1964.

Fage, René. *Le diocèse de Corrèze pendant la Révolution.* Tulle, 1889.

Faucheux, Marcel. *L'insurrection vendéenne de 1793.* Paris, 1964.

Fernandez, James. *Persuasions and Performances: The Play of Tropes in Culture.* Bloomington, Ind., 1986.

Ferté, Jeanne. *La vie religieuse dans les campagnes parisiennes (1622–1695).* Paris, 1962.

Flandrin, Jean-Louis. *Familles, parenté, sexualité dans l'ancienne société.* Paris, 1976.

Fox, Edward. *History in Geographic Perspective: The Other France.* New York, 1971.

Friguglietti, James. "The Social and Religious Consequences of the French Revolutionary Calendar." Ph.D. diss., Harvard University, 1966.

Froeschlé-Chopard, Marie-Hélène. *La religion populaire en Provence orientale au XVIIIe siècle.* Paris, 1980.

Fryer, W. R. *Republic or Restoration in France.* Manchester, Eng., 1965.

Furet, François. *Interpreting the French Revolution.* Trans. Elborg Forster. Cambridge, Eng., 1981.

Furet, François, and Jacques Ozouf. *Lire et écrire: L'alphabétisation de Calvin à Jules Ferry.* 2 vols. Paris, 1977.

Furet, François et al., ed. *Livre et société dans la France du XVIIIe siècle.* 2 vols. Paris, 1965–70.

Gallerand, J. *Les cultes sous la Terreur en Loir-et-Cher, 1792–95.* Blois, 1928.

Garrett, Clark. *Respectable Folly: Millenarians and the French Revolution in France and England.* Baltimore, Md., 1975.

Gaugain, Ferdinand. *Histoire de la Révolution dans la Mayenne.* 4 vols. Laval, 1919–21.

Geertz, Clifford. *The Interpretation of Cultures: Selected Essays.* New York, 1973.

_____. *Local Knowledge: Further Essays in Interpretive Anthropology.* New York, 1983.

Genovese, Eugene. *Roll, Jordan, Roll: The World the Slaves Made.* New York, 1972.

Girardot, Jean. *Le département de la Haute-Saône pendant la Révolution.* 3 vols. Vesoul, 1973.

Giraud, Maurice. *Essai sur l'histoire religieuse de la Sarthe de 1789 à l'an IV.* Paris, 1920.

Godechot, Jacques. *La contre-Révolution: Doctrine et action (1789–1804).* Paris, 1961.

_____. *Les institutions de la France sous la Révolution et l'Empire,* 2d ed. Paris, 1968.

_____, ed. *Les constitutions de la France depuis 1789.* Paris, 1970.

Godel, Jean. *La réconstruction concordataire dans le diocèse de Grenoble après la Révolution (1802–1809).* Grenoble, 1968.

Godineau, Dominique. *Citoyennes tricoteuses: Les femmes du peuple à Paris pendant la Révolution française.* Aix-en-Provence, 1988.

Gonnet, Ernest. *Essai sur l'histoire du diocèse du Puy-en-Velay (1789–1802).* Paris, 1907.

Gutton, Jean-Pierre. *La sociabilité villageoise dans l'ancienne France.* Paris, 1979.

Hanley, Sarah. "Engendering the State: Family Formation and State Building in Early Modern France." *French Historical Studies* 16 (1989): 4–27.

Hilaire, Yves-Marie. *Une chrétienté au XIXe siècle? La vie religieuse des populations du diocèse d'Arras, 1840–1914.* Villeneuve-d'Ascq, 1977.

——. "Notes sur la religion populaire au XIXe siècle." In *La religion populaire.* Paris, 17–19 octobre 1977. Colloques internationaux du Centre national de la recherche scientifique, no. 576. Paris, 1979: pp. 193–98.

Hoffman, Philip T. *Church and Communty in the Diocese of Lyon, 1500–1789.* New Haven, Conn., 1984.

Holton, Robert. "The Crowd in History: Some Problems of Theory and Method." *Social History* 3.2 (1978): 219–33.

Hood, James. "Protestant-Catholic Relations and the Roots of the First Popular Counterrevolutionary Movement in France." *JMH* 43 (1971): 245–75.

Hufton, Olwen. *Bayeux in the Late Eighteenth Century.* Oxford, 1967.

——. "Women in Revolution, 1789–1796." *Past and Present* 53 (1971): 90–108.

——. "The Reconstruction of a Church, 1796–1801." In *Beyond the Terror: Essays in French Regional History, 1794–1815.* Ed. Gwynne Lewis and Colin Lucas. Cambridge, Eng., 1983: pp. 21–52.

Hunt, Lynn. *Revolution and Urban Politics in Provincial France.* Stanford, Calif., 1978.

——. *Politics, Culture, and Class in the French Revolution.* Berkeley, Calif., 1984.

——, ed. *The New Cultural History.* Berkeley, Calif., 1989.

Hutt, Maurice. "The Role of the Curés in the Estates-General of 1789." *Journal of Ecclesiastical History* 6 (1955): 190–220.

Isambert, François-André and Jean-Paul Terrenoire. *Atlas de la pratique religieuse des Catholiques en France.* Paris, 1980.

Jolivet, Charles. *La Révolution en Ardeche.* Lyon, 1930.

Jones, Peter M. "Parish, Seigneurie, and the Community of Inhabitants in Southern Central France during the Eighteenth and Nineteenth Centuries." *Past and Present* 91 (1981): 74–108.

——. *Politics and Rural Society: The Southern Massif Central, c. 1750–1880.* Cambridge, Eng., 1985.

——. *The Peasantry in the French Revolution.* Cambridge, Eng., 1988.

Julia, Dominique. "La réforme post-tridentine en France d'après les procès-verbaux de visites pastorales: Ordre et résistances." *La società religiosa nell'eta moderna: Atti del convegno studi di storia sociale e religiosa. Cupaccio-Paestum, 18–21 maggio 1972.* Naples, 1973: pp. 311–97.

Kaplan, Temma. "Female Consciousness and Collective Action: The Case of Barcelona, 1910–1918," *Signs: Journal of Women in Culture and Society* 7 (1982): 545–66.

Kates, Gary. *The Cercle Social, the Girondins, and the French Revolution.* Princeton, N.J., 1985.

Kennedy, Michael. *The Jacobin Club in the French Revolution: The First Years.* Princeton, N.J., 1982.

Kreiser, Robert. *Miracles, Convulsions, and Ecclesiastical Politics in Eighteenth-Century Paris.* Princeton, N.J., 1978.
Kselman, Thomas. *Miracles and Prophecies in Nineteenth-Century France.* New Brunswick, N.J., 1983.
Lacouture, Joseph. *La politique religieuse de la Révolution.* Paris, 1940.
La Gorce, Pierre de. *Histoire religieuse de la Révolution française.* 5 vols. Paris, 1909–23.
Lagrée, Michel. "Piété populaire et Révolution en Bretagne: l'exemple de canonisations spontanées (1793–1815)." In *Voies nouvelles pour l'histoire de la Révolution française.* Colloque Albert Mathiez–Georges Lefebvre, 1974. Paris, 1978: pp. 265–79.
Landes, Joan B. *Women and the Public Sphere in the Age of the French Revolution.* Ithaca, N.Y., 1988.
Langlois, Claude. *Le diocèse de Vannes, 1800–1830.* Paris, 1974.
_____. "Permanence, renouveau, et affrontements (1830–1880)." In *Histoire des catholiques en France du XVe siècle à nos jours.* Ed. François Lebrun. Toulouse, 1980: pp. 291–368.
Langlois, Claude, and Timothy Tackett. "A l'épreuve de la Révolution, 1770–1830." In *Histoire des catholiques en France.* Ed. François Lebrun. Toulouse, 1980: pp. 215–89.
Latreille, André. *L'Eglise catholique et la Révolution française.* 2 vols. Paris, 1946–50.
Le Bras, Gabriel. *Introduction à l'histoire de la pratique religieuse en France.* 2 vols. Paris, 1942–45.
_____. *Etudes de sociologie religieuse.* 2 vols. Paris, 1955–56.
Le Bras, Hervé, and Emmanuel Todd. *L'invention de la France: Atlas anthropologique et politique.* Paris, 1981.
Lebrun, François, ed. *Histoire des catholiques en France du XVe siècle à nos jours.* Toulouse, 1980.
Ledré, Charles. *Le diocèse de Rouen et la législation religieuse de 1795 à 1800.* Paris, 1939.
_____. *Le culte caché sous la Révolution: Les missions de l'abbé Linsolas.* Paris, 1949.
_____. *L'église de France sous la Révolution.* Paris, 1949.
Lefebvre, Georges. *Les paysans du Nord pendant la Révolution française.* Paris, 1924.
_____. *The Thermidoreans and the Directory.* Trans. Robert Baldick. New York, 1964. Original ed. 1937.
Le Goff, T. J. A. *Vannes and Its Region: A Study of Town and Country in Eighteenth-Century France.* Oxford, 1981.
Le Goff, T. J. A., and Donald Sutherland. "Religion and Rural Revolt in the French Revolution: An Overview." In *Religion and Rural Revolt.* Ed. Janos M. Bak and Gerhard Benecke. Dover, N.H., 1984: pp. 123–45.
Le Grand, Léon. *Les sources de l'histoire religieuse de la Révolution aux Archives nationales.* Paris, 1914.
Lemasson, Auguste. *Les paroisses et clergé du diocèse actuel de Saint-Brieuc de 1789 à 1815.* 2 vols. Rennes, 1926–28.

Le Roy Ladurie, Emmanuel. *Carnival in Romans.* Trans. Mary Feeney. New York, 1979.

Leveque, Pierre. "Vigne, religion, et politique en France aux XIXe et XXe siècles." In *Du jansénisme à la laïcité: Le jansénisme et les origines de la déchristianisation.* Entretiens d'Auxerre, 1983. Ed. Léo Hamon. Paris, 1987: pp. 139–66.

Levy, Darlene Gay, Harriet Branson Applewhite, and Mary Durham Johnson. *Women in Revolutionary Paris, 1789–1795.* Chicago, 1979.

Lewis, Gwynne. *The Second Vendée: The Continuity of Counter-revolution in the Department of the Gard, 1789–1815.* Oxford, 1978.

Luria, Keith. *Territories of Grace: Cultural Change in the Seventeenth-Century Diocese of Grenoble.* Berkeley, Calif., forthcoming.

Mack, Phyllis. "Women as Prophets during the English Civil War." *Feminist Studies* 8 (1982).

McManners, John. *French Ecclesiastical Society Under the Ancien Regime: A Study of Angers in the Eighteenth Century.* Manchester, Eng., 1960.

_____. *The French Revolution and the Church.* New York, 1969.

_____. *Church and State in France, 1870–1914.* New York, 1972.

Marcilhacy, Christianne. *Le diocèse d'Orléans au milieu du XIXe siècle.* Paris, 1964.

Margadant, Ted W. *French Peasants in Revolt: The Insurrection of 1851.* Princeton, N.J., 1979.

Marion, Marcel. *Dictionnaire des institutions de la France aux XVIIe et XVIIIe siècles.* Paris, 1923.

Mathiez, Albert. *La théophilanthropie et le culte décadaire.* Paris, 1904.

_____. *Contributions à l'histoire religieuse de la Révolution française.* Paris, 1907.

_____. *La Révolution et l'église.* Paris, 1910.

_____. *La question religieuse sous la Révolution française.* Paris, 1929.

Mellor, Alec. *Histoire de l'anticléricalisme français.* Paris, 1978.

Meyer, Jean-Claude. *La vie religieuse en Haute-Garonne sous la Révolution (1789–1801).* Toulouse, 1982.

Meynier, Albert. *Les coups d'état du Directoire.* 2 vols. Paris, 1927.

Michelet, Jules. *Histoire de la Révolution française.* 2 vols., 2nd edition. Paris, 1868.

Minoret, Maurice. *La contribution personnelle et mobilière pendant la Révolution.* Paris, 1900.

Mitchell, Harvey. *The Underground War against Revolutionary France.* Oxford, 1965.

Mousnier, Roland. *Les institutions de la France sous la monarchie absolue.* 2 vols. Paris, 1980.

Muchembled, Robert. *Culture populaire et culture des élites dans la France moderne.* Paris, 1978.

Necheles, Ruth. "The Curés in the Estates-General of 1789." *JMH* 46 (1974): 425–44.

Norberg, Kathryn. *Rich and Poor in Grenoble, 1600–1814.* Berkeley, Calif., 1985.

Ozouf, Mona. "De thermidor à brumaire: Le discours de la Révolution sur elle-même." *Revue historique* 243 (1970): 31–66.

———. *La fête révolutionnaire, 1789–1799.* Paris, 1976.

Patry, Raoul. *Le régime de la liberté des cultes dans le département de Calvados pendant la première séparation, 1795 à 1802.* Paris, 1921.

Perin, Nicole. "La religion populaire: Mythes et réalités. L'exemple du diocèse de Reims sous l'ancien régime." In *La religion populaire.* Paris, 17–19 octobre 1977. Colloques internationaux du Centre national de la recherche scientifique, no. 576. Paris, 1979: pp. 221–28.

Pérouas, Louis, and Paul d'Hollander. *La Révolution française: Une rupture dans le christianisme? Le cas du Limousin (1775–1822).* Treignac, 1989.

Perrot, Michelle. "La femme populaire rebelle." In *L'histoire sans qualités.* Ed. Christiane Dufrancatel, Arlette Farge, and Christine Faure. Paris, 1979: pp. 123–56.

Peter, Joseph, and Charles Poulet. *Histoire religieuse du département du Nord pendant la Révolution (1789–1802).* 2 vols. Lille, 1930.

Pierre, Victor. *La déportation ecclésiastique sous le Directoire.* Paris, 1896.

Pillorget, René and Suzanne Pillorget. "Les messes clandestines en France entre 1793 et 1802." In *Histoire de la messe, XVIIe au XIXe siècle: Actes de la troisième rencontre d'histoire religieuse de Fontevraud.* Angers, 1980: pp. 155–67.

Pisani, Paul. *L'église de Paris et la Révolution.* 4 vols. Paris, 1908–11.

Pitocco, Francesco. "La costruzione del consenso rivoluzionario: La festa." In *La Rivoluzione francese: Problemi storici e metodologii.* Milan, 1979: pp. 159–210.

Plongeron, Bernard. "Autopsie d'une église constitutionelle: Tours de 1794 à 1804." *Actes du 93e Congrés national des Sociétés savantes* (Paris, 1968), 2:147–201.

———. *Conscience religieuse en révolution: Regards sur l'historiographie religieuse de la Révolution française.* Paris, 1969.

———. *Théologie et politique au siècle des Lumières, 1770–1820.* Geneva, 1973.

———. *La vie quotidienne du clergé français au XVIIIe siècle.* Paris, 1974.

———. "Le procès de la fête à la fin de l'ancien régime." In *Le christianisme populaire.* Paris, 1976: pp. 171–98.

———. "Le fait religieux dans l'histoire de la Révolution: Objets, méthodes, voies nouvelles." In *Voies nouvelles pour la Révolution française.* Colloque Albert Mathiez–Georges Lefebvre, 1974. Paris, 1978: pp. 237–64.

Plumet, Jules. *L'évêché de Tournai pendant la Révolution française.* Louvain, 1963.

Pommeret, Hervé. *L'esprit public dans le département des Côtes-du-Nord pendant la Révolution, 1789–1799.* Saint-Brieuc, 1921.

Préclin, Edmond. *Les jansénistes du XVIIIe siècle et la Constitution civile de clergé.* Paris, 1929.

Quéniart, Jean. *Les hommes, l'église, et Dieu dans la France du XVIIIe siècle.* Paris, 1978.

Quinn, Mary Ann. "Pratiques et théories de la coutume: Allodialité et conflits de droits dans la seigneurie de l'Isle-sous-Montréal au XVIIIe siècle." *Etudes rurales* 103–4 (1986): 71–104.

Rappaport, Roy. *Ecology, Meaning, and Ritual.* Richmond, Calif., 1979.

Ravitch, Norman. "Abbé Fauchet: Romantic Religion during the French Revolution." *Journal of the American Academy of Religion* 42 (1974): 247–62.

Reddy, William A. "The Textile Trade and the Language of the Rioting Crowd at Rouen, 1752–1871." *Past and Present* 74 (1977): 62–89.

Reinhard, Marcel. *Le département de la Sarthe sous le régime directorial.* Le Mans, 1936.

——. *Religion, Révolution, et contre-Révolution.* Paris, 1960.

La religion populaire. Paris, 17–19 octobre 1977. Colloques internationaux de Centre national de la recherche scientifique, no. 576. Paris, 1979.

Ricoeur, Paul. "The Symbol Gives Rise to Thought." In *Ways of Understanding Religion.* Ed. Walter H. Capps. New York, 1972: pp. 309–17.

Roche, Daniel. *Le siècle des Lumières en province.* 2 vols. Paris, 1978.

Root, Hilton. *Peasants and King in Burgundy: Agrarian Foundations of French Absolutism.* Berkeley, Calif., 1987.

Rose, R. B. "Eighteenth-Century Price Riots and Public Policy in England." *International Review of Social History* 6 (1961): 277–92.

Rosenfield, Leonora Cohen. "The Rights of Women in the French Revolution." *Studies in Eighteenth-Century Culture* 17 (1978): 117–38.

Roux, Marquis Marie de. *Histoire religieuse de la Révolution à Poitiers et dans la Vienne.* Lyon, 1952.

Rudé, George. *The Crowd in the French Revolution.* Oxford, 1959.

Ruether, Rosemary, and Eleanor McLaughlin. *Women of the Spirit: Female Leadership in the Jewish and Christian Traditions.* New York, 1979.

Sauzet, Robert. *Les visites pastorales dans le diocèse de Chartres pendant la première moitié du XVIIe siècle.* Rome, 1975.

——. "Présence rénovée du catholicisme (1520–1670)." In *Histoire des catholiques en France du XVe siècle à nos jours.* Ed. François Lebrun. Toulouse, 1980: pp. 75–145.

Scott, James. *Weapons of the Weak: Everyday Forms of Peasant Resistance.* New Haven, Conn., 1985.

Scribner, R. W. "Interpreting Religion in Early Modern Europe." *European Studies Review* 13.1 (1983): 89–105.

Sévestre, Emile. *Les problèmes religieux de la Révolution et l'Empire en Normandie, 1787–1815.* 2 vols. Paris, 1924.

Shennan, J. H. *The Parlement of Paris.* Ithaca, N.Y., 1968.

Sicard, Augustin. *Le clergé de France pendant la Révolution.* 3 vols. Paris, 1912–17.

Soboul, Albert. "Sentiment religieux et cultes populaires pendant la Révolution: Saints patriotes et martyrs de la liberté." *AHRF* 148 (1957): 193–213.

Starobinski, Jean. *Les emblèmes de la raison.* Paris, 1979.

Surrateau, René. "Heurs et malheurs de la 'sociologie electorale' pour l'époque de la Révolution française." *Annales: Economies, sociétés, civilisations* 28 (1968): 556–80.

———. *Les élections de l'an VI et le coup d'état du 22 floréal (11 mai 1798).* Paris, 1971.

Sutherland, Donald. *The Chouans: The Social Origins of Popular Counter-revolution in Upper Brittany, 1770–96.* Oxford 1982.

Tackett, Timothy. *Priest and Parish in Eighteenth-Century France.* Princeton, N.J., 1977.

———. "The West in France in 1789: The Religious Factor in the Origins of Counterrevolution." *JMH* 54 (1982): 715–45.

———. *Religion, Revolution, and Regional Culture in Eighteenth-Century France: The Ecclesiastical Oath of 1791.* Princeton, N.J., 1986.

———. "Women and Men in Counterrevolution: The Sommières Riot of 1791." *JMH* 59 (1987): 680–704.

Tackett, Timothy, and Claude Langlois. "Ecclesiastical Structures and Clerical Geography on the Eve of the French Revolution." *French Historical Studies* 11 (1980): 352–70.

Tallett, Frank. "Religion and Revolution: The Rural Clergy and Parishioners of Doubs, 1780–1797." Ph.D. diss., University of Reading, 1981.

Taveneaux, René. *La vie quotidienne des jansénistes aux XVIIe et XVIIIe siècles.* Paris, 1973.

Thompson, E. P. "The Moral Economy of the English Crowd in the Eighteenth Century." *Past and Present* 50 (1971): 76–136.

———. "Rough music: Le charivari anglais." *Annales: Economies, sociétés, civilisations* 27 (1972): 285–312.

Tilly, Charles. *The Vendée: A Sociological Analysis of the Counterrevolution of 1793.* Cambridge, Mass., 1964.

Tilly, Louise A. "The Food Riot as a Form of Political Conflict in France." *Journal of Interdisciplinary History* 2 (1971): 23–58.

Tocqueville, Alexis de. *The Old Regime and the French Revolution.* Trans. Stuart Gilbert. New York, 1955.

Turner, Victor. *The Ritual Process: Structure and Anti-Structure.* Chicago, 1969.

———. *Dramas, Fields, and Metaphors: Symbolic Action in Human Society.* Ithaca, N.Y., 1974.

Turner, Victor and Edith Turner. *Image and Pilgrimage in Christian Culture.* New York, 1978.

Ultée, Martin. "The Supression of Fêtes in France, 1666." *Catholic Historical Review* 62 (1976): 181–99.

Underdown, David. *Revel, Riot, and Rebellion: Popular Politics and Culture in England, 1603–1660.* Oxford, 1985.

Van Kley, Dale. *The Jansenists and the Expulsion of the Jesuits, 1757–65.* New Haven, Conn., 1975.

———. "Church, State, and the Ideological Origins of the French Revolution." *JMH* 51 (1979): 629–66.

———. *The Damiens Affair and the Unraveling of the Ancien Regime, 1750–1770.* Princeton, N.J., 1984.

Viguerie, Jean. "La dévotion populaire dans la France des 17e et 18e siècles." In *Histoire de la messe: Actes de la troisième rencontre d'histoire religieuse de Fontevraud.* Angers, 1980: pp. 7–23.

_____. *Christianisme et Révolution: Cinq leçons d'histoire de la Révolution française.* Paris, 1986.

Voies nouvelles pour l'histoire de la Révolution française. Colloque Albert Mathiez-Georges Lefebvre, 1974. Paris, 1978.

Vovelle, Michel. *Piété baroque et déchristianisation en Provence au XVIIIe siècle.* Paris, 1973.

_____. *Religion et Révolution: La déchristianisation de l'an II.* Paris, 1976.

_____. *La Révolution contre l'église: De la Raison à l'Etre Suprême.* Paris, 1988.

Williams, William. "Jansenism and the Pre-revolutionary Clergy." In *Studies in Eighteenth-Century Culture* 7 (1978): 289–302.

Woloch, Isser. *Jacobin Legacy: The Democratic Movement under the Directory.* Princeton, N.J., 1970.

Regional Studies on the Yonne

L'abbé Lebeuf et le jansénisme. XXXI Congrès de l'Association bourguignonne des Sociétés savantes. Auxerre, 20–22 mai 1960. Auxerre, 1962.

Auclerc, Henri. *Les curés d'Avrolles pendant la Révolution française.* Auxerre, 1949.

_____. *La déportation ecclésiastique dans le département de l'Yonne sous le Directoire (1797–1800).* Auxerre, 1958.

Baudiau, Jean B. *Le Morvan, ou Essai géographique, topographique, et historique sur cette contrée.* 3 vols. 3d ed. Paris, 1965, Orig. ed., Nevers, 1865.

Blin, Ernest. "La charité d'Avallon." *BSSY* 59 (1905): 85–107.

Blondel, Poulin. *Vie des saints du diocèse de Sens et d'Auxerre.* Sens, 1885.

Bonneau, Gustave. *Notes pour servir à l'histoire du clergé de l'Yonne pendant la Révolution, 1790–1800.* Sens, 1900.

Bontin, C. de, and Laurent Cornille. *Les volontaires nationaux et le recrutement de l'armée pendant la Révolution dans l'Yonne.* Auxerre, 1913.

Boussard, Abbé. *Le docteur Paradis et sa famille.* Auxerre, 1903.

Bouvier, Henri. *Histoire de l'église et de l'ancien archidiocèse de Sens.* 3 vols. Paris, 1906–11.

Brémond, Henri. "Une guerre de religion." *Revue de Paris* 38 (1931): 241–60.

Bruley, J. *Le Morvan, coeur de la France.* 3 vols. Paris, 1964.

Casimir, André. "Etienne-François Housset: Un républicain auxerrois." *BSSY* 105 (1973): 153–78.

Challe, Ambroise. *Histoire des guerres du calvinisme et de la ligue dans l'Auxerrois, le Senonais, et les autres contrées qui forment aujourd'hui le département de l'Yonne.* 2 vols. Auxerre, 1863–64.

Charleux, Jean. "Les routes de la sortie sud d'Auxerre sur la rive droite de l'Yonne au XVIIIe siècle." *BSSY* 114 (1982): 63–70.

Cornat, P. *Histoire de la ville de Ligny-le-Châtel.* Sens, 1866.

Corvol, Andrée. "L'affouage au XVIIe siècle: Intégration et exclusion dans les communautés de l'ancien régime." *Annales: Economies, sociétés, civilisations* 36 (1981): 390–411.

_____. "L'homme et l'arbre sous l'ancien régime." Thèse d'état, Université de Paris IV, 1983.

Courtaut, M. "Etudes sur l'esprit public du Tiers Etat du bailliage d'Auxerre en 1789." *BSSY* 4 (1850): 265–368.

David, Gaston. "Tableaux de l'histoire d'Auxerre de 1789 à 1817." *Echo d'Auxerre* 69–93 (1967–69).

Delasselle, Claude. *L'Yonne pendant la Révolution, 1789–1799*. Dossier des Archives départementales de l'Yonne, no. 14. Auxerre, 1987.

Demay, Charles. "L'évêque d'Auxerre et le chapître cathédral au XVIIIe siècle." *BSSY* 52 (1898): 5–222.

_____. "Confréries de métier, de charité, et autres établies à Auxerre avant 1789." *BSSY* 56 (1902): 197–243.

_____. "L'instruction primaire à Auxerre pendant la Révolution de 1789." *BSSY* 58 (1904–5): 145–85.

Desfarges, Dom Bénigne. *La Puisaye: Son terroir, son histoire*. N.p., 1977.

Dinet, Dominique. "Les ordinations sacerdotales dans les diocèses d'Auxerre, Langres, et Dijon (XVIIe–XVIIIe siècles)." *Revue de l'histoire de l'église de France* 66 (1980): 211–41.

_____. "Administration épiscopale et vie religieuse au milieu du XVIIIe siècle: Le bureau pour le gouvernement du diocèse de Langres de Gilbert de Montmorin." *Revue d'histoire ecclésiastique* 78 (1983): 721–74.

_____. "Le jansénisme et les origines de la déchristianisation au XVIIIe siècle: L'exemple des pays de l'Yonne." In *Du jansénisme à la laïcité: Le jansénisme et les origines de la déchristianisation*. Entretiens d'Auxerre, 1983. Ed. Léo Hamon. Paris, 1987: pp. 1–34.

_____. "Les visites pastorales du diocèse de Sens aux XVIIe et XVIIIe siècles." *AB* 49 (1987): 20–55.

Drouot, Henri. "Le culte laïcal: Sa persistance après la Révolution." *AB* 22 (1950): 204–5.

Dupéron, P. *La question du pain dans l'Yonne sous le règne du maximum*. Paris, 1910.

Durr, René. *Répertoire bibliographique de l'Yonne (1931–1963)*. Dijon, 1964[?].

Forestier, Henri. "Les campagnes de l'Auxerrois et la déchristianisation, d'après la correspondance d'E. A. Rathier." *AB* 19 (1947): 185–206.

_____. "Le culte laïcal." *AB* 24 (1952): 105–10.

_____. "Le culte laïcal. Messes blanches à Auxerre." *AB* 24 (1952): 175–77.

_____. "Le culte laïcal à Chablis." *BSSY* 97 (1957–58): 338.

_____. *L'Yonne au XIXe siècle*. 4 vols. Auxerre, 1959.

_____. "Catholiques et théophilanthropes dans l'Yonne à la veille du Concordat." *Echo de Saint-Pierre d'Auxerre* 35 (1961): 3–5.

_____. "Le 'culte laïcal' et la crise des effectifs dans le clergé diocésain (1801–1821)." *Echo de Saint-Pierre d'Auxerre* 36 (1961): 3–6, and 37 (1962): 3–6.

_____. "Le culte laïcal dans l'Yonne (1795–1828)." In *L'abbé Lebeuf et le jan-*

sénisme: 23e congrès de l'Association bourguignonne des Sociétés savantes, Auxerre, 20–22 mai 1960. Auxerre, 1962: pp. 237–44.

———. "Nicolas Chamon, fileur de laine et ministre de culte à Butteaux (an VII)." *Echo d'Auxerre* 40 (1962): 11–13.

Fourrey, Abbé René. *Dans la cathédrale Saint-Etienne d'Auxerre.* Auxerre, 1934.

———. *Trois martyrs des pontons de Rochefort: Les chanoines Hunot de l'ancienne collègiale de Brienon.* Sens, 1936.

Franjou, Edmond. "La Celle-Saint-Cyr pendant la Révolution française." *BSSY* 96 (1953–56): 111–28.

Gally, Michel. "Notices sur les prêtres et religieux de l'ancien arhdiaconé d'Avallon." *Bulletin de la Société d'études d'Avallon* (1898): 13–177.

Gazier, André. *Les écoles de charité du faubourg Saint-Antoine: Ecole normale et groupes scolaires (1713–1887).* Paris, 1906.

Giraud, Abbé. "La ville d'Avallon pendant la période révolutionnaire d'après les procès-verbaux de l'administration municipale." *Bulletin de la Société d'études d'Avallon* 52–53 (1910–11): 135–698.

Grossier, Pierre. *La grande histoire en Puisaye.* Sens, 1938.

Guérin, P. "Inventaire des documents relatifs à l'histoire religieuse et civile de Sens." *Bulletin de la Société archéologique de Sens* (1878).

Hamon, Léo, ed. *Du jansénisme à la laïcité: Le jansénisme et les origines de la déchristianisation.* Entretiens d'Auxerre, 1983. Paris, 1987.

———, ed. *La Révolution dans le département de l'Yonne.* Entretiens d'Auxerre, 1988. Paris, forthcoming.

Hermelin, Camille. "Histoire de la ville de Saint-Florentin (seconde partie, 1789–1816)," *BSSY* 92bis (1938).

Heurley, Charles. *Avallon ancien et moderne.* Avallon, 1880.

Hohl, Claude. "Les fêtes à Auxerre durant la Révolution." *BSSY* 106 (1974): 125–58, and 107 (1975): 127–45.

———. *Le jansénisme dans l'Yonne.* Les cahiers des archives, no. 4. Auxerre, 1986.

Lanfrey, André. "L'évolution de la vie religieuse dans le nord de l'évêché, d'Autun de 1667 à 1710." Mémoire de mâitrise, Université de Lyon II, 1971.

Leboeuf, Abbé. "Etat des travaux sur le jansénisme dans l'Yonne." In *Du jansénisme à la laïcité: Le jansénisme et les origines de la déchristianisation.* Entretiens d'Auxerre, 1983. Ed. Léo Hamon. Paris, 1987: pp. 35–87.

Leviste, Jacques. "La régularisation de la situation des prêtres mariés durant la Révolution." *BSSY* 103 (1969–70): 241–63.

Locatelli, Jean-Pierre. "La vie matérielle et l'enseignement dans le diocèse d'Auxerre de 1672 à 1712." Mémoire de mâitrise, Université de Paris I, 1970.

Moiset, Charles. "Les usages, croyances, traditions, superstitions, etc., ayant existé ou existant encore dans les divers pays du département de l'Yonne." *BSSY* 42 (1888): 1–157.

———. "Les corporations d'arts et métiers dans les pays qui forment aujourd'hui le département de l'Yonne." *BSSY* 44 (1890): 353–416.

_____. "La théophilanthropie dans le département de l'Yonne." *BSSY* 52 (1898): 235–59.

Monceaux, Henri. *La Révolution dans le département de l'Yonne (1788–1800): Essai bibliographique.* Paris, 1889–90.

Moreau, Georges. *Tonnerre pendant la Révolution.* Tonnerre, 1890.

Moreau, Jean-Paul. *La vie rurale dans le sud-est du bassin parisien.* Paris, 1958.

Netter, Marie-Laurence. "Alphabétisation et scolarisation dans l'Yonne et dans la Haute-Garonne de la fin du XVIIIe siècle à 1833." Thèse du troisième cycle, Université de Paris 1 et l'Ecole Pratique des Hautes Etudes en Sciences Sociales, 1980.

Noirot, Alype-Jean. *Le département de l'Yonne comme diocèse.* 2 vols. Auxerre, 1979.

Ordioni, Pierre. *La résistance gallicane et janséniste dans le diocèse d'Auxerre (1704–1760).* Auxerre, 1932.

_____. *La survivance des idées gallicanes et jansénistes en Auxerrois de 1760 à nos jours.* Auxerre, 1933.

_____. "Les origines gallicanes de l'anticléricalisme en Auxerrois." In *Du jansénisme à la laïcité: Le jansénisme et les origines de la déchristianisation.* Entretiens d'Auxerre, 1983. Ed. Léo Hamon. Paris, 1987: pp. 167–88.

Pallier, E. "Recherches historiques sur l'histoire de Châtel-Censoir." *BSSY* 34 (1880): 5–192.

Porée, Charles. *La formulation du département de l'Yonne en 1790.* Paris, 1905.

_____. *Cloches et fondeurs de cloches: Enquête campanaire dans l'Yonne.* Paris, 1911.

_____. "Les communautés des métiers dans la région de l'Yonne." *BSSY* 71 (1919): 283–386.

Quantin, Max. *Histoire de l'instruction primaire avant 1789 dans les pays qui forment le département de l'Yonne.* Auxerre, 1875.

Ribière, Hippolyte. *Essai sur l'histoire de l'imprimerie dans le département de l'Yonne.* Auxerre, 1858.

Richard, J. "Le culte laïcal." *AB* 34 (1962): 205–7.

Rocher, Jean-Pierre. "Une séquelle des querelles jansénistes au XVIIIe siècle à Saint-Fargeau (1818–19)." *BSSY* 101 (1967): 25–32.

_____. "Essai statistique sur les prêtres abdicataires du district de Saint-Fargeau." *Actes du 39e Congrès de l'Association bourguignonne des Sociétés savantes.* Toucy, 1968, 31–49.

_____. "La Révolution." In *L'histoire d'Auxerre à nos jours.* Ed. Jean-Pierre Rocher. Auxerre, 1984: pp. 271–301.

_____. "La vie religieuse aux XVIIe et XVIIIe siècles." In *L'histoire d'Auxerre à nos jours.* Ed. Jean-Pierre Rocher. Auxerre, 1984: pp. 253–70.

_____. "L'évolution politique et religieuse du département de l'Yonne pendant la Révolution." In *Du jansénisme à la laïcité: Le jansénisme et les origines de la déchristianisation.* Entretiens d'Auxerre, 1983. Ed. Léo Hamon. Paris, 1987: pp. 89–109.

_____. "Aspects de l'histoire religieuse du département de l'Yonne pendant la Révolution." In *La Révolution dans le département de l'Yonne.* Entretiens d'Auxerre, 1988. Ed. Léo Hamon. Paris, forthcoming.

Roudil, Pierre. "La vie religieuse et mentalité collective dans le diocèse d'Auxerre de 1672 à 1712." Mémoire de maîtrise, Université de Paris I, 1970.

Roussel, Charles-François. *Le diocèse de Langres: Histoire et statistique.* 4 vols. Langres, 1873–79.

Schmitt, Thérèse-Jean. *L'organisation ecclésiastique et la pratique religieuse dans l'archdiaconé d'Autun de 1650 à 1750.* Autun, 1957.

Tartat, Pierre. "L'application de la constitution civile du clergé à Avallon." *AHRF* 22 (1950): 221–46.

———. *Avallon au XVIIIe siècle—la Révolution, 1789–1799.* Auxerre, 1953.

Viard, Georges. "Les visites pastorales dans l'ancien diocèse de Langres." *Revue d'histoire de l'église de France* 68 (1977): 235–72.

Regional Journals

Several regional historical journals provided many other useful articles on the Revolution in the towns and villages of the Yonne.

Annales de Bourgogne

Annuaire de l'Yonne

Bulletin de la Société archéologique de Sens

Bulletin de la Société d'études d'Avallon

Bulletin de la Société des sciences historiques et naturelles de l'Yonne

Echo d'Auxerre or *Echo de Saint-Pierre d'Auxerre*

Index

Paris (*cont.*)
  205, 217; influence of, 32, 54, 69, 86–89, 163–64
Paris Basin, 6, 9, 23–29, 37, 39, 51, 81, 120–21, 224
Pays-d'Othe, 33–35, 59, 67
Périgord, 164
Perin, Nicole, 223
petitions, 124–48, 158–63: on behalf of priests, 112, 126, 128, 131–32; in counterrevolutionary regions, 158–62; and gender, 198, 205, 208; and law, 125–26, 133; 139–40; for lay ministers, 96, 106–7, 113; and local authorities, 128, 133–35, 144–45; model, 132, 161; Old Regime, 41, 124–26, 128, 135; process of, 126–29, 132–34; profile of signers, 129–33; to reclaim churches, 17, 95–96, 126, 130–31, 134, 137, 139, 143–45, 154–55, 157, 162, 189, 198; regional variation of, 57–60, 63, 68, 70, 73–74, 128–29, 132, 158–61; rhetoric of, 1, 10–11, 15, 111, 122–24, 136–50, 153–63, 228–30; urban-rural contrast, 73–74, 132
Picardy, 5, 23, 29
Pierre, Saint, 136, 176n17
pilgrimages, 37, 39, 40, 44, 174, 224
Pius VI, 6, 79
Pius VII, 13
Plessis-du-Mée, 189
politics. *See* assemblies; coup d'état; electoral politics; government officials; Jacobins; national religious policy; petitions; Republicans; sections
Pont-sur-Yonne, 101, 111, 145, 188–89
popular culture: and fusion with revolutionary culture, 2, 14–15, 22–23, 77, 110–12, 167, 183–88, 215, 219–20, 222–23; mockery or ritualized hostility, 72–73, 107, 109, 167, 169, 179–84, 188–89, 198, 203. *See also* charivari; dances; festivals (Catholic), (revolutionary); revolutionary culture; riots; singing
Popular Societies, 9, 51, 54–55, 126, 153, 203. *See also* Cercle constitutionnel
Popular sovereignty: authority of, 111, 135, 167, 184–85, 228; and claims for religious practice, 15, 74, 101, 122–24, 126, 135–36, 142–44, 148, 150, 160–62, 184–86, 229
population, 32, 58–59, 68, 71n56

posters, 136, 142–43, 145–47, 163
Pourrain, 44
Précy, 101
Précy-le-Sec, 99
Préhy, 99, 141, 191, 211
Prix, Saint, 62n47, 201
processions, 16–18, 28, 123, 215, 224; and Catholic Reformation, 42–43, 49–50, 120; and clergy, 194–97; and lay cults, 93–94, 112; and local officials, 193; and riots, 169, 173–74, 177–78, 183, 222; and women, 211–12. *See also* festivals (Catholic)
Protestantism, 40, 113, 116
Providenciennes, 36
Puisaye (Yonne), 32–33, 35–37, 41, 45–46, 50, 53, 59, 63, 66n48, 68–70, 100, 115, 128, 193. *See also* Saint-Fargeau: district
Puits-de-Bon, 75, 182
purification: of churches, 86, 97–98, 217; of priests, 86
Pyrénées, 217–18

Quakers, 211n89
Quarré-les-Tombes, 35

Rathier, national agent Edme-Antoine, 54–57, 92, 113, 153
Ravières, 198
Reason: cult of, 9–10, 53–54; goddess of, 9, 176, 212; as revolutionary ideal, 6, 8–10, 53, 55, 112, 228; Temple of, 112, 147, 153
rectory, 168, 181–82, 189, 192, 194, 198, 201, 203–4
refractory clergy. *See* clergy: refractory
regional variations: of religious activism, 23–29, 50–75, 128–29, 132, 158–62, 192–93. *See also* dechristianization; festivals (Catholic); lay cults; petitions; riots; Theophilanthropy; urban-rural contrasts
relics, 16, 42, 176
religious orders, 5, 36–41, 43, 46–48, 79, 84, 220–21
Rennes, 160–61
Republicans: compatibility with Catholicism, 15, 71, 112–13, 145–49, 153–59, 161–64, 198, 207, 227, 229–30; in conflict with Catholicism, 7–13, 72–73, 168, 179–84, 189–94, 203, 227. *See also* revolutionary culture

Library of Congress Cataloging-in-Publication Data

Desan, Suzanne, 1957–
  Reclaiming the sacred : lay religion and popular politics in revolutionary France /
Suzanne Desan.
      p.   cm. — (The Wilder House series in politics, history, and culture)
  Includes bibliographical references and index.
  ISBN 0–8014–2404–6 (alk. paper)
  1. Religion and politics—France—History—18th century.   2. France—History—
Revolution, 1789–1799.   3. France—Religion—18th century.   I. Title.   II. Series.
BL875.F8D47   1990
261.7′0944′09033—dc20   90–55120